Role of Media in Society

Role of Media in Society

Mittika Singal

RANDOM PUBLICATIONS
NEW DELHI (INDIA)

Role of Media in Society

ISBN 978-93-5111-215-0

Published in 2014 in India by
Reprint 2020

RANDOM PUBLICATIONS
4376-A/4B, Gali Murari Lal, Ansari Road
New Delhi-110 002
Phone : +91-11-43580356, +91-11-23289044
e-mail: randomexports@gmail.com, sales@randompublications.com,
info@randompublications.com

Type Setting by : Keystoneprintads, Delhi-110051
Printed at : Mehra Printers, Delhi-110 092

Preface

Media plays a significant role in our society today. It is all around us, from the shows we watch on television, the music we listen to on the radio, to the books and magazines we read each day. Media can contribute a lot to a society. It can change opinions because they have access to people and this gives it a lot of strength. This strength can either be used constructively by educating the people or it can be used destructively by misleading the innocent people, the most important use of media is to educate the people about the basic human rights. The dilemma of the developing countries is that people are not fully aware of their basic rights and if they know, they don't know about what to do and where to go. They don't know their collective strength. Even they don't know how to protest and what is the importance of protests. Media plays a very important role in the building of a society. Media has changed the societies of world so much that we can't ignore its importance. Media is a source of information or communication, media includes sources like print media and electronic media. Newspapers, magazines and any other form, which is written or printed, is included in print media and in electronic, media radio, television and Internet etc. are included.

In this age when there are so many channels and newspapers we cannot ignore its importance in the society. Media has lot of responsibility on its shoulders as today's society is very much influenced by the role of media. We believe in what media projects to us. We change our minds according to the information provided through it. In the past when the media was not so strong we were quite ignorant about what is happening around us, today we come to know very quickly what is happening around us. We have the access to all the international news channels that provide us the facts and figures. Considering this fact that media has the power to influence society, it should know its responsibility towards society. It should feel its responsibility to educate the society in a positive way. It should be giving us fair analysis and factual information. Media plays a vital role our society and is a part of our life. Media is a bridge between the governing bodies and general public. It is a powerful and flexible tool that influences the public to a great extent. Media is voice of the voiceless and a great force in building the nation. The media affects people's perspective. Too much intervention of media in everything is a matter of concern. Media can be considered as "watch dog" of political democracy. Through the ages, the emphasis of media on news has camouflaged. Media these days, tries to eye the news, which could help them to sell the information that is gathered worldwide, so that they could pave a way of success and fame of their respective channels. Fm radios, newspapers, information found on net and television are the mass medias that serve to reduce the communication gap between the audience, viewers and the media world. For the sake of publicity and selling, important figures, their lifestyles are usually targeted. Unimportant and irrelevant news, that usually have no importance are given priority and due to a reason or the other, they get onto the minds of the viewers and in this ways many a times, important political, economical, and sociological news get neglected and gradually, lose their importance!

I believe, if the media identifies its responsibility and work sincerely and honestly, and then it can serve as a great force in building the nation. This book is a sincere approach to make all the readers specially students, awareness of media and its role in the society.

I thank all members of my team who have helped in the preparation of the book. My special thanks go to "Random Publications" who have published the book.

– ***Mittika Singal***

Contents

Preface .... *v-vi*

1. **Introduction** **1**

Mass Society and Mass Culture 3
Mass Culture and Mass Media 6
The Voice of the Artist 8
Dilemmas of Reform 12

2. **The Intellectual and the Mass Media** **15**

The Mass Media Lack Originality 16
Parallel Paths 25

3. **The Role of Media in Public Disengagement from Political Life** ... **31**

Political Participation and Social Capital 31
The Role of Media in Political Socialization 32
The Role of Media 37
Conditioning Factors 38

4. **Media Relations in Risk Communication** **41**

Media's Role Must be Understood 42
Hazards of Risk Communication 43
"Hazards get Headlines" 43
Informed Press = Informed Citizenry 44
Seven Steps to Heaven: You're Opportunities for Success 45
Transitions and the Mass Media 48
Transitions from Authoritarian Regimes and Mass Communications 49
Economic Problems 57
Pluralization of Society 58
Democratic and Authoritarian Ideals 60

5. **Investigation of Media Framing** **65**

Intimate Partner Violence in Botswana 65
Media Framing of Intimate Partner Violence 66
Optimizing Media Relations in Public Affairs Programming 78

6. **The News Media Accountable** 80

Nation - Community and Identity 90

7. **International Bio-diplomacy and Global Ethical Forms** 99

Critical Modalities 102
From Diploma to Dialogue 106
Emerging "World Conversations" 108
Bio-diplomacy Among Ethics Strategists 109
Publics of Bio-diplomatic Commons 113
Bio-diplomatica Futures 117

8. **Role of Advanced Communication Technologies** 119

Technology, Presence, and Flow 124
Discussion 127
Conceptual Framework 129
Research Model and Hypotheses 132
Discussion 140

9. **The Role of Technology in Preparing Youth** 145

Terminology 148
Roles of Technology For Students With Disabiuties 150
Legislation 152
Accommodations vs. Universal Design 153
Full Participation in Academic and Employment Offerings 155
Work-based Learning 157
Implications for Practice 158

10. **Media Involvement in Explaining Internet Dependency** 161

Motivation 163
Media Involvement 164
Media Dependency 165
Links Among Motivation, Involvement, and Dependency 166
Research Questions and Hypothesis 168
Data Analysis 173
Clarifying the Muddle 178
A Vulnerable Theory 183
The Empirical Turn of the Law 186
The Dangers of Anecdotalism 188
Conglomerate Support of Fascism 189
The Rules of Inference 191
Systematic Measurement 192
The Enterprise of Measurement 193
The Role of Editorials and News 195
The Normative and The Personal 197
The Vibrant Role of Empirical Legal Studies 199

11. **Role of Advertising Media in Society** 202

Media Management 202

Cable Advertising 203
Online advertising 204
Mobile marketing 209
Collaborative Filtering: Advertising Efficiency 214
Shock advertising 218

12. The Role of Media Communications in Developing Tourism 220

British war-time Premier Sir Churchill saw the "Pearl of Africa" 221
The Challenges and Issues in Developing Eco-tourism Policy 221
Peace and Security Issues in Uganda's Tourism Eco-industry 223
Prospects and Problems of Eco-tourism Development Activities in Uganda 224
ICTs Public Campaigns and Policy Strategies for Sustainable Tourism 226
The Effects of Mass Media on the Contemporary Culture and Society 227
Media Communications Issues, Culture, Eco-tourism and Environment 229
Teaching Tourism, Image and Media Relationships 237
Effects of Negative Media Events on Tourist's Decisions 245
The Media and the Development of the Tourism Industry 254
Contribution of the Media to Expectations of Space Tourism 262
International Tourism and Media Conference 270
The Effects of Online Social Media on Tourism Websites 279
Conclusion 285

Index **286**

1

Introduction

Over the last thirty years much has been written about mass society, mass culture, and the mass media. One is the composition of the group of contributors. There are some of the expected names: Gilbert Seldes who, in 1927, with his book *The Seven Lively Arts,* put the mass media on the agenda of intellectual discussion and has contributed to it ever since; Bernard Berelson, one of the empirical research specialists, who, over the last two or three decades, has made mass communication one of the best documented aspects of the American scene.

In the world of today, media has become almost as necessary as food and clothing. It is true that media is playing an outstanding role in strengthening the society, it's a mirror of the society. Its duty is to inform, educate and entertain the people. They help us to know whats going on around the world. They put their lives in danger during attacks or a natural disasters, just to inform us of the situation. It is partly because of them that awareness is spreading in the society. It is the media who shape our lives. Our lives would be incomplete without the media. Media is the watch dog of the political democracy.

If it plays its role honestly, it will be a great force in building the nation but now a days, media has become a commersialised sector eying only for news that is hot and sells. Instead of giving important information and educative programmes, all that one gets on television is sensational depiction of all news stories, their only goal being gaining television rating points (TRPs). Every issue is hyped for a day or two, so much so that you switch to any channel, they all will be flashing the same story but then when the heat is over there is no following of the case.

The news then jostles for space with other stories that are carrying the heat then. Inspite we all cannot think of a world without television sets, media has become so much a part of us that to recognise its impact, we need to step back and consciously think about how they shape our lives and what they are saying. The media affects people's perspective not only through television, but also through radio and newspapers. In this way, even many messages, with which we cannot agree, inevitably coming to us from diverse constellations of media.. They can even be turned to our benefit by whetting our understanding and articulation of what we believe, today news channels and even some newspapers are mouthpiece of some political parties.

Their work then, limits only to spread the ideology of the party rather than give correct news. People have to judge on their own by looking and listening to different channels for the same news and then form a conclusion. Media is an integral part of our society, but that's also a fact that its too much intervention in everything is a matter of concern. Sometimes, just for making money, an insignificant news is given so much priority that the real news is not even brought into notice. Yes, it does also entertain but again it's a debatable issue because by 'entertainment' we mean healthy entertainment and not those nonsense TV serials.

So at last, like science it is a tool, which we have to use by our judgment to provide maximum satisfaction side by side without harming ourselves. Sometimes, some channels also broadcast and publish the messages in such situation that the real messages are left beyond our hands. The other disadvantage is that some times they also publish or broadcast some vulgar news, and sometimes unessential activities are served as very important news and broadcasted again and again. This does not broaden the reach of media.

In spite of being sensational and biased, the significant of media can not be ignored, especially in an age, in which globalisation and liberalisation have become the order of the day. In this globalised world, task and duties of media are increasing day by day. There is still a lot to be done by the media for the betterment of the society. The mass media themselves are mainly represented through spokesmen who have had serious research backgrounds: Frank Stanton, who has done some of the pioneering work in radio research and who is now president of the Columbia Broadcasting System; Leo Rosten who, with his *Washington Correspondent*, made one of the early contributions to the study of the "communicator," and who is now an influential policy adviser for *Look Magazine*.

Three other types of participants are not usually represented in this kind of symposium. We find professional historians of prominence in their own fields. Then, there are three well-known philosophers: Ernest Nagel and Charles Frankel from Columbia, and Sidney Hook from New York University. Most unusual, however, is the participation of artists. This is the first time people who write about culture and those who create it have confronted each other. Among the participants are: Randall Jarrell, the poet; James Baldwin, the novelist; and Arthur Berger, the composer.

The second interesting feature of this volume is a very careful record of the discussion which followed the original presentation; it gives an additional element of depth to what is offered in the formal papers. Many discussants made important contributions but wrote no papers. Some of those whose prepared statements are included in this volume often said more personal, and therefore more important, things in the discussion.

MASS SOCIETY AND MASS CULTURE

It is important, however, to distinguish two strands in it. Shils gives a coherent presentation of almost all the issues, but at many points he also adds his own observations of the situation. The reader might do well to separate these two aspects and to consider first the formal structure of Shils' contribution.

He begins with a brief description of what he considers the essence of mass society. One should not worry too much about the definition. We all know from direct experience that tremendous growth of the population, the complexity of urban life, the mechanization of the productive system, and a changed political structure have engendered in many countries a way of life quite different from the one existing, say, a hundred years ago.

We have to add the rapidly rising standard of living and the development of a large entertainment industry. What the essential features of this new type of society are and how they affect human existence is, as we shall see, one of the major topics of this symposium. The main facts are known to everyone and only the term "mass society" might be new to some. Shils describes the culture of this mass society; he distinguishes three levels of culture which in colloquial terms are often called highbrow, middlebrow, and lowbrow culture.

The classification, although vague, is useful and perhaps inevitable. When we talk of highbrow culture we think of enduring works of art and the contemporary efforts of avant-gardists who deserve respect because of the seriousness of their intentions. We think of the average movie, the family magazine, or the respectable television programme when we use the term middlebrow. By lowbrow we mean such things as comics, detective stories, and vaudeville. It is no coincidence that the examples are cultural products offered to people rather than activities in which they themselves engage.

Little was said at the symposium about lowbrow culture. But a distinction between the first two levels is crucial. For in a nutshell one can say that everyone is concerned with two main problems: What happens *to* highbrow culture in mass society? And what does the great increase in middlebrow culture *do* to people? The focal point at which both these problems can be unraveled appeared to Shils to be the mass media.

All through the symposium this emphasis on the mass media is hardly ever questioned, and yet I shall try to show that this is not a completely obvious point of view. Shils also deals with the consumers and the producers of the various forms of cultural products. He briefly summarizes what is known of the social stratification of "audiences." It is useful to learn that a simple classification of the population by education or by some index of social economic status permits reasonably safe predictions of what people will select on their television sets or do with their free time.

But Shils adds an observation which has rarely been made. The cultural activities of young people at least in this country are much less related to their social status. Here he implies an interesting problem indeed: Will these *young* people twenty years hence recreate the stratified pattern of their parents or should we expect greater homogeneity of cultural interests in the future?

There is the question of historical comparisons. Certainly many more people participate in "culture" today than took part, say, one hundred years ago, and that has necessarily made for lowering the level of the average supply. But if we were to look at strata comparable to the upper class and aristocracy of the nineteenth century, would the same be true? The tendency toward and the difficulty of seeing historical trends are very marked in such discussions.

Handlin's paper in this volume provides a characteristic example. He sees a great difference between the folk art of the past and today's mass culture. But a careful reading of his contribution shows that what he means by folk art could have played only an occasional role in people's lives. What did they do on long winter evenings?

Were they desperately bored? Or is boredom itself an experience which has developed in industrial society? From Handlin's personal remarks one gathers that historians know very little about how people used to spend their time, so comparisons become speculations. But Shils correctly raises a second question: Is there an inherent threat to highbrow culture in mass society? Where does this threat come from? Are commercial interests corrupting the public? Or is it that a mediocre audience, which can afford to pay for entertainment, is distracting valuable talent from more worthy pursuits?

Is there a withering away of elites who are a necessary breeding ground for cultural innovations? The keynote paper also introduces a notion of "*mediocre intelligentsia.*" These are the men and women who, while highly trained themselves, produce the middlebrow culture. We shall later see that they are a special problem for the creative artist.

Shils is optimistic on most of the points and it was this strongly expressed optimism which obscured for many participants the merits of his general formulations. Both Van den Haag and Arendt more or less explicitly stressed that Shils had omitted one important category.

Their argument was that Shils had omitted one look at the nature and content of the cultural supply; one should be much more concerned with the way it is received. Van den Haag argues that people in mass society have lost the ability to take cultural issues seriously. The whole idea is symbolized in a statement by T. W. Adorno: "Radio has made of Beethoven's Fifth Symphony a hit tune which is easy to whistle."

The theme of Miss Arendt's contribution is related; she says popular culture has made of the classics something to be consumed rather than understood. In a way, Handlin's paper belongs in the same group. When he compares the folk culture of an earlier period with the mass culture of the industrial age, he finds a change in function. Folk art was not necessarily better but it was much closer to people's daily lives and their social traditions; "it dealt with the complete world intensely familiar to its audience and permitted a direct rapport between those who created and those who consumed this culture."

Nathan Glazer suggested that from a combination of the content level of the cultural product and the way it is received, one should derive four types of situations.

In an oversimplified form, these are:

- Serious work seriously received;
- Serious work denatured by the attitude of the "consumer" —looking at the reproduction of a great painting inserted in a picture weekly, listening to a Mozart aria preceded and followed by some popular bit in the frame of a television set;
- Mediocre works received in a serious mood as exemplified by a woman who listens to a day-time drama in order to understand her family problems better or the Book-of-the Month Club subscriber who honestly wants to improve himself;
- Finally, there is bad stuff consumed to fill empty time, this being the enemy of the people.

Each of these situations might have been discussed in its own terms, but it would take a long time to explore them systematically. In retrospect, I can only urge the readers of this volume to penetrate in their own way and as best they can this notion of functional variation in *reception* which is the common theme of Handlin, Arendt, and Van den Haag.

Attention should be drawn to characteristic differences between various contributions. The social scientist Van den Haag e.g., in the last part of his contribution, gives a list of properly numbered indictments of the deterioration of human relations in mass society: we have lost the taste for privacy and contemplation, have replaced sincere personal contacts with an empty gregariousness, and so on.

Randall Jarrell, the poet, in the first part of his paper, uses—purposely, he says—a stream of metaphors and impressive aphorisms which he feels communicate more. One other comparison should not be missed.

Shils characterizes mass society in terms which show his basic optimism: Social participation has increased, the rights of each individual are more respected, rationality is more widespread. Van den Haag, in the second part of his paper, takes up all these points and so to say reverses their sign: Social participation is uninformed and vulnerable to slogans, individualism has broken all human bonds, rationality comes about at the expense of deep and sincere experiences.

The interchange might give some readers the feeling which Hughes at one point expressed only half facetiously: that whomever he listens to he has to agree with. Perhaps the fact that positive and negative elements are so interwoven in the contemporary scene is one of its most characteristic features.

MASS CULTURE AND MASS MEDIA

The first papers in the symposium, while supposed to deal with mass culture in general, devote much space to the mass media. As the sequences progress, the mass media increasingly become the centre of attention, with television receiving the major share. By the end of the volume, one can tell that they have become the main topic of the programme. In some ways this should not cause surprise. Since the participants are mostly people who make their living from writing, problems of communication are nearest to their hearts. Still this bias deserves some further comment. I have for a long time noticed the intensity with which topics related to broadcasting and to a lesser degree movies and the printed media are discussed in the United States.

"Twenty or thirty years ago liberal organizations were concerned almost exclusively with questions of social betterment—child labour, woman suffrage, economic insecurity, the exploitation of workers, and so on. These same liberal organizations are today almost as exclusively concerned with the danger of radio, the danger of newspapers, and the bad effects of motion pictures. Broadcasters think of themselves as honest, hard-working, and decent people; why is it then, that doctors and preachers and teachers dislike them? The liberals of today feel terribly gypped. For decades they and their intellectual ancestors fought to attain certain basic goals—more leisure time, more education, higher wages. They were motivated by the idealistic hope that when these goals were reached, the "masses" would develop into fine human beings. But what happened?

After the liberals had won their victories, the people spent their newly acquired time and money on movies, radio, magazines. Instead of listening to Beethoven, they listen to Johnny Mercer, instead of going to Columbia University, they go to the Columbia Broadcasting System. The situation of the liberals is much like that of the high school boy who, after weeks of saving, accumulates enough money to buy a bracelet for a girl, and who then learns that the girl has gone out with another boy to show off her nice new trinket."

It seems that this interpretation is still valid today. And the position of the spokesmen for the mass media has also remained unchanged. Rosten and Stanton stress that they make considerable contributions to adult education. Of course they are first of all responsible to their stockholders but they plow much of their profits back into public service features. The manager of and advisers to the mass media feel that their economic success is proof that they do "what the people want"—and that in addition they provide cultural leadership. Interestingly enough, a similar attitude is reported as characteristic of the attitude of businessman even if their own profits are not involved.

One contributor to this volume, Mr. Sweeney, at the time Director of the Museum of Modern Art, blames the board members of many museums for resorting to mass appeal when it is not economically necessary. Museums have the double function of serving the trained mind and being educational agents for a broader public. it is regrettable that no expert in adult education was included in the symposium. His opinion would have helped to develop further Mr. Sweeney's interesting observations. The emphasis on the mass media is characteristic of the American scene and obscures certain other aspects of mass culture. This can be somewhat remedied by a short digression into the way similar discussions are conducted in another country, France. In one respect the French and the American situations are like one another.

The social scientist and the man of letters in both countries are likely to be politically left of centre. But in France, because they have as a frame of reference strong labour parties, they debate cultural values more in their relations to political militancy. The central theme in discussion of mass culture is usually the use of leisure time. Mass media only play a marginal role. sThe great symbol of the first labour government under Leon Blum in 1936 was the enactment of laws guaranteeing paid vacations and regulating details of week-end arrangements. Equally characteristic are a number of government supported activities like the popular theatre and the youth sport movement. The issue hidden behind the intensive theoretical discussions about leisure time is whether it will lead to an independent labour class culture or whether it will end in assimilation of all workers into a middle-class pattern.

One gets a good picture of this climate of thinking through an issue of the magazine *Esprit* which appeared in June, 1959, simultaneously with the symposium, which led to the present volume. The issue is devoted to "*Le Loisir*." The theoretical papers are primarily concerned with the relation bteween leisure time and participation in social movements. Empirical studies analyse bow the legally guaranteed vacation period is utilized by various groups of employees. Data on mass media exposure are used to bring out the sociological meaning of various types of work. Thus, for instance, one study compares two groups of white collar people who have about the same income but differ according to the degree their work is mechanized.

The group with more interesting work shows a normal distribution of activities like movie attendance or listening to the radio. Those who have monotonous work show bimodal behaviour, they either engage in an excessive amount of mass media activities or they retreat into an isolation, which takes them either to the saloon or leads to an impoverished family life. It is this retreatism which is considered the main cultural danger by many authors. One has the impression that mass media exposure is looked on as a hopeful sign of incipient concern with the larger world.

Quite a number of other aspects are often crowded out from discussions of mass culture among American intellectuals. Only Hazard in this symposium points out that the objects of daily use have an aesthetic aspect which is definitely part of the surrounding culture. He seems to feel, for instance, that by and large the design of home equipment achieves quite high standards. The social scientist might make a distinction between objects which have high social visibility and lend themselves to social competition and which are often in bad taste—some types of cars would be a good example. Other objects like refrigerators and dictating equipment are more easily left to the control of the professional designer, and do indeed often display considerable taste. In poorer countries, alcoholism is usually an important topic in mass culture discussions.

THE VOICE OF THE ARTIST

While the scope of this symposium is restricted in one direction, it is enlarged in another. Included in the present volume are the statements of three creative artists and the record of the discussion includes the comments of some others. I have tried to extract from all this a statement of their position. They all agree that the goal and task of the artist is to interpret human experience. There is some disagreement as to whether he does so mainly by describing other people's lives or by being especially articulate about himself. But they have no doubt that life for everyone would be much harder if art didn't help to make sense out of it.

Some idea of a division of labour is implied. Not every human being can, by himself, add this kind of depth to what happens to him. Only the artist is in a position to perform this task because he lends all his efforts to it; but throughout history he has done this at a great sacrifice. Because the artist's social function is intangible and its importance not easily appreciated, he is usually economically insecure and the contact with his audience, if it exists, is precarious and frustrating. Today additional difficulties are added because of the nature of mass society, the role of the mass media, and in the United States also because of some consequences of its economic system.

On the first point the main complaint is that the mass man is unreceptive to contemplation; that a complete separation has come about between artistic production on the one hand and occupational and community life on the other; that it has become less and less clear for whom the creative artist is working; and that he is often restricted to addressing himself to just a small group of experts. The mass media complicate the matter in a variety of ways. By providing endless diversion, they corrode people's willingness to pay attention to serious thought. The mass media emphasize the fleeting events of the moment and weaken people's connection with the past, as it is expressed in myths and the kind of symbolism which epics or the Bible provide. This has grievous consequences for the artist, for his creativeness consists essentially in providing new variations on pervasive themes.

The record is most explicit on two dreaded features of the American scene. The one could be called institutional temptation. It is true that artists are not likely to starve as they did a century ago; there are fellowships, foundation grants, and teaching positions at the universities. But they all require the artist to do a great many things that are not essential to him. He is rarely paid for performing his mostcreative function. The objection was made that nothing keeps him from starving as his ancestors did and working on what the spirit moves him to. But I think there was real understanding that in an overpowering institutional setting such individual solutions are hardly possible.

The second target of the artist's complaints—and also pointed out at length by Miss Arendt—is the role of the popularizers. The existence of a large audience wanting some easy information and eager to pay for it creates a new group of technicians who take the original and make it palatable, be it fashioning a movie out of a drama or a magazine article out of a serious piece of analysis. This again increases the sense of despair for the serious artist. In terms of fame land material success, he finds himself pushed into the background as compared to the mass communicator; compared with the past, he suffers less absolute and increasing relative deprivation.

This point lends additional complexity to the debate with the defenders of the mass media. Rosten in his paper points out how hard he and his colleagues try to popularize important subject matters. However, the artist can more easily condone the ineptness of a bad writer than the slickness of a popularizer. The grievance, incidentally, does not seem to be restricted to the artist. The physicist Holton mentioned in the discussion that he and his colleagues resent the image of the scientist portrayed by the mass media. It was surprisingly difficult to get artists to talk in terms of their own experience. Notice, for instance, how Mr. Jarrell's paper clearly falls into two parts. In the first he describes mass society mainly in the same detached way as any social scientist would—but his style is different from Van den Haag's.

Only in the second part of his paper does he write about his own experiences. And the most personal and revealing remarks of Mr. Baldwin are found in the record of the discussion and not in his paper. Perhaps in such a symposium the artists resent playing the role of guinea pigs. In this sense then the presence of the creative writers was a noble experiment but not a complete success. The partial failure shows, however, how important it would be to pursue the effort further. What is needed are men and women who are willing to talk to us social scientists about themselves as artists in the world of mass culture, rather than about the nature of art.

Interestingly enough, it is the musician Arthur Berger who is most specific and articulate. Perhaps it is reading and explanation of musical scores which gave him analytical training. He makes many interesting points. Among these is the idea that one should not be overjoyed by the extensive performance of classical music over radio, because the unanticipated effect might be a freezing of musical taste.

The trend in artistic style has always been toward increasing complexity, and it usually takes a new generation of laymen to accept what was considered revolutionary and unharmonious in their parents' day. Such acceptance might now take much longer because broadcasting puts all its weight behind works which people are accustomed to bearing. Berger singles out quite a number of other impediments which are built into the technology and social structure of the mass media.

New works, e.g., are difficult to play and require a great deal of rehearsal. But because of union rules and other traditions developed in broadcasting, lengthy rehearsals become almost prohibitive today. Incidentally, magazines too develop a style of their own, and television has producers who are believed to know what the medium requires. All this means that in many areas professional techniques interpose themselves between the artist and the public. Whatever the need for or the justification of this trend, the artists do not seem to take it kindly.

Berger suggests concretely that broadcasters should make unconditional grants to modern writers and composers. Their contribution should not be linked to the suitability of a work for television or radio. It should rather be looked on as an additional tax, because a broadcasting license turns over a public property—the airwave—for the benefit of a private businessman. While he did not put it quite this way, the remarks of A. W. Brown went in the same direction. A former president of the Metropolitan Educational Television Association (which provides educational television stations with programme material), he pointed out that, because of lack of funds, only about 50 education channels have been put in operation out of 250 available channels.

More such stations would give artists a larger number of outlets. If one adheres to the formula that commercial broadcasters should make somewhat less money than their franchises permit in the free market, it is easy to conclude that they should give active financial support to educational television. I might be permitted to add one remark which is personal in the sense that it concerns only my own professional specialty. The artists in the symposium request effort and respect for difficult modern art. At the same time they are impatient when they are confronted with the corresponding problem in the social sciences. Mr. Jarrell said at one point that he loved anthropologists but hated sociologists.

The context made it quite clear that what he dislikes are statistical tables difficult to read and what he is pleased by are essays on cultural subjects more akin to poetry. Two men who took pessimistic positions in the discussion have a similar record. *The Reporter*, of which Mr. Kristol was the Managing Editor, and *Commentary*, of which Mr. Glazer is a frequent contributor on social sciences, have been consistently hostile to all modern trends in the social sciences.

As Mr. Hazard put it in an aside, empirical social research might be the counterpart of atonal music. It seems to create the same hostility among modern artists which their work creates among the general public. And yet there is one type of research which might help on some of the problems which the artists brought up. I mentioned above that the way people receive or "consume" cultural products is of con siderable concern to some of the participants. Seldes, for instance, comments on the passivity of modern audiences; Hook, on the other hand, insists that he does not understand what is meant by this frequently used term.

Now it so happens that mass communication research has developed sophisticated interviewing techniques which bring out what people feel while they watch a movie or television programme, at what points they are involved, where they misunderstand the content, and so on. Such analysis of the listening experience has been used mainly for the purpose of improving the effectiveness of propaganda, commercial or otherwise. There is no reason, however, why it should not be used for more objective ends.

As a matter of fact, such an effort was made once by I. A. Richards, who was one of the pioneers of the "New Criticism" which started in England after the First World War. His Cambridge group was mainly interested in substituting for the romantic approach to the personality of the author a structural analysis of the work of art itself. Richards wanted, in addition, to look at the other side of the coin and to study the structure of the readers' experience. He developed a procedure which seems to be little known and to which more attention should be given.

Richards asked a number of his students to read carefully and repeatedly an array of poems ranging from serious pieces to conventional trash. He then requested them to describe in detail all the reactions, associations and opinions they had. These reports he analysed and classified carefully. The main product is a detailed description of what today we would call the audience experience. The purpose of Richards' experiment as well as the organization of his book is best described in his own formulation of his three aims:

"First, to introduce a *new kind of documentation* to those who are interested in the contemporary state of culture whether as critics, as philosophers, as teachers, as psychologists or mainly as curious persons. Secondly, to provide a new technique for those who wish to discover for themselves what they think and feel about poetry (and cognate matters) and why they should like or dislike it. Thirdly, to prepare the way *for educational methods* more efficient than those we use now in *developing discrimination* and the power to understand what we hear and read." [Emphasis supplied]

Perhaps it falls in a no-man's land between psychologists and students of literature. Perhaps Richards' rather primitive techniques seem disappointing. But as the studies quoted above show, we now know that one can give a very good picture of how a specific type of person understands a work of art, how he is affected by it, and how it fits into the stream of his personal experiences.

A convergence of these research techniques with serious artistic concerns be more widely tried. Obviously, the goal is not the custom tailor creative production to the wishes of the man in the street. But a great many interesting and mostly unpredictable outcomes can result from a systematic confrontation of the artist with his actual and potential audiences. To say the least, the type of controversies which the present symposium exemplifies could be referred to a firmer body of facts.

DILEMMAS OF REFORM

Stuart Hughes takes the position that one cannot have political without cultural democracy; we are paying for our freedom of opinion by letting the people have the freedom of choice in cultural matters. Phillips in the discussion objects: he does not see any necessary connection. A somewhat different formulation might make the issue more concrete. The expression "paying for" is indeed somewhat vague and perhaps fatalistic. What actually happens is that, in the mass media field, we are confronted with a set of basic values which we hold equally dear but which cannot be all fully realized. Schlesinger, for instance, argues for a stronger role of the government in broadcasting policies. Even if television is accepted as a business, the idea of free enterprise does not preclude some government regulation.

He correctly points out that at many points in our economic system we have laws on wages and hours and similar business decisions. In the communications field, however, we run into a conflict with the First Amendment which specifically precludes government interference in the realm of ideas. Even if this difficulty could be resolved by stating that television, like the movies, conveys mainly entertainment and, therefore, doesn't fall under the First Amendment, a realistic problem remains. American broadcasting is really quite free so far as political controversy goes. It is questionable whether the opposition party would have a fair chance in a government controlled system. One would, therefore, have to look for a form of regulation which affected cultural matters only.

Once this is conceded, another question comes up. In a democracy, is there any justification for imposing elite standards on the whole country? In this connection a distinction which is often overlooked must be made. The realistic issue is not whether the majority should accept what the intellectual minority prefers. The problem is whether *within* the realm of what was referred to mudlebrow culture standards could be developed and should be maintained. The Federal Communications Commission, for instance, receives many complaints about the abundance of violence in television dramas. The question then arises whether one does not find less violence there than, for instance, in *Hamlet*. Everyone has an uneasy feeling that this is a specious argument, but it would be difficult to articulate clearly under what conditions an overbundance of violence is regrettable.

While there is no answer on this specific problem, there are similar issues on which communication research can provide answers. Everyone is familiar with the programs called "soap operas." They are about families which get into trouble, solve a predicament somehow, only to start a new episode of difficulties. It is certainly not high art, but it is sometimes entertaining and listeners should not be deprived of this kind of relaxation.

However, even if one accepts the basic formula, one can point to some specific deficiencies. Arnheim has analysed a score of such plots and has shown that the troubles in which the families find themselves are usually created by men while the happy solution is provided by women. It is not difficult to understand the purpose of this tradition: it makes the soap opera more attractive to women, and this is the audience in which the advertisers are primarily interested. But the same type of entertainment could be provided without such elements of bias and this would be an intrinsic improvement.

What I am trying to say is that even if we accept the legitimacy of middlebrow culture, it is still possible to develop standards which make for improvement on its own terms. The role of the elite then would not be that of dictators but of advisers. Concretely this role can take a variety of forms. Hyman's contribution to this symposium describes what he as a college teacher does to influence the standards of his students. On another occasion Robert Hutchins stressed the importance of periodic reviews. One of the proposals of his Commission on the Freedom of the Press was that the content of mass media be sampled under appropriate categories so they could be subjected to the limelight of public opinion. This is supposed to make for improvement without specific regulation. The success of such a scheme depends very much of course on the introduction of creative descriptive ideas like the ones exemplified by Arnheim's study.

A third dilemma which deserves attention is due to a special piece of broadcasting legislation. The Federal Communications Act provides that, in order to avoid collusion on the setting of advertising rates, the anti-trust laws should apply to broadcasting. On this it proved ineffectual. But in present application it also precludes concerted action on programme content. Stanton in his paper points with justified pride to the many fine programs one finds in an average week on CBS. Competing networks could make the same claim. But what would be overlooked is the fact that for competitive reasons all of these programs are usually heard at the same time. The value of the existing programme supply could be greatly enhanced by a very simple procedure. Now the networks pit against each other programs with mass appeal at one time and programs with elite appeal at another time.

Nothing but legal traditionalism prevents an arrangement by which on some days one network has a large audience and another network has a smaller number of connoisseurs: on other evenings the situation would be reversed by agreement. It is not so much the commercial nature of broadcasting but a narrow interpretation of commercial competition which accounts for some of these difficulties.

Since this symposium was held, interest in the problematics of the mass media has extended, at least temporarily, to broader public groups. It is rather characteristic that this interest was not aroused by the cultural critics but by moral indignation over cheating on a television, show. This raises the question whether discussions like the one published in this book have any practical utility at all.

And here we can once more turn to the teachings of history. The contribution of Leo Lowenthal shows that every technological innovation the field of communication was experienced by some people as a cultural danger: the less expensive book, the lending library, the magazine and so on. It is really startling how timely the discussions which Lowenthal reports from the 17th and 18th century sound today.

Stimulated by his material, I went back to the first recorded discussion of mass communication: Plato *Phaedros,* the dialogue concerned with the skills and the social implications of the public orator. Socrates, of course, takes the position which the pessimistic critics in this volume take and he, too, goes back to history. He feels that the misery started with the discovery of writing.

"For this discovery will create forgetfulness in the learners' souls, because they will not use their memories; they will trust to the external written characters and not remember of themselves. They will appear to be omniscient, and will generally know nothing; they will be tiresome company, having the show of wisdom without the reality."

In spite of this dire foreboding, writing, orating, printing and now broadcasting have spread, and society still survives. Matters often look bad, but somehow they always stop short of being disastrous. True, as in other fields, especially in social legislation, it was often an accidental event which triggered an improvement. But this would not have happened if a continuous stream of criticism had not kept us prepared to take advantage of such opportunities. It is the tragic story of the cultural crusader in a mass society that he cannot win, but that we would be lost without him.

2

The Intellectual and the Mass Media

Most intellectuals do not understand the inherent nature of the mass media. They do not understand the process by which a newspaper or magazine, movie or television show is created. They project their own tastes, yearnings, and values upon the masses—who do not, unfortunately, share them. They attribute over-simplified motivations to those who own or operate the mass media. They assume that changes in ownership or control would necessarily improve the product. They presume the existence of a vast reservoir of talent, competence, and material which does not in fact exist.

A great deal of what appears in the mass media is dreadful tripe and treacle; inane in content, banal in style, muddy in reasoning, mawkish in sentiment, vulgar, naïve, and offensive to men of learning or refinement. I am both depressed and distressed by the bombardment of our eyes, our ears, and our brains by meretricious material designed for a populace whose paramount preferences involve the narcotic pursuit of "fun." Why is this so? Are the media operated by cynical men motivated solely by profit? Are they controlled by debasers of culture—by ignorant, vulgar, irresponsible men?

Many intellectuals think so and say so. They think so and say so in the face of evidence they either do not examine or cannot bring themselves to accept: that when the public is free to choose among various products, it chooses—again and again and again—the frivolous as against the serious, "escape" as against reality, the lurid as against the tragic, the trivial as against the serious, fiction as against fact, the diverting as against the significant. To conclude otherwise is to deny the data: circulation figures for the press, box-office receipts for the movies and the theater, audience measurement for radio and television programs.

The sad truth seems to be this: that relatively few people in any society, not excluding Periclean Athens, have reasonably good taste or care deeply about ideas. Fewer still seem equipped—by temperament and capacity, rather than education—to handle ideas with both skill and pleasure.

The deficiencies of mass media are a function, in part at least, of the deficiencies of the masses. Is it unfair to ask that responsibility for mental laziness and deplorable taste be distributed—to include the schools, the churches, the parents, the social institutions which produce those masses who persist in preferring pin-ball games to anything remotely resembling philosophy?

Intellectuals seem unable to reconcile themselves to the fact that their hunger for more news, better plays, more serious debate, deeper involvement in ideas is not a hunger characteristic of many. They cannot believe that the subjects dear to their hearts bore or repel or overtax the capacities of their fellow citizens. Why this is so I shall try to explore later.

At this point, let me remark that the intellectual, who examines his society with unyielding and antiseptic detachment, must liberate himself from the myths (or, in Plato's term, the royal lies) by which any social system operates. It is ironic that intellectuals often destroy old myths to erect and reverence special myths of their own. A striking example is found in the clichés with which they both characterize and indict the mass media. Let us consider the principal particulars in that indictment.

THE MASS MEDIA LACK ORIGINALITY

They certainly do. Most of what appears in print, or on film, or on the air, lacks originality. But is there any area of human endeavor of which this is not true? Is not the original as rare in science or philosophy or painting as it is in magazines? Is not the original "original" precisely because it is rare? Is it not self-evident that the more that is produced of anything, the smaller the proportion of originality is likely to be? But is the absolute number of novel creative products thereby reduced? Are we dealing with Gresham's Law—or with imperfect observation?

The mass media are not characterized by endless inventiveness and variation. But they are considerably more varied and inventive, given their built-in limitations, than we give them credit for. Consider these limitations: neither life nor truth nor fiction offers infinite choices: there is only a limited number of plots or stories or themes; there is only a limited number of ways of communicating the limited body of material; audiences develop a cumulative awareness of resemblances and an augmented resistance to the stylized and the predictable; and even the freshest departures from routine soon become familiar and routine.

Besides, originality is often achieved at the price of "balance" or proportion: the most arresting features in, say, The New Yorker or Time often incur the displeasure of scholars precisely because they prefer vitality to a judicious ordering of "all the facts." The artist, of course, wrests freshness and new insight from the most familiar material; but true artists, in any field at any given time, are so rare that their singularity requires a special word-"genius."

The mass media are cursed by four deadly requirements: a gargantuan amount of space (in magazines and newspapers) and time (in television and radio) *has* to be filled; talent—on every level, in every technique—is scarce; the public votes, i.e., is free to decide what it prefers (and it is the deplorable results of this voting that intellectuals might spend more time confronting); and a magazine, paper, television or radio programme is committed to periodic and unalterable publication.

Content would be markedly improved if publications or programs appeared only when superior material was available. This applies to academic journals no less than to publications or programs with massive audiences.

"The mass media do not use the best brains or freshest talents." Surely the burden of proof is on those who make this assertion. The evidence is quite clear that talent in the popular arts is searched for and courted in ways that do not apply in other fields: seniority is ignored, tenure is virtually nonexistent, youth is prized. In few areas is failure so swiftly and ruthlessly punished, or success so swiftly and extravagantly rewarded.

And still—talent is scarce. It is a woeful fact that despite several generations of free education, our land has produced relatively few first-rate minds; and of those with first-rate brains, fewer have imagination; of those with brains and imagination, fewer still possess judgment. If we ask, in addition, for the special skills and experience involved in the art of communicating, the total amount of talent available to the media is not impressive.

"The best brains" in the land do not gravitate to the media—if by brains we mean skill in analyzing complexities, or sustaining abstract propositions for prolonged intellectual operations. But the best brains would not necessarily make the best editors, or writers, or producers, or publishers—at least they would not long survive in a competitive market. The media are enterprises, not IQ tests. They feed on inventiveness, not analytic discipline. They require creative skills and nonstandardized competences. Their content has, thus far at least, resisted the standardized and accumulative statement of propositions of a Euclid or an Adam Smith.

"The mass media do not print or broadcast the best material that is submitted to them." To edit is to judge; to judge is, inevitably, to reward some and disappoint others. The assumption that a vast flow of material pours into the editorial offices of the media—from which publishers or producers simply select the worst—is simply incorrect. A huge proportion of what finally appears in magazines, radio, and television was "dreamed up" inside the media offices, and ordered from the staff or from freelance writers. And as often as not, even when the best talent is employed, at the highest prices, and given complete freedom, the results disappoint expectations. Excellence is not necessarily achieved because it is sought. "The mass media cannot afford to step on anyone's toes."

The following recent articles in popular magazines most conspicuously stepped on quite powerful toes: What Protestants Fear About Catholics;

Cigarettes and Lung Cancer; Birth Control; The Disgrace of Our Hospitals; Fee-Splitting by Doctors; Agnosticism; Financial Shenanigans and Stock Manipulations; A Mercy Killing; The Murder of Negroes in the South.

The movies and television recently offered all but the deaf and blind these scarcely soporific themes: miscegenation; adultery; dope addiction; white-Negro tensions; the venality of television; the vulgarity of movie executives; the cowardice of a minister, a banker; hypocrisy in business and advertising; big business and call girls; the degeneracy of Southern whites.

It was long assumed that the most sacred of sacred cows in a capitalist society is the Businessman or Big Business as an institution. But in recent years we have been exposed to a striking number of revelations about Business. Advertising men and methods, presumably too "powerful" to expose, much less deride, have been raked with coals of fire—in media which depend upon advertisers and advertising. "The Man in the Grey Flannel Suit" became a symbol of conformity to the masses, no less than the intellectual, through the mass media.

It is worth noticing that the sheer size of an audience crucially influences the content of what is communicated to it. Taboos, in movies or television, are not simply the fruit of cowardice among producers (though their anxiety is often disproportionate, and their candor unnecessarily hampered by pessimistic assumptions of what public reaction will be). Taboos are often functions of audience size, age-range, and heterogeneity. Things can be communicated to the few which cannot be communicated (at least not in the same way) to the many.

Books, magazines, and newspapers can discuss sex, homosexuality, masturbation, venereal disease, abortion, dope addiction, in ways not so easily undertaken on television or film. The reader reads alone-and this is a fact of great importance to those who write for him. "The mass media do not give the public enough or adequate information about the serious problems of our time."

Never in history has the public been offered so much, so often, in such detail, for so little. I do not mean that Americans know as much as intellectuals think they ought to know, or wish they did know, about the problems which confront us. I do mean that the media already offer the public far more news, facts, information, and interpretations than the public takes the trouble to digest.

I find it impossible to escape the conclusion that, apart from periods of acute crisis, most people do not want to be *involved*, in precisely those areas which the intellectual finds most absorbing and meaningful.

Do intellectuals find it unnoteworthy that, year after year, four to five times as many citizens in New York City choose the *Daily News* as against the New York *Times* or *Herald Tribune*? Or that for decades the citizens of Chicago have preferred the Chicago *Tribune* to competitors closer to the intellectuals' heart? Or that for decades the people of Los Angeles have voted in favour of the Los Angeles *Times*, at the expense of less parochial competitors?

"The aesthetic level of the mass media is appalling: truth is sacrificed to the happy ending, escapism is exalted, romance, violence, melodrama prevail." The mass media do not attempt to please intellectuals, on either the aesthetic or the conceptual plane.

Some commentators believe that if the media offered the public less trivia, the taste of the public would perforce be improved. But if the media give the public too little of what they want, and too much of what they don't want (too soon), they would simply cease to be mass media—and would be replaced by either "massier" competitors or would drive the public to increased expenditures of time on sports, parlor games, gambling, and other familiar methods of protecting the self from the ardors of thought or the terrors of solitude.

The question of proportion (how much "light stuff" or staple insipidity to include as against how much heavy or "uplifting" material) is one of the more perplexing problems any editor faces. It is far from uncommon to hear an editor remark that he will run a feature which he knows will be read by "less than 5 per cent of our readers.,"

I suspect that intellectuals tend to judge the highbrow by its peaks and the nonhighbrow by its average. If we look at the peaks in both cases, how much do the mass media suffer by comparison? American movies, for instance, caught in staggering costs (and, therefore, risks), have produced, in a short span of time, such films as The Bridge on the River Kwai, Marty, The African Queen, Twelve Angry Men, The Defiant Ones, High Noon, The Sheepman, Seven Brides for Seven Brothers, etc.

Television, beset by the problem of a heterogeneous audience, and submitting to the disgraceful practice of advertisers permitted to exercise editorial censorship, has produced some extraordinary news and documentary programs, and such dramas as: Middle of the Night, Patterns, Little Moon of Alban, Days of Wine and Roses, The Bridge of San Luis Rey, The Winslow Boy, Requiem for a Heavyweight. CBS's "Camera Three" recently presented, with both skill and taste, three programs dramatizing Dostoevski Notes from the Underground, A File for Fathers (scenes from Lord Chesterfield, Lewis Carroll, Oscar Wilde), *Père Goriot*, Chekhov The Proposal.

In my opinion, some of the more insightful work of our time can be found in the mass media, for example, the comic strip *Peanuts*, which throws an original and enchanting light on children; the comic strip *Li'l Abner*, which is often both as illuminating and as savage as social satire should be; the movies of, say, William Wyler, George Stevens, Jules Dassin, John Huston, David Lean, Delbert Mann.

Intellectuals generally discover "artists" in the popular arts long after the public, with less rarefied aesthetic categories, has discovered them. Perhaps there is rooted in the character structure of intellectuals an aversion, or an inability, to participate in certain sectors of life; they do seem blind to the fact that the popular can be meritorious. This changes with time. And a Jack Benny or Phil Silvers may yet achieve the classic dimension now permitted the Marx Brothers, who—once despised as broad vaudevillians—have become the eggheads' delight.

"The mass media corrupt and debase public taste; they create the kind of audience that enjoys cheap and trivial entertainment." This implies that demand (public taste or preference) has become a spurious function of manipulated supply. Here the evidence from Great Britain is illuminating: for years the government-owned BBC and the admirable Third Programme offered the British public superior fare: excellent music, learned talks, literate discussions. For years, the noncommercial radio defended the bastions of culture. Yet when the British public was offered choices on television, it dismayed Anglophiles by taking to its heart the same silly quiz shows, panel shows, Westerns, melodramas, and "situation comedies" which the critics of daily newspapers deplore both in London and New York.

Or consider what happened in March 1959 when the Granada TV network, a British commercial chain, presented The Skin of Our Teeth with no less a star than Vivien Leigh—and in her first appearance on television. The noncommercial BBC ran, opposite the Wilder play and Lady Vivien, a twenty-five-year-old American movie, Follow the Fleet, with Ginger Rogers and Fred Astaire.

The English critics sang rare hosannahs for Thornton Wilder's play, its glamorous star, the script, the direction, the production. But for every seventeen homes in London that chose the Pulitzer Prize play, sixty-six preferred the twenty-five-year-old musical. Outside of London, the ratio was even more depressing. Viewers by the millions, reported Reuters, switched their dials away from Wilder and Leigh to Fred and Ginger. The head of the Granada network even castigated the BBC in the press, urging that it be "ashamed of itself" for seducing a public that might have adored Art by offering it Entertainment. (A similar contretemps occurred on American television when the magnificent production of Green Pastures lost viewers by the millions to the ghastly Mike Todd Party in Madison Square Garden.) The final and crushing irony lies in the fact that *Follow the Fleet* put a BBC programme among the first ten, in popularity, for the first time in the year.

Doubtless the mass media can do more, much more, to elevate what the public reads, sees, and hears. But the media cannot do this as easily or as rapidly as is often assumed. Indeed, they cannot get too far in front of their audiences without suffering the fate of predecessors who tried just that. There is considerable evidence to support the deflating view that the media, on the whole, are considerably *ahead* of the masses—in intelligence, in taste, in values, e.g., the vocabulary in almost any popular journal, not excluding fan magazines, is often too "highbrow" for its readers.

It seems to me a fair question to ask whether the intelligence or taste of the public is really worse today than it was before the mass media came along. "The mass media are what they are because they are operated solely as money-making enterprises."

Publishers and producers are undoubtedly motivated by a desire for profits. But this is not *all* that motivates them. Publishers and producers are no less responsive than intellectuals to "ego values"; they are no less eager to win respect and respectability from their peers; they respond to both internalized and external "reference groups"; they seek esteem—from the self and from others.

Besides, producers know that a significant percentage of what they present in the mass media will not be as popular as what might be substituted—but it is presented nonetheless. Why? Partly because of nonpecuniary values, and partly because of what critics of the crass profit-motive seem blind to: the fact that part of the competitive process involves a continuous search for products which can win favour with audiences not attracted to, or satisfied by, the prevailing output. New and minority audiences are constantly courted by the media, e.g., the strictly "egghead" programs on television, the new magazines which arise, and flourish, because they fill a need, as *Scientific American, American Heritage.*

Whenever profits, used as either a carrot or a stick, are criticized, it is tacitly assumed that reliance on other human impulses would serve man better. Is this so? Do virtue, probity, self-sacrifice guarantee excellence? It seems to me that most of the horrors of human history have been the work not of skeptical or cynical or realistic men, but of those persuaded of their superior virtue.

To replace publication for profit by publication via subsidy would of course be to exchange one set of imperfections for another. The postal system offers scant support to those who assume that nonprofit enterprise is necessarily better than private competition.

It should be noted, parenthetically, that anyone who enters the magazine or newspaper field in the expectation of high profits is either singularly naïve, extremely optimistic, or poorly informed: few areas of American business show so high a mortality rate, are plagued by such unpredictabilities, promise so many headaches, and return so low a net profit. Successful magazines earn as modest a profit as three per cent on invested capital. To the purely profit-minded, business has long offered innumerable opportunities outside of publishing which far surpass it in profitability, security, or potential.

"The mass media are dominated—or too much influenced —by advertisers." The influence of advertising is often too great—even if that influence is one-tenth as potent as many assume it to be. The editorial function should be as entirely free of non-editorial influences as possible. But publishers, producers, and editors would respond to power or influence *even if all advertising were abolished*. It is an inescapable fact of human organization that men adjust to power (that, indeed, is one of power's attributes); that men consider, or try to anticipate, the effect of their acts on those who hold most of whatever is most prized in a society.

There is a reverse and paradoxical angle to advertising: when a newspaper or magazine, a radio or television station becomes successful, the advertiser needs it as much as the other way around. Revenues from many advertisers increase the capacity to resist pressure from individual advertisers. Organs which can be "bought" nearly always decline in prosperity and influence. Purely professional calculations often override vested interest. Some news or stories are so significant that it is impossible to prevent their publication.

The instance of the cigarette industry, mentioned above, is worth notice. Tobacco companies represent one of the largest and most consistent sources of national advertising revenue. Yet within an hour after medical reports appeared linking cigarette smoking to lung cancer, they were fully and dramatically presented to the public-not only on the front pages of newspapers but in radio and television reporting as well.

The news was simply too big, too "newsworthy" to be suppressed (even though several discussion programs shied away from the subject). The deficiencies of automobiles, where safety is concerned, have been analysed in magazines which receive huge advertising revenues from automobile companies. This is not to say that all truths which threaten power—in business, in the arts, even in the groves of academe—always gain as swift and public an airing as they deserve. They often do not. They do not because men, even men in power, are often timid, or weak, or frightened, or avaricious, or opportunistic, or unwise, or short-sighted. Some media operators, like some politicians, some clergymen, some labour leaders, some economists, are overly sensitive to the side on which their bread is buttered.

There is another and telling body of evidence about advertising on which no one, so far as I know, has commented: motion pictures accept no advertisements, never did, never depended on it, and were never "at the mercy of advertisers." Yet of all the mass media, it is the movies which have been most parochial and timorous. Is it because movies do depend entirely on box-office receipts, and have no advertising revenues to subsidize independence?

Advertisers seem to me to exercise their most pernicious influence in television. For in television, advertisers are permitted to decide what shall or shall not appear in the programs they sponsor. This seems to me insupportable. An advertiser in a newspaper or magazine buys a piece of space in which to advertise his product. He does not buy a voice on the news desk or at the editorial table. But the television advertiser buys time both for his commercials and for *the time between commercials*; he becomes a producer and publisher himself. I am convinced that this is bad for the public, bad for television, and (ultimately) bad for the sponsors.

"The mass media do not provide an adequate forum for minority views—the dissident and unorthodox." Producers and publishers give more space and time to minority views (which include the *avant-garde*) than numerical proportions require. They feel that it is the function of specialized journals to carry specialized content. The popular media carry far more material of this kind than anyone would have predicted two decades ago.

The democratic society must insure a viable public forum for the dissenter—in politics, morals, arts. That forum will never be as large as the dissenters themselves want. But I know of no perfect way to determine who shall have what access to how many—at the expense of whom else—except to keep pressing for as free a market as we can achieve.

It may seem to some readers that I have substituted an indictment of the masses for an indictment of the mass media; that I have assigned the role of villain to the masses in a social drama in which human welfare and public enlightenment are hamstrung by the mediocrity, laziness, and indifference of the populace. I hope that detachment will not be mistaken for cynicism.

I should be the first to stress the immensity of the social gains which public education and literacy alone have made possible. The rising public appreciation of music, painting, ballet; the growth of libraries; the fantastic sales of paperback books (however much they are skewed by *Peyton Place* or the works of Mickey Spillane), the striking diffusion of "cultural activities" in communities throughout the land, the momentous fact that popular magazines *can* offer the public the ruminations of such nonpopular minds as Paul Tillich or Sir George Thomson—the dimensions of these changes are a tribute to the achievements of that society which has removed from men the chains of caste and class that hampered human achievement through the centuries. I, for one, do not lament the passing of epochs in which "high culture" flourished while the majority of mankind lived in ignorance and indignity.

What I have been emphasizing here is the inevitable gap between the common and the superior. More particularly, I have been embroidering the theme of the intellectual's curious reluctance to accept evidence. Modern intellectuals seem *guilty* about reaching conclusions that were once the *a priori* convictions of the aristocrat.

It is understandable that twentieth-century intellectuals should dread snobbery, at one end of the social scale, as much as they shun mob favour at the other. But the intellectual's snobbery is of another order, and involves a tantalizing paradox: a contempt for what *hoi polloi* enjoy, and a kind of proletarian ethos that tacitly denies inequalities of talent and taste.

The recognition of facts has little bearing on motivations and should surely not impute preferences. The validity of an idea has nothing to do with who propounds it—or whom it outrages. The author is aware that be is inviting charges of Brahminism, misanthropy, a reactionary "unconscious," or heaven knows what else.

But is it really heresy to the democratic credo for intellectuals to admit, if only in the privacy of professional confessionals, that they are, in fact, more literate and more skillful—in diagnosis, induction, and generalization, if in nothing else—than their fellow-passengers on the ship of state?

Perhaps the intellectual's guilt, when he senses incipient snobbery within himself, stems from his uneasiness at being part of an elite, moreover, a new elite which is not shored up by ancient and historic sanctions.

For intellectualism has been divorced from its traditional *cachet* and from the majesty with which earlier societies invested their elites: a classical education, Latin or Greek (in any case, a language not comprehensible to the untutored), a carefully cultivated accent, the inflection of the well born, the well bred, or the priestly. One of the painful experiences spared intellectuals in the past was hearing Ideas discussed—with profundity or insight—in accents which attest to birth on "the other side of the tracks."

It may be difficult for shopkeepers' sons to admit their manifest superiority over the world they left: parents, siblings, comrades. But the intellectual who struggles with a sinful sense of superiority, and who feels admirable sentiments of loyalty to his non-U origins, must still explain why it was that his playmates and classmates did not join him in the noble dedication to learning and the hallowed pursuit of truth.

The triumph of mass education is to be found not simply in the increment of those who can read, write, add, and subtract. It is to be found in a much more profound and enduring revolution: the provision of opportunities to express the self, and pursue the self's values, opportunities not limited to the children of a leisure class, or an aristocracy, or a landed gentry, or a well-heeled bourgeoisie. The true miracle of public education is that no elite can decide where the next intellectual will come from.

Each generation creates its own devils, and meets its own Waterloo on the heartless field of reality. The Christian Fathers blamed the Prince of Darkness for preventing perfectible man from reaching Paradise. Anarchists blamed the state. Marxists blame the class system.

Pacifists blame the militarists. And our latter-day intellectuals seem to blame the mass media for the lamentable failure of more people to attain the bliss of intellectual grace. This is a rank disservice to intellectuals themselves, for it dismisses those attributes of character and ability—discipline, curiosity, persistence, the renunciation of worldly rewards—which make intellectuals possible at all. The compulsive egalitarianism of eggheads even seems to lure them into a conspicuous disinterest in the possible determinism of heredity.

Responsibility increases with capacity, and should be demanded of those in positions of power. Just as I hold the intellectual more responsible than others for the rigorous exploration of phenomena and the courageous enunciation of truths, so, too, do I ask for better and still better performance from those who have the awesome power to shape men's minds.

PARALLEL PATHS

The mass media are tempting targets: they are big, they are conspicuous, they are easily distorted, they invite bright and brittle condemnations—and they do have built-in limitations of their virtues. They have shown themselves inefficient warriors, and on the whole have tended to be too little concerned with what the intellectuals have had to say. On the other side, the fondest attachment of the intellectuals is to theory not to practice; more importantly, there is among many intellectuals an uncongeniality with some of the basic ingredients of a democratic society and, in many cases, a real distrust of them.

Democratic procedures, to some extent even democratic values, necessarily involve quantitative considerations, about which intellectuals are always uneasy. This uneasiness is not restricted to cultural matters. For example, it influences their view of the legislative processes and of economic interplays in our society.

The intellectual is highly impatient of much that is imperfect but also inevitable in democracies. But despite these differences between intellectuals and the mass media, I think that they have something in common, that their efforts are fundamentally going toward the same general goal but along different paths. I take it to be the distinguishing characteristic of civilized man that he is concerned with the environment and destiny of himself and his kind. The end of all scholarship, all art, all science, is the increase of knowledge and of understanding. The rubrics of scholarship have no inherent importance except in making the expansion of knowledge easier by creating system and order and catholicity.

The freedom of the arts has no inherent value except in its admitting unlimited comments upon life and the materials of life. There is no *mystique* about science; its sole wonder exists in its continuous expansion of both the area and the detail of man's comprehension of his physical being and his surroundings. The ultimate use of all man's knowledge and his art and his science cannot be locked up into little compartments to which only the initiate hold the keys. It cannot be contemplated solely by closeted groups, or imposed from above. If vitality is to be a force in the general life of mankind, it must sooner or later reach all men and enter into the general body of awarenesses. The advancement of the human lot consists in more people being aware of more, knowing more, understanding more.

The mass media believe in the broad dissemination of as much as can be comprehended by as many as possible. They employ techniques to arrest attention, to recruit interest, to lead their audiences into new fields. Often they must sacrifice detail or annotation for the sake of the general idea. Although it may be presumptuous, perhaps I can suggest a general contrast in the position of the professional intellectual: he feels that knowledge, art, and understanding are all precious commodities that ought not to be diluted. He believes that if things were left to him this dilution would not happen, because the doors of influence would be closed to the inadequately educated until they had earned the right to open them, just as he did. His view is that if standards remain beyond the reach of the many, the general level will gradually rise.

In this respect, I dissent from Mr. Rosten's conclusion that the intellectuals "project their own tastes, yearnings, and values upon the masses." * I do not believe there is such an irreducible gap between the tastes, yearnings, and values of the intellectuals and those of the masses. The difficulty is that the intellectuals do not project at all to the uninitiated. Their hope is to attract them, providing that it is not too many, too fast. They would wait for more and more people to qualify to the higher group, although they themselves want to stay a little ahead of the new arrivals.

This accounts, I believe, for the intellectuals' fear of popularization. The history of the Book-of-the-Month Club illustrates this point. Intellectuals have repeatedly made statements (not entirely characterized by a disciplined array of evidence), that the book club would bring about an "emasculation of the human mind whereby everyone loses the power of his determination in reading," and that the club's selections were "in many cases, not even an approximation to what the average intelligent reader wants."

Yet a study by a Columbia University researcher found that over an eighteen-year span the reaction of reviewers, critics, and professors to the Book of-the-Month Club selections was far higher in terms of approval than their reaction to random samples of nonselections. By comparing the two heaviest book selections of the club in 1927 to their two lightest ones in 1949 (without other evidence) Stanley Edgar Hyman suggests that the standards of selection are deteriorating.

Yet he makes no mention of the fact that in 1949 the Book-of the-Month Club for the first time in its history distributed a serious contemporary play, *Death of a Salesman,* that it distributed a serious discussion of a vital issue in Vannevar Bush *Modern Arms and Free Men,* that it put into hundreds of thousands of homes William Edward Langer's *Encyclopedia of World History,* that it brought to its subscribers George Orwell *Nineteen Eighty-four,* Winston Churchill's *Their Finest Hour,* and A. B. Guthrie Pulitzer-Prize novel, *The Way West.*

Let me press what Mr. Hyman regards as evidence of "deterioration" of the Book-of-the-Month Club selections to the conclusion at which he himself arrived, that in the decade since 1949 "the selections seem to have continued to deteriorate." Even a glance at the evidence would refute this slashing generality. Indeed, the books distributed by the club throughout the 1950's suggest some high levels of excellence: in fiction there have been three books by William Faulkner, three by James Gould Cozzens, two by John Hersey, seven plays by Shaw, six by Thornton Wilder, Eugene O'Neill *Long Day's Journey into Night,* novels by Feuchtwanger, Salinger, Thomas Mann,

Hemingway, John Cheever, and James Agee; there have been eight historical works by Churchill, two by Schlesinger, two by Van Wyck Brooks, others by Morison and Nevins, Dumas Malone, Bernard DeVoto, Catherine Drinker Bowen's life of John Adams, Toynbee *Study of History*, two of Edith Hamilton's studies of ancient Greece, and Max Lerner *American Civilization*; in poetry, Stephen Vincent Benet, and *The Oxford Book of American Verse*; from the classics, Bulfinch *The Age of Fable*, Frazer *The Golden Bough*, the Hart edition of Shakespeare, a new translation of *The Odyssey*, works by Dostoevsky, Gustave Flaubert, and Mark Twain; in art, Francis Henry Taylor's Fifty Centuries of Art, John Walker Masterpieces of Painting from the National Gallery, and Art Treasures of the Louvre; in reference works, Fowler *Modern English Usage*, Palmer *Atlas of World History*, Audubon *Birds*, and Evans' *Dictionary of Contemporary American Usage*.

To turn to television, I hear over and over such generalities as, "there is nothing but Westerns on television," or "Television is all mysteries and blood and thunder." Such charges usually come from people who do not look at television, but that does not modify their position. As in the case just cited, there is no uncertainty about this exaggeration; one can look at the actual record.

Let us take by way of example the week of February 15 to 21, 1959, on the CBS Television Network, because that week had nothing exceptional about it. During the preceding week, there were such outstanding broadcasts as Tolstoy Family Happiness and a repetition of the distinguished documentary, The Face of Red China. In the following week, the programs included the New York Philharmonic and the Old Vic Company's Hamlet. Returning to the unexceptional week of February 15, about 4½ hours, or 18 of CBS Television's total programme content of 75½ hours, were devoted to Westerns; about 5 hours, or 15, were taken up by mysteries.

On the other hand, 7¾ hours, or about 10 of the total number of hours, were devoted to news and public affairs. Altogether, some 78 per cent of the evening programing was occupied by drama, fairly evenly divided among serious, comedy, mystery, Westerns, and romance-adventure.

Looking at the record for the first five months of 1959, I find on the CBS Television Network alone four Philharmonic concerts; 90minute-long productions of plays by Shakespeare, Barrie, and Saroyan, adaptations of Shaw and Ibsen, full-length productions of *The Browning Version*, Melville *Billy Budd*, Henry James' *Wings of the Dove*, Hemingway *For Whom the Bell Tolls*, and many distinguished original dramas; thirteen conversations with people of such diverse minds and talents as James Conant, Sir Thomas Beecham, and James Thurber; nine historic surveys of great personalities or developments of the twentieth century; and nine specially scheduled programs inquiring into major issues in public affairs, such as the Cuban revolution, the closing of integrated high schools, statehood for Hawaii, and the Geneva Conference.

I am citing these for two purposes. One is to show how, by using selected examples, it can be as easily proved that television is exclusively instructive as that it is exclusively diverting. My other purpose is by way of considering a practical response to the complaints that the intellectuals voice about all the mass media. What do the intellectuals really want? Do they want us to do *only* serious programing, only programs of profound cultural value? Or do they just want us to do more?

And if so, what is more? Do they want the Book-of-the-Month Club to distribute only heavy reading, or just more? Does the club do harm because it has included books of humour among the thirty to forty selections, alternates, and dividends it distributes each year? Is there any serious belief anywhere that among the paperback books we ought to censor what we consider culturally insignificant and allow only what we consider culturally enriching? Or do not the intellectuals really want to stake out reserves, admission to which would be granted only on their terms, in their way, at their pleasure?

Television occupies the air waves under the franchise of the American people. It has a threefold function: the dissemination of information, culture, and entertainment. There are different levels and different areas of interest at which these are sought by a hundred and fifty million people. It is our purpose—and our endlessly tantalizing task—to make certain that we have enough of every area at every level of interest to hold the attention of significant segments of the public at one time on another.

Therefore we do have programs more likely to be of interest to the intellectuals than to others. We can try to include everybody somewhere in our programme planning, but we cannot possibly aim all the time only at the largest possible audience.

The practice of sound television programing is the same as the practice of any sound editorial operation. It involves always anticipating (if you can) and occasionally leading your subscribers or readers or audience. The "mass of consumers" does not decide, in the sense that it initiates programs, but it does respond to our decisions.

A mass medium survives when it maintains a satisfactory batting average on affirmative responses, and it goes down when negative responses are too numerous or too frequent. But so also does the magazine with a circulation of five thousand—as the high mortality rate of the "little magazines" testifies. Success in editing, whether a mass medium or an esoteric quarterly, consists in so respecting the audience that one labors to bring to it something that meets an interest, a desire, or a need that has still to be completely filled.

Obviously, the narrower and the more intellectually homogeneous your audience, the easier this is to do; and conversely, the larger it is and the more heterogeneous, the more difficult. I must dissent from the unqualified charge that "advertisers today exercise their most pernicious influence in television."

The basis of this charge is that, while an advertiser buys space in a magazine with no power of choice as to the editorial content of the magazine, on television he allegedly controls both the commercials and what programme goes into the time space.

The matter is not so simple. In the first place I categorically assert that no news or publicaffairs programme at CBS, however expensive to the sponsor, has ever been subject to his control, influence, or approval. There is a total and absolute independence in this respect.

An advertiser in magazines does have the power to associate his advertising with editorial content by his choice of a magazine. If he makes a household detergent, he can choose a magazine whose appeal is to housewives. In television, he can achieve this association only by seeking out kinds of programs, or, more properly, the kinds of audience to which specific programs appeal.

This is of course why a razor blade company wants to sponsor sports programs. But this does not mean that the company is going to referee the game or coach the team. In television, for the most part, advertisers are sold programs by networks or by independent producers, somewhat in the sense that space in the magazines is sold by sales efforts based on the kind of audience the magazine reaches.

At the same time, we are perfectly aware that in the rapid growth of television the problem of the advertiser's relationship with programme content has not yet been satisfactorily solved. It is an area to which we are going to have to devote more thought and evolve new approaches. I return to a central point: that some sort of hostility on the part of the intellectuals toward the mass media is inevitable, because the intellectuals are a minority, one not really reconciled to some basic features of democratic life. They are an articulate and cantankerous minority, not readily given to examining evidence about the mass media and then arriving at conclusions, but more likely to come to conclusions and then select the evidence to support them.

But they are an invaluable minority. We all do care what they think because they are a historic force on which our society must always rely for self-examination and advancement. They constitute the outposts of our intellectual life as a people, they probe around frontiers in their splendid sparsity, looking around occasionally to see where-how far behind—the rest of us are. We are never going to catch up, but at least we shall always have somewhere to go.

As for the mass media, they are always in the process of trying, and they never really find the answers. They also are the victims of their pressing preoccupations, and can undoubtedly improve their performances, better understand their own roles, learn more rapidly. I feel that intellectuals and the media could really serve one another better if both parties informed themselves more fully, brought somewhat more sympathy to each other's examinations, and stopped once in a while to redefine their common goals. We in the mass media have probably been negligent in not drawing the intellectuals more intimately into our counsels, and the intellectuals, by and large, have not studied the evidence carefully enough before discussing the mass media. The mass media need the enlightened criticism, the thorough examination, of the intellectuals. When the latter are willing to promise these, we shall all make progress faster and steadier.

3

The Role of Media in Public Disengagement from Political Life

The current political system is plagued by dramatically declining political participation, civic engagement, and political trust. Some scholars argue that this cynicism and alienation from civil society may correspond with the emergence of television as a leisure activity, replacing collective with individual interests, while others contend that this process results from specific attention to news genres.

Alternatively, communication technologies and messages may not be directly promoting or constraining participation, but instead facilitating such engagement for groups with access to social, political, and economic resources. This study begins by examining the connections between political participation and social capital, manifest through civic engagement and political trust.

These relationships are then explored in terms of television viewing and news genres. This work builds on sociological discussions of participation and social capital, and communication scholarship on the role of media in political socialization.

POLITICAL PARTICIPATION AND SOCIAL CAPITAL

Political participation, civic engagement, and political trust have declined. These trends are evident in observing proportionately fewer people voting in elections in the last thirty years, while proportionately more people report distrust of the government. Analyses demonstrate that distrust grew from less than one-third in 1975 to 75 per cent in 1992.

While citizens appear to be less engaged with their political community, they are also less likely to be involved in community networks. Over time memberships in support groups and secondary associations (such as AARP and NOW), where people do not know each other personally, have been increasing, whereas community association memberships have been decreasing.

The nature of the relationship between people who belong to these tertiary associations, united through sharing certain symbols, values, and identities, is assumed to be qualitatively different from the type of bond enacted between people who work together directly in local organizations. Schudson offers a valuable critique of this argument by reconceptualizing "civic participation."

Measuring participation in "conventional forms" misses critical factors, such as level of involvement, as opposed to number of organizational memberships, or even participation in other types of groups, such as commercial, professional, or advocacy organizations. Further, Schudson suggests that, instead of characterizing this trend as a "decline," perhaps it represents a return to "normalcy".

According to other observers, the noted decline in political participation is directly related to eroding social capital. This view assumes that a democratic system requires a strong and active civil society, through which members build social connections. These social connections, facilitating social networks, norms, and trust, constitute social capital.

Social capital serves as an important resource, used by participants to pursue political and economic gain. Sources of social capital, based in structures of social relations and internalization of community norms, (lifter from social capital itself, indicating the benefits accrued through memberships in social structures and other networks, and from potential consequences of social capital (such as social control and support).

Focusing on social capital recognizes the importance of social context, in addition to economic and human resources, in understanding human behaviour. According to Bellah, some indices of social capital may include membership in community organizations and trust in public institutions.

Although political distrust may be described in terms of cynical attitudes toward government representatives and agencies, it is important not to conflate distrust with apathy or cynicism with skepticism. While conceptually linked with political alienation, apathy, indicated through low involvement in political processes, and distrust hold different relationships with voting intentions; Austin and Pinkleton demonstrate that distrust can motivate people to vote under certain conditions.

Capella and Jamieson suggest that cynicism, as an all-knowing critical stance, be differentiated from skepticism, as a critical mode of asking questions. This nuance is critically important in understanding political attitudes, though perhaps difficult to capture in many measures of political distrust.

The initial set of assumptions to be tested address this relationship between political participation and social capital, conceived as civic engagement and political trust. Before attempting to address connections with media technologies and genres, these initial dynamics need to be established.

THE ROLE OF MEDIA IN POLITICAL SOCIALIZATION

While some scholars are concerned with the role of television viewing in general, others focus on the contributions of television news, newspapers, and computers to the political socialization process. Although media may provide news, persuasive information, socialization, and entertainment, some researchers emphasize the entertainment function of television when they contend that television viewing may explain the decline of democratic processes and of social capital, by creating more superficial community experiences.

Television, according to this argument, facilitates the privatization and individualization of leisure time, which then inhibits possibilities for civic engagement. This position assumes that television erodes social capital by displacing time spent on community activities with private, individual behaviors, and by negatively influencing viewers' attitudes and actions. Although this sense of civic and political engagement seems to favour interpersonal connections, Schudson counters that it is not interpersonal conversation that constitutes democratic life, but rather media that contribute to public memory.

As multidimensional forces in our social and political worlds, media do more than provide sources of information, but also serve to legitimate and perpetuate political and social communities. Other scholars differentiate genres and channels in explaining the extent of political participation. For example, some blame the nature of news coverage, emphasizing political scandal, for emerging cynicism. Distrust of political institutions appears to correspond with distrust of the media, which tends to be associated with membership in civic and professional associations.

Attempting to distinguish differences in political socialization according to channel use, research generally confirms that reading newspapers and watching television news tend to be associated with political knowledge, though the relationship between media use and political participation is less clear. Pinkleton and Austin propose a more nuanced approach, acknowledging the potentially positive benefits of media use, by providing information and inspiring interest, which may reduce cynicism and increase participation, as well as the potentially negative consequences, when media sources frustrate viewers who want information, thereby increasing cynicism and lowering participation.

Recent literature on political communities has suggested the importance of emerging computer technologies, as a link between the government and the public, and as a bridge across constituents. Kellner contends that new technologies, such as computers, may promote democratic debate and participation.

Even though these scholars admit that access to this channel is restricted to an elite, they believe that computer technologies have the capacity to foster social capital and citizenship, as an interactive technology that may serve as an alternative to dominant media systems. One key factor that may differentiate this medium is its potential for interactivity, thus blurring traditional boundaries between mediated and interpersonal communication. In order to address concerns with the role of media in political socialization, this study explores a variety of media uses in relation to political participation, civic engagement, and political trust. In this study, media use is analysed in terms of general television viewing, television news viewing, newspaper reading, and using computers to seek political information.

CONDITIONING FACTORS

Situating political participation within a broader structure, some individuals have greater access to social capital than others, and are thus afforded more political and economic opportunities. Studies of voting demonstrate clear differences across gender, socio-economic status, and other demographic variables. Similarly, civic engagement appears to be a luxury activity among those with higher incomes, serving as a way to reduce the government's responsibility for problematic social conditions. Another important factor to consider is level of education.

Putnam and others demonstrate the importance of education in explaining political and civic engagement, assuming that those with more education are more likely to participate in formal political processes due to their closer access to powerful social networks. This research accounts for the structural positions of individuals as potential conditioning factors in attempting to understand political participation, civic engagement, and political trust. Given that dominant values in the United States privilege white, male, and upper-class constituents, the intersections across gender, race, ethnicity, and education constitute potential degrees of power among select groups.

Media contribute to the political socialization of community members, legitimizing political and economic systems, and promoting ideological values that serve the interests of dominant groups in society. With these concerns in mind, background variables are meant to represent potential conditions of marginality, which themselves may tend to correspond with lower levels of social capital and political participation.

RESEARCH QUESTIONS AND HYPOTHESES

The first set of research questions explores the relationship between political participation and social capital, operationalized as civic engagement and political trust. It is speculated that increased indices of social capital may be associated with increased levels of political participation.

Specifically, those who are more active in civic affairs may be more likely to engage in formal electoral processes, while those who are more distrustful may be less likely to do so. The next set of research questions addresses the role of media use in explaining political participation and social capital. It is hypothesized that higher levels of television viewing may be associated with lower levels of political participation and indices of social capital, but that specific attention to news genres (television news, newspapers, and computers) may correspond with higher levels of civic and political engagement, and of political distrust.

Finally, it is hypothesized that participating in political rituals and holding social capital may be conditioned by participants' relative social conditions (including level of education, identification as White and as not Hispanic). Although gender was included in initial models, these results are not presented here because findings were consistently not significant.

METHOD

In order to explore relationships across political participation, social capital, and media use, survey research was conducted in November 1996, following the national election. This work was supported by a Special Research Grant from the University of Texas at Austin, coordinated by the Office of Survey Research of the University, and conducted for class credit by students in a research methods course. Random digit dialing, based on proportions of known prefixes, was used to approach a random sample of adult residents of Texas (N=257), achieving a response rate of approximately 41 per cent. Interviewers telephoned 848 randomly constructed telephone numbers.

Based on other polls conducted through this organization in Texas, we estimate that approximately 29 per cent of an RDD sample is not eligible for household survey research, being businesses, fax machines, or numbers not in use. Given this estimate, approximately 641 of the original list were believed to be appropriate for this survey, with 13 per cent not reached after three separate attempts and the remaining refused. Other polls in this state, using these techniques, have typically achieved a 43 per cent completion rate. Appropriate respondents included only those household residents who identified themselves as U.S. citizens and were at least 18 years old, in order to focus the sample on eligible voters.

Hypotheses were tested through bivariate analyses, and through analyses of variance as a multivariate approach to assess the relative effects of individual factors on degree of political participation and levels of social capital. In different analyses, political participation, civic engagement, and political trust served as dependent variables, with media variables as independent factors and background variables as covariate factors. In some bivariate analyses, gamma was used as an appropriate statistic for ordinal-level variables, when cases did not tend to fall in one row or column.

Scales were created to measure political participation, civic engagement, and political trust, while separate variables were selected to indicate media use and background factors. Many of these measures were recoded in standardized form in order to conduct multivariate analyses. Political participation was measured with an original scale characterizing formal participation in electoral politics. The scale of political participation includes belonging to a political party (39 per cent), being registered to vote (83 per cent), voting in the recent national election (79 per cent), and voting in an earlier local election (76 per cent). The scale has moderate reliability.

The emphasis on formal characteristics of electoral political participation corresponds with a narrow conceptualization grounded in the literature reviewed above, lending face validity to this scale. The scale is recoded into low (0-2 points), medium (3 points), and high (4 points) categories. Most respondents claim to have acted in three of these four ways (median=3), while about one-third report conducting all four of these activities.

Social capital is operationalized, as suggested by Bellah, as involvement in community activities, membership in community organizations, and trust in political institutions. About two-thirds (68 per cent) report being actively involved in their communities in a five-point Likert scale, while almost half (43 per cent) of the studied sample report belonging to some type of community organization, separate from their membership in a religious organization.

These two variables are combined into a scale of local community involvement (r=.31, p [is less than].01): 25 per cent are categorized as having low, 38 per cent as medium, and 37 per cent as high involvement. A separate scale to assess level of political distrust was created by combining answers to three five-point Likert items, including whether people report trusting the government to enforce laws (52 per cent), trusting the current President (39 per cent), and having confidence in the political system (54 per cent).

These items are included in a scale of political trust (alpha=.59; Eigenvalue of first factor =1.65, explaining 55 per cent of the variance) and then recoded in dichotomous form for subsequent analyses. About half (51 per cent) are categorized as having trust in the political system. The alpha value for this scale is slightly below a more desirable.60 to establish reliability. Results from factor analyses, however, lend some justification that these three factors work together toward a unidimensional variable.

Several media variables are included in this model. First, respondents were asked how many hours of television they had watched the day prior to the interview (mean = 2.7 hours) in order to assess; extent of television viewing; this variable was recoded in subsequent multivariate analyses to distinguish less frequent (0-1) from more frequent (2+) viewers.

Then, respondents were asked specifically whether they had watched television news (65 per cent) or read a newspaper (58 per cent) the day prior to the interview. In order to understand whether computers were used as a channel for seeking political information, respondents were also asked whether or not they had used a computer to learn about the recent political campaign (7 per cent reported using this technology at some time during the campaign season).

Several background factors are used to assess structural position of respondents. These include level of education (11 per cent have less than high school education, 54 per cent have a high school degree, and 35 per cent have a college degree), self identification as a member of the Hispanic community (20 per cent), and self identification as non-White (28 per cent).

SOCIAL CAPITAL AND POLITICAL PARTICIPATION

The first set of analyses concerns the basic premise that indices of social capital may be associated with political participation. Multivariate analyses use political participation as a dependent variable, with civic engagement, political trust, and media variables as main independent factors and background variables as covariate factors.

Civic engagement and political distrust appear to be among the stronger predictors of political participation. First, findings confirm the first hypothesis that people who perceive themselves to be actively involved in their communities and in community organizations, as one indication of social capital, are more likely to participate in electoral politics than those who do not.

Only about one-fifth (22 per cent) of people with low community involvement engage in a high level of political participation, compared to one-third (34 per cent) of people with moderate levels and almost one-half (44 per cent) of people with high levels (F=5.57, p [is less than].05, eta squared=.247).

However, the second hypothesis, that people with political trust would be more likely to engage in political participation, is not supported by these results. While civic engagement appears to be associated with political participation in a positive direction, political trust appears to work in a negative direction: people who voice their distrust of the President, government, and political system are more likely to engage in electoral politics (40 per cent) than people who are more trusting (29 per cent; F=4.14, p [is less than].05, eta squared=.215).

Given the different directions of these relationships, confidence in political institutions, and figures serves as a different factor than involvement in local civic activities and organizations. Confirming this conceptual distinction, these two constructs, civic engagement and political trust, bear no statistical association. Consequently, these variables are analysed separately rather than as integrated components of social capital.

THE ROLE OF MEDIA

Analyses explore how experiences with television, television news, newspapers, and computers might be related to political participation, civic engagement, and political trust. In this section, political participation is first explored as a dependent variable with indices of social capital and media use as main independent variables and background factors as covariates; next, civic engagement and political trust are each used as dependent variables in separate analyses.

Multivariate analyses demonstrate that media factors do not appear to mitigate the associations between civic engagement and political participation, or between political distrust and political participation. However, two media variables appear to hold their significance in this model predicting political participation: watching television news and reading the newspaper.

These findings confirm hypotheses that people who attend to television news or newspapers are more likely to participate in electoral politics than those who do not. For example, about twice as many people who watch television news participate fully (41 per cent) compared with those who do not watch television news (21 per cent).

Contrary to some scholars' expectations, the extent of television watching bears no relationship with tendency to participate in the political system. Thus, hypotheses suggesting that people who watch more television will be less likely to engage in political participation, or that people who use computers to seek political information will be more likely to engage in political participation, are not confirmed.

When focusing on civic engagement or political distrust, none of the media variables appear to be statistically significant when controlling for other factors. Thus, hypotheses concerning media use and social capital are not supported. It is worth noting that in bivariate analyses, however, people who report using a computer to learn more about recent elections are about half as likely to have political trust (26 per cent) than those who do not; however, multivariate analyses establish this dynamic to be in part a product of educational status.

CONDITIONING FACTORS

It was hypothesized that people in relatively more marginal conditions might be less likely to engage in civic or political participation, or to hold political trust. Bivariate analyses confirm assumptions that people with higher levels of education, who identify themselves as White and not Hispanic, are more likely to participate in civic life and in electoral politics than their counterparts. However, multivariate analyses suggest that education appears to be the most critical factor when controlling for other conditions, while race and ethnicity appear to be less consistently significant; the exception here is the relationship between race and trust, described below.

More than half (52 per cent) of the respondents with college degrees engage in civic activities compared to about one-third (30 per cent) of those with high school degrees, and one-fifth (18 per cent) of those with less formal education. Participating in electoral politics holds a similar trend.

Although the educated class appears to be more likely to join formal community organizations and to participate in the electoral system, this group does not trust the current political system or its leaders. Rather, this elite group appears more likely to be skeptical about the government than those in relatively more marginal conditions.

Less than half (39 per cent) of people with college degrees report political trust, compared to 55 per cent of people with high school degrees, and 70 per cent of people with less formal education. In addition, those who identify themselves as not White are more likely to hold political trust (68 per cent) compared with others who identify themselves as White, contrary to expectations.

DISCUSSION

This study confirms an initial premise that political participation is associated with civic engagement. People who are more involved in local community affairs are more likely to be engaged in the political process as well. Thus, civic engagement may reinforce political participation, particularly among people with human capital. Conceptualizing social capital as civic engagement demonstrates clear relationships with political participation, but not when conceived as political trust. It was posited that a lack of social integration would be associated with lack of trust in public institutions, and that this distrust would contribute to a lack of political participation.

However, political distrust is more likely to lead to political participation, rather than to discourage it. Instead of viewing distrust as a problem within a system that requires consensus, distrust may be a valuable part of a political process. Distrust may indicate a reasonable frustration with the political system, as well as a belief in one's self-efficacy.

A model of democratic participation that builds on conflict may place more value on the role of skepticism among participants. Given that distrustful constituents are more likely to vote than people who are more complacent, perhaps another tactic to improve political engagement might be to educate people toward having a critical perspective. These results suggest that people with higher levels of education and those who identify themselves as White, despite having greater access to social and political networks, are more likely to be distrustful, as well as involved in civic activities and the political process. One might see education as part of a socialization process that encourages civic and political participation.

As a form of human capital, education facilitates social position through networking, or access to social capital. The educated classes may participate because they have more opportunity to do so, and with more to gain. However, if political participation has decreased over time among the educated class, this may imply that the network of power has become even more exclusive.

Despite current theoretical interest in the role of computer technologies in our political processes, this remains an exclusive information source for the elite. Moreover, blaming television for public disengagement from political life appears to be too simplistic. Television exposure, in general, does not appear to be related to political participation or social capital. Instead, watching television news and reading the newspaper are more likely to be associated with political participation than watching television in general. These two channels need to be considered separately. First, it is less clear what content a newspaper reader may focus on than a television news viewer. Second, while reading the newspaper is highly associated with level of education, watching television news appears to transcend educational distinctions. Newspapers may then perpetuate the interpretations and practices of an elite, while television news may be an appropriate vehicle to encourage political participation among diverse groups.

As for further research, longitudinal analyses of political participation, civic engagement, political trust, and media use, based on a nationally representative sample with a higher response rate, would contribute more solid evidence of these relationships. Future research may also need to reconceptualize conventional theoretical assumptions regarding the nature of media use, social capital, and political participation. Assumed relationships between trust and participation, as well as media use and engagement need to be reconsidered. Conceiving of social capital as political trust may be unfounded.

Shifting frameworks of social capital from a micro-level to a macro-level analysis would allow us to envision potentially negative consequences, such as the exclusion of some groups and the reinforcement of others. The changing nature of political participation may be situated within the rise of individualism in our ideological values and in our political practices. The survival of the democratic process may be contingent upon understanding the value of political action based on skeptical thinking.

4

Media Relations in Risk Communication

Since passage of the Superfund Amendment Reauthorization Act of 1986 (SARA), Title III, Section 313 of which required companies to inform the public about chemical emissions, much has been written about the role of "risk communication" in a relatively new field, "risk management." Scholarly and professional research has been undertaken, seminars and workshops presented, and articles written about how to explain environmental risk.

Academics have offered thoughts on what "models" of communications should be used, and even how to design communications for "risk-takers"—those willing, even eager, to take chances. A cottage industry in environmental risk communication consulting has taken root in less than half a decade, giving prominence to research-oriented major players and number of others. The literature continues to grow exponentially and risk communication seem assured of a pre-eminent role in industry and government public information and risk management programs for many years to come.

Therefore, it would behoove public relations professional with risk communication responsibilities to become intimately familiar with current literature in the field, as well as understand past failures and success in communicating environmental and other forms of risk. To that end, following the chapter below, a selected bibliography and list of references id offered, which might be a good starting place for those wanting to immerse themselves in easily-available literature. While the following draws upon research in risk communication, it is not purely theoretical, nor is it merely a "laundry list" of how to deal with the news media (although some "basics: of good news media relations will be inherent).

Utilizing a number of studies and proven concepts, this chapter looks at and analyses to some degree the media relations aspect of risk communication strategies, how journalists tend to treat the subject of "risk," and offers suggestions to help improve communication with and through the news media. Because reporters act as "filters" for your messages, the media are the crucial link in disseminating risk messages to key publics.

While risk communication can be thought of as reporting on the hazards of everyday life, organizations face their own "hazards of communication."

Among them are: not fully understanding how to present the facts to the news media; the problem of making journalists understand or care about your particular risks; and, perhaps most important, understanding journalists' limitations and what to do about them.

It has been written that risk communication shouldn't be left solely to public relations "technicians." Instead, goes this thinking, it should be an integral part of risk management and thus the responsibility of plant managers and environmental officials. In reality, though, risk communication is a public relations function; and it's especially true in media relations, clearly the purview of the communications professional (although other managers should be schooled in such concepts).

We are becoming ever more wary and fearful of risks involving real or imagined safety and health hazards. We can almost play "Risk of the Day' as we watch television (especially during "Sweeps Week"), read local or national periodicals, listen to state and federal governmental agencies and watchdog and environmental groups and others who regularly bring us the latest in bad tidings about threats to our health and well-being—from the disappearing ozone layer to the latest tainted food product.

MEDIA'S ROLE MUST BE UNDERSTOOD

Who tells us about these hazards? Most often it's the news media, usually staffed by underpaid, overworked journalists, one of whom may have been covering city council meetings prior to being put on the "toxicology beat" the day before calling you about the latest perceived hazard your organization presents to the city's health. And, expect this journalist to display a certain ingrained skepticism and adversarial outlook that must be understood and dealt with if your message or response is to be accurately conveyed by the news media to your publics. Before your organization has a chance to be deemed "a menace to the public health"—whether by the news media, activist group, government agency, or a combination of all three—anticipatory, skillful, frequent and truthful communication can often mitigate such charges.

Understanding what journalists need to get the story right the first time is a key to successful risk communication through the news media. For whatever reasons, if your communications efforts with the media have been non-existent, lax, or less than truthful, you run the risk of suddenly being on the defensive and put in the position of:

- Saying nothing, and explaining that your lawyers are looking at the charges; or
- Offering hastily-contrived explanations which could be misconstrued to mean you believe profits and jobs come ahead of safety and health issues.

While your management may even endorse such responses, they can damage credibility with the news media and lead to unwanted headlines, such as: "Menace to Public Health Not Denied," or "Profits Above Safety at Local Plant." This is not to say similar headlines and stories won't result with even the best-managed risk communication, but why take the chance?

HAZARDS OF RISK COMMUNICATION

The following media relations "don'ts" may seem self-evident, but it's amazing how often they've become staples of unsuccessful attempts at risk communication.

To employ these methods is to ensure media enmity:

- Disseminating self-serving data
- Making irrelevant comparisons/downplaying risk potential
- Using technical jargon
- Employing non-credible or incompetent sources
- Taking an adversarial posture
- Stonewalling or inaccessibility
- Ignoring public concerns

As mentioned earlier, not making such mistakes won't ensure accuracy by the news media, but could go a long way toward building a solid and "symmetrical" media relationship. Writing in The New York Times, Peter Passell noted that "To make sensible choices between greater safety and the alternatives...need more and better information, presented in ways that stimulate a sense of perspective."

It follows, then, that we must communicate essential facts from which the public can make these choices, such as how much risk to balance against benefits—economic or otherwise. It also follows that journalists have a measure of responsibility to interpret and convey such communication, while keeping their traditional posture of "unbiased observer," skeptic and "friendly adversary."

"HAZARDS GET HEADLINES"

The above axiom is found in scholarly research as well as anecdote-based reports on risk communication. While seemingly obvious, the concept is an integral part of understanding how the news media is likely to respond (or not) to your communication efforts. If we anticipate how and why journalists might react to risk issues, we may be able to anticipate and/or mitigate damage caused by inaccurate or incompetent reporting.

A good starting place would be to understand that "risk" isn't a news story, while "hazard" is. Once a hazard has been established, the risk becomes news, and the media's job becomes one of reporting, not education about some potential or future risk. In short, the news media are best at reporting "risks" that become "hazards"-and, eventually, "crises".

Along with a tendency to ignore risk and report on hazards and their negative consequences, journalists generally emphasize those hazards that are both serious and relatively rare. And, there seems to be a "lack of congruence between the size of the risk and amount of media attention." Thus, in dealing with the news media, risk communicators should be aware of and anticipate three "maxims" often governing perceived newsworthiness:

- Rare hazards are more newsworthy than common ones (e.g., "toxic shock syndrome" affected just.01 per cent of menstruating women).
- New hazards are more newsworthy than old ones (e.g., the Alar controversy).
- Dramatic hazards (sudden and/or mysterious) are more newsworthy than long-familiar ones (e.g., Legionnaire's Disease; the radon controversy).

INFORMED PRESS = INFORMED CITIZENRY

One could just as well place a question mark after the above heading, inasmuch as communications research often indicates such an equation is at best only wishful thinking on the part of communicators. Nonetheless, educating the news media about risk and your organization's efforts in risk management is at least a solid starting point in keeping your publics informed. The more we try to understand journalists—their idiosyncracies, their biases (What? But the media are supposed to be unbiased...), their likes and dislikes—the more success we're likely to have in risk communication. Or, at the very least, we'll have fewer surprises.

Drawing from research and more than 25 years working with the news media, I offer the following observations about journalists and their modus operandi when it comes to reporting on risk. Along with each observation are potential solutions to these dilemmas facing risk communicators. The news media will generally ignore your organization's experts in favour of government or activist sources, especially people they already know. A number of studies have shown industry spokespeople are used far less frequently than "outsiders" to respond to risk-related questions.

This adds still another potential "filter" to messages you're trying to get to your publics. One Solution: Establish outside credible sources, imbued with knowledge about your organization and its risk management programs. Get them with "beat" journalists early and often. (Be aware, however, that no matter how solid the credentials of your "outside sources" may be, there's still the chance the news media will treat them as "tools" of your organization.)

Journalists often lack knowledge of anything past "who, what, when, where, why and how," as opposed to understanding risk assessment fundamentals or environmental science as a whole. This often makes them susceptible to "pro" and "anti" arguments, with no shades of grey or room for interpretation.

According to the Foundation for American Communications (FACS), journalists desperately need increased education in science-related areas, especially risk assessment. Increasingly "event-centered," the news media must develop analytical skills about the beats they cover. And, as noted above, yesterday's court reporter may well need to be today's epidemiology expert.

Therefore, FACS produces educational seminars and research materials for journalists—something their publishers often don't have the time, inclination or funding to do—such as its new "Toxicology Study Guide." One Solution: Develop credible, objective and simplified background materials for the news media, especially that new "beat" reporter; and support independent organizations such as FACS and The Media Institute in their efforts to improve journalism education.

Journalists tend to "personalize" risk-related stories. This drives your experts and technical sources crazy, but in media parlance, it makes for a "good read," or "good TV." Editors ask reporters to "bring dead issues to life; to focus on real people facing real decisions." So live with it. The story will be covered; you just might disagree with format and focus. One Solution: Be prepared with answers; try to do your own "personalizing" of the situation (if management and/or your lawyers will allow it; even something as hokey as drinking a glass of allegedly "tainted" beverage, or other dramatization of the risk situation in question).

Eschew jargon; offer metaphors and good, solid, meaningful comparisons. (NOTE: Be careful here, and use only "like" comparisons-not voluntary vs. involuntary risks. Don't be perceived as trivializing risk potential: And don't get caught with comparisons such as: "It's much safer working in our mines than being at home;" the miner's spouse might disagree.)

SEVEN STEPS TO HEAVEN: YOU'RE OPPORTUNITIES FOR SUCCESS

Despite the potential pitfalls in dealing with news media "filtration" of your risk communication activities, there are some things you can do to prepare yourself and your management.

Here are seven steps to consider when planning your risk communication programme:

- Recognize risk communication as part of a larger risk management programme and understand the whole is based on politics, power and controversial issues, which encompasses more than just "open and honest" communication.
- Get your management in the "communications loop," and help train them to deal effectively with the news media; especially those tapped as "official spokespersons."
- Develop credible outside experts to act as "news sources" for journalists. Train them, also.
- Know your stuff; become an expert in your area of risk to instill a measure of credibility into your relations with journalists covering your organization.

- Go to local, regional or national news media with solid facts and figures before they have to come to you. Make certain your data:
  - Has statistical significance;
  - Can be successfully duplicated by other research;
  - Is specific as to what "conditions" it causes or problems it presents;
  - describes potential research weaknesses; and
  - Is understandable and easily translatable into newspaper or broadcast copy.
- Research perceptions of your organization by the media and other publics to gauge credibility and help determine if your messages will be believable. It's generally understood that the credibility of the message-sender is crucial to communications effectiveness, so why not see where your organization stands and be prepared to adjust accordingly.
- Understand your target audiences and how the news media can help you effectively communicate. For example, is there an unusual preponderance of "risk-takers" in your target population? What kind of messages/media and frequency will it take to reach them?

Regardless of your understanding of the news process or the likes and dislikes of journalists, it' wise to keep in mind that effective risk communication generally will come from perception of your organization's actions. Put another way, in the long run it's not so much words as deeds that count in communicating risk.

On March 1, 1995, Vladislav Listyev, a prominent Russian journalist was gunned down outside of his apartment in Moscow. What had transpired to make a journalist the target of such an act in a country where the mass media has traditionally been subordinate to the state? On the whole, specific journalists have not been singled out. The role of the media is changing.

In Russia and Poland since the fall of communism, there is hesitancy to place the mass media in their former position as a mouthpiece for the government, but, on the other hand, there may be even greater hesitancy to give them the liberal freedom dictated by an increasingly democratic orientation.

What has the role of the mass media been in these transitions from authoritarian rule? What will it be in the future? The government institutions and leaders who have been placed in power have not reacted to the mass media consistently. These relationships have ranged from attempts at near complete, communist-like control to indifference and attempts to court the mass media for their own "public relations" purposes.

This chapter presents the results of a comparative study of Poland, from the fall of the communist government in 1990, and Russia, from the election of Boris Yeltsin in 1991, to the present. Utilizing research on media effects in society combined with the general theoretical framework suggested by transition theorists, discuss the role of the media in forming governmental institutions, though not necessarily democratic ones.

After a brief historical overview, I will examine some of the obstacles which the media will face in the future, such as economic problems, the pluralization and fragmentation of society, the rising emphasis on democratic-oriented journalism. Finally, I will propose possible roles (based on Harold Lasswell's classic work describing the social functions of communication), which media systems could adopt in the future. The research will show that the media systems will not be able to choose these roles independently for there are numerous other factors which affect their function and even their existence.

The mass media, as well as other institutions and systems within these countries, are in a definitional period. As the institutions within the political, economic and social systems in these nations become more concrete, the mass media find a role within those systems. The opposite is also true. The mass media will take an active, dynamic role in shaping these institutions in order to find a place within them. There is never a complete consensus of the mass media's role because of the high degree of political, ideological and social differentiation in these countries. Yet the mainstream, elite mass media will begin to follow a general path which is acceptable (not necessarily in action, but in role) to themselves and the institutions around them.

Because of their past and probable future global importance, as well as their current instability, questions concerning Russia and Poland are crucial items on the international agenda. As the core of a former power in a bipolar system, Russia will, in the next few decades, attempt to regain its position economically and politically. The Cold War mind-set has not entirely faded and "Russia-watching" will continue. Poland also will assert itself as an example of how free market and democratic reforms might be beneficial to itself and the region. The mass media systems in both countries have the potential to help and hinder these processes, often simultaneously.

This study will be limited to the print media in the form of newspapers and magazines. Using sources of the media and current events, such as Editor and Publisher, Current Digest of the Post-Soviet Press, Radio Free Europe/ radio Liberty daily bulletins (now the Open Media Research Institute), and The New York Times, among others, this research focuses on the media as a connecting - and often catalytic - factor between the political, economic and social institutions currently in the process of finding a place in Russian and Polish society.

Electronic media are equally important, especially because of their wide exposure and the immediacy of their coverage. In fact, there is significant desire and action on the part of the Russian and Polish governments to retain control of television and radio. But, because of the different dynamics between the electronic and print media or press, and the durability and accessibility of the written word, anything other than general references to radio and television will be left for a later analysis.

TRANSITIONS AND THE MASS MEDIA

To understand the relationship between the media and the political institutions during a transitional period, it is useful to look at the theories behind transitions. This places the overall events of the last few years in Eastern and Central Europe into a more generalizable context of social change (specifically transition research on Latin America and Southern Europe).

Literature along these lines tends to fall into two broad categories which are separated by their ends: (1) transitions to democracy and (2) transitions from authoritarian regimes. Both are open-ended theories, but one is open at the beginning (i.e., the genesis of democracy) and the other is open on the outcome (i.e., the end result of transitions from an authoritarian regime).

TRANSITIONS TO DEMOCRACY AND THE MASS MEDIA

First, the literature on transition theory that leads to democracy focuses on the conditions which are necessary for a democratic end. Francis Fukuyama claims all roads eventually lead to liberal democracy because the world and the individuals in it will want it so, Robert Dahl addresses the global conditions which are necessary for democracy, including civic participation, equal representation and appropriate institutionalization. The role of the media in this type of transition has been the subject of thousands of pages, most noticeably from scholars in democratic societies. Since the acceptance of the role of the printed word in the French and American revolutions, the mass media, and especially the print media, have been utilized as a forum for democratic thought and a mechanism for the transfer of democratic ideals.

This is often associated with Western, and particularly American, mass media. Russia and Poland have become a new proving ground for Western journalists seeking to promote the democratic ideals of speech and press freedom. U.S. journalists and academics have been instrumental in media assistance programs and financial aid for the former Soviet bloc. It does not necessarily follow that implementing democratic press reforms will lead to a democratic form of government, though it has seemed to help.

Journalist Walter Lippman believed the purpose of newspapers is not to mirror the world, just signalize events. They cannot "perform the functions of public enlightenment that democratic theory requires." As will be seen, Lippman was right to a certain extent. The mass media can contribute to democratic political systems, but there are other factors which also contribute to the transition process, for which the mass media are an underlying connector. By itself, the press is less powerful.

TRANSITIONS FROM AUTHORITARIAN REGIMES AND MASS COMMUNICATIONS

The second type of transition theory, transitions from authoritarian societies, is much more apropos to our geographical area of focus. Both types attempt to explain transitions in political, social and economic structures, but the first is much more normative. The second group does not claim democracy as the only possible outcome. "What [was] overthrown [in the former Soviet bloc countries] is much clearer than the answer to question of what will have to replace the obsolete and outmoded structures. Or...'transition from what?' is quite clear, whereas 'transition to what?' will for some time remain an open-ended issue." This lack of predictive capability with, the authoritarian transition literature has been accepted.

The most serious impediment to the accumulation of scientific knowledge about social reality is the prospect that different causes could produce the same effect. In other words, there are different roads in the process of political and economic transition that might lead to the same outcome and, conversely, there are similar roads which might result in different outcomes. I have attempted to synthesize the literature on transitions from authoritarian regimes into themes. First, there are many ways to pass through this transitory period. In 1986, a collection of authors discussed these various roads through the time of transition. At the time, these transitions were occurring primarily in Southern Europe and Latin America and each of these cases had diverse characteristics which affected the transition.

Some of these ideas can also apply to the cases in Eastern Europe. Second, there are various conditions which led to the transitory period. Adam Przeworski focuses on the factors leading to the breakdown of authoritarian regimes and the causes of their liberalization. Third, typologies of transitions exist, but they are never all inclusive. Situations may overlap with others, have unique characteristics or both.

Schmitter and Karl recently attempted to include the Eastern European countries in the general authoritarian transition literature. They proposed a matrix of Weberian "ideal-type" transitions, with space in the centre for the overlapping situations. Finally, transitions take time. it is difficult to analyse effectively a situation as it is happening. it is much easier in retrospect. Yet, there are ways to measure aspects of the transition.

A key issue in the establishment of a new type of government after one has fallen is the speed and strength of the institutionalization process. If democratic institutions are established more quickly, there seems to be a greater chance that some form of democracy will ensue. It is the same with more socialistic institutions. Karl and Schmitter believe the arrangements crafted by key political actors during a regime transition establish new rules, roles and behavioural patterns which may (or may not) represent an important rupture with the past.

These, in turn, become the institutions shaping the prospects for regime consolidation in the future. In short, looking at institutionalization, as well as specific roles and actors can be an indicator of the transitional process and, sometimes, the direction. The mass media institutions are part of the communications processes existing and operating in and around these factors leading to transition. In the same way the mass media has been studied as a facilitator of democracy, the role of the mass media in these transitions from authoritarian regimes (as well as research on the media and social change more generally) is important to consider. Research on this subject has not been as completely covered as other types of institutionalization during transition.

For purposes of this study, the most relevant writings can be described by the general category of communications systems (including interpersonal, as well as media and technology) and social change. The subject of social change is so broad that its relationship to communications systems is difficult to define in concise terms. Yet, intuitively, there can be a correlation between the expansion and reach of the mass media and types of social change, though the strength and causal links of that correlation can only be speculated. Theories can clarify these relationships.

Denis McQuail has categorized communications and social change theories into five groups:

- Theories of mass society which "suggest that the mass media encourage and make viable a rootless, alienated, form of social organization in which we are increasingly within the control of powerful and distant institutions";
- Marxist theory which presents the "mass media as a powerful ideological weapon for holding the mass of people in voluntary submission to capitalism";
- Theories which describe communications as a force for both integration and for dispersion and individualization within society;
- Theories demonstrating the effects of mass media and their capacity to take over the cultivation of images, ideas and consciousness in an industrial society and, by so doing, forming new bases for collective thought and action; and
- The "Global Village" of Marshall McLuhan in which a worldwide community, which supersedes existing boundaries, is established through direct and common experience from primarily television.

From these theories, Joseph Klapper proposed some generalizations about the effects of mass communication on social change which can apply to Russia and Poland. Mass communication does not usually serve as a necessary and sufficient cause of something, but rather functions with other factors and influences.

This is important to our study as mass communications alone seems to have little or no effect. These other factors and influences use mass communication in the process of change. For example, institutions, such as Solidarity and the Catholic Church in Poland, are willing to utilize the power of mass communication.

On the occasions that mass communication is used in the service of change, one of two conditions are likely to occur:

- The other factors and influences are likely to be inoperative and the media effect will be direct or
- The other factors and influences, which normally reinforce the status quo, will be found to favour change.

The second option seems much more likely in these cases. There are always situations in which mass communication will produce direct effects or serve psychophysical functions. There are some things which mass communication can do that other factors cannot do, such as the continued presence of printed material in an individual's home. The effects of mass communication on change are affected by the nature of the media and communications themselves (i.e., aspects of textual organization, the source and medium, public opinion).

One common thread running through these theories and generalizations is that what we experience is increasingly indirect and mediated and that, whether by chance or design, more and more people are receiving a similar version of the world through similar types of mass media. The differences come in the "versions" of reality proposed by the various media and theories. It is: very clear that the mass media do have important consequences for individuals, for institutions and for society and culture. That we cannot trace very precise causal connection or make reliable predictions about the future does not nullify this conclusion.... All that remains is to discover not whether the media have power and how it works, but who has access to the use of this power.

Generally this means asking questions about ownership and other forms of control, whether political, legal or economic. The question, then, is one of power. How effective are the mass media? If they are effective, who should control them or should they be controlled at all? Does the entity which has control over the mass media control other parts of society? This question of power is key in Russia and Poland during their political, economic and social transitions. The conflict arises as the mass media assert their own power and the political institutions attempt to arrest that power in their own manner. The media do not want to be controlled, but the political structure must harness and use their power for its own benefit if it is to succeed and survive.

Contemporary literature which looks both at the mass media and its effects in Russia and Poland is scarce. These two nations, which have begun to liberalize their political systems, have used and reacted to their respective mass media in different ways. Poland had an extensive samizdat press which was highly influential during the 1980s.

Since the official collapse of the ruling communist party in 1990, the media has been decreasing in its social relevance, cohesiveness and power. The Polish mass media are in need of direction and definition in regards to ownership, role and power. In Russia, the Soviet press was the epitome of the Marxist propaganda arm. Its liberalization process has been quite slow. Though it is still economically dependent on the state, the Soviet press also is now in a "limbo," but coming from a different direction than the Polish press, it is gaining social relevance, cohesiveness and power while at the same time searching for some identity and role.

There has been very little written about the role of the press in these types of societies. Many questions have been left unanswered, but the issue continues to persist. Russian journalists George Vachnadze and Elena Androunas have recounted the more recent experiences of the Russian press as it has attempted to liberalize itself. But these are more narratives and anecdotes and have not placed present experiences into the broader theoretical context. An edited volume by Sarah Sanderson King and Donald Cushman and Slavko Splichal's work have begun to look at communications systems at the transitional level, but have not specifically linked the use of the mass media in transitional countries to social and economic change. Instead, they have focused on the media and political stability.

Before looking at the contemporary relations between the government and media, it is useful to examine the history of such relations in each area. The history of communications systems within Poland and Russia has a strong relationship to the communist press systems which were imposed on their societies, but the reactions were different. The Soviet press was able to maintain its monopoly on mass media-disseminated information whereas the Polish press succeeded in creating underground communications networks for the dissemination of more credible information. Because the present identity crisis in the media is linked to those communist systems, the historical overview will focus principally on the point at which these authoritarian systems were implemented.

RUSSIA

The communist press system had its origins in Lenin's implementation of communism as the ideological foundation of the Soviet single political party system. As described by Schramm et. al, the communications system in communism, like every other system and institution in a Soviet state, existed to do only what it is specifically assigned to do by the leaders of the state. In communist states the leaders seek to ensure their power through control of key organizations: trade unions that discipline the workers, collective farms that organize the peasantry, and writers' unions that keep intellectuals in line.

Schramm says this idea is at the root of the communist press theory. It stems from general ideologies of control in Karl Marx's writings, then it was adapted by Lenin and Stalin, stating that the media can be a useful tool in fomenting revolution. Even today, the theory has been interpreted differently than Lenin applied it seventy years ago. "But the key to the whole system is control of the media through which the negative sanctions wielded by mass organizations are positively reinforced by the propagation of communist ideology and policies."

The media, in a communist system, can be crucial to the ruling elite in times of crisis. Lenin understood the central role of the press in 1901 when he offered his now famous dictum that "a newspaper is not only a collective propagandist and a collective agitator, but also a collective organizer." Stalin declared twenty-one years later: "The press is the most powerful instrument with which the party daily, hourly, speaks with the laboring class in its own vital language. There exists... no other such flexible apparatus." Brezhnev in 1967 reiterated that the mass media were "... a powerful means of rearing the people and propagandizing the party's ideas."

This attitude about the role of the media led to a contradiction. If the purpose of the press was to agitate people toward revolution as Lenin had proposed, what was its purpose after the revolution? They would respond that its new purpose would be to motivate revolutionary change in other parts of the world. They subsequently embrace an authoritarian approach to the press for their own countries and use the media to reinforce and maintain the status quo. Some countries began to see the paradoxical decisions and began to utilize the media as a weapon to fight the existing structure.

During the period from 1917 to 1985, the communists were able to maintain effective control over the media. Journalistic alternatives were scarce. "For decades up to 1991, the role of the opposition press in the USSR was played by the foreign mass media. Bauer discusses the importance of secondary channels of information (of which Western media are a part), often found in societies based on Soviet ideology, which substantiate or refute known information.

A wide variety of sources attest to the importance and pervasiveness of informal, unofficial communications in the Soviet Union [and its satellites].... The regime itself tacitly acknowledges the importance of such [unofficial] media not only in its propaganda against rumor mongering but, and more directly, in its use of informers, arrests for "alien" ideas, and intellectual "delousing" of Soviet citizens and soldiers to the West.... More important, however, is the fact that so many of them [informants] go on to report that much of what they knew of day-to-day events and policies in diverse areas of Soviet life came to them via the unofficial, word-of-mouth channel.

These unofficial channels of communication were in the form of mass media in many instances as well as word-of-mouth communication as with the academic and some religious publications. The Russian people found that the literary form of the written word was another effective tool for the circulation of "truthful" information. Authors and playwrights banned by the Soviets - such as Pastemak, Solzhenitsyn and Medvedev - told the truths of Russian history or, through metaphor and allegory, parodied the Soviet system. "There is a world of difference in Soviet and Russian culture between the writer (pisatyel) and the journalist (zhurnalist).

The former has a social and political influence with no exact parallel in contemporary Western societies." Copies of literary works and other types of print media found their way through the country. Millions of copies of the outlawed Bible and Koran managed to work their way into Russia. Then the mass media found a chance to break away from the control. Mikhail Gorbachev was made party secretary and began to actively promote the ideas of glasnost and perestroika.

Irena Maryniak believes this "glasnost brought a breath of air into Soviet public life, it released the Soviet people from a fear entrenched for three generations. It acted, too, as a form of collective therapy to help heal nearly 70 years of state-induced amnesia." She believes that journalists facilitated this therapy with the publication of generally known, but suppressed, truths.

For example, the liberal magazine Ogonyok (Flame) printed documentation "about the fate and work of repressed writers from the archives of the KGB." From 1985 until 1991, open opposition in the print media to political institutions increased. In fact, "the Soviet press... is leading the processes of perestroika." Then, in 1991, the fall of Communist Party paved the road to more liberal media systems.

POLAND

Over the years, the Polish media has been at the forefront of political and social movements in the country. This does not happen in every country, but the tradition of the pre-world War II Polish media was "a good heritage of a pluralistic media system."

When the communists took over they attempted to destroy this legacy, but it kept rising against all obstacles again and again to oppose and finally aid in overthrowing the regime that was repressing it. Since the 1950s, the Polish press system has been a communist press system as described earlier. Yet it has also been as much a product of its history and the shifting demands that have been placed upon it, as it has been a product of the Soviet model of the ideal Marxist-Leninist press.

The Marxist charge for the press was to serve as a collective organizer, agitator and propagandist for the masses, raising them up through education and images of correct behaviour. For the most part, the traditional Polish press was focused on a limited intellectual audience. Historically, there was little local capital for an extensive and permanent mass press, and there was a high level of illiteracy in Poland, as elsewhere in Eastern Europe, until after World War II. The Polish system during the past 40 years, in both its structure and emphasis, has reflected all of this. It has focused on discussion, analysis, and culture — addressed primarily to the intelligentsia and only secondarily to the desires of the mass population.

Furthermore, whenever possible, press names and images hearken back to their non-communist, prewar predecessors. Even the writing award of the Association of Polish Journalists (a communist organization) is named after a leading Polish publicist of the early 1900s because he was one of the only heroes the Polish journalists felt they could emulate.

But, in the late 1940s and early 1950s, because of the then-unknown communist way of thinking, the Polish press was different. It was directed to be written primarily for and by workers and peasants. The prewar journals of non-communist political groups, religious organizations, and intellectual or professional associations were closed down as power was secured by the communists.

During the 1980s, it was this unbending Soviet control that led the Poles to turn to other places for more credible sources of information. The publications by the Committee for Social Resistance (KOR) were some of the nation's most widely circulated documents. Solidarity's publications, from the Tygodnik Solidarnosc to sporadic bulletins describing situations throughout the country, were also widely read and discussed.

But the government-sanctioned press also had a voice. Because it felt it had total control of the Polish information systems, even the ruling communist regime claimed the Poles believed the existing press. In an article in the World Marxist Review, Jerzy Urban, the Government Minister and Press Spokesman for Poland, said the purpose of the press is to tell the public the truth about what the government is doing. In the best sense of the phrase, it is a "public relations" arm of the government.

According to Urban, in May of 1989, the state was conducting five public opinion polls a week to determine changing attitudes toward government policy. During 1988, the government had discovered that people did not believe the government's claim that wages grew faster than prices during the previous year. Yet, "when we expose past mistakes and criticize our own record, the public believes us absolutely," Urban said.

There is evidence to place this assertion in doubt. The Poles turned to other sources of information. This led to the rise of the samizdat or underground press, which was born in the mid-1970s as Solidarity began to take root. Samizdat literally means "self-publishing."

The striking feature about these samizdat publications was "their sheer quantity, their variety, the length of the individual publications, [and] the openness with which the editors and contributors to those publishing enterprises carried out their activities." The role of the underground press in eroding communist power in Poland over the last 15 years is often overlooked in the West. "Ninety per cent of those interned during the martial-law crackdown of 1981 were not union or political activists, but those responsible for writing, printing and distributing opposition pamphlets." It can be safely asserted that the cause of the 1989 break up of the communist monopoly was not singular, but the role of the media was great.

To be sure the new media were an agent of the several revolutions, but at the same time it was disillusionment both with the old media and the regimes they represented that fueled support for change.... The samizdat press was the thread that wove together the [revolution's] disparate social elements. These uncensored publications were only a part, but the most important part, of a general self-defence of society against the totalitarian apparatus of a state whose goal was the control of all human activity, whether political, cultural or economic. The result... was the breaking of the communist state monopoly of information.

These underground newspapers had another audience, sympathizers in Western nations. "It was, I think, the role of things like the East European Reporter and the links that were made between the Czech dissidents, the Hungarian dissidents and the Polish dissidents" that made the West sits and up and take notice.

Newspapers were not the only type of media to make a mark. Literary magazines, such as Kultura, loudly voiced opposition and dissidence throughout the decades. Kultura editors describe risks taken by many who read Kultura at night, the "chain of readers all eagerly awaiting their turn" (because the publication has a print run of only 7,000 copies) and the disappearance and reappearance of copies of Kultura in places that caused alarm to the Polish authorities. "Kultura was so feared by Polish authorities that it became the target of fierce press attacks and was used as evidence in trials."

Solidarity's national newspaper Tygodnik Solidarnosc, which appeared in the spring of 1981, had 500,000 copies printed in its first edition, but "it was read by far more people." This was the case for much of the print media during this time. This expansion of print media continued through the delegitimation of communism in the late 1980s and early 1990s. Then, as society became more pluralized, the print media followed.

CURRENT SITUATION OF THE RUSSIAN AND POLISH PRESS

Now the media have reached a similar point in both countries: a need to define their role in relation to the political, economic and social institutions which are being created in the wake of communism's delegitimation.

As Russia and Poland form the institutions needed to stabilize their political infrastructure; create the institutions necessary for a more liberal economy; and mobilize into institutions such as political parties to solidify the social strata, the media seem to be reforming, creating and mobilizing as well.

There are several obstacles which the mass media in Poland and Russia will have to surmount in order to define a role that works for them as well as for those who read, fund and criticize them.

- First, they will confront the economic problems stemming from the path taken toward a freer market economy.
- Second, they will have to deal with the pluralization and fragmentation that is taking place within their own structure and within society itself.
- Third, they will need to recognize the democratic ideals about communication which conflict with those they have become accustomed to over the past decades.
- And fourth, they will need to find the role(s) which suit them ideologically and economically.

ECONOMIC PROBLEMS

First, with the trend toward a more liberal free market economy, the print media are plagued by economic problems. The tradition of being subsidized by the government has created a false sense of security. In a freer world, the Russian and Polish press want to change their image as puppets of an authoritarian regime to one of greater autonomy and control.

But, they are discovering that independence also means a greater difficulty in obtaining the funding necessary for continued printing. Founded in 1917 as the official mouthpiece of the Soviet legislature, Izvestia (News) is an example of the economic hardships which threaten the Russian print media. In 1991, Izvestia announced its independence from its editor in chief and the Supreme Soviet for which it had disseminated information for 74 years. "Reporters paraded their liberation from party and state sponsorship in pieces that openly criticized even the highest Soviet and republic leaders and bodies."

The result was increased circulation and a ban from the authorities. Enforcement of such governmental action was becoming more and more difficult in the open society, so the government turned to another form of coercion. Izvestia discovered that independence came with a heavy price — loss of funding and preferential treatment from the communist party and the state.... [It] had long been insulated from the practical problems of supply, production and distribution... [and], to make matters worse, nearly all of the essential publication services remained under governmental monopoly.

Results of this situation were disheartening, and Izvestia was not the only publication affected. The combined effects of economic price liberalization and the monopoly on publications services nearly led to a collapse of large print media in Russia. For example, the financial director of Moscow News said that "the government-monopolized printing plants charge prices equal to about 30 per cent of a newspaper's cover price, whether the press run is 2,000 or 2 million — a basic contradiction of the tenets of economy of scale."

Because of this, the Moscow News has had to cut its press run nearly in half. There is a similar set percentage in the distribution system. If the paper decides to raise its price, its printing and distribution costs are automatically increased. In February 1992, Boris Yeltsin proclaimed a "Decree on Additional Measures of Legal and Economic Protection for the Periodical Press and State Book Publishing." By so doing he provided some relief, but the loss of circulation and the cost of printing will continue to be a factor in newspaper size and content.

In the euphoria of the transformation of 1989, Polish media proliferated, despite the fact that the communications industry was "reeling" from both increases in printing costs and plummeting sales because of increased cover prices. "Before, it was clear — the censor, the party, those were our enemies.

Today it's the price of newsprint, distribution, all those things that our Western colleagues know all about, but we are just beginning to discover." The Russian newspapers and public felt these price increases as well. O'Clery believes it is a conscious process on the part of the government to retain control of the print media. The Russian government has raised "the price of paper, printing, and delivery. This has forced newspapers to increase the price they charge readers, and they are losing circulation.... Since Ogonyok raised its charge from forty kopeks to one ruble, its circulation has fallen to 1.5 million, a drop of 35 per cent."

The Russian and Polish print media are dealing with these economic challenges in various ways. Moskovsky Komsomolets (The Moscow Young Communist) is selling advertising space and other newspapers are publishing classified ads. Reporter's salaries are slim, but there are perks, such as dividing up "five or six free trips abroad... each month, in return for giving a tourist agency free advertising space."

Some publications have pursued relationships outside their borders. The Polish government daily Rzeczpospolita (circulation 250,000) has reached an investment agreement with the French publishing group Hersant. Gazeta Bankowa, a financial weekly, has established a joint venture with French, U.S. and Spanish publishers.

PLURALIZATION OF SOCIETY

Despite these economic obstacles, the number of publications in both countries has increased. The increase has reflected a second obstacle to the print media: a pluralization of purpose, scope and ideology. In an open society there is more acceptance of comment, criticism and feedback and, therefore, there will be more avenues for those activities. The Russian government has budgeted 30 billion rubles to help 400 publications.

"The top priorities are children's, scientific, cultural and other special journals that are ill-equipped to survive in a market economy." In Poland during the first year after the fall of communism, the number of journals and newspapers increased by 600 in five months. More than just creating new publications, the Poles also began to provide avenues for publishing. New publishing companies were formed to replace the Robotnicza Spoldzielnia Wydawnicza (RSW, the Workers Cooperative Publishing House), the organization that had control 80 per cent of Polish publications for 40 years. "So we form new publishing companies. We expect within a year more than 500 new small local newspapers to be in print," said Stefan Bratkowski, director of the newly legalized Polish Journalists Association.

This pluralization is also reflected in the social and political realms of Russia and Poland. In both countries, the number of political parties, representing thought across the political spectrum, and grass-roots movements has mushroomed. As mentioned earlier, Klapper explains that one of the characteristics of mass communications and social change is they will not usually serve as a necessary and sufficient cause of something, but rather function with other factors and influences. There is a connection between the print media and these disparate groups and ideas.

Vladimir Orlov, a journalist from Moskovsky Novosti, said that Yeltsin fears the media because he knows that there is always the possibility that "strong opposition newspapers can mobilize marginal groups" and that is not a pleasant prospect. In 1991, 60 new Russian journals were launched and "45 of them have flourished to become even more outspoken critics of the president and the Party." The political leadership has dealt with this attitude in the mass media in two different ways: following the democratic process of regulation through legislation and falling back on the old authoritarian habit of total control of the mass media.

For example, in February 1994, the Duma (Russian Parliament) passed an act which would dictate the media's responsibilities in the coverage of its activities. This was to ensure what the Duma believed should be more positive coverage of Russia's political processes. Poland has also enacted legislation to control the actions and ownership of the mass media.

An example of the second type of reaction came in October 1993. In response to a coup attempt, Boris Yeltsin declared a "state of emergency" and imposed censorship on 13 newspapers and the television show "600 Seconds," which he felt would foment the opposition. "Publications and broadcasts carried by these newspapers have to a great extent promoted the destabilization of the situation during mass disorders in Moscow and the end of September and early in October, and the organization of the revolt," the Russian Press and Information Ministry is quoted as saying. The reaction was unprecedentedly explosive and Yeltsin repealed the order after only two days.

Regarding the event, Orlov said that "the old system of censorship couldn't work" in this new society. Sevoydna (Today) wrote that there was no logical cause for the censorship because there was the belief among the print media that "under the present circumstances, only guaranteed freedom of speech can save the regime from degeneration and tyranny."

DEMOCRATIC AND AUTHORITARIAN IDEALS

This leads to the third area of challenge for the future, the implementation of more liberal press freedoms in nations which have become habituated to authoritarian systems and thinking. The concept of the freedoms of speech and the press for society, journalists and the government is different in Poland and Russia than it is in the West. As stated earlier, the West (especially the United States) has been at the forefront in providing programs to Russian and Polish journalists which emphasize the importance of a free press in the newly-emerging political systems. In fact, freedom of the press has often been the battle-cry for movement and the outcry against attempts at control. Foster believes that the justifications for the freedom of the press were strikingly similar to those in the United States.

Proponents argued that an independent Fourth Estate would expose and check potential abuses and mistakes by executive, legislative and judicial branches; provide the citizenry with the full and objective information essential for democratic self-governance; assist in the spiritual liberation of the population from the shackles of socialism; offer a forum for introduction, comparison, and debate of reform proposals; and consolidate Russian citizens in support of their embattled government during a time of most difficult sociopolitical changes and economic trials. [That] reality has diverged markedly from these high-sounding phrases.

It seems that the post-soviet era has been characterized by continued clashes between the governments of Poland and Russia and the mass media, both electronic and print. Both the journalists and the government are learning to relate to each other on a new level. The superficial declarations of speech and press freedom will have no effect unless the principles implicit therein are adhered to. Lidiya Kalinina, writer at the magazine Domostroi, has said, "We have no censorship now, but the main body of people working in the media are conformists whose views will change with the prevailing wind."

There are exceptions with publications such as Moskovy Novosti and Moskovsky Komsomolets, which are outspokenly critical of Russian politics and are increasing their circulations as well. But, many mainstream journalists are afraid for their jobs. As previously discussed, the government is fearful of a powerful mass media and is hesitant to deal with them on the level of a democratic, free press.

When newspaper analyst John Morton attended a conference in Russia entitled Free Economy and the Mass Media" he was concerned to hear numerous complaints from journalists that "the government, despite its announced devotion to a free press, is subtly distinguishing in dispensing newsprint and official information between `pure' media operations (those friendly toward the government) and `impure' ones (those that are critical)." One of the principal obstacles in the improvement of this relationship is the history of censorship within communist societies. This form of control has become associated with communistic media theories since Lenin's time. In Russia, the Bolsheviks took control of the media as a necessary source of propaganda.

Censorship naturally accompanied this type of mass media use. Censorship was introduced in Poland by temporary decree in 1946 and lasted unchanged until Solidarity's uprisings in 1981. "In July 1981 the Polish Parliament finally passed legislation that invalidated the 1946 decree and substantially liberalized censorship.... On December 13, however, martial law was introduced and the law was suspended." Actions involving what more liberal mass media analysts would call censorship or prior restraint of news, are a part of the flow of information in both Russia and Poland. "Vladimir Solodin, who had had the job of defending freedom of the press in the Yeltsin government, switched to be the chief of censorship [during the October 1991 coup attempt] without a visible qualm."

Some of the confusion in the relationships between the mass media and political institutions can be explained with the idea of enemy imaging. In the late 1950s and early 1960s, both Kenneth Boulding and Ole Holsti introduced research on the subject, principally emphasizing the relationship between the United States and the then Soviet Union. In a paper regarding his now famous research on John Foster Dulles, Holsti writes, "The relationship of national images to international conflict is clear: decision-makers act upon their definition of the situation and their images of states - others as well as their own."

He continues by saying that these images must coincide with "commonly-perceived reality" in order to be supported. There is great value in enemy imaging. By classifying something as an enemy, "one's own values are enhanced, the cohesion of the group is strengthened, [and] the indistinct inner fear can be projected out onto some specific cause."

This is what happened to the media in Poland, especially during the 1980s when it was linked to the Catholic Church and the Solidarity movement. For the communist press, the enemy was capitalism and inside the Soviet Union, the government itself was the enemy of the literary movement. As the new political systems learn to relate to the new mass media, they, too, must find new enemies. With the collapse of the communist ideology, the enemy is no longer the world. It must be something within the society such as crime, social and economic progress or the environment.

These governments are discovering that the mass media can play an integral role in the process of finding and focusing on a new enemy. Unfortunately, the mass media are wary, given the past history of such relations.

FINDING A ROLE

Finally, there will be a need for the print media in each country to define its role. In a classic essay, Harold Lasswell, a political scientist and a pioneer in communications study, identified three social functions of communications:

- Surveillance of the environment,
- Correlation of the different parts of society in responding to the environment, and
- Transmission of social heritage from one generation to the next.

Since Lasswell, scholars have suggested that entertainment as a social function of communications would be added as a fourth category, but this function is only beginning to be observed in Russia and Poland. These social functions identify the choice (or a combination of choices) of roles which the mass media in Russia and Poland can play: (1) information giver (surveillance of the environment), (2) an agenda setter and mobilizer (correlation of parts of society) and (3) a reinforcer of values transmission of cultural heritage (transmission of social heritage).

The first role is as an information giver seems to be the most talked about. Russian and Polish journalists want to be able to disseminate what they feel is more objective and truthful information. Orlov said this is one of the principal desires of the post-Soviet press. "The role of the press in Russia today is the same as it is the United States: make investigations, do interviews, report what happens, criticize and analyse."

But the content of that news is being examined. Orlov believes that Russians are becoming tired of negative political news. "The public is not so interested anymore in the media as a news source. They want entertainment." According to Lev N. Gushchin, editor of weekly Ogonyok, "In general, the readers are tired of politics, tired and disappointed with the political changes that have not brought about any real changes" and newspapers are responding by turning to entertainment, crime, sports and pop culture.

The feeling in Poland is that journalism is just a by-product of the authoritarian system and journalists will have to relearn news-gathering skills. "We in Poland have forgotten how to take an interest in the rest of world," laments Ernest Skalaski, an editor at Gazeta Wyborcza. Journalists had forgotten how to exchange information. More than that, this generation of journalists had never really learned how to look for stories, cover beats and sniff out news.

The next role of the media could be as an agenda setter or mobilizer. According to George Gerbner, the agenda setting process can be seen in the dominant agencies of communications which produce the message systems that cultivate the dominant image patterns. They structure the public agenda of existence, priorities, values and relations.

People use this agenda to support their ideas and actions in ways that tend to match the general composition and structure of message systems provided that there is other environmental support for these choices and interpretations. In other words, people use the information in the press to justify and motivate their mobilized activities.

In both Russia and Poland this is currently seen in the fragmented political parties and mobilization on a local level (though Zhirinovsky may be an exception). To set the agenda there is one important prerequisite: media access. Most senders are professionals and if journalism remains in the hands of professionals, others tend to be excluded as potential journalists/senders from having access to this media which is the means to reach the rest of the public.

Grassroots discussion among citizens tends to be displaced, in the mass communications situation, by discussion among columnists, public relations practitioners, and other professionals, or among experts or political figures debating one another. Currently the dialogues are taking place on this level. As mentioned before, Orlov feels the general interest, in political dialogue at least, is minimal.

Finally, the media can be a reinforcer of values and ideas and, as McQuail mentioned earlier, can also cultivate images, ideas and consciousness. This is the goal of the marginal right and left wing publications. Again, Zhirinovsky is a good example. His nationalistic movement hopes to cultivate an alternative approach and reinforce those ideas. Yeltsin sees the print media as a forum for his government as well.

On March 4, 1994, he created a new presidential information department with the goal to "provide the public in Russia and abroad with objective information on Russian government policy." Orlov said these new information strategies are part of a larger public relations campaign to improve the Yeltsin government's image with the public and the press. To a certain extent, the press relies on these organizations for information and reciprocally, the organizations rely on the press for the dissemination of it. In this way, the institutions become more beneficial to each other.

Russia and Poland can provide useful information for studies on the mass media in transitions from authoritarian rule and, should they eventually reach some type of democracy, they will be increasingly valuable as case studies in this area as well. Their history and cultures are different from other countries which have already experienced this transition, but some general trends can be delineated. First, transitions from authoritarian systems, and especially from hard-line communism as in the case of Russia and Poland, usually result in a period of flux while the mass media acts differently than it did under the authoritarian regime.

For example, the large samizdat press in Poland had to change its focus, and the print media in Russia moved out from under state control. Secondly, this transition period is marked by a fragmentation of society, which is reflected both in the numbers and orientations of the press. Third, political, economic and social institutions are fluid and constantly changing together with the goal of great stability (though how that stability will be attained is in question). The press is changing with society, attempting find a role that will fit it economically and ideologically or it is actively promoting a certain course of action, as with the Westernization (democratization) of the press or the nationalistic movements.

It can be argued that society is always in a state of change so the above assertions would not be significant. Yet, there are relative levels of stability. The mass media will continue to look for a role in society - in relation to other systems and institutions - where it fits in with other societal institutions. There is no clear threshold to discern when comfort becomes stability or vice versa, but that is the beauty of comparative politics. Comparing both geographical areas and general trends, can provide indications of stability as the world has come to define it. An additional thought is that stability does not last.

There is a place for opposition, even in societies where institutions feel relatively comfortable. But, if that opposition becomes too strong and is able to mobilize portions of the populace, the political structures will surely attempt to silence it. Then the political structures, if they were more democratic, will be changing as well.

The mass media never seem to lay down and let current political institutions abuse their power, but there are indications that the ebb and flow of the political, economic and social tides of a nation have an impact on them. But the reverse is also true. The mass media will continue to give a voice to the wide spectrum of mainstream and marginal thoughts which are sure to be a part of Poland and Russia during this transition from communist rule.

5

Investigation of Media Framing

Despite increasing attention from the international community, violence against women (VAW) remains a global public health and human rights issue, and continues to impact the physical, mental, sexual and reproductive health of women. According to the World Health Organization, one of the most common forms of VAW is that committed by a male husband or partner. This intimate partner violence (IPV) is not limited to violent acts or threats-intimate partner homicide (IPH) comprises a subset of this violence.

In Botswana, a country in sub-Saharan Africa, these homicides are locally referred to as 'passion killings,' and are increasingly prevalent. Despite their brutal nature, little attention has been paid to the so-called passion killings in the research literature; however, media reports provide information about, and insight into, these crimes. This study endeavored to investigate the portrayal of IPH and passion killings in Batswana news media, in order to expand understanding of IPV in Botswana.

INTIMATE PARTNER VIOLENCE IN BOTSWANA

Though limited, the published research literature provides some discourse around IPV in Botswana. According to this literature, IPV is widespread, and in part stems from the patriarchal gender role system of traditional Tswana culture, where this violence was considered acceptable and commonplace. Phaladze and Tlou identify the important role of past Batswana cultural norms in understanding the current situation of women in Botswana. For example, under Batswana customary law, women were traditionally considered a minor and under their husband's sole guardianship.

Though this law no longer stands, it has consequently continued to "entrench women's subordination to men", and must be considered when investigating the prevalence of IPV. Maundeni continues this discourse in his study of wife abuse in Botswana. In his discussion of the social stigma attached to women experiencing domestic violence, he postulates that among other things, cultural factors not only play a key role in ongoing IPV, but are also primary reasons why women stay in abusive relationships; that is, women are socialized to accept their inferior status in society and their subordination to men. Several authors emphasize the importance of recognizing the impact of conservative gender norms on cultural acceptability of partner abuse in patriarchal societies; in Botswana, as in other sub-Saharan African countries, women's violation of these norms is seen as justification for the perpetration of IPV.

Only one published study was found to discuss the trend of passion killings in Botswana. According to Alao, passion killings are "viewed as a sign of patriarchal crisis", and are "directed at females, where either a husband or boyfriend decides to kill the female partner". Again, the role of patriarchy is emphasized. From this definition, it appears that the importance of the term 'passion killings' may lie in its social, as opposed to definitional, significance. In order to explore this, it was decided to examine the media framing of passion killings and IPH in Botswana.

MEDIA FRAMING OF INTIMATE PARTNER VIOLENCE

Several authors have discussed the importance of news media in bringing awareness to social issues, and in forming the social construction of a problem. According to Pan & Kosicki, news media frame stories so as to provide central organizing thoughts; Entman adds that these central thoughts serve to "promote a particular problem, definition, causal interpretation, moral evaluation, and/or treatment recommendation", and that framing involves "selecting some aspects of perceived reality and making them more salient in a communicating text".

Through this process of framing, the media influence the issues citizens are concerned about, and how urgent they view the problem to be. Berns discusses the importance of analyzing media framing because "individuals draw on these sources when constructing their understanding of issues"; in her study, she demonstrated that the media served to resist attempts to place domestic violence within a patriarchal framework by degendering the problem.

Furthermore, the construction of a problem can affect whether or not the public believes it is a social problem worthy of change. Several studies have examined media framing of domestic violence, and all generally agree that women, the probable victims, are portrayed as being at fault for the violence. Meyers suggests that the media encourage the continuation of IPV by maintaining the idea of male supremacy.

Given the role media framing plays in how particular issues are constructed and understood, it is critical to investigate how the local media portray IPH and passion killings to the Batswana public.

Specifically, this study set out the following research objectives:

- Determine how IPH are characterized by the Batswana media (e.g., what cases were presented? who was involved?);

- Explore the media framing of these homicides by analyzing articles discussing specific cases of IPH; and
- Explore the label 'passion killings,' in order to determine when and how it is used, and if these killings differ from IPH in any important way.

METHODS

The research team, not being located in Botswana, was reliant on Batswana newspapers that were electronically available and that had electronically available archives. As such, four newspapers - Botswana Guardian, Daily News), Midweek Sun, and Mmegi - were selected because they had electronic archives accessible within the public domain.6 A six month sampling timeframe was selected as a half year was considered sufficient for the purposes of exploration.

Criteria were developed to aid in the selection of media articles from within the determined timeframe for inclusion in the study. Articles were selected if they discussed a specific case of IPH, or were an opinion or general information article that specifically discussed passion killings. To be included as a case specific article, the article had to discuss a death, an attempted murder or a reported threat-to-kill (included as it appeared to be a precursor to cases of IPH), and the persons involved in the violence had to be current or former romantic partners, with the relationship specified in the article.

The homicide could have involved a male perpetrator and female victim; a female perpetrator and male victim; a male perpetrator and male victim; or a female perpetrator and female victim. However, it was expected that no articles would be found on same-sex violence, as homosexuality is illegal in Botswana. Cases that fit the above criteria were selected whether or not the article contained the phrase passion killing(s).

Including cases that fit the criteria of IPH but were not labeled as a passion killing allowed for a determination of any critical differences between the two. To be included as an opinion article, the article had to contain the phrase passion killing(s) or a clear reference to these killings (alternate labeling such as love killings), and the primary focus of the article had to be on this subject. General information articles also had to contain the phrase passion killing(s), or a clear reference, but the article did not have to focus on passion killings specifically (e.g., could briefly mention prevalence).

Each edition of the four selected newspapers published within the sampling timeframe was reviewed for articles that fit the study criteria. Some newspapers published daily and some weekly. For case specific articles, both initial reports on the case, as well as information about the trial, if applicable, were included. To supplement the research and ensure that Objective 3 was fully explored, an additional search was performed for historical opinion/general information articles written between January 1, 2003 and July 31, 2006 and containing the phrase passion killing(s).

An academic paper on passion killings in Botswana suggested there was an increase in the annual number of killings beginning in 2004, so the start date for the "historical" search was chosen to collect information from just before this period through to the start date of the "current" search, to potentially allow an exploration of reasons for the increase in these crimes.

To conduct the historical search, the term passion killing was entered into Google (TM) Botswana, and articles returned in this online search that fell within the desired date range and fit the criteria for an opinion/general information article were selected. Although this search was initially intended to find opinion/general information articles, it was noted that several of the articles also mentioned specific cases. The research team decided that additional information about these cases might provide data relevant to the study, and thus allow a more thorough response to the research objectives.

Therefore, the name(s) of victims and/or perpetrators of a passion killing mentioned in the historical opinion/general information articles were also put into a search performed in Google (TM) Botswana, and articles returned that fit the criteria for either a case specific article or an opinion/general information article, and fit within the historical search dates, were selected. This iterative search process was intended to identify all relevant articles. From the current search, 32 articles were found: 18 case specific articles and 14 opinion/general information articles. The historical search returned an additional 17 articles that fit the study criteria: 6 case specific articles and 11 opinion/general information articles. In total then, 49 articles (case specific (n=24) and opinion/general information (n=25)) were included in the sample for this study.

The majority of articles (n=45) came from two of the newspapers, Daily News and Mmegi. All the articles were imported into the QSR N6© computer programme for qualitative data analysis and coding was done by one of the research team members. Each article was coded as a whole (i.e., titles and subheadings were not coded separately), and a sentence was designated a text unit. In total, 993 text units were coded.

Articles were analysed through ethnographic content analysis (ECA) informed by a theory of framing. As described by Altheide, ECA is a "reflexive analysis of documents" that "supports a theoretically informed account of media content". According to Entman, content analysis informed by framing "avoid[s] treating all negative or positive terms...as equally salient and influential". For this study, it was important to determine the framing of the articles, as content analysis without framing may have missed key media messages that are perceived by the audience. ECA was performed on all selected articles to determine what words and themes were common to the discussion of IPH and/or passion killings.

Prior to coding, two templates, a facts template and a frames template, were created by the research team based on previous research in media framing, and applied to both sets of articles (case specific and opinion/general information). During coding, the facts template remained as initially developed, while the frames template developed through an iterative process.

RESULTS

Objective 1: The Characterization of Intimate Partner Homicides

CHARACTERISTICS

In the 24 case specific articles analysed, a total of 23 cases of IPH were reported. All cases except two involved a single male perpetrator and a single female victim. In the cases that deviated, one included male and female perpetrators and female and male victims (i.e., the perpetrators killed their ex-intimate partners - his girlfriend and her boyfriend). In the other, the female victim committed suicide, as opposed to being murdered by the male perpetrator.

While suicide was not originally included in the criteria for IPH, this suicide appeared to be the result of ongoing IPV by the perpetrator. Furthermore, while the article described the death as a suicide, it was not entirely clear that this was actually the cause of death; it may have been a homicide reported as a suicide. Therefore, it was decided that this death would be included as a case of IPH. In 4 of the 23 cases, the perpetrator committed suicide following the murder.

REASONS FOR LACK OF INTERVENTION PRIOR TO IPH

From the analysis of these articles, it became clear that there existed a general lack of intervention to protect these victims of violence either prior to or during an IPH. Reasons for this lack of intervention were interpreted as stigma, social silence and fear. Twenty-four of the 49 total articles contained some allusion to stigma, either surrounding the crimes themselves (e.g., do not occur in Botswana) or around the perpetrators and victims.

Victims were the most heavily stigmatized, and allusions to victim provocation (e.g., she terminated the relationship, she spent too much money) were found in 12 of the 24 case specific articles. The theme of social silence, or unwillingness to discuss or acknowledge the existence of IPH, was found in 5 of the 49 total articles. Examples of social silence included the beliefs that "Botswana culture...does not permit the type of killings that have been witnessed here" and that Botswana is a "nation of peace and tolerance". Finally, 3 of the 49 total articles discussed fear as a reason why a person who either witnessed or was told about the violence, or the victim herself, did not intervene.

Persons outside the violence discussed fear of repercussion as a reason for lack of intervention (i.e., killer would come back and kill them if they intervened), whereas the victim's fear of repercussion resulted in withdrawal of cases reported to the police.

Objective 2: Media Framing of Intimate Partner Homicides Blame Frame. One broad frame, referred to here as the blame frame, was consistently used to convey the problem of IPH in Botswana. This frame, which served to assign responsibility for the existence of these crimes, and in so doing diagnose the cause of the problem, was used in 44 of the 49 total articles.

Within this overarching frame, several underlying sub-frames were found: a frame that blamed gender or gendered structures; a frame that blamed broader social structures; and a frame that blamed outside factors without implicating the victim or perpetrator specifically.

As stated previously, all of the cases involved female victims (one by suicide), and all but one perpetrator was male; thus, victim and perpetrator blaming appeared to represent blaming of females and males, respectively. As such, it was felt that the victim and perpetrator blaming most appropriately fell within the gender frame. Of the three sub-frames, the gender frame was used most often, and was found almost equally in both sets of articles.

Victim blaming occurred not only in the majority of articles using the gender frame, but also in just over half of the total articles (n=25). Victims were blamed explicitly for terminating the relationship, or 'ditching' their partners, and implicitly for causing an argument or misunderstanding that led to the murder.

In one case, the article discussed an argument the victim had supposedly caused, as the perpetrator "had seen his girlfriend talking to another man and this could have stirred the trouble", and in another, the victim's "uncontrolled expenses" had led to a "running misunderstanding with her boyfriend". In a case involving arson of the victim's home, where the victim survived but five other family members were killed, the victim was blamed by her relatives for having a relationship with a "criminal". These articles also tended to exonerate the perpetrator, by blaming victim provocation for the perpetrator's actions.

As stated by one article, "[the perpetrators] often make the decisions because they fail to handle rejection. Sometimes it is not all about the fear of rejection but they wonder how they would cope after being left by their lover". Several articles using the gender frame did blame the perpetrator, either in combination with the victim, or on his/her own. However, articles that seemingly blamed the perpetrator generally spent more time discussing why perpetrators committed these crimes (e.g., due to anger management issues, impulse control, emotional stress) then what he or she did.

In this way, articles that 'blamed' the perpetrator represented another way to excuse the perpetrator for his or her actions. Articles using this frame also blamed gendered social institutions, such as the family unit (e.g., not counseling children well, encouraging children to live together prior to marriage) and traditional culture, as well as power relations between the perpetrator and victim. Articles using the social structure frame (n=4) primarily blamed civil society as a whole for the existence of this violence; for example, for not "taking the issue of passion killings seriously" and for not coming up with strategies to "eliminate all these gruesome killings".

The police and justice systems were also blamed for the continuation of this violence, primarily due to lack of protection of victims. Two of the articles discussed cases in which either the victim or her family had tried to protect themselves by reporting the perpetrator to the police; however, in both cases, the perpetrator was released and the victim killed shortly thereafter.

In these cases, the police were blamed for not preventing the violence. In addition to the police and justice system, other social structures blamed for both the violence and the lack of protection of victims included the government, the West, economics and development, and the media.

Finally, several articles used a frame that blamed outside factors, and not any particular person, group, institution or system, for the occurrence of IPH. These factors included witchcraft, alcohol and mental illness. Of these, alcohol was blamed most often. Upon analysis of the different frames used by the articles, it was noted that several articles used a combination of the gender, social or outside sub-frames when assigning blame.

Primarily, both gendered and social structures were blamed (e.g., the victim and the police and justice system). In one article, perpetrators were blamed for letting their anger reach the "boiling point," while the media were blamed for portraying the "perpetrators of violence as heroes". Overall however, the gender frame alone was used in the overwhelming majority of articles included in this study.

POLICE FRAME

The five articles not using the blame frame used what Bullock and Cubert refer to as the "police frame". As they describe it, the police frame conveys a "just the facts approach", where there is "no speculation about the nature of the relationship between the perpetrator and the victim and no indication that the killing or its attempt was part of a larger problem between those involved". This frame was only used in articles discussing specific cases of IPH, and blame was not placed on either party.

STIGMA FRAME

Finally, a stigma frame, that is, the perception that this violence only happens to certain people, was evident in several of the articles (n=2). Rather than explicitly specifying what type of people would be expected to experience this violence, however, the articles using this frame presented two homicides as shocking or surprising because of who was involved.

In one, the perpetrator was a respected Botswana Democratic Party (BDP) councilor, described as a "humble person who was slow to anger," and the victim his wife. In the other, the victim was portrayed as a promising young university student who was engaged to her perpetrator. By their focus on the shock that these women could be murdered, the articles suggested that IPH is unexpected among those who are successful, or those in a committed relationship.

In the case specific articles (n=24), the phrase passion killing(s) was not used in any of the current articles, but was used in 4 of the historical articles. In these 4 articles (number of text units=98), the phrase passion killing(s) was found in 11.2 per cent of text units (n=11).

This finding is important as neither the current nor historical case specific search criteria required that the case be described as a passion killing, so any use (or non-use) of this phrase in these articles represents a choice by the author, and not a result biased by search methods. The percentage of text units containing the phrase passion killing(s) in opinion or general information articles was not determined, as, to be included in the study, these articles had to contain either this or a similar phrase (e.g., love-related killings).

COMMON BELIEFS

Common beliefs about the nature of passion killings were identified by analyzing the 25 opinion/general information articles. In these articles, passion killings were often associated with love, and were referred to as "love-inspired", "love-related", "love killings", and as "love turning sour".

Only one article discussed the discord of the association of these crimes with love, and with characterizing them as a crime of passion. Despite the strong association of these crimes with love, they were also described negatively throughout the articles, using terms such as brutal, femicide, disturbing, inhumane, cynical, barbaric, horrific, gruesome, cruel, ghastly, sadistic, outrageous, fiendish, painful and abominable.

Eighteen of the 25 opinion/general information articles acknowledged the increasing prevalence or occurrence of passion killings in Botswana. Two of the 25 articles compared the severity of passion killings to the HIV/AIDS pandemic that is currently affecting Botswana. Though statistics were not available from any national agency, statistics about the number of passion killings per year were reported in news articles (via a member of the local police and a member of the Batswana government's Men's Sector) and in a recently published academic paper.

Finally, all articles that provided a definition for a passion killing characterized the crime as being perpetrated by a male, where the victim was almost always female, and where the killer was likely to commit suicide following the crime.

DISCUSSION

The analysis of the selected articles provided a consistent pattern of IPH in Botswana, and aided in clarifying the label 'passion killing.' In this study, no characteristic was found that distinguished a passion killing from an IPH; therefore, this label appears to represent a particular social construction. This is discussed in further detail below.

In terms of the characteristics of IPH in Botswana, the analysis of case specific articles suggested that they generally occur between current, or recently separated, nonmarried intimate partners, and are perpetrated by the male. Many of the partners were listed as living together at the time of the killing, but further study would be required to determine if this is a significant correlation.

The finding that most IPH occur between non-married partners was also interesting, but again, cannot be determined as significant here as it is possible that a husband killing a wife (or vice versa) is less likely to gain media attention due to stigma. In the future, police records of all reported crimes could be looked at to determine if either of these findings is significant.

Contrary to the common and strongly held Batswana social belief that perpetrators of IPH commit suicide following the murder, the majority of perpetrators in the case specific articles were not reported to have committed suicide. Due to the social stigma surrounding suicide, it is possible that cases involving a suicide are less likely to be reported, or that media reports would mask this trend within their reporting of cases.

This represents an important topic for future study, as the occurrence of perpetrator suicide may be a defining characteristic of a 'passion killing' and a reason for the use of this label, while also a characteristic that may keep passion killings out of public documents. Finally, no articles discussed a previous history of physical violence between the two partners prior to the IPH, an exclusion that likely serves to represent these cases as isolated incidents of 'passion.'

As discussed by Bullock and Cubert, making incidents isolated removes association of these crimes with a larger social problem. Based on statistics found in this study, one to two killings occur each week; however, the majority of these cases are not reported in the media. The under-reporting of IPH in Batswana newspapers is significant.

Due to the lack of information typically given about perpetrators and victims in the articles, it cannot be validly discerned why some cases are reported, while others are not; however, based on common themes found in the analysis, it is likely that the overall lack of reporting revolves around stigma, patriarchy and social silence. Stigma is entrenched in social myths and stereotypes, including the belief that IPV is the fault of the victim.

Because myths and stereotypes blame the victim for her death, they in turn make IPH less newsworthy, and hence less likely to be reported. In addition to victim blaming, the patriarchal gender role system found in Botswana likely represents a key reason why these crimes are so rarely covered.

Globally, the majority of victims of IPH are women, and the perpetrators men; as was shown by cases of IPH in the articles analysed, this trend is no different in Botswana. Since, in traditional patriarchal Botswana culture, men are the dominant sex, violence against women may not be considered especially newsworthy.

Indeed, two of the most heavily reported cases involved violence against a man. In one, a mob beating of the perpetrator occurred following the killing of his pregnant ex-girlfriend, and in the other, a female and male had killed their former partners. Finally, social silence is likely implicated in the lack of reporting.

Several of the articles discussed portraying Botswana as "a nation that other nations would envy" and one that is "healthy and responsible". If IPH were widely publicized, this would disrupt the desire to portray Botswana as a nation of "peace and tolerance". These possibilities for the under-reporting of IPH deserve the attention of future research, as reasons for lack of reporting may also be implicated in lack of protection of victims.

As shown in the results of the article analysis, victims, who are primarily female, are most commonly blamed for this violence. This finding was not surprising, and is corroborated by previous studies. However, the emphasis on gendered blaming further affirmed the key role of gender in understanding these killings.

Several articles cited changing gender roles, stemming from an increased emphasis on gender equality, a shift from patriarchal beliefs, and increased socio-economic freedom and opportunities for women, as reason for the increase in IPH in Botswana. Within this context, Denbow and Thebe discuss how Batswana men still consider themselves the head of the household, and "remain uncomfortable if their wives have more education, earn more money, or hold more prominent positions in the workforce than they do".

From this theory, it can be hypothesized that changing gender roles, and women becoming more central in society, may leave men feeling that their authority is threatened; in response to this threat, violence is used to regain power and control. While this idea represents an overly simplified explanation for killings that are the result of complex and interacting issues, it should nonetheless be explored in future research as a key component of IPH in Botswana.

Finally, this study attempted to understand the unique label 'passion killings.' In general, there appears to be a persistent association of these crimes with love. By constructing these crimes as love-related, the media not only remove culpability from the perpetrator, as the crime is committed out of his great passion for the victim, but also may affect how the public views their role in the prevention of these crimes.

If these crimes are the result of passion and love, positive and private emotions, what place does the public have to intervene? Furthermore, the media present these crimes as occurring with no warning signs of prior violence, further constructing passion killings as a problem outside the reach of public intervention because there is no signal of need or opportunity.

While the media do use negative adjectives to describe these crimes, their underlying connection with love and passion underwhelm these descriptors. Since the use of the label 'passion killing' by the media provides a particularly detrimental construction of IPH to the public, it is of utmost importance that these killings are reframed as crimes of violence and control.

Given the media's construction of IPH as a love-based crime, the lack of use of the term 'passion killing' when describing specific cases is noteworthy. Despite the fact that cases of IPH as described in current case specific articles fit the definition of a 'passion killing' (as presented in opinion/general information articles and given by Alao, none of these articles used this term. A discord exists, then, between willingness to discuss passion killings and willingness to apply this label to actual murders; the same newspapers that wrote opinion and general information articles about passion killings never labeled specific IPH cases as such.

Why this discord exists, and what it represents, remains to be explored. As several historical case-specific articles did use the term passion killing to describe cases of IPH, it may be that a shift in the use of this term has occurred; however, more historical case articles would need to be examined before any definitive conclusions can be drawn.

The results of this study must be considered in light of its limitations. Firstly, the inability to access Batswana newspapers that were not electronic, or that did not have electronic archives, may have led to a biased sample. Several newspapers, inaccessible at the time of the study, now have electronic archives, and so should be included in future studies.

Secondly, because a fairly short, convenience sampling timeframe was used, important articles may have been missed. However, due to the iterative nature of the search, as well as the inclusion of historical articles, it is felt that the sample was robust for that particular time period, and that the sampling frame did not negatively impact the results.

In spite of the aforementioned limitations, these finding have implications for both future studies and prevention programming. Firstly, further investigation into social beliefs surrounding this violence is warranted, and, if gender is found to be central as predicted by this study, it must be incorporated into programming.

Specifically, programming focused on gender roles, both traditional and changing, should be considered potentially important to the prevention of this violence. Secondly, the construction of IPH as a love-based crime, and specifically the use of the label 'passion killings,' must be halted, so that a proper construction of these crimes, specifically one that presents them as the violent acts they are, is presented to the public.

From late 1993 to mid-1994, a middle-aged couple did something that professional lobbyists could only dream about: They visited all 535 members of Congress without an appointment, and without ever leaving home. "Harry and Louise" may have been only actors in a widely watched series of television ads portraying a couple concerned about President Bill Clinton's proposed health care programme, but their impact on reform debate in Congress and elsewhere was no act.

Created by the Health Insurance Association of America (HIAA), the ads "skewered" the Clinton Administration's proposed programme, with spots airing even before the plan had been presented to Congress in September 1993.

But it wasn't even the ads per se that turned the tide against the Clinton programme. According to at least one observer, it was the overall media attention resulting from Hillary Clinton's "frequent and biting attacks" which gave the ads "recognition that no amount of money could buy." That, along with a carefully orchestrated multi-million dollar public relations effort, "turned a popular idea into a political millstone."

One reporter even named "Harry and Louise" the "political couple of the year," beating out Bill and Hillary. The fictional twosome contributed as much to the health debate of 1994 as "Murphy Brown" and Dan Quayle did to the "family values" controversy the news media had fun with in 1992.

The HIAA's campaign goal was to make certain the spots were seen by "those who will shape the debate." Thus, the campaign's impact was not on the citizenry at large, but "on the people who make the decisions." The HIAA had a definite target market in mind: Congress.

And the organization went about a decidedly "traditional" public affairs programme — to influence pending legislation — in a decidedly "new breed" fashion: The news media played as crucial a role in the programme as "old breed" lobbying tactics, which often involve only face-to-face Congressional visits and backroom machinations.

Granted, the "old breed" style is not to be dismissed, but as long-time Washington lobbyist Tom Korologos points out, "new breed" lobbying definitely includes public relations and the news media. The role of media relations in a professionally organized grass roots lobbying programme is not only smart in an era when Congressional representatives are "more publicity prone and more responsive to (their) district," but essential.

MEDIA CRUCIAL TO PROGRAMME SUCCESS

While it still may be true that "nothing beats a personal visit" with your legislator, Victor Kamber cautions that "to win in Washington, you must increasingly fight public affairs battles as if they were political campaigns," including utilizing the news media. If today's public affairs officers don't think the news media play a crucial role in the success of their programs, they'd need only be reminded of numerous cases where companies either misunderstood or underestimated the media's importance or simply didn't care, whether because of corporate culture or a total reliance on "old breed" lobbying methods.

Classic public policy issue campaigns such as the one mounted by the American Bankers Association (ABA) to repeal legislation which would have allowed withholding from individual savings accounts are often successful largely because a media relations component was built into the programme from the beginning.

And conversely, companies ignoring the news media — or underestimating its power to help "set the agenda" on public issues — have lost their cases on Capitol Hill as well as in the court of public opinion. "High visibility can have a wildfire effect on legislation," whether it be a media plan utilizing controlled communications such as the advocacy advertising Mobil has placed on op-ed pages since the early 1970s, or uncontrolled methods such as news releases and talk-show appearances. However, before embarking on a media relations effort, public affairs managers must also be aware that while the media's impact on sensitive issues can be vital to a public policy programme, "negative (media) coverage, especially coming from an undecided legislator's district, can significantly weaken your ability to gain that legislator's vote."

However, the rewards of including a well-focused media relations component in your public affairs programme far outweigh the risks. In effect, it's being sure your organization has "married public affairs with public relations," something Richard Armstrong, former head of the Public Affairs Council, called for back in 1982. A decade later, Washington public affairs counselor Peter Hannaford told of the need to consummate the public affairs-public relations marriage, and outlined how crucial it is to include a "media element" in public affairs planning.

Most public affairs strategies, he wrote, "benefit from close coordination between the public affairs staff and those who deal in the art of strategic communications." At the very least, he noted, working with the news media will result in "an increased exposure of the merits of your case."

MEDIA'S POWER CAN INFLUENCE ATTITUDES

Today, the power of the news media in the public policy arena is unquestioned, whether one believes the media actually do "set the agenda," or as Bernard Cohen wrote in 1963: The media don't tell us what to think, but they tell us what to think about. From the pioneering underpinnings of Lazarsfeld and Merton's 1948 research into the mass media and its ability to "confer status on public issues" to Ehling and Dozier's work more than four decades later revealing that publicity "can change deeply rooted and complex patterns of mass behaviour," it's clear "the power of the press to set the agenda for public debate...is unmistakable."

While it's equally clear that "it is almost impossible to reverse a trend of public opinion through communications efforts alone," and that "publicity" itself is never the solution to a public policy problem or opportunity, a media relations strategy should have a "place at the management table" and be effectively combined with overall decisionmaking.

OPTIMIZING MEDIA RELATIONS IN PUBLIC AFFAIRS PROGRAMMING

Public affairs managers must educate CEOs and other top executives to the benefits (as well as the dangers) of media relations as an integral component to the public policy campaign. Even though a 1994 study discovered some 70 per cent of CEOs surveyed named "media relations" as a qualification "most valued" in their communications officers, research indicates most business executives continue to fear, distrust and misunderstand the news media.

So with the above discussion in mind, the following guidelines are offered to help ensure that media relations plays a successful part in you public affairs programme:

- Assess your organizational culture/structure. Is public relations linked to public affairs? Where does a media relation fit in the overall communications programme? A communications audit can answer these questions and more. Determine if pro-active media relations is supported by top management as well as the public affairs unit. Then seek to make the organization even more open to the media as well as other constituencies. Organizational culture will play a crucial role in the success or failure of these efforts as you seek to adapt your campaigns to fit the organization's philosophy and mission."
- Assess and understand the news media. Know what constitutes news (local angle, timeliness, human interest, etc.). Some reporters say up to 90 per cent of information they receive isn't news; it goes right into the circular file. Understand what the media think about your organization (regular contact, feedback); and cultivate beat journalists and others who cover your business and its issues. Good media relations involves a two-way relationship, established long before your campaign (or crisis) begins.
- Train your management and other spokespeople. Whether by in-house communications professionals or an outside firm specializing in media relations training, it's imperative that those expecting to be on the front lines of contact with newspeople be given instruction in how to successfully conduct themselves when doing interviews with print or broadcast journalists. While some larger corporations and trade associations have the luxury of in-house video studios

and staff communications professionals, smaller organizations can take advantage of the many specialists who've created a cottage industry in media training in recent years. Many are former print and broadcast journalists who bring a "real-world" view into the training sessions. There are also a number of excellent books on how to prepare and conduct media interviews. Having such a text on hand for management referral might be a good investment.

- Establish your organization's source credibility by developing informative and relevant background materials. Frame your materials in understandable terms; clarify confusing jargon. Don't provide only self-serving propaganda and information that doesn't allow constituencies to make an "informed decision" — a doctrine David Martinson refers to as "substantial completeness." Remember, journalists are on the lookout for fresh new sources. The Washington Post, for example, has gone on the record as seeking to avoid "dependence on the same academics or public figures" for its stories.
- Establish accessibility and visibility of management and other spokespersons. Assuming organizational culture will permit it, take a proactive stance in your media relations activities. Offer your management as experts in those subjects crucial to the media's understanding of your public policy issues. While research has shown that journalists will often seek out third-party sources before going to your organization for information on issues of importance to you, you can stay in the loop by giving signs of your availability, knowledge of the subject and willingness to cooperate.

In the "Harry and Louise" situation, one observer faulted the Clinton Administration for its late start in the health-care communications effort, noting an earlier appointment of a White House spokesperson as media focus would have helped "solidify the message."

Establish feedback for your programme. Effective communication is a two-way proposition. It's not enough simply to send your messages and assume they're being heard, let alone understood. And don't let the ease of today's technology in allowing you to get the message out lull you into false security about the effectiveness of your communication. Make sure you have resources in place to measure your program's effectiveness. The best public affairs programs involve not only clear, concise messages, but a willingness to listen and react to information feedback. Even feedback from the media can help modify a company's programme, initiate a policy change or head off a problem.

6

The News Media Accountable

News media-newspapers, magazines, broadcast journalism, and websites with journalistic content-usually start worrying about ethics only in times of crisis, says French scholar of mass communication Claude-Jean Bertrand. In fact, codes of ethics, ombudsmen, press councils, and journalism reviews have been created during times of great social disaffection and "increasingly angry disillusionment" among the public about the news media, when people have "a growing sense of being baffled and misled," as Walter Lippmann once put it. For example, the first code of ethics for journalists was created in 1923, shortly after World War I, following criticism about the influence of political propaganda and the advertising industry on news media content.

Ombudsmen, press councils, and local journalism reviews, meanwhile, flourished in the United States during the social upheavals of the late 1960s and early 1970s. They all can be called instruments of media self-regulation because ombudsmen and authors of journalism reviews and of codes of ethics, as well as members of press councils, are generally media professionals who engage in monitoring, investigating, and analyzing developments in journalism and in the media business.

As such, they expose mistakes, point toward potentially harmful developments, and encourage attention to ethics among journalists. Bertrand describes press councils, codes of ethics, journalism reviews, ombudsmen, and some nongovernmental institutions concerned with media issues as "media accountability systems," defined as "any non-State means of making media responsible towards the public." Since the State should not participate in monitoring the news media, "except by delivering the threats that media often need to start the process of selfregulation," Bertrand urges media owners, media professionals, and media consumers to hold the news media accountable.

But then, because media consumers often prove too "apathetic or unorganized," Bertrand emphasizes the importance of self-regulation by media owners and media professionals, who are asked not only to hold politics, business, and other systems of society accountable, but also to inquire if media professionals fulfill their primary responsibility, which is "to provide a good public service." The goal of media accountability systems is thus to "improve the services of the media to the public; restore the prestige of media in the eyes of the population; diversely protect freedom of speech and press; obtain, for the profession, the autonomy that it needs to play its part in the expansion of democracy and the betterment of the fate of mankind."

To reinforce media accountability by means of media self-regulation, media professionals are limited to "moral pressure." "But their action can be reinforced by the authority of media executives or persisting legal obligations," adds Bertrand.

In addition to the "systems" mentioned before, Bertrand includes "media reporting" and "media criticism" in his list of media accountability systems. He emphasizes that specialized journalists should monitor the news media and write critically about them for a mass audience. Since the news media "have become one of the nervous systems in the social body, the public needs to be informed about them.

Some journalists must specialize in that field so as to cover its news well and investigate uncompromisingly." But Bertrand says: "With exceptions (usually due to ideological animus or business rivalry), media do not criticize each other: blind eyes are turned on the failings of colleagues. Self-criticism is almost unknown.... In this profession, as in others, solidarity sometimes verges on collusion." Although written more than fifty years later, his conclusion recalls the 1947 Hutchins Commission's critique, issued after its inquiry into the social responsibility of the media: "We recommend that the members of the press engage in vigorous mutual criticism.

Professional standards are not likely to be achieved as long as the mistakes and errors, the frauds and crimes, committed by units of the press are passed over in silence by other members of the profession." Bertrand's accusation about a lack of media criticism is no longer valid. Since the mid-1990s, there has been "an absolute explosion of the genre" of media reporting and media criticism in the United States. Leading newspapers like the New York Times, the Washington Post, and the Boston Globe now regularly report about developments in journalism and the media business, as do magazines like Time and The New Yorker.

Howard Kurtz of the Washington Post, David Shaw of the Los Angeles Times, Felicity Barringer of the New York Times, and Cynthia Cotts of the Village Voice have become well-known for covering the news media. They call their relatively new beat the "media beat" and describe themselves as "media reporters," "media writers," "media critics," or "media columnists," while they speak about their journalistic work as "media reporting" or "media criticism."

Today, media issues are also discussed in the broadcast media like CNN's "Reliable Sources," the National Public Radio's weekly "On the Media," and productions with a regional focus, such as "Beat the Press" in the Boston area. Finally, many online media have been established for such critiques.

Among them are media consumers' sites like Mediachannel.org and Websites for media professionals, such as Jim Romenesko's MediaNews, now part of the Poynter Institute's Website. In a special edition of the Columbia Journalism Review describing the booming media beat in March 2000, James Boylan concluded: "At the turn of the century, media critics are blossoming like spring."

It could be argued that the impetus for this increase in media reporting and media criticism has again been a growing public discontent with the news media. For example, the excessive reporting about the O.J. Simpson case and about the affair involving former President Bill Clinton and White House intern Monica Lewinsky stirred intense criticism. The news media might have reacted by monitoring each other more intensely; at least, many of the "media scandals" discussed in the late 1990s have been investigated and publicized by the news media themselves.

For example, the Boston Phoenix was involved in exposing Mike Barnicle's and Patricia Smith's plagiarism and invention of quotes in the Boston Globe. When the Los Angeles Times entered a profit-sharing agreement with one of the subjects of its reporting, the sports centre "Staples Arena," the paper was caught by one of its local competitors-and the L.A. Times reacted with the publication of an in-depth, self critical report about its own failure. Similarly, the Ncii' York Times published long, self-critical pieces recently after reporter Jayson Blair was discovered to have fabricated quotes and interviews. Obviously, not all "mistakes and errors" have been "passed over in silence."

Media economics also helps explain the increase in media reporting. The last decade was marked by numerous big-time media mergers involving, for example, CBS and Viacom, or AOL and Time Warner, and by a boom in the media business due to new media technologies like cable and satellite television and the Internet.

Finally, media professionals themselves have increasingly become a topic in the news media. Jonathan Yardley already laments: "The good intentions... have gone seriously awry. The laudable idea that the press should police itself in the best way it knows how-by covering itself with the same objectivity and thoroughness it tries to bring to all other subjects-has been twisted, and diminished into just another variation on the culture of narcissism, celebrity and gossip." While many more media professionals now write and comment on the media, little research has been done so far on media reporting and media criticism as a media accountability system. The bulk of academic literature available deals with the history of media reporting and media criticism, or with single high-profile media critics. Half a dozen content analyses examine how the news media covered the news media's work with reference to specific events, such as a war or political campaigns.

Merger and acquisition activities have also been studied. Pieper and Hughes found that Time and CNN generally restricted their coverage of the merger of their parent companies to the business aspects of the transaction, i.e., the consequences for the stock market. They left it to competitors like the Washington Post and The Nation to question the consequences of the deal for the independence of the newsrooms at Time and CNN.

Similarly, Turow found allusions to "self-censorship" in the newsroom of Time with regard to the company's business strategies. Robinson's 1983 content analysis of articles on media issues in leading newspapers found that most news media, with the exception of the Washington Post, shied away from criticizing themselves.

Instead, print media emphasized the problems of the broadcast media, while national organizations covered the local media. Northington, having surveyed two dozen journalists on how they reacted to being criticized in trade magazines like the Columbia Journalism Review, found that journalists generally did not change their professional behaviour. The media reporters and media critics specifically have not been studied so far, but ombudsmen have been surveyed several times. Research indicates that the ombudsmen's interest in remaining on good terms with their peers and the news organization can interfere with their potential as instruments of self-regulation.

Also missing in the context of media reporting and media criticism are studies about media owners and media managers as well as media consumers- if and how they follow the "media beat," and what they make of the information they receive there.

METHOD

This exploratory study of leading media reporters and media critics in the United States involved interviewing media reporters and media critics about three key issues:

- How do these journalists cover peers and employers; are "blind eyes" still turned on the failings of colleagues and bosses?
- Do they address a general audience, an "insider audience" of media professionals, or both?
- To what extent do they regard media reporting and media criticism as a media accountability system?

The total number of media reporters and media critics in the United States is small. A comprehensive list on the website MediaNews names 32 "media people" (media reporters and media critics) and 37 media critics from "alternative weeklies." For this study, 30 media reporters and media critics were selected.

This sample included: (a) journalists presumed to have widest reach within the peer group, because their papers or magazines are most widely read by other journalists, according to Weaver and Wilhoit; and (b) journalists who have been proven "innovators" in the field of media reporting and media criticism: for example, the media critic from the Village Voice, which was a pioneer in media criticism in the 1970s; Jim Romenesko, whose website Media News has been ground-breaking in providing online articles on media issues; and one of the editors of the now-defunct Brill's Content, which sought to pioneer as a "media consumers' magazine."

In addition, journalists from the Columbia Journalism Review (CJR) and the American Journalism Review (AJR) were interviewed because, in contrast to the other interviewees, they explicitly address an insider audience with their trade magazines. From the sample of 30, 21 journalists agreed to be interviewed in person. None of the full-time TV and radio media reporters responded or agreed to participate in the study. The interviews took place in the United States in November and December 1999. The average length of the interviews was 50 to 60 minutes, with the longest one taking about two hours. The tapes were later transcribed by the author.

Nine interviewees described themselves as "media writers" or "media reporters," with the task of objective reporting about the content of the news media and the development of the media industry. They will henceforth be referred to, for the sake of brevity, as "media reporters." For example, Felicity Barringer, of the New York Times, described herself as "a media reporter." "That involves covering journalism, the business, and lots of other things, but I abhor commenting on my colleagues and my profession. I just describe what they do.... What's happening with corporate earnings and mergers... what's happening in the coverage of a major news event...."

Twelve interviewees emphasized their critical approach by describing themselves as "media critics" or "media columnists." They will be described as "media critics." They said their task was to comment on the content of the news media and the structure of the media industry; they offered "critiques" or "opinions," or provided "checks and balances" on the news media, as the New Yorker's Ken Auletta put it.

However, no clear-cut distinction between the two role models has yet emerged in this nascent beat. For example, at one point media reporter Mark jurkowitz also referred to himself as a "media critic." All but 2 interviewees covered or criticized the news media full-time. Of the 21 journalists, 17 wrote for leading newspapers, magazines, and online publications, and could therefore potentially reach large audiences. Two interviewees, Mark jurkowitz and Geneva Overholser, reported having worked as ombudsmen for some years, but both had stopped doing that long before the interviews took place.

FINDINGS

Peers and Employers as the Subject of Media Reporting and Media Criticism. As discussed earlier, the work and the decision-making processes of journalists have become a more frequent subject in the U.S. news media in the last decade. Many media professionals react to the public criticism with high sensitivity, according to most interviewees. For example, Howard Kurtz of the Washington Post said "you inevitably anger and alienate many people in the business who would otherwise be your friends. People are wary around you, even in your own newsroom...." Dan Post said that as the San Francisco Chronicle media critic he would face "a lot of scrutiny" by the fellow journalists who followed his columns. "So you have got to make sure that you got it right."

Establishing a professional distance from peers was described as being difficult by the interviewees, because they already knew many of the people they write about. This was very different from covering a foreign country, for example, or a government agency. "[Y]ou've been through a lot of what they've been through," said Felicity Barringer, the New York Times media reporter.

Dan Kennedy, the Boston Phoenix media critic, stated that it took him "an awful long time really getting comfortable and confident in going after other journalists. I know how difficult the job can be. Sometimes you are going after people who are more accomplished than you are. But then you have to step back and think, gee, if a movie critic just trashes a Stanley Kubrick film, that doesn't mean that the critic thinks he should be a better director than Stanley Kubrick. I have to put myself in the same slot."

Many interviewees indicated that they felt a responsibility for the consequences of their writing. Cynthia Cotts of the Village Voice expressed sympathy for the use of anonymous sources on the media beat because "simply to be suspected of being a source for someone like me could jeopardize that person's job." Likewise, freelance journalists who she criticized had to fear for their livelihood afterwards, which made her more cautious when criticizing their work. Similarly, Mark Jurkowitz was aware of his influence on peers and other media organizations, and was cautious to criticize small publications, for example. On the other hand, Cynthia Cotts described "puff pieces that media journalists do, including me." She explained that writing only critical pieces "diminishes the chance of anyone ever talking to me."

Many interviewees identified strongly with fellow journalists. David Shaw, the Los Angeles Times media reporter, said: "Actions that I might have previously regarded as a result of some carefully calculated decision, or perhaps even a conspiracy,... are very often a product of ignorance and stupidity and inefficiency...." Like most other interviewees, Ken Auletta was convinced that mistakes made by journalists were often a result of the high business pressure in today's media companies, led increasingly by managers unfamiliar with journalism.

Covering one's own employer was likewise described as a challenge, since "you are certainly aware of your relatives." However, all interviewees stressed their efforts to avoid the impression that "you're trying to further the interest of your own newspaper or company that owns your newspaper." Howard Kurtz always disclosed his affiliations, and said he would make an effort to be tougher on CNN as well as the Post, because of his connection there. David Shaw said that he would sell the Los Angeles Times shares he regularly received as soon as possible.

On the other hand, the interviewees also reported that although they were "inside the building," they were treated no differently by their own employers than any other reporter. Mark Jurkowitz recalled covering the scandals involving his colleagues at the Boston Globe, Mike Barnicle and Patricia Smith: "You are hoping that your own publisher will talk to you, which sometimes he didn't.... I got the same press releases...." Dan Post's experience covering the sale of the San Francisco Chronicle was similar.

Still, these journalists conceded that their employers' business interests might influence the way they covered the problem of media concentration. All regarded media concentration as dangerous for journalism. Nonetheless, journalists from smaller publications who were not part of a large media conglomerate, like the Village Voice, the Boston Phoenix, the former Brill's Content, and the trade magazines AJR and CJR, seemed more eager to tackle the issue of ownership and its consequences.

They also complained about the quality of media reporting in the major news media: "It is always the business implications-what does this mean for stockholders.... It's never, what is this going to do with the diversity of opinion...." Meanwhile, media reporters from large newspapers like the New York Times and the Boston Globe doubted that media concentration would be a number-one topic for their audiences.

Mark Jurkowitz said that since "the public has never really cared about this issue," writing about the stories that do not get covered was difficult: "You are trying to prove the negative." He added: "My problem with it is, I just don't see how you turn back the clock any more.... Everything's been deregulated." In sum, the interviews indicate a high degree of peer orientation. The media reporters and media critics considered the implications of their work on fellow journalists arguably more than they might when they covered politicians or businesspeople, with whom they did not share a professional background. This does not necessarily imply that they are softer on media professionals.

The harsh reactions of media professionals to Howard Kurtz, for example, indicate that he is hard-hitting. And the account the interviewees offered about how they strove to cover their own employers as objectively as possible can be taken as proof that they seek to achieve impartiality even under difficult circumstances. On the other hand, only a few interviewees were as frank as Cynthia Cotts, who even admitted to writing "puff pieces."

And many interviewees conceded to producing "too little coverage of the commercial interests of our bosses and the subtle pressures that that imposes on journalism," because these journalists apparently assumed that this would interfere with the business interests of their employers. Additional research will be needed to determine whether journalists apply the same ethical standards to members of the Fourth Estate as they do to representatives of other social groups. Media Users and Media Professionals as Target Groups of Media Reporting and Media Criticism. Of course, the journalists from AJR and CJR focused on a professional audience. But many interviewees adhered to Bertrand's thesis about a relatively passive general audience.

The majority of both media critics and media reporters doubted the public's interest in media reporting and media criticism, generally because they received little feedback from the popular audience, and a lot of feedback from insiders. Tim Jones, for example, was firmly convinced that the majority of his Chicago Tribune readers were "more interested in complaining about the media than reading about and understanding the media." Few of the interviewees reported a high degree of feedback from the general audience. One exception was Howard Kurtz: "Those who think that my primary readers are simply other journalists... totally misconstrue how interested the general public is in media coverage and media criticism."

Mark Jurkowitz said he wanted to "train" the media users to skepticism towards the news media by "treating it like a consumer beat in some ways." Slate's Scott Shuger, who also reported considerable feedback from lay users, described his goal: "Readers should ask themselves: Whose interests are being served by this story told in this way and whose are being left out?" The varying degrees of response from the general audience may result from different ways of covering media issues. Several interviewees said they could attract larger audiences among media professionals with insider stories about media celebrities. Sean Elder, former Salon media critic, gave an example: "Tina Brown: Just mentioning her name-always gets hits.... [T]hings that are considered a little more fringe, like... supermarket tabloids... don't get that much interest."

While few interviewees admitted explicitly that they pander to media professionals, quite a few seemed to do it-and a glimpse onto MediaNews confirms that much "media gossip" is published in the news media every day. Mark Jurkowitz commented: "A lot of the media writing is inside baseball. It's about us, it's for us, it's gossip about our industry." He added: "The public is... interested. But if you only talk about your own industry gossip, they are not going to be interested."

Those who exploit their peers' craving for gossip without regard to the interest of the general public usually get away with it, since media reporters and media critics seldom go after other media reporters and media critics. It could even be assumed that "media gossip" and "insider reporting" is encouraged by some news medi a executives, if one considers Dan Post's account of how his own column was created: "I think that is also part of the idea behind having that type of a column in the paper, to be perfectly candid.... By writing about the media, it is sort of a way to get other media reading your paper. [I]t helps the newspaper's reputation...." In sum, the majority of the interviewees received more feedback from media professionals. This apparently tempts many media reporters and media critics to pander to their professional audience by providing insider news. Those who strove to choose topics relevant and understandable for a popular audience also reported substantial feedback from average media consumers. It could be argued that media reporters and media critics need to watch each other more closely to make sure that their peer orientation does not result in more and more "inside baseball."

MEDIA REPORTING AND MEDIA CRITICISM AS A MEDIA ACCOUNTABILITY SYSTEM

The central goals of media accountability systems, Bertrand said, are improving the news media's service to the public, restoring the news media's prestige among the public, and preserving its autonomy from state interference. Do the interviewees use "moral pressure" to further these goals? While most interviewees said they had an impact on peers, many said they doubted they have any influence on the media owners and media managers, or the media business in general.

Few interviewees were fully confident that they could help improve the news media's service to the public by holding the media accountable. Those who believed they had influence were the best-known and most respected media reporters and media critics in the United States. For example, The New Yorker's Ken Auletta said he wanted to "educate" corporate leaders to be more sensitive toward ethical matters. The Washington Post's Howard Kurtz stated that the "essence" of his job was "to hold journalists and news organizations accountable."

He added that he had often been described by other editors and reporters as having had "a bit of an impact." "A former editor of Newsweek once wrote a memo to his staff on ethical matters, and included a line, saying: Don't do anything that you wouldn't want to see in Howard Kurtz's column.... I have certainly seen instances where media outlets have changed policies, at least in part, because of something that I have written, apologized for stories that turned out to be wrong, for example."

Meanwhile, many of the younger interviewees-even those who were aware of their immediate impact on peers-considered their influence on the improvement of the news media to be limited, and took an explicitly humble approach. They wanted to be reporters, not "reformers," and could only "sometimes" help serve readers. Sean Elder, from Salon, wanted to keep "people honest," but added that he had "a little more sympathy for the point of view of the editors, who're just trying to keep their jobs and sell something." Eric Alterman, of The Nation, was convinced that "the media is large and so amorphous" that "they can absorb any criticism you make."

He said that there had never been a more important time to be a media critic-but that he would not kid himself that it made a whole lot of difference. Geneva Overholser saw too much media gossip instead of thoughtful media criticism. Therefore, she asked, "[W]hat difference does it make?" Only the two journalists from the trade magazines emphasized that they also wanted to help restore the media's prestige, at least among colleagues, by trying to "write about examples of things we've done well," as Alicia Shepard from the AJR put it. And Mike Hoyt from the CJR said that "not enough attention is given to the positive side of what journalists do."

Also, David Shaw of the Los Angeles Times, a veteran on the media beat, was the only interviewee to mention the danger of state interference when he said that media reporting and media criticism was "better than nothing. We don't have anything else. I certainly don't want any kind of government regulation." Meanwhile, the professional spectators of the news media interviewed here apparently did not regard media freedom as endangered, since almost none mentioned the danger of state interference.

In sum, media reporters and media critics disagreed about the purpose of media criticism and media reporting. A minority of journalists considered themselves "advocates" of the public and adopted a "missionary approach" to their work. Among this faction were the few well-known media reporters and media critics, who were confident that they could improve the news media's service to the public by holding journalists accountable. The two journalists from the trade magazines who saw themselves also as "ambassadors" of their profession were another exception. Many of the younger journalists emphasized that while they wanted to inform readers about the news media and teach them to analyse the media, they did not want, nor did they think themselves able, to change or even improve the news media in general, or restore their prestige.

Many long-time prejudices about a "conspiracy of silence" among media professionals can no longer be considered valid. The journalists on the still-young media beat generally strove to cover the news media, its structure, and even their own employers comprehensively and impartially. They said that as media reporters and media critics, they could have an impact on their peers who have lost jobs or were confronted with changed newsroom policies, for example, after having been criticized by them. This suggests that media reporters and media critics have a considerable potential as instruments of media self-regulation. This potential, however, is not yet fully exploited.

Many media reporters and media critics still appeared to be more reluctant to go after fellow journalists, as well as media managers and media owners, than after politicians or businesspeople, for example. The apparent reason for their cautiousness is their dependency on other media professionals as sources, colleagues, and employers. Media professionals are also the most important target group for their writing, since many media reporters and media critics lamented a lack of feedback from the popular audience. And in fact, the expansion of the media beat went along with an increase in "media gossip" in the news media. Media reporters and media critics might need to be reminded at times that their prime duty should be service to the public, and not their peers.

That said, media reporting and media criticism in the news media have emerged from the media boom of the 1990s as a promising media accountability system in the United States. Once the media beat is even more established in the news media, media reporters and media critics might also become more confident in their "watchdog roles." Some find tradition like the proverbial bag of salt on the back of the donkey which wanted to cross a river, and some others perceive it as a beauty of the past that is to be treasured forever: for some, tradition is a cataract in the eyes of humanity, while for others it is the eyes themselves.

Some tend to eulogize everything that is traditional, while others are too ready to condemn everything that is traditional. Perhaps the issue here is the relation between the past and the present, between continuity and change and the creative ambiguity inherent in the relationship, because an overcritical attitude is as harmful as blind obeisance. The object of this paper is to focus on the dynamic aspect of tradition within the context of nation, community and identity. A preliminary discussion of nation, community and identity provides a backdrop for an analysis of the dynamic aspect of tradition. In the course of this study an attempt is made to delve into the three components of tradition: the emergence of 'invented tradition', the appearance or disappearance of negative tradition and the little and great tradition with specific reference to India.

NATION – COMMUNITY AND IDENTITY

Nation is a modern phenomenon arising out of specific modern conditions providing a possibility for a large participant culture. Nation is neither immemorial nor self-generative but a construct. Nation-building, according to Karl Deutsch, was the result of the twin processes of communication and social mobilization. The emergence of nation-state is generally attributed to three related processes of centralization: "the emergence of supra-local identities and cultures (`the nation'); the rise of powerful and authoritative institutions within the public domain (`the state), and the development of particular ways of organizing production and consumption (`the economy')".

Setting aside the various disputes1 regarding the nature of the relationship between these three processes, it can safely be remarked that the forging of identity - more specifically in a pluralistic society, simultaneously creates diversity. As it is evident from the break up of the former Soviet Union, the anti-national rebellions in giving birth to new nation states have attained respect and recognition as successful nationalist movements.

In the words of Peter van der Veer, "the centralizing force of nation building itself sprouts centrifugal forces that crystallize around other dreams of nationhood: nationalism creates other nationalisms - religious, ethnic, linguistic, secular - but not common culture." The differences in pluralistic societies and the consequent attempts towards centralization and homogenization contain also the seeds of heterogenization because of the explosive dimension inherent in the tradition of smaller communities. The explosive nature of their traditions irrupts powerfully when they are pushed to the periphery and when their very existence is under threat.

Smith speaks of two overlapping concepts of nation. The first view - civic or territorial - is very much a western conception. As per this understanding, the following four vital spheres constitute a nation: territory, law, economy and education. The other view perceives nation as named human populations with claims to a common ancestry, a democratic solidarity, common customs and languages and a common native history. The features that figure in the latter conception of nation are, according to Smith, precisely those features of community which define ethnicity and ethnic identity. He defines an ethnic community as "a named human population possessing a myth of common descent, common historical memories, elements of shared culture, an association with a particular territory and a sense of solidarity". Smith's view provides a more general perspective.

It accepts the fact that a nation is a modern construct found only in modern conditions, and on the same vein asserts that it is not a wholly modern construct because it requires pre-modern ethnic elements. Hence, nations are formed out of civic and ethnic components. Obviously Avijit Pathak is right in stating that a nation remains abstract and empty without a living, concrete experience like family, ethnicity, religion and language. The story of the new nations like India, Indonesia and Nigeria manifested the necessity of creating overarching loyalties that would transcend the more primordial ones like ethnic membership, religious affiliation and linguistic identification.

But these loyalties are neither blind nor are they easily replaceable. Apter rightly points out, "Race, ethnicity, religion, and language are the means whereby people identify themselves, organize their community, find meaning for their sentiments and express their beliefs. All critical elements of man in society appear to be touched in some important manner by each of these matters". Indeed it is a community that gives its members an identity and thus provides a situs in which to define themselves individually.

Identity is perceived in a dialectical process or experience: how a community sees itself or is seen by others, how it contrasts itself and its character as against each `other,' and how it perceives and selects its history. Thus identity indicates who some one is and also provides one a sense of belongingness while simultaneously setting one apart from various 'others'. In different words, "Identity is a matter of the outs as well as the ins.... ethnic identification arises out of and within interaction between groups". Jenkins finds significant similarity of perspective in the views of Everett Hughes and Clifford Geertz. For Hughes, an ethnic group is one wherein "people in it and the people out of it know that it is one; because both the ins and the outs talk, feel and act as if it were a separate group".

Geertz's elegant definition of ethnicity reflects the dialectic polarity between ins and outs, and between similarity and difference. Ethnicity is the `world of personal identity collectively ratified and publicly expressed' and `socially ratified personal identity'. Clifford Geertz calls these 'loyalties' primordial sentiments. He asserts that a state is built on fellow-feeling, which is a feeling of corporate sentiments of oneness. When the members of a state are charged with corporate sentiments of oneness they begin also to experience their belongingness to one another.

This fellow-feeling, or `we-ness' binds together those who have it strongly, overriding all differences arising out of economic conflicts or social gradations and as well severs them from those who are not of their kind. The existence of this fellow-feeling or we-ness, Geertz understands, as the foundation of a stable and democratic state. Probably, to hold the view that the sense of nation emerges powerfully as a tangible experience when it is confronted with the 'other' is also not far-fetched. For instance Rupert Emerson holds the view that when the chips are down a nation effectively mandates its members' loyalty, setting aside the claims of the smaller communities within it and those ties which cut across it or potentially enfold it within a still greater society.

TRADITION

The term 'tradition' is studded with innumerable interpretations. Without going into different definitions of tradition, it suffices here to say that in the common usage the term tradition means the same as `something from the past'. Durgan and Sinha characterize tradition as the accumulated experience of a community which provides a base as well as guidelines to its members through its beliefs, rituals, attitudes, values, customs and institutions.

Tradition comes into play whenever one refers to any link between the present and the past. Jerzy Szacki, a Polish sociologist, perceives tradition not simply as any type of link between the past and the present, because only that aspect of heritage that is viewed as necessary and relevant can in reality force its way into the present. In the words of Szacki, "Only that is remembered and preserved which is actually important to the group, and the whole rest is irreparably forgotten".

The subjectivist element in Szacki's conceptual scheme of tradition appears clearly when he stresses the highly malleable nature of tradition and the way each generation can select a certain heritage, evaluate, reform and adjust to its present needs. According to this perspective, a tradition must be continually reshaped and revalued to meet the changing situation of a group if it is to survive as tradition. Further, when heritage fails to supply convenient items, these may even be invented. The invented ones may be in opposition to the sentiments of the inherited tradition; what is important is that they are attuned to the prevailing psychological climate.

A useful illustration of how a generation selects a certain aspect of its heritage and attempts to adjust it to its present need is the way Lokmanya Tilak, a great nationalist leader, used the feast of Ganesh caturthi during the freedom struggle. Ganesh is the elephant-faced God in Hinduism. This Ganesh caturthi feast is celebrated in August-September every year. Tilak revived this feast as a means to bring the hindu community together. Although Tilak belonged to Chitpavan community, a priestly class in the hierarchical hindu caste system, he did not choose the Saraswati feast, which has its origin in the great tradition, but instead chose the Ganesh feast which belongs to minor tradition.

He selected it from the cultural heritage of the masses in order to fit the specific needs of his time. Tilak realized the necessity, in the words of Pradhan, "of giving a deep-rooted cultural basis to the political movement by breaking through the routine of the somewhat academical nature of the Congress movement, and he strove to bridge the gulf between the present and the past and to restore continuity to the political life of the nation". Tradition consists of three components: how a tradition is transmitted, what is being handed over, and the nature of involvement of the participants.

Szacki speaks of these three dimensions of tradition as three complementary concepts of tradition: Social transmission (tradition in the functional sense), Social heritage (tradition in the objective sense) and Tradition (in the subjective sense) respectively. The first focuses on the act of transmitting certain values of a given community from generation to generation. The way these values are transmitted can take innumerable forms, for instance, orally or through the press, mass media, performing arts and the celebration of festivals. The second dimension of tradition emphasizes the content of tradition. It is the accumulated and accumulating storehouse of a community's systems of beliefs and rituals, values, attitudes, customs and institutions.

The third stresses neither the act nor the object of transmission but the attitude of a given generation to the past and consequently its approval or disapproval of a certain aspect of its heritage. For instance, the disapproval shown by the British public toward the traditional practice which ruled against hoisting the flag over Buckingham Palace following the death of Diana, the Princess of Wales, was no secret.

The importance of the third dimension of tradition comes from the conviction that it is illusory to believe in the possibility of being into faithful to one's earlier generations, as that would mean living in their socio-cultural world. Tradition is often taken for granted in common parlance as something which man uses to replace reason, but frequently it happens to be an object of complex intellectual operations. Szacki points out two types of intellectualization. He ascribes one to E. Husserl and the other to Bert F. Hoselitz The intellectualization of tradition on the strength of the statement that a given pattern would be good even if it were not traditional goes to Husserl's credit, whereas the other type, namely, the intellectualization of tradition qua tradition is attributed to Hoselitz However both these processes of intellectualization take place in the social consciousness.

Szacki points out another process of intellectualization which is unlike the above-mentioned two types. He explains briefly: We have a rational pattern of behaviour, and we try to provide it with a tradition of its own. Behaviour patterns which for some reasons are accepted as rational must for some other reasons be presented as complying with patterns to be found in the past. It is so because, a community has a tendency to accept something more willingly when it is shown as rooted in the past and this tendency is more prevalent in traditional societies. L. Krzywicki's concept of historical substratum, which Smolicz refers in his article, is here in place.

According to him it is a sum total of passive factors in one's social heritage, which is capable enough to arrest the rise of new social movements by restricting the freedom of the individuals. His understanding of social change seems to be too narrow and in opposition to social change and new innovations. The dynamic concept of tradition perceives tradition not as a sum total of historical substratum, inevitably bound to be backward looking and conservative, but as a forward-looking activity which seeks its basis in the accumulated experience of earlier generations.

"It is tradition which offers a framework in which to breathe, and an invitation to play our own part.... The very wholeness of tradition in which we live certainly demands much of us". Tradition as a forward-looking activity in a dynamic continuity with the past is free from suffocation and superfluity.

For, openness without rootedness is superfluous, and rootedness without openness is fanaticism. Therefore tradition is not necessarily to be seen in opposition to social change and innovation. "A tradition can only survive the vicissitudes of time and continue to flourish if it accommodates itself to the present".

A healthy relationship of the past (tradition) with the present is brought into being through three processes: through a reinterpretation or modification of cultural heritage to the contemporary situation, through the influence of other cultures, and through the influence of creative developments and inventions within the given society. When a society is open to these processes its tradition will cease to be a burden of the past.

The relationship between the past and the present should not be viewed as a one-way traffic directed towards modification of the past. A healthy relationship between the past and the present also implies that the present is confronted and challenged by the past - by the core values of the nation's culture. Thus cultural continuity between the past and the present gives due respect and importance to both the present and the past, allowing the necessary space and freedom for processes that are mutually complementary.

The notion of cultural continuity brings us to the question of the fundamental elements of culture or the core values of a given culture. When one perceives of culture as a static concept, then the core values of a culture appear to be immutable in nature; but when culture is perceived as a continuing accumulation of social heritage then one comes to the conclusion that the core values of a culture also undergo changes in their nature and as well in accordance with the interpretation given to them by successive generations.

Thus, referring to Hinduism, Dalmia and von Stietencron explain tradition as "an entity that is neither a permanent unchanging heritage of the past, nor entirely fictitious, but constantly being selected and modified in response to social change and to visions of the future". The questions that have to be honestly faced are the following: what are the core values and how important are they for the identity of a given society? How stable or fragile are such core values in the contemporary time? How persistently they are activated or reconstructed?

The subjectivist interpretation of tradition understands the term 'handing down' in a metaphorical sense because of the modification a culture undergoes in the process of social transmission. Each generation makes its own selection of elements from its heritage, making the new elements again and again the basis for valuation, changing approvals into disapprovals and vice versa, or simply becoming indifferent to what used to be key issues. Consequently, this view admits the possibility of creating tradition that would be not the valued part of the actual heritage, but the valued part of an alleged heritage. There are examples of traditions which are either pure fantasy or which have little agreement with the past.

Eric Hobsbawm and Terence Ranger call this phenomenon "inventing tradition". Inventing tradition is essentially a process of normalization and ritualization characterized by reference to the past. According to Hobsbawn `invented tradition' includes both traditions that are consciously constructed and formally instituted and traditions that emerge in a less easily traceable manner but which establish themselves with great rapidity. The goal of invented tradition is generally to establish continuity with a suitable historic past, a continuity that is largely fictitious,

The earlier part of this chapter referred to the phenomenon of modern nations as largely artificial constructs, and also pointed to the search for establishing 'overarching loyalties' in the process of such contemporary nation-building. Consequently the modern nations of the world cannot be adequately understood without paying careful attention to the invention of tradition. The nation-state, national-symbols, histories, and multi-ethnic societies are comparatively recent historical innovations. Hobsbawm points out that plenty of today's political institutions, ideological movements and groups were so unprecedented that even historic continuity had to be invented; entirely new symbols and devices came into existence as part of the attempt to create these modern national movements and states.

On the richness of these emotionally and symbolically charged, invented symbols, Hobsbawm says, "The national flag, the national anthem, the national emblem are the three symbols through which an independent community proclaims its identity and sovereignty, and as such they command instantaneous respect and loyalty.

In themselves they reflect the entire background, thought and culture of a nation". No in-depth study of national phenomena can be achieved without giving due attention to the 'invention of tradition'; the modern 'nation' is a construct which relies heavily on the possession of appropriate symbols. Another important aspect of the subjective interpretation of tradition is the negative evaluation of tradition. Members in a group never shape their attitudes in a vacuum; while developing their attitudes they also take into consideration the attitudes of other members. George Allan in an autobiographical tone writes, "I live together with other human beings in a community that has distinctive traditions.

Those who comprise my social group share particular conditions and undertake or permit characteristic activities. We believe certain things to be significant, and we act on the assumption that certain things are right or useful or opportune. Other communities of people arrive at quite different conclusions, accepting beliefs which we reject, legitimating actions which we prohibit". Different social groups tend to espouse different traditions and if such groups are in an antagonistic relationship to each other, the positive tradition of group A becomes a negative tradition of the members of group B.

Three points must be mentioned with regard to the negative evaluation of tradition:

- In a plural society there is never a shortage of such alternative and competing traditions.
- Changes in these evaluations do not remain constant. They depend on the political, social and economic status of the group. This partly explains why the content of cultural tradition grows continually, so that each social group within a society comes to be particularly influenced by systems of ideas belonging to different periods in its development. Consequently what was greatly esteemed in one period may not enjoy equal favour among all groups in another period.
- Changes in the negative traditions of the various groups in a given society are probably an excellent indicator of inter-group relations and also of the status of a given group within a given society.

In a plural society, minority groups usually manifest a tendency to abandon their traditions in favour of the majority group's tradition. Szacki calls the minority groups the new recipients of currently respected tradition of a wider community. The process of Sanskritization in the history of social change in India can be cited as an example.

Popper holds the view that this break from one's tradition is in reality not a freeing from the bonds of tradition but only a change from one brand of tradition to another. A particular group's interest in switching its loyalty to another tradition has to be seen within its historical context.

However, one should note that highly complex plural societies with different ethnic strands seem to underplay the value of cultural continuity, precisely because the reconstruction of the past often tends to be incoherent. Therefore competition between different traditions makes any appeal to cultural continuity and to the past unattractive and ineffective. The wider the cultural diversity in a given population, the greater will be the difficulty in attempting to see its past as a monolithic block.

The first of the above-mentioned three observations, namely, 'plural society with alternative and competing traditions' leads us on to consider Robert Redfield's comments on 'little and great traditions'. Redfield asserted that every civilization consists of traditions. That of the elite, of the reflective few who give it formal articulation, he termed 'great tradition'.

That of the unlettered mass of the folk, he christened 'little tradition'. Redfield assumed that all civilizations began with an orthogenetic or primary process of growth and kept on transforming themselves through heterogenetic contacts as they moved toward a more universal form of civilization. Milton Singer and McKim Marriot applied Redfield's approach to study the social change in India.

Milton's statements about cultural change in India can be formulated in the following way:

- He asserts the continuity of India's great tradition with the little tradition because he holds the view that India's primary or indigenous civilization had been fashioned out of pre-existing folk and regional cultures.
- This cultural continuity is an outcome of a common cultural consciousness, which most Indians have in common and which they express in essential similarities of attitudes and ethos.
- He attributes the formation of this common cultural consciousness to the influence of certain shared factors and processes, such as common sacred books and objects, and a shared appreciation of a special group of literati and other agents of cultural transmission.
- In countries like India, cultural continuity with the past plays an enormous role that even modernizing and progressive ideologies had to be traditionalized.

Further, he also concluded that the resilience of the Indian tradition is such that changes take place in it through selective adaptation rather than basic transformation. Dube criticized Singer's dichotomization of traditions as insufficient, stating that traditions in India are organized not in a bipolar but in a multi-polar system.

Dube postulated a six-fold classification of traditions. They are: the classical tradition, the emergent national tradition, the regional tradition, the western tradition, the local and sub-cultural traditions of social groups.\ However, Yogendra Singh, a sociologist from Delhi, criticized Dube's classification as unsatisfactory because his classification stands again on an ad hoc and nominalistic principle. Singh remarks further that in substantive realm the emphasis is more on culture than on social structure.

Tradition is a social fact and it has been understood differently. The course of this study has sensivitized to the different dimensions of tradition, highlighting the fact that tradition cannot be regarded as simply any type of link between the past and the present. It also requires an active display of sentiments of acceptance or rejection. The relationship between continuity and change in tradition primarily depends on the key issue of core values of a given society.

The future debates centered around the question, "Was it (tradition) the repetition of earlier patterns, or the recognition that the past is a story of change, accepting the invitation to develop what we inherit in certain ways?" and consequently the discussions on the nature of tradition, its boundaries and viabilities for change and development cannot be conceived without reference to the nature and viability of core values of a given society. Indeed, an understanding of nation, community and identity is more intimately related to the dynamic concept of tradition than one ordinarily perceives it to be.

7

International Bio-diplomacy and Global Ethical Forms

One of the most powerful and under-explored ideas amongst Edward Said's final reflections can be attributed to the humanism of intellectual vocation: the notion that the virtues of good office-harnessed in the potential energy of democratic criticism-may be evidenced as practical missions. Aligning passion with dispassion, the figure of the public intellectual as "lookout" consolidates a type of mission work-makes the engaged life of the mind a particular vocation, so to speak.

Social anthropologists of course have always been native lookouts of one kind, or another, but the job done well is no easy one. We know ourselves as professionals through the service of critical observation and participation: what we see of "culture" shapes what we make of our interventions-how we proceed ethnographically and collaboratively, what we do with theory, the terms whereby we draw up the world.

This reflexively engaged missionary work, which is quite separate from an earlier proselytising in the name of conversion and is also distinguishable from the modern missions underpinning science and human rights endeavours, might even be said to make anthropology one of the most-if not the most-authentic "lookout" for the humanities and social sciences. Referring here quite specifically to a body of work in political critique currently organizing around "public anthropology" which examines the mission of engagement as public reasoning, public interest and public policy intervention forms, be it for political emergency and disaster relief or quotidian welfare.

This chapter offers a new direction for anthropology's involvement in the public arena of science and societal engagement: it is a speculative snippet culled from the particular "missions" that inform contemporary diplomacy in the age of biological politics and medical science. The argument proceeds by putting forward the novel notion of "biodiplomacy" in order to examine the following three sets of issues.

- Biodiplomacy relations for international science. Emerging forms of governance in international science, I suggest, require analytical strategies for detailing the complexities by which active interventions in biodiplomacy can come to be known: how citizens, professionals and para-state entities are discerned and invested with socio-political value. While an explicitly cultural focus on knowledge biodiplomacy depends in part on empirical exegesis for its descriptive future, this is a topic notably overlooked by some of the most sophisticated debates in critical theory and social anthropology today. The ethics of power, assemblages and arbitration over diverse life-forms have not been approached as the anthropological ethics of knowledge "biodiplo-matica" and there are at last two reasons why this needs redress:

- Despite the fieldworker's best efforts at detached engagement, it cannot be incidental that the role of the critical anthropologist-in seeking to sharpen up such debate for global fora and for the anthropology of globalization-is allied with, if not enchained within, certain force-fields of mediatory power. For diplomacy, as it came to be instituted in the West from the time of Greek city states through to the Renaissance and the modern nation state, has always been about the perilous missions of [relational] mediation. In brief, the writing of diplomatic history by former "in-service" diplomats, social economists, historians and military strategists testifies to the constancy of movements across space and time, territorial acquisition and loss, and pathways of commerce. Quite specifically, there can be no diplomacy-no ground for diplomatic relations-without the mediations of the envoy. At least before the age of virtual communication, nothing could be imagined to happen without the skill, intercultural awareness and political receptivity of the messenger who moves between sending and receiving states, and thereby personifies a potential interface for the negotiation of international relations.
- In the scholarly literature, mainstream reviews of diplomatic politics tend to be elided with historical, military and economic accounts of international relations; and all such accounts are premised largely on liberal and neo-liberal theories of the ascendant state as rational actor. That is to say, mainstream Western diplomatic discourse tends to recount possibilities for mediation and "intervention" in the official or semi-official language of rationality and rational action. Hence, the capacity to intervene is justified as the political norms of détente, entente, bargaining powers, defence positions, and such like. Furthermore, within the official cultures of bureaucratic summitry, the positions and counter-positions of "negotiation" are taken as potentially representative of the rationality of entire

states or even trans-regions ("blocs"). In contrast, this chapter asks: how might insights from social and political anthropology break that bargaining fixture to offer other kinds of "interventions" into the dynamics of (bio)diplomatic culture? What kind of new comparative studies are needed to accomplish these missions?

- Modalities of intervention, withdrawal and extrication. I am interested, however, not simply in documenting instances of intervention, but in probing how forms of action (types of engagement, participation, mediation, advocacy and so on) in the biodiplomatic realm are apparent also as relations of disengagement. Global ethical forms must be also examined as relations of withdrawal: how are these movements to be conducted and analysed as social critique? And what might this mean for our understanding of global and intellectual processes more broadly? I should explain that the following reflections originate in my own attempted passage back and forth among the UK academy, various national and international ethics councils, and non-governmental organizations concerned with issues of science, biomedical innovation and regulatory politics. Somewhat by chance, I recently found myself charged with the professional responsibility of "representing" the public face of academic anthropology at bioethics discussion fora and closed policy meetings sessions. It is in these contexts, as an itinerant knowledge diplomat, that my interest came to be fostered in modalities of extrication, intervention and mediation. In the age of virtual superpowers beyond the nation and outside the purview of territory, and against a climate of adjudication by international organizations and UN conventions, is the diplomat simply the eyes and ears of "the state" with no real power and influence? If so, where now is the figure of the mediator to be located and how can s/he intervene in and report back across disparate knowledge bases? What is an ethics of extrication without undue compromise? How, and for whom, can the modalities of intervention and mediation be practiced, written up, presented and re-presented as public knowledge?
- Inter-governability and inter-disciplinarity. What possibilities exist for the bringing together of practical and theoretical missions? My own fieldwork suggests that a significant conceptual challenge here for the social sciences and humanities entails the operation of "transaction spaces" between two ideals: those that relate to practices of inter-governability and those that go by the name of inter-disciplinarily. When relations across geopolitical borders are refracted through knowledge relations across disciplinary borders,

what kind of nexus exists between globalization and kinship in these social spaces? Facilitating diplomatic conventions across states on the one hand and following the exchange of ideas between subject fields on the other, what relations of analogy can be said to exist between inter-governability and inter-disciplinarily? How apparent are these framings and by what means are they encompassed by the figure of the field worker?

All these questions prompt further inquiry into the global ethical forms of international biodiplomacy or "biodiplomatica," and it is with the intention of moving away from Foucauldian-inspired analyses of "biopower" that the following discussion proceeds to offset some (bio)diplomatic maneuverings from divergent sources. First, I consider an instance of political withdrawal from a site of humanitarian action.

This is offset against a plea for the politics of science democratization as interventions of the social. But what of the intellectual effects of the juxtaposition itself-how are these to be reckoned and what effects do they produce? Critical mission work in this instance, provides a profitable backdrop for re-evaluating what counts as the shifting interface between written and oral encounters in the history of diplomacy; and in turn, the gain offered by the maneuver comes by way of a little re-organized skepticism-namely, some insights on the limits of conversation as a future political resource for biodiplomatic engagement.

CRITICAL MODALITIES

In July 2004, Médecins sans Frontières, the international medical NGO, announced it had decided to pull out its humanitarian operations from Afghanistan. The withdrawal marked a political crisis for an agency that had sought since the early 1970s to validate its interventions by appeals to independence: action relief "beyond borders" (sons frontières). This event (the withdrawal) also marked a symbolic watershed for the wider international community that began to ask questions about the terms of engagement by which an ethics of humanitarian assistance would define its missions of the future.

So, why the retreat? It was not just that five MSF workers had been killed in northwestern Badghis province the preceding month, ostensibly at the command of a local warlord, explained an agency spokesperson. It was not just that the Taliban had been circulating accusations that MSF members were operating clandestinely as spies for the US. All in all, it was not the mobilization of terror endangering loss of life, continued the spokesperson.

Rather, the root of the crisis turned upon the way relations between different professionals and professional identities had become entangled-so dangerously caught up with one another-that this had made for grave compromise on the ground. In brief, the presence of the US-led military coalition and the proliferation of its so-called "provincial reconstruction teams" had put non-partisan humanitarian volunteers at risk by blurring the line between soldiers and aid workers. Close up, the "cooptation" of aid work by foreign troops involved in infrastructure reinforcement had had the effect of politicizing the humanitarian effort such that it appeared as aid efforts themselves constituted a furtive intelligence gathering technique.

Hence the leaflets depicting food-bags that were air-dropped at the Afghan Pakistan border in Zabul province incited mixed suspicions and loyalties (and no doubt many fears too) because flying downwards to the war-wounded one would have seen a conditional string of words: "In order to continue the humanitarian aid, pass over any information related to Taliban, al-Qaida or Gulbuddin (the renegade warlord) to the coalition forces."

Whether from air or ground, the real obstacle was the difficulty that all parties faced in effectively telling people apart. "We all the look the same" commented a Christian Aid volunteer as he described how humanitarian workers in comfortable clothes could be mistaken for nonuniformed soldiers who also did "life-saving" work with civilians. "Nobody knows who is doing what, why and when," he went on to add.

As kinship theorists know, not being able to tell people apart can invoke strong metaphorical allusion. In this case, the problem was a matter of noncorresponding symbolic forms, nor did it have to do with joint claims to preserve a "shared" relation of common substance. Nor indeed was it symptomatic of any lack of specialization. Rather, it had to do with the apparent ease with which particular skills, roles and responsibilities had been borrowed across professional domains. If looking the same was about being seen to be doing "like-wise," it was also about making use of another's knowledge set without explicit acknowledgement of the borrowing.

Humanitarian neutrality had been compromised by the local "reconstruction" teams run by the US military and the "co-optation" of bona fide aid workers. If indeed MSF could no longer see the world as a borderless place for its medical operations-nor, most importantly, envision itself as exemplar of an efficacious organizational presence within that world-it was because claims to the loss of impartiality were as much about the failure to recognize the necessity for singularity (read: "professional distinctiveness") as they were about freedom, democratic rights and acting in the name of independence.

Almost exactly at the same time as MSF was pulling out from Afghanistan, Bruno Latour's latest critique on political ecology came into print as its first French-to-English language translation. The Politics of Nature, subtitled "How to Bring the Sciences into Democracy," sets up a counter case to the process of withdrawal-the act of disengagement. This time the ground for negotiation lies in knowing how to move from one imputed field of indigenous expertise into several other social fields. This idea of bringing science into democracy is neither peculiar to the persona of Latour nor to French intellectual public life, but is in fact a common characteristic of recent Anglo-European critiques in the social sciences that seek to reframe what is distinctive about the engaged, participatory relationship between "science and society."

In brief, these reframing endeavors typically negotiate the terms of a new consensual "contract" for the knowledge economy-the science and society dyad giving way to mutual recognition and interdependent co-evolution as new organizational forms of complexity and relational knowledge. To see science at work in the agora-this being the Greek term Helga Nowotny and colleagues use to denote the social space where science is opened up to the public and where the market and politics intersect-means challenging traditional assumptions of scientific authority, especially the notion of impartiality attributable to a value-free objectivist science. And this is why the movement of science into the public arena hopes to become a powerful formula on at least two counts.

First, scientific expertise is seen as socially distributed: it brings in plural perspectives-from moralists, policy makers, politicians, economists and others. second, in order to keep engaging its multiple publics, science embeds itself in various public legitimization activities-whether this be through so-called "transparency measures" or a combination of tactics such as identifying, addressing, diverting, pacifying or delaying the different user needs of the citizenry. Both of these developments make science ostensibly more "democratic" because, contrary to human rights organizations and non-governmental activists, scientists cannot withdraw from society the traces of their past interventions. The applications of scientific knowledge are enduring because technological inventions can never be un-invented. In cultural terms, their effects are irreversible.

This chapter abstracts these two moments-the attempt to bring the sciences into democratic governance and the decision to move humanitarian operations out of Afghanistan-as parallel framing devices. The aim, as intimated above, is to use those events as symbolic media through which to consider other problems to do with the political ethics of engagement, mediation, disengagement, and extrication. But first I'd like to say a little more about Latour's Politics and the extent of its provocations.

The chief challenge, it would seem, is the claim made in relation to what the text defines as "experimental anthropology." The term, obviously a suggestive one, appears to be aimed at discrediting the theoretical premise of "nature" as an edifying, unifying force on the grounds that to all past anthropological engagement can be attributed, Latour contends, the error of "mononaturalism" (namely, an analytic over-investment in a single Nature at the expense of public life).

Latour's suggested remedy comes by way of the notion of the "pluri-verse"; an analytical intervention which reframes the concepts of "social" and "society" as meaningless other than outside of a [so-called] "New Constitution": a constitutional ecology, we are told, that would be founded through collective experimentation.

This remains the text's collusive ideal for nowhere is there application to the realities and imaginations that make experimental form the stuff of people's hard-won "alternative worlds." But the precise location of the provocation, however, comes with what finally gets tagged on to the text's extrapolation of the collective (i.e., the author's working through of "experimentalist anthropology" as democratic science). For it is, Latour says, the diplomat, in the person of the skilful negotiator, who "succeeds the anthropologist" in instituting a new common world (of essential requirements) as a new scene of "first contacts".

While some might find the idea of new "first contacts" appealing, it would be a gross oversight of contemporary research-engaged practice by political anthropologists (and others) to presume any such succession comes at the cost of our epistemic or disciplinary relinquishing. I suspect many a scholar-public advocate of postcolonial science studies also would be moved to adopt a more skeptical line. But the point I want to highlight here concerns what already has been withdrawn from Latour's own Politics.

For there is no mention in the text that modern field-based anthropology has, in a certain sense, always been about [doing] diplomacy. More to the point, there is no acknowledgement in Latour's analysis that the study of diplomacy is anthropological.

In its description of sociality as matters of peacekeeping and intertribal warfare; in the evidence left by the peace treaties of wampum beadwork by North American Indians; in its observance of diplomatic relations maintained through the practice of gift giving; in all that we know about the announcements between communities of forthcoming marriages, feasts, election, or death notification-it is anthropology that can potentially act as the genuine and critical "lookout" for diplomatic culture.

Furthermore, the "forest diplomacy" of the Iroquois, the preference for oral transmission of messages, the symbolism of "wampum" paths and chains-all provide counter-examples to the Western emphasis on communication through the written word.

It may be the case then that the long range element in negotiations, where the messenger had to be sent on his travels to plead this or that case and had to carry on his person a document as proof, is not so easily transposable to the mediations by orators in inter-community altercations. In the next section, I turn to consider how the historical trajectory of diplomatic verification has evolved from a type of science into the political value of world conversations for bio-diplomats. Yet if ethics is seen to get attached to the values of a more participatory "global talk," at the same time it is apparent there are limits to the resource of conversation itself.

FROM DIPLOMA TO DIALOGUE

Derived from the ancient Greek verb diploun (to double) and from the Greek noun diploma, referring to an official document written on double leaves (diploo) joined together and folded (diplono), diplomacy was originally linked to the written production of ancient diplomas. Produced on parchment and given to heralds as evidence of their status, these objects subsequently evolved into letters of recommendation, especially passport-type documents that enabled the messenger-traveller to use the public post.

In medieval times the diploma concept extended to a category of official document that conferred privileges with foreign communities, and it was in conjunction with this broadened usage that one also starts to see during the 16th and 17th centuries an emerging science of diplomatics. The link between diploma and diplomatica was exacting. It turned on the scientific study of handwriting, requiring the detailed analysis of the hand of the paper scribe. Diplomacy came to be about the inscription, arrangement and authentication of diplomas, especially the classification of different types of diplomatic script (i.e., writing styles) by nationality according to which nations could be known.

This newly "inter-national" character of diplomatica entailed the simultaneous materialization of a new class of "res diplomatica" (diplomatic objects): in effect a whole industry of diplomatic business was serviced by trained clerks until the late 17th century-professional archivists who undertook the science of verifying and deciphering ancient and contemporary documentation (coins, scrolls, medallions, treaties, and so on).

But it is only towards the end of the 18th century that one starts to see a shift from the science of handicraft to the politics of statecraft. Diplomatic exchange channelled through the representative of the state made statecraft a matter of external affairs-international relations regulated through the personalized exchange of diplomas and diplomats. This early politicization of diplomacy, linked closely to the idea of the official mission, had the effect of diverting attention away from the form or style of the diploma-document to its particular contents-to the specific nature of the messages contained by so-called "letters of credence" (lettres de créance).

After the end of the Cold War and the crumbling of the socialist and nonaligned blocks, diplomatic relations can no longer be confined to ambassadorial business between heads of state and their representatives. In the global polity, the significance and form of diplomacy again undergoes cultural change. On the one hand, diploma has become familiar as dialogue, as in the scheduled dialogues of "summit culture." But diploma has also become the reification of dialogue. The allusion here is not simply to the diplomatic convention: "jaw jaw is better than war war." There is both an intensification and romanticization attached to acts of dialogue, whereby it would seem as though it is almost the whole world that wishes to be seen engaged in the activity of continuous "conversation."

That is to say, it is dialogue-or rather the "multi-logue" in its various forms-that is believed to facilitate not only the idea of a common world, but a good common world-namely, a world comprised of ameliorative imagination. It is of course not the case that the written word has become a superfluous medium, but rather that it has been superseded in diplomatic culture by particular norms for ethics codification whose validation is tied explicitly to the public life of organizations.

Further, in tying these norms to organizations, the nation is bypassed; dialogue becomes essentially internal as well as external, and the government [state] starts looking like another organization. Relatedly, and at the same time, a multi-polar, multi-state diplomacy is presenting itself as a new ideal: as a type of "commons"-and here one can go back to Latour's "collective experimentation"-framed in part on an ethics of inclusiveness-an ethics whose raison d'être is the reconstitition of the "corps diplomatique" through the voice of multiple agents.

The notion of corps diplomatique that once represented the older ideal of a "family of diplomats" and that modelled itself on principles of commensality, exclusivity and knowledge specialization-based on social values instituted through the guild, collegium or as practices of freemasonry-is now the diffusion of an open, more participatory "global talk": actors attempting to converse with each other, and across multiple institutional (and indeed virtual) sites make for the possibility of diplomatic encounters between international organizations, NGOs, activist groups, and intergovernmental agencies.

Looking to the UN for instance, it is not by accident that a Declaration designated 2001 the "International Year of Dialogue among Civilizations". The point is that these new diplomatic "missions" turn the representative delegate into the ubiquity of conversation: this too can be seen as another instance of cultural borrowing-a recasting across the professions.

Where once the traditional profile of the diplomat meant he was received as reliable polyglot and polymath, as the cross-specialist conversant in many languages who, incidentally, was neither a generalist nor a specialist but nonetheless looked like a modern day inter-disciplinarian simply because he could be counted upon as always knowing something about something; it is now conversation itself that has become literally partible. I am referring here to the idea of conversation as action extendible across persons as though it were one continuous engagement with relational knowledge.

What this tells us is that anyone can acquire, or at least assume they may acquire, the title of diplomat as a type of "common name" pertaining to the "multitude". While that may sound liberating, new diplomacy creates at the same time conditions for the collective production of a realist Utopia: for what is being gathered together is the illusion of the emerging "world conversation." All this talk about the global diffusion of talk is diplomacy under another guise.

EMERGING "WORLD CONVERSATIONS"

Take, for example, the "Intercultural Dialogue" initiative of the International Association of Universities. Established by UNESCO after the Second World War, the IAU is headed by the mission statement "Universities of the World Working Together" and in 2002 it set up a dedicated Working Group for the promotion of intercultural dialogue.

Its aim was to foster collaboration in higher education across various international, regional and national learning institutes with a view to..."examining the qualities that are needed to live together in communities that are increasingly defined by cultural complexity." Its stated ideal is the promotion of diversity, divergent opinion and fostering mutual understanding: belief in the idea one can teach or learn for intercultural understanding, human rights, cultural peace.

Consider how inclusiveness is signalled by breadth of enrollment. To date, organizations as diverse as the International Centre for Dialogue Among Civilizations based in Tehran, and the Council of Europe's "Intercultural Dialogue and Conflict Prevention" project have enlisted to the initiative. One may though be inclined to ask: Where is the dialogue?

What is the conversation? In one sense, intercultural dialogue appears to have spawned its own pedagogic industry; a new diplomatic commerce based on the literal re-issuing of the diploma as the paper form of degree certificate from universities across the globe.

Yet if conversation has become an "expansive moment" in which the ubiquity of dialogue makes speech both more valued and more mundane, does it follow that more "cross-talking" with the other always means more understanding and better channels of communication?

How international organizations and NGOs in science governance talk to each other is precisely the problem borne out by the recent growth of bioethics committee bodies. On the one hand, the vast proliferation of ethical protocols in science, the attempt by various international organizations to generate universal codes and written guidelines of science ethics-all these one might recognize as modern day "relics" of the parchment diploma.

As evidence, one could point to various UN initiatives in science and technology, such as UNESCO's Universal Declaration on the Human Genome and Human Rights or, more recently, the Declaration on Universal Norms in Bioethics.

Drafting conventions, as Riles observes, involve endless revisions, deletions, addenda and para-setting, and it is through the endless process of revision that states too can impress themselves upon each other-becoming literally "recognizable entities." Similarly, though outside the purview of the law, bioethics committees operate as institutional fora for bringing together plurally conceived views: they are reliant on processes of information gathering, information exchange, and consultation.

Whether they work as self-contained endogenous units or look outwards beyond themselves through the orchestration of such things as public consultation exercises, it is in the final analysis the resource of conversation that is needed to bring together the disparate views.

In this sense, the origins of modern biodiplomacy for a postdependent world turn, in large part, on the critical realization that the values of principlism underpinning mainstream Western bioethics (i.e. autonomy, beneficence, non-maleficence, justice) cannot necessarily make ethics protocol "stick." More is needed than a normative framework and formulaic ethics codes to hold up the interventions of regulatory discourse and to make science "democratic."

BIO-DIPLOMACY AMONG ETHICS STRATEGISTS

Let me introduce at this point a "local" case of a kind. It is local insofar as I am referring to the anthropologist who engages with members of code-generating professional bodies; and specifically to the ethnographer's entrance as academic anthropologist into the life of bioethics committee subculture. In early 2003, KRAFT-a pseudonym for an international science NGO based somewhere between Belgium and Switzerland-announced that it was to set up a new working group to conduct a review on the topic of "The Rights and Responsibilities of Science and Society."

The aim of the review was described as "strategic": it would entail specific interventions into national and international policy formulation and have as its identifiable output the production of a Report intended for wide dissemination amongst the international science community. The drafting of the Report was to be preceded by a year-long deliberative process, and the deliberations were to be an occasion for critical debate amongst a wide range of invited participants. This group would constitute itself as the "Working Party" (WP) which would meet for stretches of two to three days at a time.

Now KRAFT was quite aware of the reasons why such an enterprise might seem distinctive when compared to the working methods of other international bodies. During its own early planning meetings to review design, the Council Directorate apparently had given great thought to the membership of the new group, and it wanted to include not only a strong mix of natural scientists but also, most notably, to bring in multiple perspectives from the social sciences, Interdiscplinarity, in other words, was accorded auspicious value as good bargaining power.

When I happened to find myself at the first review meeting in October 2003, an external observer could have been excused for thinking that members of the WP looked the picture of intercultural dialogue. Next to the social anthropologist sat, if I may repeat the introductions: a science and technology studies scholar with a special interest in environmental politics; an engineer working on pattern recognition and artificial intelligence; a representative from a science-based NGO with training in law and medical ethics; a physicist who had been instrumental in the 1999 World Conference on Science; a civil engineer; a researcher specializing in environment and sustainability issues; a philosopher of science and ethics; a retired surgeon; a biochemist whose speciality was tropical parasites; and a research immunologist of infectious diseases.

We were complemented by our Chair, who held a Professorship in astrophysics, our Deputy Chair, who had published widely in science and technology studies, and the KRAFT Deputy Director who offered a background in biochemistry and neuroscience. In one sense these alignments of persons and disciplines were quite contrived, yet it was precisely the contrivance of the conversational process that turned us all into "envoys"; less as notional ambassadors from our respective countries, than as diplomats who originated from our disciplines and spoke for our various knowledge affiliations.

In pressing forward our respective positions, each of us would be required to act as knowledge intermediaries: how to intervene and when to withdraw from a position, what to pull together as a shared viewpoint-all such discursive negotiation promised to give new inter-institutional pertinence to the old values encoded in the expression "universality of science". At the same time, contrivance was also manifest in the way a vision of international bioethics could be imagined, both practically and conceptually, as though it were a new civilising mission (for instance, the instrumentality attached to development agendas via such initiatives as capacity-building programs).

At the second meeting of the Working Party in February 2004, discussion was devoted in large part to the concept of the "universality of science," a principle that has underpinned KRAFT's working ethos since its founding in the 1930s. Up to the present time this term has been written into the organization's Statutes in a quite specific sense: the idea of "universality" being synonymous with the protection of certain rights and freedoms of bonafide scientists, ' such as free circulation across geopolitical borders for the conduct of scientific work; free association for research communication and publication.

During the session debate on these points, some of the social scientists ventured to put forward for consideration a slight shift in emphasis. Though the substantive focus on human rights was not unimportant, they remarked, the term "universality of science' could be seen as overloaded and some members went on to speculate whether it might benefit from further critical review. To convey a sense of these critical interventions, here are some unattributed comments made in response to a pre-circulated First Draft of the Report. What seems to be missing [from the First Draft Report] is a clear statement of how recent science-society developments require a reconsideration of the way KRAFT has "stood for" the concept and practice of universality.

The term now needs much further elaboration and qualification if it is to make any meaningful sense in the wider "science and society" framework, and especially in a truly internationalist, cross-cultural context. The challenge now for KRAFT turns on maintaining its professional identity as a non-political organization (one that protects the principle of non-discrimination) So, of course you still want to safeguard the right of scientists from all parts of the world to participate in your [the Organization's] activities regardless of race, religion, political philosophy, ethnic origin and so on.

But how is the organization going to navigate between its institutional mission statement-what it says about its professional identity-on the one hand, and the realities of global inequality as this relates to scientific practice and policy on the other? Things like the politics of resource provision, access to essential medicines, the ethics of pharmaceutical R&D prioritization etc-divisions especially pert between developed and developing countries.

The wider point, though, is that the "universality of science" needs to be understood as the process of producing and translating ideas-as the movements of knowledge through cultures and time. It is ideas as well as scientists that circulate across geophysical space. Moreover, this isn't really a "new" question: one would be equally justified to ask what meaning Archimedes in Greek or Newton in Latin has for (say) 21st Chinese scientists, as one would to enquire into the relevance of the algebra of al-Kwarizmi (in Arabic) for Renaissance Europe, or for that matter, contemporary AI-Qaeda.

While some of the natural scientists responded positively to these concerns and wanted to press forward this line of thinking, others tried to push aside any conceptual redefinition of the universality thesis. In brief, the latter argued that a broadened definition of "universality" could undermine the work of KRAFT that had been invested for so long in the task of human rights protections-especially the sensitive appeals and documentation work relating to individual scientists' visa applications.

Perhaps it may only have been symbolic of the beginning of epistemic breakdown that our Chair, who had steered the first meeting, was unable for personal reasons to attend this second meeting. In his absence, informal concern was expressed at the end of the first day about the apparent circularity of comments-the way committee conversation appeared to keep looping back on itself. This quality of recursivity seemed to some to be indicative of an unproductive expenditure of meeting time that had failed to draw out and specify key issues. Conversely, other panel members noted in private (to myself and one other member) the view that discussion had gone off at too much of a tangent; there had been indirection, inconsistency of thinking, and people were using key terms such as "society," "human" and "rights" at cross-purposes. Conversation lacked bite: it was "flabby" and "loose." Later over supper, more informal comments were passed around that had the effect of stirring up the immixture.

Speculating in private over why particular review members had been selected for participation in the Review, some said they were concerned they had not seen evidence of others' credentials. If a particular panelist's grasp of the issues was not evident to peer members, how had KRAFT gone about recruiting people, they wondered, and what kind of expertise was needed for a member's "representativeness" to be recognised by others? Why, in other words, had one been positioned to act as a potential mediator?

At our third meeting, in June 2004, nobody turned up. A fortnight before we were due to assemble a generic email from KRAFT was circulated to WP members with apologies and reasons for the cancellation. The Chair could not be present and, despite everyone's best intentions, the drafting of the Report had not yet been finished. In any case, continued the message, travel distance for some members is considerable and given that the "main substance" of the review is already in place, "a meeting at this point might not be time well spent."

The plan was now for the Deputy Chair and Deputy Director to finish off the drafting, and once complete, this emended version of the Report would then be circulated electronically to us all for final comments. The final revised version would then go off for submission to the KRAFT Executive Board for its "closed" consideration. Much is revealed by this foreclosure of conversation and the reversion to the written word, albeit in electronic form as virtual communiqué.

Where the grounds for withdrawal in the case of Medicines sans Frontières were precipitated by the recognition that different persons looked too alike-there was too much similarity-the need for face-to-face dialogue of the KRAFT review process was withdrawn prematurely because it seemed members displayed too much difference. Ours had appeared a bodily constitution that was too international, too interdisciplinary-in other words, too diverse in its origins-to carry us through as one common (recognizable) entity. Suddenly, everything that still had to be done and that belonged to the future came to look as though it were already behind us.

The tasks, in a sense, had un-done themselves even though it was recognized much revision work remained on the table. We, the main body of the Working Party, had been extricated from the Report-though not detached completely from it since it was inferred "ownership" of the resulting document would rest in our hands. Thus the Report could not go forward to the Board Committee until each WP member pledged his/her acceptance of the written contents and thereby acquiesced to the quality of its contents.

In retrospect, however, when one goes back in real time to the initial designs of the Council Directorate, it was always part of the original plan to see our professional interactions as evidence of the working of relational knowledge. Hence, the active recruitment search for particular members and the careful planning that went into the attempt to put us together (whereby the intergovernability ideal is exposed as contrivance). This gap between interdisciplinarity as the preferred procedural model and the unpredictability of the actual outcome-namely the way past collaborative effects are taken up as new knowledge for other (previously unspecified) ends whether by one particular discipline, researcher, research group or constellation of practitioners-might be identified as yet another doubling effect of diplomacy.

In other words, what this review process had shown up is that there is no necessary or obvious correspondence between the original plan for collaboration and the manner of its applications. Such a lack of correspondence might be said to mimic the conventional science-technology divide whereby science/scientists retain the independence to keep doing the experimentation to which their vocational mission directs them. In this sense doing diplomacy involves the paradox of engagement through forms of neutrality; extending one's frame of reference by sharpening up one's independence. Interdisciplinarity (facing multiple sides at the same time like the diplomat who partners with non-sovereign subjects) may be more about disciplining disciplina rity (one's home base) as modes of exceptionality.

For in the return passage, the anthropologist as diplomat takes back as much new knowledge to familiar bases-ideally sharpening these in the process-as s/he takes outwards for possible exchange the offer of new grounds of conversation.

PUBLICS OF BIO-DIPLOMATIC COMMONS

But biodiplomacy is not just about the collaborative aspirations of mediated cross-talk. It is also about defining the philosophical and practical problem of what extra-legal "privileges and immunities" should be given to vulnerable communities whose livelihoods may be affected by certain health, environmental and scientific hazards.

Within this bracket, biodiplomacy is a particular field or set of practices involving the transnational movement across borders of persons, bodily samples, viruses, research grants or other resources, often between different country scientists. For example, pandemics and drug-resistant infectious diseases that cross geo-political borders require certain kinds of justifications for the pre-emptive isolation or containment of contagious persons.

The same would apply in the case of the intentional release of bio-agents used for sabotage as precision weapons of terror, as in ethnically targeted germ-warfare, or in espionage bioterrorism. Both involve the continuous revision of boundary lines, culturally and spatially conceived, as well as how these lines can be enforced and sustained since the danger of infectivity runs past identifiable populations: it is impossible to keep the zone of contagion exclusive.

Similarly, transnational flows of biodata or biosamples demand justifications about the kind and extent of restrictions to be placed on sample procurement and data sharing between research teams. In such contexts, biodiplomacy concerns negotiation over medically sensitive information and the range of release: whether information does or does not run away making knowledge itself the potentially infectious agent. And, as intimated earlier, the biodiplomacy of humanitarian assistance asks how we arbitrate the protections and entitlements to be given to frontline medical aid workers in international conflict zones.

Another case involves the ethics of partnership between sponsor and host countries in the context of international clinical trials and human subject experimentation. Issues around equitable access to medicines and the recruitment of subjects for experimental research become a matter for biodiplomacy when they concern the transfer of knowledge, personnel and resources between developed and developing countries.

There is at least the hope that the globalization of clinical trials may open up possibilities for new "first contacts" that turn on an ethics of collaboration between sending and receiving states-between those research communities who bring in externally sponsored funds for experimentation, ostensibly to introduce a relationship of beneficence-and those resource-weak countries affected by HIV/AIDS, malaria and tuberculosis.

That hope might be naive and may well be stymied by various constraints, but one important point about seeing these issues through the biodiplomatic lens has to do with the way due process in the extra-legal sense can be given to the value of equivocation.

Conceding to the power of ambiguity also accords its own epistemic privileges. Indeed, it has been said that "the essence of good diplomatic drafting is, where possible, to avoid saying anything that admits of only one meaning" and when we observe further notes on etymological origins, this may not be surprising. Aside from the link already mentioned to diploma, it is possible to trace a semantic connection to the crafts of the double hand and the process of doubling (diploo): notably, the doubling of authority and sovereignty that comes with the double "mace" of diplo-macy.

Mace evokes the messenger's ceremonial staff that represents authority, authorising the agent as an official medium; and diplomacy-as the doubling of the mace-is tied to double versions: to equivocation, economies of duplicity and plurality of position: hence, to official and unofficial secret missions. It is precisely the question of double standards in medical research that has erupted into a diplomatic "zone for mediation" between sponsor-host relations.

One recent, much-cited case-involving Western researchers and research communities in Africa-concerns the prevention of perinatal (maternal-fetal) transmission of HIV from pregnant women to their unborn babies. At issue has been the ethics of Zidovudine clinical trials, also known as AZT, and interpretations over parity of treatment tied to the notion and application of so-called best standards.

The "controversy," as it circulated within the international medical community, polarized between two sides: those who argued against the trials ("the protagonists") and those in favour. The protagonists argue that no patient participating in a trial sponsored by US funds should be denied the "standard of care" available in developed countries. Advances in scientific research should not be at the expense of withholding treatment from one patient sub-group, and it would be unethical, they claim, to deny a proven course of treatment to the [placebo-administered] experimental control groups.

The opposing view argues experimental feasibility trials are necessary so as to compare interventions under local conditions with current standard local therapy, even if that standard is no care at all. Since HIV-affected women in some parts of the world routinely receive no treatment, how-they ask-could inclusion to a trial worsen subjects' health? One would not be putting mothers or infants at any increased risk.

The dispute itself famously collapsed into charges and counter charges against so-called "health ethics imperialism"-namely, the justifications or otherwise of importing both standards and concepts from the West to nonWestern healthcare settings. But these differences of opinion cannot always be mapped along area-specific lines of intervention. Several non-Western commentators, whose local communities so-called "ethical imperialists" would gloss as potentially "captive" and exploited populations, directed their criticisms towards the "equivalence" thesis of the moral universalists.

Health workers from Uganda and local representatives from the Thai Red Cross Society, to name just a few, could all be heard stressing the significance of specific social contexts for the ethical determination of appropriate health interventions. As one Gambian health worker remarked: "Stopping trials in Africa that are trying to help improve the health of poor people so that those in affluent countries can have peace of mind seems a tortured form of ethical logic."

Now this charge of "health ethics imperialism," as it tallied back and forth between the different sides, might give the illusion of an emerging world conversation-one that is open and free, part of a democratic dialogue. But it was through a broader social agenda focused on post-trial welfare and distributory justice that some faint sense of an inclusive, participatory "biodiplomatic commons" started to open up.

NGOs and treatment access activists involved in campaigns for affordable drugs exposed and challenged the profit monopolies of global pharma, and in so doing spoke up to resist "globalization from below." However, in the attempt to negotiate a multilateral framework that could recognize the role of the pharmaceuticals industry in the political economies of the placebo, international biodiplomacy played itself out against another doubling. It mediated another controversial backdrop.

Charges of "health ethics imperialism" are, after all, rooted in cultural memory and in both official and unofficial histories of human experimentation abuses, especially past violations of informed consent. Insofar as it exposed (once again) the ineffectual basis of international bioethics regulation, the Zidovudine controversy testified to an appalling record of social suffering. Policy regulators reminded themselves that "bioethics" had emerged as a new field in the 1940s, largely in response to the Nazi wartime atrocities.

But staring back in the light of that reminder was the unsettling persistence of the record and the recruitment of unsuspecting research subjects, more or less the world over: poor African-Americans enlisted to the 40 year Tuskegee Syphilis study in Alabama; the use of Egyptian women as research subjects for Norplant contraceptive trials funded by the US Food and Drug Administration; the movement of human organs along social fault lines, from the poor to the rich.

Activist campaigners, bioethicists, scientists and policy makers all know that, so far as the future is concerned, there is another side to be told about international collaborations and the ethics of research experimentation. This would be based on defendable evidence: not necessarily legally enforceable matters as such, but the piecing together of legitimate practice.

Now that Western scientists are receiving huge grants to conduct large experimental studies on that condition that developing country trial recruits have given expressly their prior informed consent (financial support being otherwise withdrawn), it is the anthropologist, if anybody, who may step in as biodiplomat to play the role of critical knowledge mediator "look-out" between sponsor [sending] and host [receiving] states.

Take the case of recruits enlisted onto a genetic epidemiological study. Are such persons "genuine participants" if their own predominantly a-genetic understandings of inheritance belie non-Western notions of disease transmission?

When trial participants who have not had educational schooling in the germ theory of disease causation explain the sudden death of a relative as the effects of witchcraft and evil spirits, and say they therefore have no need to be enrolled onto a study, will Western-trained scientists in the field respond with the kind of skepticism that greeted President Thabo Mbeki's original opposition to the provision of AIDS drugs in South Africa on the grounds that the medicines were toxic, and that it was not HIV disease but poverty that was the prime cause of AIDS?

It may not always be clear what the shape of intercultural dialogue looks like in these contexts, however it is possible to see why the current consideration of biodiplomacy between sponsor and host countries challenges the work that existing "guiding" ethical precepts are supposed to do.

When we look to the ways that emergent values are recognized as locally conceived and enforceable outside of their originary [Western] frame of context, then inter-community altercations-and their trade-offs between multiple stakeholders-are just as much a part of the bargaining process (i.e.

in the sense of interventions, withdrawals, extrication) as the "pre-negotiation" framings informing traditional diplomatic summitry. Beyond the rules, norms, clauses and conventions, it is equivocation, ambiguity and double standards that make such conversations relational and global and, at times, transposable across the boundaries of the singular discipline.

BIO-DIPLOMATICA FUTURES

This chapter has suggested that modern biodiplomacy needs new peripatetic theorists; that anthropologists may play a role in developing new public engagement models for inclusive cultural ambassordship; and that a (bio)diplomatic commons does not simply take knowledge back to source ("back to the people" as the idea of a country's sovereign subjects), but involves a potentially participatory ethics of continuous and open engagement. As we saw however in the vignette on "emerging world conversations," such engagement may seem at times more illusory than real in its discursive effects.

This insight affords yet another perspective-one, moreover, that is germane to a relational ethics of knowledge translations. Namely, it lets us see how the political contours of public anthropology can make important "interventions" into the processual, temporal dynamics of diplomatic culture through new comparative studies. In terms of seeking to engage a critically reflexive anthropology of bioethics, I have argued that missions of critique involve translational debate about the origins of modern biodiplomacy both in and for a post-dependent world.

Such "translocational" work brings with it the critical realization that the values of principlism underpinning mainstream Western bioethics (i.e. autonomy, beneficence, non-maleficence, justice) cannot necessarily make ethics protocol "stick" and that more is needed than a normative framework and formulaic ethics codes to hold up the interventions of regulatory discourse and to make science "democratic."

Thus, in future bioethics scholarship, an anthropologically informed, cross-cultural focus on the knowledge entanglements of people, objects, trade routes and financial flows, for example, may look to re-work the Western emphasis on "handling negotiation," "conflict resolution" or confrontational modes of "brinkmanship" in order to extend conventional renditions of the legal parameters of world diplomacy.

For instance, further to Hardt and Negri's study of the new global Empire, alternative conventions for the mobility of the "multitude," as situated within the new internationalist "global commons" (and beyond US constitutionalism), would need an anti-utopian analysis of anthropological ethics to address ethnographically modalities of intervention and extrication in the context of new world threats, insecurities and unresolved "diplomatica."

A background theme of this chapter, then, is that political associations and connections between international science, international relations and international ethics deserve elucidation not just in terms of the idea of diplomacy, but also as the diplomacy of the idea. Working through the diplomacy of the idea means seeing how the condition of epistemic authority is rooted in a kind of aboriginal embassy comprised of persons formerly known as "theors."

If we can act responsibly by giving due respect to that original position, then the public anthropology of science and society cannot be just about engagement as the virtue of knowledge application or applicability; anthropology becomes distinctively "public" because it is about engagement as lived relations constitutive of social critique.

In alliance with this, and contra Latour's claim, it is-perhaps of all the social humanities available for study today-critical social anthropology, for its diverse publics, that can claim to be most rightfully heir to that travelling theoretical legacy.

8

Role of Advanced Communication Technologies

The International Classification of Functioning, Disability and Health of the World Health Organization defines disability as a "condition in which people are temporarily or definitively unable in performing an activity in the correct manner and/or at a level generally considered 'normal' for the human being." According to this definition, disability is considered a specific situation in which a person is not able to fully exploit his or her relationship with everyday contexts rather than a characteristic of the individual.

For these reasons, technological rehabilitative tools have to move from a specific activity-centered approach to a general user-centered one. In particular, the focus of technology should be the improvement of the quality of the life of the individual, through its effective support of his or her activity and interaction.

In this chapter, we consider the role of two emerging technologies-virtual reality (VR) and ambient intelligence (Ami)-in rehabilitative care. These technologies may be capable of enhancing quality of life for a variety of rehabilitation populations because of their ability to enhance the user's feeling of presence, defined as the "feeling of being in a world that exists outside the self".

More specifically, VR and Ami can be used for a new breed of rehabilitative applications focused on a strategy described as "transformation of flow." Debilitating illnesses such as Alzheimer's disease often draw individuals into themselves, and to counteract this tendency VR and Ami technologies are used to evoke a feeling of presence or engagement in the external world. The flow experience is one of feeling highly engaged with the world, a feeling that many diverse groups report as empowering.

VIRTUAL REALITY AND AMBIENT INTELLIGENCE: TWO PRESENCE-ENHANCING TECHNOLOGIES

VR can be considered the leading edge of a general evolution of communication interfaces such as television, computers, and telephones.

Unlike historical communication interfaces, VR provides full immersion of the human sensorimotor channels (auditory, visual, and kinesthetic), thereby creating a vivid and global experience. VR is an advanced human-computer interface that has recently been used in rehabilitation to allow people to "interact with and become immersed in a computer-generated environment in a naturalistic fashion". Subjectively speaking, it is the feeling of presence that distinguishes VR from other interface technologies.

These aspects of VR offer two main advantages to rehabilitators. First, patients receive immediate feedback about their performance in a variety of forms and sensory modalities. This allows for the creation and provision of more ecologically valid assessment and rehabilitation scenarios. Furthermore, it allows the provision of "cuing" stimuli or tailored sensory modality presentations designed to improve availability of assessment and rehabilitation.

In other words, the creator of the VR environment has the capability to build in systematic assessments that provide ongoing feedback regarding improvements over base-rate performance. second, the therapist/rehabilitator using VR can create and control a dynamic and interactive 3-D scenario within an immersive environment.

Thus, VR allows for complete performance capture and the availability of a more naturalistic/intuitive performance record for review and analysis. Furthermore, it offers the capacity to pause assessment, treatment, and training for discussion and/or integration of other methods. In a computer-generated environment such as VR, the full range of behaviour-including overt behaviour as well as physiological measures such as heart rate and galvanic skin response-can be captured and correlated with the subjective experience of research participants.

In summary, VR provides a new human-computer interaction paradigm in which users are no longer simply external observers of images on a computer screen but are active participants within a computer-generated 3-D virtual world. In a particular virtual environment created with VR technology, the patient has the possibility of learning to manage a problematic situation related to his or her diagnosis in a more realistic and ecologically valid context than is typically provided in most clinical settings.

The term ambient intelligence refers to a specific vision of the Information Society Technologies Advisory Group (ISTAG) of the European Community according to which humans will be surrounded by intelligent interfaces supported by advanced technologies distributed everywhere and embedded in everyday objects such as furniture, clothes, vehicles, and roads.

Although the term ambient technology may be specific to the ISTAG, its concepts, methods, technologies, and interfaces are shared by different groups all over Ae world. Some examples are the smart medical home concept introduced by the Centre for Future Health, the notion of pervasive human-centered computing proposed by the Oxygen MIT project, and the ubiquitous computing vision detailed by Georgia Tech. For example, the Smart Medical Home Research Laboratory is a five-room house equipped with infrared sensors, computers, biosensors, and video cameras.

The goal is to develop an integrated personal health system where all technologies are integrated seamlessly, allowing people to maintain health, detect the onset of disease, and manage existing diseases. To illustrate, the Centre for Future Health provides a video of an older person asking the system whether or not she can take an aspirin and what may be causing her headaches.

The system asks her questions about her condition, recalls her physician's advice, and notes that headaches may be a symptom of her other medications. On the practical side, Ami may be roughly described as the flip side of VR: VR puts people inside a computer generated world, and Ami puts the computer inside the real world to help us.

If combined with mobile technologies, Ami may enhance the activity of a mobile user by embedding one or more interactive Ami objects (e.g., holograms, videos, images, texts, sounds) in his or her clothes, automobile, or even a bicycle. Through "tangible user interfaces," it is possible to employ physical objects, surfaces, and spaces as specific embodiments of digital information.

For example, one can imagine an Ami interface built into a bicycle that provides information about the grade of upcoming hills, traffic approaching from all directions, and rider fatigue, and makes recommendations to the rider or even occasionally assists with pedaling. Following this paradigm, we can embed an active interface in any assistive device, helping the user to understand how to use it effectively. In this way, tangible interfaces may transform the ambient environment (e.g., walls, desktops, ceilings, doors, windows) into an active interface between the user and his or her activity.

According to the Ami metaphor, people will live in enriched environments in which the technology is sensitive to their needs, personalized to their requirements, anticipatory of their behaviour, and responsive to their presence. Considering the Ami-enhanced bicycle described above, such an interface would need not only to sense objective conditions such as hill grade and weather conditions, but also to assess the subjective preferences of individual riders at each particular moment.

Different riders are likely to find different kinds of information useful and be more or less willing to receive help at different times. Presumably, this assessment is made on the basis of a combination of previous experience with specific riders, sensory inputs from the present environment, and judicious questioning of the rider.

Recently, Riva introduced a psychological definition of Ami based on the experience of the user: "Ami is the effective and transparent support to the activity of the subjects through the use of information and communication technologies". This definition suggests that the role of Ami in rehabilitation is related to its ability to support action. It also identifies effectiveness (defined as attainment of the objective of the activity) and transparency (defined as an absence of breakdowns during the activity) as the main characteristics of any rehabilitative Ami system.

Following this vision, the most important reason for developing Ami assistive tools lies in their potential to compensate or expand the activity of users through new forms of human-computer interaction. For instance, an Ami system may identify the impairment of a blind man and signal him by voice the instructions presented on a wall. Furthermore, Ami assistive tools may use gaze analysis to expand possibilities of interaction in paralyzed subjects.

PRESENCE AND AGENCY

We argue that the key feature of both VR and Ami technologies is that they offer an effective support to the activity of the subject by activating a stronger sense of presence. Presence is usually defined as the "sense of being there" or the "feeling of being in a world that exists outside the self". A growing group of researchers considers presence as a neuropsychological phenomenon, evolved from the interplay of our biological and cultural inheritance, whose goal is to increase emotional fidelity and perceptual accuracy to produce a strong sense of agency and control.

Some VR researchers consider the subjective sense of presence in VR worlds simply a "perceptual illusion of nonmediation". However, recently some VR researchers have conceptualized presence more broadly to address the question of why people feel a sense of presence in any setting, computer generated or otherwise. In these works, presence is conceptualized as a continuous variable, so that individuals may feel different degrees of presence in different situations depending on the degree of meaning experienced in an environment.

Thus, an inhabitant of the Amazon rainforest, rich in ethnobotanical knowledge, may feel a fuller sense of presence while walking through die forest than might an urban visitor admiring the beauty. Similarly, a computer-literate person may feel a greater sense of presence while surfing the Web than might a computer novice. From this point of view, presence has a simple but relevant role in our everyday experience: Ë is the control of agency through the unconscious separation of "internal" and "external."

The sense of presence allows the nervous system to differentiate between internal and external states. As infants develop, they learn that some aspects of their perceptual worlds (such as the movements of their arms) are part of the "self" and that other aspects of the environment (such as the movements of a mobile) are not "self." Were it not for the development of the sense of presence, it would be impossible for the nervous system to reference perceptions to an environment beyond our boundaries. As we will see below, the meaning of "internal" and "external" is related not only to the body but also to the social, emotional, and cultural space (situation) in which the self is embedded. If this sounds far-fetched, consider the subjective experience of driving a car.

For experienced drivers, the car becomes an extension of the self. Statements such as "she's too close to my rear" or, worse, "he hit me" reveal the subjective sense of internalizing the dimensions of the car. This subjective recalibration of boundaries facilitates the greater sense of control experienced by good drivers. From this point of view, it is important to distinguish between presence as process and presence as feeling. Presence as process is the continuous activity of the brain in separating "internal" and "external" within different kinds of afferent and efferent signals.

As emphasized by de Vignemont and Fourneret, the double sense of agency depends on the same mechanisms of action control: It results from the unconscious comparison between different kinds of afferent and efferent signals. Therefore, these monitoring systems allow one to automatically distinguish one's own actions and those of the other. Thus, presence as process can be described as a sophisticated form of monitoring of action and experience, transparent to the self but critical for its existence.

As Russell further clarified,Action-monitoring is a subpersonal process that enables the subjects to discriminate between self-determined and world-determined changes in input. It can give rise to a mode of experience (the experience of being the cause of altered inputs and the experience of being in control) but it is not itself a mode of experience. For this reason, presence as feeling is not separated from the experience of the subject but is related to the quality of our actions. It corresponds to what Heidegger defined as "die interrupted moment of our habitual standard, comfortable being-in-the-world" Subjectively, a higher level of presence as feeling is experienced by the self as a better quality of action and experience.

However, sometimes we become aware of presence as a feeling of being separate from our being-in-the-world, as during either breakdowns or optimal experiences. Winograd and Flores refer to presence disruptions as breakdowns: A breakdown occurs when, during our activity, an aspect of our environment that we usually take for granted becomes part of our consciousness. If this happens, we shift our attention from action to the object or environment in order to cope with it.

To illustrate, imagine sitting outdoors engrossed in reading a book on a pleasant evening. As the sun sets and the light diminishes, one continues reading, engrossed in the story, until one becomes aware that the light is no longer suitable for reading. In such conditions, before any overt change in behaviour, what we experience is a breakdown in reading and a shift of attention from the book to the light illuminating the book.

It is interesting to consider why we experience such breakdowns. Our hypothesis is that breakdowns are a sophisticated evolutionary tool used to control the quality of experience, which ultimately enhances our chances of survival. As a breakdown occurs, we experience a lower level of presence as feeling, which reduces the quality of experience and leads us to confront environmental difficulties.

On the other end of the spectrum are optimal experiences. According to Csikszentmihalyi, individuals preferentially engage in opportunities for action associated with a positive, complex, and rewarding state of consciousness known as optimal experience or flow. There are some exceptional situations in real life in which the subject's activity is characterized by an unusually high level of presence. In these situations, the subject experiences a full sense of control and immersion.

When this experience is associated to a positive emotional state, the result is the feeling of flow. An example of flow is the case in which a professional athlete is playing exceptionally well (positive emotion) and achieves a state of mind in which all attention is focused on the game (high level of presence).

For Ghani and Deshpande, the two main characteristics of flow are total concentration on an activity and the enjoyment that one derives from the activity. Significantly, these authors identified two other factors that affect the experience of flow: a sense of control over one's environment and the level of challenge relative to a certain skill level.

TECHNOLOGY, PRESENCE, AND FLOW

A critical corollary of our vision of transformation of flow in rehabilitation is design-technologically mediated situations that elicit a state of flow by activating a high level of presence. In particular, we argue that VR and Ami are the best technologies for facilitating optimal flow experiences. In this section, we will explain the rationale behind this claim. Immersive VR is the medium most capable of activating the highest level of presence and allowing flow when connected to positive emotional experiences.

The work of Gaggioli supports this vision. Gaggioli compared the experience reported by a user immersed in a virtual environment with the experience reported by the same individual in daily situations. To assess the quality of experience, the author used a procedure called the experience sampling method, which is based on repeated online assessments of the external situation and internal personal states of consciousness.

Results showed that VR experience was the activity associated with the highest level of optimal experience (22 per cent of self-reports). Reading, television viewing, and the use of other media-in the contexts of both learning and leisure activities-yielded lower percentages (15 per cent, 8 per cent, and 19 per cent of self-reports, respectively) of optimal experiences. The successful use of VR exposure in therapy highlights the possibility that a high level of presence elicited by the use of technology may help facilitate rehabilitation. VR has been used in a number of therapeutic contexts, including therapy for phobias, posttraumatic stress disorders, and pain reduction in burn patients.

Ami could be a powerful tool for increasing the level of presence in natural environments. This can be achieved by providing tools or cues that directly or indirectly support the action of the subject. Ami offers the user new tools or targeted cues that make his or her action simpler (e.g., an interactive map to make it easier to reach the clinician's office in the hospital). It also offers indirect support by providing cues that improve the meaning given to the situation (e.g., a narrative describing the history of a church we are visiting, along with the times of church services and information about the congregation).

Authentic rehabilitation implies the active participation of patients in their contexts, their exposure to opportunities for action and development, and their freedom to select the opportunities that they perceive as most challenging and meaningful. In response to this vision, a critical asset potentially offered by VR to the rehabilitation process is the possibility of triggering optimal experiences.

Optimal experiences cultivate individual development within a given skill domain. As Massimini and Delle Fave noted, to replicate a flow experience, a person will search for increasingly complex challenges in the associated activities and will improve his or her skill, accordingly. This process has been defined as cultivation; it fosters the growth of complexity not only in the performance of flow activities but in individual behaviour as a whole.

This process can also be activated after a major trauma. As Delle Fave explained, to cope with dramatic changes in daily life and in accessing environmental opportunities for action, individuals may develop a strategy defined as transformation of flaw, a person's ability to build upon optimal experiences to identify and exploit new and unexpected resources and sources of involvement.

We hypothesize that it is possible to use VR and Ami to activate a transformation of flow to be used for rehabilitative purposes. The proposed approach begins with identification of an enriched environment that containsfanctional real-world demands. The use of real-world demands is critical to creating a connection between subjective experience and true agency. Then, we use the technology to enhance the subjective level of presence in the environment and to induce an optimal experience. Linking agency and presence promotes cultivation by linking an optimal experience to particular abilities.

This transformation of flow not only provides positive experiences but also guides and motivates fuller engagement beyond the scope of particular VR sessions. It is interesting to note that the proposed approach can be considered an advanced technological version of the multisensory environment approach used in the rehabilitation of the learning disabled and of older people with dementia.

Multisensory environments are purpose-built units or rooms utilized for the application of multisensory stimulation, whose goal is the stimulation of the primary senses to generate pleasurable sensory experiences in an atmosphere of trust and relaxation without the need for intellectual activity. Exposure to multisensory stimulation occurs through the agency of the care provider, nurse or therapist who facilitates the development of a relaxing and supportive environment.

The results from a recent randomized controlled trial (N = SO) showed the efficacy of this approach in the treatment of older people with dementia. In particular, the use of a multisensory environment appeared to have a greater influence on aspects of communication in comparison with one-to-one activity, and also appeared to lead to improvement in behaviour and mood at a 4-week follow-up.

We hypothesize that the VR experiences we propose will have a greater impact because they rely on the agency of the participant rather than on that of the care provider. To verify the link between advanced technologies and optimal experiences, the V-Store project was recently carried out to investigate the quality of experience and the feeling of presence in a group of 10 patients with frontal lobe syndrome involved in VR-based cognitive rehabilitation.

On one hand, during the project the experience sampling method was used for repeated online assessments of these patients' external situations and the emotional, cognitive, and motivational components of their daily experience during 1 week, which included traditional cognitive rehabilitation and sessions of exposure to the V-Store VR environment. On the other hand, after the VR experience the ITC-Sense of Presence Inventory was used to evaluate the feeling of presence induced by the VR sessions.

Findings highlighted the association of VR sessions with both positive affect and a high level of presence. In particular, during the VR sessions "spatial presence"-the first scale of the ITC-Sense of Presence Inventory-was significantly correlated with the positive psychological feelings of "being free" and "being relaxed".

The transformation of flow may also exploit the plasticity of the brain, producing some form of functional reorganization. Optale and his team used a transformation-of-flow approach to treat male erectile disorders. They found that 30 of 36 patients with psychological erectile dysfunction and 28 of 37 clients with premature ejaculation maintained partially or completely positive response at a 6-month follow-up.

The most interesting aspect of their work is the PET scan analysis. Optale et al. used PET scans to analyse regional brain metabolism changes from baseline to follow-up in the experimental sample. The analysis of the scans showed different metabolic changes in specific areas of the brain connected with the erection mechanism. These findings suggest that this approach may hasten the healing process and produce lasting neurological changes. The relationship between VR-based therapy and neurological functioning is an exciting avenue for further research.

Recent experimental results from the work of Hoffman and his group in the treatment of chronic pain also might be considered to foster this vision. Few experiences are more intense than the pain associated with severe burn injuries. In particular, daily wound care-the cleaning and removal of dead tissue to prevent infection-can be so painful that even the aggressive use of opioids (morphine-related analgesics) cannot control the pain.

However, it is well-known that distraction-for example, having the patient listen to music-can help to reduce pain for some people. Hoffman, Doctor, Patterson, Carrougher, and Furness conducted a controlled study of the efficacy of VR as an advanced distraction by comparing it with the efficacy of a popular Nintendo video game.

The results showed dramatic reductions in pain ratings during VR in comparison with those during the video game. Furthermore, using an fMRI scanner, they measured pain-related brain activity for each participant during conditions of VR and without VR in a study in which order was randomized.

The team studied five regions of the brain that are known to be associated with pain processing: anterior cingulate cortex, primary and secondary somatosensory cortex, insula, and thalamus. They found that during VR all these regions showed significant reductions in activity. In particular, they found direct modulation of pain responses within the brain during VR distraction. The degree of reduction in pain-related brain activity ranged from 50 per cent to 97 per cent.

DISCUSSION

In this chapter, we suggest the possibility of using two emerging communication technologies-Ami and VR for a new class of rehabilitative applications based on a strategy described as "transformation of flow." The vision underlying this concept arises from positive psychology. According to this vision, existing professional treatments should include positive peak experiences because they serve as triggers for a broader process of motivation and empowerment.

Within this context, transformation of flow can be defined as a person's ability to draw upon an optimal experience and use it to marshal new and unexpected psychological resources and sources of involvement.

We identified the feeling of "presence"-the feeling of being in a world that exists outside the self-as the theoretical link between the technology and transformation of flow. The technology is used to trigger a broad empowerment process within the flow experience induced by a strong sense of presence. Two emerging technologies, VR and Ami, may facilitate these processes. By inducing a feeling of presence, VR and Ami may support a person's actions, allowing a greater subjective sense of personal efficacy.

An avenue of research that we are currently exploring concerns the use of this technologically based transformationof-flow protocol to fight the onset of Alzheimer's disease. In particular, we hypothesize that this approach could be used to target mild cognitive impairment, a pathological state that differs from normal aging characterized by objective evidence of memory impairment.

However, despite the significant advances in computer and graphic technology and the development of different VR and Ami applications, their rehabilitative use is still limited by the maturity of the systems available today. No off-the-shelf solutions are currently available. Our experience is that rehabilitation research with VR and Ami requires much patience for dealing with conflicting hardware and software. Nearly every VR system requires a dedicated staffer at least one computer technician to keep the system running smoothly.

Testing the available technology is an important and ongoing process, so therapists and researchers must continue to investigate the application of these tools to their day to-day research and clinical practice. Finally, it is still the case that in most circumstances, today and in the foreseeable future, the clinical skills of the rehabilitator are the key factor in the successful use of any technology.

Job search is a concept that has attracted a lot of attention from scholars and practitioners. Most of the research on this issue has focused on processes and causes that determine the organizational choices of job searchers. Less research has attempted to examine the processes and determinants of what can be termed sectorial choice, namely choices between working in the public or the private sector regardless of the specific organization.

The issue of sectorial choice is an important one both for individuals seeking jobs and for policy makers in the public sector in search of qualified applicants. Yet, very little research has investigated the process of job search by looking at the sector rather than the organization as the main concept of inquiry. Two works are exceptional in this regard. Kilpatrick, Cummings and Jennings examined work values and image of employees in the Federal Service.

Their book attempted to shed some light on the issue of sectorial choice, but limited research directly followed the issues raised by it. A more recent work by Blank examined and compared demographic characteristics of employees in the public and private sectors. The main finding of that paper was that groups protected by federal laws, such as minorities and veterans, tended to work in the public sector.

One goal of this study is to stimulate more research that may make conceptual as well as practical contributions. Instead of elaborating on the limitations of research on this topic, we adopted use some of the ideas of the two studies mentioned above. Kilpatrick et al.'s notion of the importance of the image of the public sector is applied here by using the concept of public sector image as one of the main determinants of tendency to work in the public sector.

Blank's study was the first to propose a model of factors that determines whether one is a public or private sector employee. Some of the determinants proposed by Blank are applied here. While Blank's model is based on demographic determinants, our model includes psychological as well as experience variables together in addition to the public sector image variables.

Although this study of final-year Israeli students was exploratory, three specific research questions were advanced and tested. First, what are the determinants of public sector image; second, what are the determinants of the tendency to work in the public sector; third, do the determinants of tendency to work in the public sector relate to it directly or indirectly through the mediating effect of the public sector image.

The answers to these research questions were expected to contribute to the literature by providing new data about an issue that has been inadequately examined. Beside the expectation that the findings of this study will stimulate more research on the issue, the data provided here may provide policy makers in the public sector with new ideas and ways to attract qualified applicants to the public sector.

CONCEPTUAL FRAMEWORK

The concept explained here is the tendency to work in the public sector. Ajzen and Fishbein and Ryan argued that intention to behave in a certain way is the linkage between attitudes and behaviour. That is, understanding the reasons for high versus low tendency to work in the public sector has important implications for understanding the actual decisions of applicants whether or not to work in a public sector organization.

A concept advanced by Perry and Wise, the closest concept to tendency to work in the public sector, is motivation to work in the public sector. Perry and Wise proposed three categories of reasons that are related to such motivation: rational motives, such as participation in the process of policy design, normative motives, such as willingness to serve the public interest, and emotional motives, such as commitment to the public sector resulting from an inner believe in its social importance.

The concept examined here, tendency to work in the public sector, is similar to the one proposed by Perry and Wise but is more suitable for our target population, namely final-year students. Because our interest here is what causes prospective employees to decide to work or not to work in the public sector, tendency to work in this sector seems to be a more appropriate concept for examination. Another reason to prefer this concept is that the relationship between tendencies toward a given behaviour and the actual behaviour is not always close. Thus one may have a low tendency to work in the public sector, but in the absence of any real alternative in the private sector may decide to work in the public sector regardless. Note that a person may choose a job not in accordance with his or her preferences because when the organizational choice had to be made no employment alternatives existed in the preferred sector.

In this research we were particularly interested in the tendencies, not necessarily on the actual behaviour. We wished to explore possible reasons why job in the public sector seemed attractive. As stated, this in itself can provide scholars and policy makers with important information on how to attract employees to the public sector. Once we determined that the concept of under investigation here was the tendency to work in the public sector, it was only natural that the conceptual framework for developing a model of proposed determinants of this tendency would be based on the literature of job search and job choice.

Moss and Frieze contended that the process of job choice has two main parts: first, early socialization, when the individual develop expectations and accumulates information on alternative jobs; second, the actual job search and job choice. Lord and Kerman argued that information on the prospective job and organization is collected before the entry into the organization.

Individuals collect and process information on different jobs from childhood onward. Gatewood et al. explained that the process of job choice is one of information evaluation. Individuals collect information from two main sources to decide whether to seek work in a given organization: (1) informal, such as family and friends; (2) formal, such as newspaper ads and employment agencies. Getewood et al. argued that information from informal sources is more important for people than that from formal sources.

The above studies suggest that the roots of decisions on employment in the public sector might be found very early in a person's life. An interesting research question in this regard is how the process of accumulation of information on employment alternatives affects one's image of the public sector. The role of socialization mentioned by Gatewood et al. seemed to be closely relevant to the research subject at hand, namely tendency to employment in the public sector, so aspects of socialization were examined in this respect.

The literature on job search and job choice has naturally concentrated on the organizational level. Two concepts from this research seemed to be most relevant to this research and were integrated into its conceptual model. The first is the concept of person-organization fit, which refers to the fit between one's personality, values and beliefs and the strategic needs, norms, and values of the organization. The fit is created partly by the organization in the selection process and partly by the organizational socialization process. The literature has emphasized several aspects of fit between the individual and the organization: fit between one's knowledge, qualifications, and abilities and one's job requirements; fit between one's needs and the organizational structure as well as its support systems; fit between one's values and the organization's culture and values; fit between one's personality and the organizational perceived image or personality.

The concept of person-organization fit provides the conceptual framework for this research. It leads to the idea that prospective employees gather information about the public sector and evaluate the fit between their characteristics and those of the public sector. The outcomes of this evaluation affect their decisions whether to consider the public sector as an employment alternative favorably or not. This assumption is in line with Cable and Judge, who argued that the theory of person-organization fit can explain employment decisions of prospective employees. Bowen et al.'s approach to the concept of person-organization fit emphasizes the organizational image as an important component of the fit.

Organizational image is the second important concept adopted for this research from the job-choice literature. Rynes defined organizational image as a general impression of the attractiveness of the organization. This impression is based on the amount of information the applicants have at the first stages of their job search, and it affects their preliminary decisions. The importance of the organizational image on employment decisions was emphasized by several scholars. The organizational image is determined by social and cultural processes. People are prepared for a realistic level of expectations of the job, and this preparation is accomplished done by a variety of socialization agencies such as school, home, community, and the media.

We are interested not so much in the organizational image as in the sectorial one, more specifically, in the image of the public sector. The literature on this issue is sparse, so some reliance on the organizational image literature was necessary. In analogy with Rynes's definition of organizational image, we defined sectorial image as a general impression of the attractiveness of the public sector, which affects employment decision.

The few studies that have looked into the issue of sectorial image are quite old, and rather limited in their methods. In some of these studies the public sector image was measured by one item and not by scales tested for their reliabilities and validated for their psychometric properties. Yet despite their limitations, the studies on sectorial image found in general that the image of the public sector was not favorable among American employees.

Jasper, who examined engineering graduates and novice engineers, concluded that the general feeling of the group appeared to be that government employment carried a stigma. The students pictured the engineer working for the government as primarily interested in security and felt that employees hired by the government were generally mediocre in ability.

The above studies found what seems to be a prevalent negative image/reputation of the public sector, particularly regarding its employees and work in its organizations.

RESEARCH MODEL AND HYPOTHESES

Following the literature, we anticipated that our research population, students before graduation, would develop expectations and gather information on various jobs. This stage is preparatory to the next, which is the actual selection. This study focused on one specific and defined question out of the many possible here, namely if there is a sectorial choice, and if so, what are some of its determinants.

Here we set out the research model and its hypotheses. Two of the main concepts of the model have been discussed above: the dependent variable, tendency to work in the public sector, and the mediating variable, public sector image. The independent variables will be described below, together with our hypotheses regarding their relationships with the mediator and the dependent variables.

The model consists of three groups of independent variables: demographic variables, background and experience variables, and personal-psychological variables. The first group of hypotheses concerns the relationship between the independent variables and the dependent variable, tendency to work in the public sector.

Because we anticipated that public sector image would be positively related to tendency to work in the public sector, we expected the same pattern of relationship between the independent variables and tendency to work in the public sector to prevail for the relationship between the independent variables and public sector image.

Therefore, in the hypotheses section we do not elaborate on the relationship between the dependent variables and public sector image but we analyse these relationships in the results section and discuss their implications in the discussion. The main hypothesis of this research was the anticipation of a mediating relationship. That is, sectorial image will mediate the relationship between the independent variables and the tendency to work in the public sector.

DEMOGRAPHIC VARIABLES

The main rationale to expect demographic characteristics to be related to tendency to work in the public sector is that deprived groups in society, such as minorities and women, will tend to work in an employment environment where they are more protected and less discriminated. The public sector is considered to be such an environment. Arabs are a deprived minority in Israel and work in the public sector was found to assist them in earning higher wages and suffering less discrimination than in the private one. It was thus logical to expect a greater tendency to work in the public sector among Arab students than among Jewish students, and for Arab students to hold a more positive image of this sector.

By the same token it could be argued that immigrants students, those not born in Israel, would also prefer employment in the public sector. Immigrants constitute an unprotected social group that will search for employment that can provide them more job security and less discrimination, namely employment in the public sector. Dolton, Makepeace, and Inchley argued that the public sector is one of the more popular employment choices among women. Their income there is higher than in the private sector and they are less discriminated there than in the private sector.

Women may be expected to demonstrate more positive image of the pubic sector and higher tendency to work there than men. Following this logic it could also be expected that married students would prefer employment in the public sector. Blank argued that the public sector attracts employees looking for job security, and married people are more vulnerable in terms of the costs of losing their jobs. Therefore the public sector can be an attractive alternative for them. Finally it could be expected that older students would tend to work in a more stable environment and be less willing to take risks in their career than younger students.

Job security would be a stronger consideration for older students and this would impel them toward employment in the public sector. Thus, according to Hypothesis 1 (H1) Arabs, immigrants, females, married, and older students will have a more positive image of the public sector and higher tendency to work there.

BACKGROUND AND EXPERIENCE VARIABLES

The literature has emphasized the role of socialization in determining one's organizational choice. Most of the variables that follow represent earlier experiences of students that could shape and affect their attitudes to employment in the public sector. One of them is the major discipline studied by the student. The difference will be between students whose major is in the social sciences and those whose major is in humanities.

The importance of this factor was advanced by Kilpatrick et al. The rationale is that social sciences students feel that they have studied something of practical value that make them more attractive in the job market and can assist them in finding a job. Students in humanities feels that what they have studied has less practical value and relatively little to offer in the private sector, so they will prefer employment in the public sector, with its reputation of being less selective than the private.

Kilpatrick et al. also argued that the average grades of students also affect their decision to choose employment in the private or public sector. Students with higher grades have more alternatives and are more valuable in the employment market, considering that new graduates generally have no work experience. This fact makes the average grades the main measure of quality graduates' as job applicants. Those with higher grades will feel more competent and confident to search for a job in the private rather than the public sector, so they will have a lower tendency to work in the latter.

Treadwell and Harrison emphasized the role of work experience as one of the main socialization agents. Students who have worked at part-time jobs in the public sector acquired a more realistic perception of the employment there, which probably be more positive than what they had before working in it. They will have acquired more accurate information about employment there, including the sector's advantages and benefits. It was thus expected that students who had worked in the public sector would have a stronger tendency to work there and a more positive image of the employment there.

By the same token we posited that students also with work experience but with higher income have experienced its benefits, and because higher income is commonly associated with employment in the private sector, such students may be expected to prefer employment in that sector. They would avoid the public sector, which is certainly not associated with high income. The role of the perception of alternative employment opportunities has been mentioned in the literature as an important criterion in the process of job search. Individuals who perceive that they have less employment alternatives and opportunities, regardless of the reasons, will tend to look for a job with more security.

In that way they will not have to go back to the job market, which is not promising for them as job seekers. Thus, according to Hypothesis 2 (H2) students whose major is in the social sciences, whose average grades are lower, who have had more work experience in the public sector, and a lower income, and who perceive that they have fewer alternatives in the job market, will have a more positive image of the public sector and will have a stronger tendency to work there.

PERSONAL PSYCHOLOGICAL VARIABLES

Leary, Wheeler, and Jenkins argued that personal characteristics are related to employment choices. Moss and Frieze explained that individuals look for jobs that will best meet their personal needs and/or values, and choose the one that has the best fit with their needs.

The rationale of person-organization fit, the main conceptual framework of this research, also supports the inclusion of personal-psychological variables as determinants of tendency to work in the public sector. Several personal variables are included here. Kilduff argued that people with low self-monitor will feel more comfortable in a work environment that emphasizes more autonomy, and more personal freedom, in comparison with people with high self-monitor who will prefer a more conformist environment. Those with low self-monitor will prefer an environment that has clear and formal expectations of their role in the organization.

Accordingly, we expected students with low self-monitor to prefer an environment with more autonomy and tolerating more self-expression, while students with high self-monitor would prefer employment in the public sector, which is considered a more conformist environment than that which they would probably find in the private sector.

It was also expected here that students with external locus of control would prefer employment in the public sector. Students with internal locus of control would attribute success to ability and performance. This would strengthen their preference for employment in the private sector, which seems to emphasize effort and results. A person with external locus of control attributes his or her success to external causes, and will prefer stable employment where the compensation and promotion systems are regulated by laws and formal procedures generated by the government.

A person with external locus of control will feel less vulnerable in employment in the public sector. Two needs variables were also included in the group of personal-psychological determinants. First, students with low need for achievement would prefer employment in the public sector. The rationale is similar to the one outlined in the psychological variables mentioned above.

Students with high need for achievement are more ambitious and value competition in order to achieve their goals. Those with low need for achievement would prefer stability and security over competition, and the public sector is considered a stable and secure environment. Finally, it was strongly expected that students with high need for security would prefer employment in the public sector. Blank argued that because the goal of the public sector is not profit it attracts job seekers with higher need for security.

Employees in the public sector are and feel more secure in terms of losing their job and it could be expected that students with a high need for need security would prefer employment in the public sector. Thus according to Hypothesis 3 (H3) students with high self-monitor, external locus of control, low need for achievement and high need for security will have a positive image of the public sector and higher tendency to work there.

THE MEDIATING ROLE OF PUBLIC SECTOR IMAGE

The research model suggests that the relationship between the above-mentioned determinants and tendency to work in the public sector is not direct but mediated by the image of the public sector. Kilpatrick et al. were among the very few researchers who examined and emphasized the concept of public sector image. Rynes in a more recent work defined public sector image as a general impression of the attractiveness of the sector, which affect employment choice. Krau and Ziv argued that the image of employment in the public service mediates the relationship between the characteristics of employment there and the employment choice of individuals.

The expectation here for a mediated relationship is based on the following rationale. Average students are in their early stages of job search, and without stable and permanent employment all they have developed is an image of different aspects of the public sector. Thus, the determinants mentioned above are related first to the perceived image of the public sector.

Demographic, work experience, and personal-psychological characteristics all function to shape the image of the public sector starting from childhood and during the years of study at university. The importance of the image is emphasized by the person-organization fit theory.

Prospective employees evaluate their characteristics and those of the organization, and choose the one that has the best fit with their characteristics. The image that is the result of these determinants is directly related to the tendency to work in the public sector. Thus according to Hypothesis 4 (H4) the relationship between the determinants and the tendency to work in the public sector will be mediated by the image of the public sector.

METHOD

The target population of this study was 1640 third-year undergraduate students of most of the departments at an Israeli university. Departments that were not included in the sample were Law, Social work, Art, Nursing, Occupational therapy, Department of Teaching and Teacher education. The reason for not including them is because in the Israeli setting the graduates of these departments do not have much of a sectorial choice.

Most of the available jobs for students in Law and Art departments are in the private sector and most of the available jobs for students in Social work, Occupational therapy, Teaching and Teacher education are in the public sector. In all the other departments graduates have more available jobs in both sectors and therefore it was decided to include in the sample only students from such departments. Therefore, all 1640 third-year students from these departments were defined as the target population and were asked to participate in the study.

Questionnaires were distributed by mail to the home address of each of them. After two waves of distributions, 660 usable questionnaires were returned, a response rate of 40 per cent, which was acceptable considering that this was a mail survey.

A breakdown of respondents by their major subject showed that 76 per cent of the sample were social sciences students, 64 per cent were females, 86 per cent were Jews, and 14 per cent were Arabs. Respondents' average age was 25.8 years (s.d.= 4.1); 84 per cent of them were born in Israel, 22 per cent were married, 70 per cent had a part-or a full-time jobs, and 50 per cent had some experience in working in the public sector.

A comparison of the sample with some characteristics of the entire population as provided by the university administration, revealed that 64 per cent were female in the target population, a percentage identical to that in the sample; 76 per cent were Jews in the target population, compared with 86 per cent in the sample; 57 per cent were social sciences students in the target population, compared with 76 per cent in the sample. The differences are reasonable, so we may generalize from the sample to the target population.

DATA ANALYSIS

The main statistical analyses in this study were multiple and hierarchical regressions. To support the hypotheses regarding the mediated relationship between the independent variables and the dependent variable, we followed Baron and Kenny and James and Brett. According to them, a mediating relationship can be supported by one or more of the following methods:

- Regression analysis,
- ANOVA or MANOVA,
- Testing for interactions.

Nevertheless, Baron and Kenny elaborated on the simplicity and the effectiveness of regression analysis, compared with the limited test for mediation in other methods such as ANOVA. Accordingly, we applied the regression analysis method, in which, as described by Baron and Kenny, to test for mediation one estimates the following three regression equations.

First, the mediator is regressed on the independent variable, whereby the independent variable must affect the mediator. Second, the dependent variable is regressed on the independent variable, whereby the independent variable must affect the dependent variable. Third, the dependent variable is regressed on both the independent variable and on the mediator, whereby the mediator must affect the dependent variable. If these conditions all hold in the predicted direction, then the effect of the independent variable on the dependent variable must be less in the third equation than in the second.

FINDINGS

First we examined the two scales for the public sector image to find whether the items of the two scales should be treated as multi-dimensional or unidimensional. Exploratory factor analysis of the 32 items of the two scales was performed, and produced three factors; 14 of the 15 items of the image of public sector employee loaded strongly on the first factor, and 13 of the 17 items of image of public sector employment loaded strongly on the second factor.

Three items of the employment image loaded on a third factor, and one item of employee image did not load on any of the factors. This finding supported in general the existence of two separate dimensions. But two other indications supported the treatment of the two dimensions as one scale. One of these was the relatively high correlation between the two scales (r=.66).

Note, however, that a correlation of.66 is still acceptable in terms of treating the two constructs as separate dimensions. The other indication was that the reliability of the 32 items was very high (.97) and supported the notion that the two scales were in fact one construct. One can see that the findings above are not conclusive in terms of making a clear decision whether to treat public sector image as a unidimensional or a multidimensional construct. Therefore, we decided to analyse and present the data with the public sector image as a unidimensional and a multidimensional construct.

The findings show good reliabilities and good psychometric properties of research variables. The correlations among the independent variables were not high except for the correlation between employment status and income. These findings support the absence of multicollinearity. Note that although the variables in this study were based on self-report data, allowing source bias or general method variance, the low correlations among the independent variables demonstrate the absence of common method error. The correlation matrix shows negative relationships between tendency to work in the public sector and the three public sector image scales.

Some consistency can be found in the relationships between the demographic variables and the public sector image variables as well as the tendency to work in the public sector. This is strongly supported for the variables ethnicity, country of origin, major studies, and average grade. The variable experience in the public sector is also related significantly to the image variables and to the variable tendency to work in the public sector. Note, too, the lack of relationship between the personal-psychological variables and the image variables. Tendency to work in the public sector was related to two psychological variables (self-monitor and need for security). In short, the correlations provide some support for hypotheses 1 and 2 and weaker support for hypothesis 3.

In each of the equations the mediating variables (public sector image of employment, employee, and the total scale) were regressed on the independent variables. Also, the dependent variable was regressed on the independent variables. The findings generally support the two terms for mediation mentioned above. First, significant relationships existed between the independent variables and the dependent variable. Variables representing each group of the independent variables (demographic, experiences, and psychological) were related to tendency to work in the public sector. As for the relationships between the mediating and the dependent variable, the findings showed significant relationships between the two that support the second term of mediation.

These relationships were stronger for the image of employee and for the total scale of image than for the image of employment. The general conclusion is that the findings meet the first and second requirement for mediation as described by Baron and Kenny. Conceptually, the findings provide stronger support for hypotheses 1 and 2 than for hypothesis 3. Hypothesis 1 predicted that demographic variables would be related to public sector image and to tendency to work in the public sector.

While the demographic variables were not related to the image of employment in the public sector, the findings show that males and Arabs had a more positive image of employee in the public sector, and Arabs had a stronger tendency to work there than Jews. This provides some support for hypothesis 1. Stronger support was found for hypothesis 2. Three of the experience variables were related to the image of the public sector. Students whose major was humanities had a more positive image of the public sector in all the three dimensions tested here. Students with higher grades had a more negative image of the public sector in all the dimensions.

Students with some work experience in the public sector had a more positive image of employee in the public sector. The above significant relationship was found for the total image scale but not the image of employment. Two of the experience variables were related to tendency to work in the public sector. Students whose major was in humanities and students with some work experience in the public sector had a stronger tendency to work there. Altogether, the findings seem to provide solid support for hypothesis 2.

Hypothesis 3 predicted that the psychological variables would be related to image of the public sector and to the tendency to work there, and it received partial support by the data. None of the psychological variables was related to any of the public sector images, and this finding was not expected. Hypothesis 3 was supported by the relationship of two of the psychological variables to tendency to work in the public sector.

As expected, students with low self-monitor, and with high need for security, had stronger tendency to work in the public sector. The variables locus of control and need for achievement were not related to the image variables or to tendency to work in the public sector. In all it may be concluded that hypothesis 3 was only partially supported by the data.

This two-step regression was proposed by Ferris, Frink, Bhawuk, and Zhou to allow a more sensitive evaluation of the third condition for mediation: the mediators must affect the dependent variable, and, more importantly, the effect of the independent variables on the dependent variable must be less in the last equation (the relationship between the independent variables and the dependent variable) than in the second steps.

As mentioned this was done twice, when first public sector was treated as multidimensional and when in a second set of equations the public sector image was analysed as one scale. The mediating factors were entered into the equation in the first step while all other independent variables were entered in the second one. The findings provide empirical support for condition. First, the data strongly show that public sector image was strongly related to tendency to work in the public sector. Most of the variance in tendency to work in the public sector was due to the effect of public sector image, while all other variables contributed 10 per cent or 11 per cent to the total explained variance.

Although this estimation was not part of the research hypotheses one should note the significant effect of the mediators on tendency to work in the public sector. This finding supports the rationale of hypothesis 4, which expected strong relationships between public sector image, as mediating factors, and the dependent variable, tendency to work in the public sector. The data strongly support hypothesis 4 when we compare the last equation with the two second step equations. The data clearly show that the effect of the independent variables was less in the regression equation than in the two regressions.

All these findings are much in line with the third condition for mediation of Baron and Kenny. In short, the findings provide empirical support for hypothesis 4, namely public sector image mediated the relationship between all the independent variables and tendency to work in the public sector.

DISCUSSION

One of the goals of this study was to draw more attention by scholars to an issue that has been overlooked for many years and to stimulate more research on this important topic. The findings of this study support most of the basic arguments advanced by this chapter. First, tendency to work in the public sector is a construct that has a meaning for students who are exploring their possibilities in the job market.

The same can be said about the concept of public sector image that was also advanced here. Moreover, the two concepts are related, and the image of the public sector mediated the relationship between the proposed determinants and tendency to work in the public sector. Thus, despite the somewhat exploratory nature of this study since very little research has been conducted on the issue, the findings show that the topic examined offers a promising and challenging research agenda for the future.

The findings of this study provide general support to the very few and somewhat old studies on this issue. Kilpatrick et al. set out the notion that the image one has about the public sector can affect one's attitudes and behaviour. This idea was elaborated here and tested by use of valid and reliable scales with more advanced methodology than that employed by Kilpatrick et al. The scales we proposed and tested captured two important dimensions of the public sector image: the image of its employees and the image of employment in the public sector.

The findings were not conclusive in determining whether public sector image is a multidimensional or unidimensional construct. While the relatively high correlation between the two suggests that perhaps they should be treated as unidimensional it seems that a multidimensional perspective was better supported by the data. Some interesting differences between their determinants supported the notion that they are distinct. For example image of employment was related only to two experience variables while image of employee was related also to gender ethnicity and country of origin. Future research should test the scales proposed here to arrive to a more definite conclusion whether image of the public sector is a unidimensional or a multidimensional construct.

Regardless of this methodological aspect in both its unidimensional and multidimensional form, the findings here showed the potential of image of the public sector as a concept able to increase understanding of prospective employees' decision whether or not to work in the public sector. The findings strongly supported the notion that public sector image mediates the relationship between determinants and tendency to work in the public sector. That is, demographic, background, and experience variables work to shape the image one has of the public sector, and this image determines one's tendency to work in that sector.

This process emphasizes the role of socialization in shaping one's image of the public sector, and supports Moss and Frieze's argument that socialization is an important component in the job search and job choice processes. The relationship between work experience in the public sector and the image of the public sector supports Lord and Kerman's argument that the information on the prospective job and organization is collected before entry into the organization.

The findings here show, as suggested by Gatewood et al., that the process of sectorial choice is one of information evaluation. Individuals collect information that assists them to decide whether to get an employment in a given organization, in this case the public sector. The findings of this study also support earlier findings of Blank, who examined demographic determinants of workers' choice between employment in the public or private sector.

Blank's study differs from this one because it examined and compared employees from both the public and the private sectors, while ours examined tendency to work in the public sector among students. Yet some similarities between the findings of the two studies exist.

First, Blank's main findings showed that non-whites and veterans, groups protected by federal employment laws, preferred the public sector but women had no statistically distinguishable preference between the sectors. Blank's finding was supported in general by the findings here. Arab students, a relatively deprived minority in Israel, preferred employment in the public sector and had a more positive image of the public sector than Jewish students.

It may be concluded that minorities prefer employment in the public sector because they feel more protected by the laws and regulations in it, regardless of culture and country. Another interesting finding is that in both studies gender had no significant effect on employees' working in the public sector in Blank's study, or on students' tendency to work in the public sector here.

This finding showed that, regarding employment in the public sector, gender becomes less important in the process of making a sectorial choice. Other characteristics affect females' decisions in both cultures whether or not to work in the public sector, not the anticipation that they will be more protected in the public sector. This conclusion needs to be tested in future research.

Another finding by Blank was that employees with lower education preferred the public sector, while those with higher education or more experience seemed to prefer the private sector. The logic of Blank's finding was in a way supported here.

Education represents human capital, and those with more of this resource felt more confident to compete in the private sector. In this study, grades and major subject represent human capital for students. It is not surprising that students whose major was in social sciences and who won higher grades thought that by having more human capital they had more options in the job market and could compete successfully in the private sector.

This was demonstrated here in the negative image that students with higher grades had of the public sector and in the stronger tendency of students whose major was in humanities to work in the public sector. The findings here provide support for human-capital theory in the sense that prospective employees with more human capital do not perceive work in the public sector as employment that will enable them to capitalize on their resources. This study's contribution is to show that what Blank found for employees can be predicted prior to their joining the workforce. Our findings in the Israeli setting accord with those of Jasper for engineering graduates and novice engineers noted above.

The findings here, almost 40 years later and in another culture, seem to support those of Jasper. Note, however, that many differences exist between the above studies, particularly between Blank's work and this one. A major difference is the inclusion in our model of public sector image, which was strongly supported by the data.

Another notable finding is the relatively weak effect of the psychological variables. These had no effect on any of the public sector image forms. This finding emphasizes the role of socialization and not personality in shaping one's attitudes to employment in the public sector. But one cannot ignore the strong effect of personality on tendency to work in the public sector.

This was demonstrated in the significant effect of self-monitor and more especially need for security, on this tendency. This finding shows that certain personalities tend to look for employment in the public sector. The strong effect of need for security shows that not only is the public sector a better environment for protected groups such as minorities, but this pattern is also relevant for those who feel unprotected whether or not they are in a protected group. These finding needs to be replicated in future research before definite conclusions can be made.

The findings here strongly support the conceptual framework of person-organization fit as appropriate to understanding of the determinants of tendency to work in the public sector. This theory postulates that what determines one's choice is the fit between one's personality, values, and beliefs and the strategic needs, norms, and values of the organization.

The findings here emphasize the fit from the individuals' point of view. Prospective employees who are from a minority group (Arabs), who are not especially trained (major in humanities and not social sciences), who have some work experience in the public sector, whose personality leans toward a more conformist formalized and dependency environment, and above all who have a strong need for security, prefer to work in the public sector.

Support for the person-organizational fit framework is reinforced by the significant effect of two psychological variables on tendency to work in the public sector. This effect supports the approach emphasizing the fit between the individuals' personality and the perceived organizational image or personality. The effect of the psychological variables was not evident in the relationship between the psychological variables and image of the public sector.

This study offers some practical implications particularly for policy makers. While all will agree on the need to increase the quality of the workforce in the public sector, this study offers new insights into how to do it. Image was found here as a key concept affecting students=tendency to work in the public sector. Some prospective employees will not choose the public sector because of its negative image. But this image can be shaped and influenced. For example, providing students with some experience in the public sector is one practical way to improve the image of the public sector and increase the tendency to work there.

Providing social sciences graduates with information on the advantages of working in the public sector is another way to attract them to the public sector. Improving the image of the public sector will probably attract more excellent students. Person-organization fit theory postulates that the fit can be created by the organization in the selection or the socialization process. The effect of the variable experience in the public sector emphasizes the ability of public organizations to use the socialization process to attract qualified employees to the public sector.

The effect of the two psychological variables suggests that the selection process can be used to detect these psychological characteristics. But first a strategic decision has to be made by organizations: do they want employees with high selfmonitor and high need for security? If not, applicants possessing these two characteristics might be rejected. Image is one of the reasons why people who feel less confident about themselves choose to work in the public sector.

Improving the public-sector image will probably result in more quality applicants wishing to work in the public sector. This study showed some ways by which the image of the public sector can be enhanced, but much more work is needed to explore other factors that shape it.

Finally, several limitations of this study must be considered. First, because this research examined students, there may be limits to the generalizability of the findings to other populations, especially employees. second, the study relied on self-report data, allowing for the possibility of same-source bias, a common problem with cross-sectional, non-behavioral measurement.

Because the multivariate analysis considered the simultaneous effects of all variables, the extent of this problem was reduced. Third, much of the work on public sector employment has concentrated on American employees, which limits ability to generalize findings across other cultures and settings. While the American data are very important, there must be more diversity in the cultures and nations that are tested. This chapter has attempted to show the usefulness of such research in another culture, the Israeli one, and also to propose some directions for nature study.

Despite the limitations, this study has some important contributions. The findings here demonstrate the importance of public sector image and tendency to work in the public sector as important considerations for understanding sectorial choice of prospective employees. The proposed model has some important conceptual and practical implications that can direct future research. More research on this issue seems warranted in light of the findings and before solid conclusions can be made on the findings here. The contribution of this study is its proposing some promising directions for research on an interesting and important issue.

9

The Role of Technology in Preparing Youth

Today, technology has become essential in almost every educational, employment, community, and recreational environment. Access to electronic and information technology can help students with a wide range of abilities and disabilities prepare for and succeed in adult life. Specifically, for people with disabilities, such access has the potential to maximize independence, productivity and participation in academic programs, employment, recreation and other adult activities. In addition, for those who have the interest and aptitude, advanced technology skills can open doors to high tech career fields that were once unavailable to people with disabilities.

Although the benefits of technology may be even greater for people with disabilities than for people without disabilities, individuals with disabilities are less than half as likely as their non-disabled counterparts to own computers, and they are about one-quarter as likely to use the Internet. In addition, the design of many Web pages, instructional software programs, productivity tools, telecommunications products, and other electronic and information technologies erects barriers for some individuals with disabilities.

For example, Web pages that do not include text alternatives that can be read by speech and Braille output systems limit information access by a student who is blind or is a poor reader; the content of a videotape that does not have captions is inaccessible to a viewer who is deaf; software with a high reading level may not be accessible to people with learning disabilities or developmental disabilities; and office equipment that cannot be operated from a seated position is inaccessible to an employee who uses a wheelchair for mobility.

Taking advantage of the power that technology offers in improving the precollege and postsecondary academic outcomes for individuals with disabilities is critically important because people with disabilities today experience far less career success than their non-disabled peers. However, these differences in achievement diminish between individuals as they gain more education.

For example, the employment rate for individuals with disabilities who do not complete high school is 15.6 per cent; for those who complete high school it is 30.2 per cent; for those with some postsecondary education it is 45.1 per cent; and for those with four years of college it is 50.3 per cent. Clearly, technology access that leads to greater success in precollege and postsecondary education has the potential to improve career outcomes for people with disabilities.

Today, individuals with disabilities are significantly underrepresented in postsecondary education and a significantly lower percentage of students with disabilities than those without disabilities eventually earn degrees. The largest and fastest growing disability among freshmen who report having disabilities is learning disability - 40.4 per cent in 2000 as compared to 16.1 per cent in 1988. Percentages of students with disabilities reporting other types of disabilities are 16.1 per cent blindness or partial sight, 15.4 per cent health-related impairments, 8.6 per cent hearing impairments, 7.1 per cent orthopedic impairments, 2.9 per cent speech impairments, and 16.9 per cent other impairments.

Even those who complete postsecondary studies are likely to have fewer work-based learning experiences than those who do not have disabilities. Lack of job skills and related experiences before graduation create additional barriers to employment for people with disabilities. The poor employment figures for people with disabilities coupled with the positive impact of postsecondary education and work-related experiences make increasing their success in these activities an important goal. The cost of failure to reach this goal, to these individuals and to society, is high.

High-tech careers are particularly accessible to individuals with disabilities because of the combined effect of the increasing use of electronic and information technology and of the advancements in assistive technology that provide access to computers and other electronic equipment for people with a variety of disabilities. A bachelor's degree or higher is a prerequisite for many of these challenging careers. Although few students with disabilities pursue high-tech postsecondary programs and careers and the attrition rate is high, those who succeed in these fields demonstrate that opportunities do exist for people with disabilities who successfully overcome the barriers imposed by facilities, electronic and information technology inadequate academic preparation, lack of role models, and negative attitudes.

In order for students with disabilities to pursue postsecondary academic and career options, they must have access to the high-tech tools available to their nondisabled peers. These include computers, websites, telecommunications products, instructional software, and scientific equipment. Full access requires that built-in barriers to these tools and resources as well as facilities in which they are housed be removed and appropriate assistive technology be readily available.

Today, the full potential of using technology to prepare young people with disabilities for postsecondary education is not being realized. Funding is reported as the top barrier by service providers and policy experts. Consumers identify the two biggest barriers to be lack of knowledge of stakeholders about appropriate assistive technology and lack of funding to purchase assistive technology.

Many graduates of teacher education programs are not adequately prepared in the general use of computer technology and in classroom applications. In addition, as reported by the National Council on Disability, "the rapid acquisition of educational technology has not sufficiently addressed the needs of students with disabilities. Access for students with disabilities is just beginning to be identified as an important factor when purchasing educational technology."

Consequently, products with inaccessible characteristics are often purchased, inaccessible electronic resources and educational software are developed and procured, and inaccessible facilities are constructed. Many computer support staff, regular education teachers, and special education teachers are not sufficiently trained to use mainstream and specialized equipment and on how these technologies can work together to maximize access to education for students with disabilities.

As summarized by Hasselbring and Glaser, "Lack of adequate teacher training has an especially strong impact on students with disabilities because technology is often a critical component in planning and implementing an educational programme for these students." Other barriers to technology access for individuals with disabilities include lack of trained professionals to evaluate assistive technology, difficulties in locating assistive technology for testing by individuals with disabilities, confusion about existing laws and policies regarding assistive technology and accessible electronic and information technology, gaps in laws and policies that fund assistive technology, and the bureaucracy of public programs and insurance companies.

In particular, because of differences in laws and funding for technology between precollege and college environments, even students who are lucky enough to gain access to empowering technology in precollege settings may not be allowed to take it with them when they exit high school. Clearly, much work needs to be done before the full potential of today's technology to promote postsecondary academic and career success for students with disabilities is realized.

Although it is easier to agree on the problems that exist than the interventions that will overcome them, most would agree that the situation would be much improved if the following three conditions were assured.

- All individuals with disabilities have access to technology that promotes positive academic and career outcomes.
- People with disabilities learn to use technology in ways that

contribute to positive postsecondary academic and career outcomes and self-determined lives.

- There is a seamless transition of availability of technology for all people with disabilities as they move from K-12 to postsecondary to career environments.

This chapter defines terminology related to the use of technology by people with disabilities. Then, it describes what specific roles technology can play in preparing young people with disabilities for postsecondary education and employment. Next, legal issues in precollege education, postsecondary academic, and employment settings are discussed.

After that, is a summary of key issues that must be addressed in order for young people with disabilities to gain the full benefits that technology has to offer as they make the transitions from precollege education to postsecondary education and employment. Finally, implications and recommendations are suggested.

TERMINOLOGY

Throughout this chapter, technology includes electronic and information technology and assistive technology that provides access to electronic and information technology. Information technology is defined as "any equipment or interconnected system or subsystem of equipment, that is used in the automatic acquisition, storage, manipulation, management, movement, control, display, switching, interchange, transmission, or reception of data or information.

The term information technology includes computers, ancillary equipment, software, firmware and similar procedures, services (including support services), and related resources." Electronic technology encompasses information technology, but also includes any equipment or interconnected system or subsystem of equipment that is used in the creation, conversion, or duplication of data or information.

Electronic technology includes telecommunications products such as telephones and office equipment such as copiers and fax machines. Many electronic and information technology products are designed in such a way that they are inaccessible to people with some types of disabilities.

For example, a person with a visual impairment may not be able to interpret instructions if they are presented only in a visual format; a person who is deaf cannot access content if it is only presented aurally; someone with who is a poor reader cannot access content that requires a high reading level. An important term to define is access, as it relates to the use of computer hardware, software, and other technology.

According to the National Science Foundation, "access implies the ability to find, manipulate and use information in an efficient and comprehensive manner". Too often even those individuals with disabilities who have a computer and Internet connection still cannot make full use of its capabilities because of the inaccessible features of hardware and/or software. They have technology, but do not have access to all of the benefits it delivers to others.

Assistive technology is defined as "any item, piece of equipment, or system, whether acquired commercially, modified, or customized, that is commonly used to increase, maintain, or improve functional capabilities of individuals with disabilities".

Assistive technology enables people with disabilities to accomplish daily living tasks; assists them in communication; and provides greater access to education, employment, and recreation. It can be used to maximize physical or mental functioning and minimize the impact of a disability. Examples of assistive technology include scooters and wheelchairs, alternative automobile controls, environmental controls, prostheses, communication aids, hand splints, hearing aids, and alternative input and output devices for computers.

An assistive technology service is defined as "any service that directly assists an individual with a disability in selection, acquisition or use of an assistive technology device". For this chapter, only assistive technology that interfaces with electronic and information technology and related services are relevant.

The process of creating products that are accessible to people with a wide range of abilities, disabilities, and other characteristics is called universal design. Universal design is defined by the National Centre for Universal Design at North Carolina State University as "the design of products and environments to be usable by all people, to the greatest extent possible, without the need for adaptation or specialized design".

At this Centre, a team of architects, product designers, engineers, and environmental design researchers established a set of principles of universal design to provide guidance in the design of environments, communications, and products. General principles include: the design accommodates a wide range of individual preferences and abilities; the design communicates necessary information effectively, regardless of ambient conditions or the user's sensory abilities; the design can be used efficiently and comfortably and with a minimum of fatigue; and appropriate size and space is provided for approach, reach, manipulation, and use regardless of the user's body size, posture, or mobility.

The concept of universal design has been applied to all teaching and learning activities. In particular, when producers apply universal design principles as they create electronic and information technology, the products are more usable by everyone, including people with disabilities.

They minimize the need for assistive technology and are compatible with commonly used assistive hardware and software. Below are a few examples of accessible electronic and information technology and its benefits to students with disabilities in educational settings.

- Accessible Web pages allow students with disabilities, including those who have sensory impairments and those with low reading skills, to access information; share their work; communicate with peers, teachers, and mentors; and take advantage of distance learning options.
- Accessible instructional software (on disks, CDs or other media) and documentation allow students with disabilities to participate side-by-side with their peers in computer labs and classrooms as they complete assignments; collaborate with peers; create and view presentations, documents, spreadsheets; and actively participate in simulations and other computer-based activities.

  Accessible telephones make communication accessible to everyone, including people with cognitive, mobility, visual, and hearing impairments.

The following section provides examples of roles technology can play in the lives of individuals with disabilities.

ROLES OF TECHNOLOGY FOR STUDENTS WITH DISABIUTIES

The following examples demonstrate how electronic and information technology can be used by students with disabilities and contribute to their independence, productivity, and participation in academics and careers.

Specifically, technology can help them in the following ways:

- Maximize independence in academic and employment tasks. Example: A student with a mobility impairment uses a hands-free keyboard and mouse to operate a computer to take class notes, access library resources, and complete papers rather than have an assistant write for her.
- Participate in classroom discussions. Example: A student who cannot speak uses a computer-based communication device to deliver speeches and participate in class discussions.
- Gain access to peers, mentors, and role models. Example: In a supported Internet community, a student who is deaf uses email to chat with other teens, gain support for college and career transition from mentors, and meet role models.
- Self-advocate. Example: A student who is deaf uses a TTY and relay service to arrange appointments regarding internship accommodations with her supervisor.
- Gain access to the full range of educational options. Example: A student who is blind and uses speech output technology fully participates in an Internet-based distance learning course that employs universal design principles to assure access to people with disabilities.

- Participate in experiences not otherwise possible. Example: a young man with no functional use of his arms and legs experiences completing a chemistry experiment through a computer simulation and observing sea life while swimming in the ocean through virtual reality.
- Succeed in work-based learning experiences. Example: A student who has no use of his hands independently operates a computer to draft and edit articles in a journalism internship at the local newspaper office.
- Secure high levels of independent living. Example: A young person who has a developmental disability uses a cell phone to maintain regular contact with caregivers as he participates in community activities. Example: A teen with a mobility impairment uses a voice-controlled system to operate the television, turn lights on and off, open doors, and perform other tasks of daily life.
- Prepare for transitions to college and careers. Example: A student with a learning disability that makes it difficult for him to read uses a computer with a speech output system to explore internship and career opportunities, take self-paced career readiness and interest tests, and research the academic programs and services for students with disabilities offered at colleges of interest.
- A girl who is blind and a boy who has no use of his hands work on the school newsletter with fellow journalism students; she uses speech output technology, he uses a voice recognition system, and other students use standard input and output devices on a local area network in the computer lab.
- Master academic tasks that they cannot accomplish otherwise. Example: A student with a learning disability uses a set of software tools to support her management of reading, writing, and study demands in a postsecondary setting.
- Enter high-tech career fields. Example: A child who shows interest in engineering at a young age, but does not have the fine motor skills to manipulate objects, gains technical knowledge using the Internet, operates computer simulations of engineering tasks, and develops a solid foundation for college studies and a career in engineering.
- Participate in community and recreational activities. Example: An adult who is blind can privately cast his vote for President of the United States because the voting booth is designed to be accessible to everyone.

These and countless other examples demonstrate the important roles electronic and information technology can play as young people with disabilities pursue postsecondary education and careers.

First, they realise the same benefits as individuals without disabilities - they write articles, develop spreadsheets, access Internet-based resources and services, work side-by-side with their peers. In addition to these benefits, however, some people with disabilities use technology as compensatory tools which allow them to do things that are otherwise impossible because of their disabilities.

For example, technology can provide a voice for those who cannot speak in the customary way; can allow people to write even though they do not have functional use of their hands; can make it possible for individuals to use the telephone even though they do not have the ability to hear. The following section summarizes key legislation related to technology access for people with disabilities in elementary and secondary schools, postsecondary institutions, and employment.

LEGISLATION

The Individuals with Disabilities Education Act mandates that each state provide a free and appropriate education for all children, regardless of their abilities or disabilities. It requires that individual education plans (IEPs) be developed for students with disabilities who meet certain criteria and that assistive technology and transition, among other things, be considered in the development of IEPs.

Section 504 of the Rehabilitation Act of 1973 prohibits discrimination against individuals with disabilities in federally-funded programs and services that receive, which include the vast majority of educational institutions. The Americans with Disabilities Act of 1990 (ADA) reinforces and extends the requirements of section 504 to public programs and services, regardless of whether or not they receive federal funds.

Precollege programs must provide access to all children, regardless of disabilities; thus, all students with disabilities, regardless of whether they have IEPs, have a right to the same technology access that is provided to students without disabilities. For qualified students who disclose their disabilities and present appropriate documentation, postsecondary institutions must provide reasonable accommodations to assure equal access to programme offerings.

Although the ADA does not specifically mention electronic and information technology, the United States Department of justice clarified that the ADA applies to Internet-based resources - "Covered entities that use the Internet for communications regarding their programs, goods, or services must be prepared to offer those communications through accessible means as well". The ADA mandates nondiscrimination in employment as well, requiring reasonable accommodations for employees with disabilities; such accommodations may include the purchase of assistive technology.

Provisions of the Carl D. Perkins Vocational and Applied Technology Education Act of 1998, the Rehabilitation Amendments of 1992 and 1993, the

School-to-Work Opportunities Act of 1994, and the Technology-Related Assistance for Individuals with Disabilities Act of 1988 further dictate programme access and support services that must be provided to people with disabilities.

Unfortunately, many elementary, secondary, and postsecondary educators and service providers have difficulty understanding and applying the maze of conflicting definitions, eligibility criteria, and policy implications of legislation that impacts the provision of technology access for individuals with disabilities.

Section 508 of the Rehabilitation Act requires that agencies of the federal government develop, purchase, and use electronic and information technology that is accessible to individuals with disabilities. The Architectural and Transportation Barriers Compliance Board (Access Board) developed standards to which these agencies must comply.

Even for those who are not covered entities under section 508, the standards developed by the Access Board provide a good starting point for organizations seeking to meet their ADA obligations. They include standards for (a) accessible desktop and portable computers, (b) Web-based resources, (c) video and multimedia products, (d) software and operating systems, and (e) selfcontained, closed systems such as photocopiers and fax machines.

Although educational institutions and employers have legal obligations to provide technology access to students and employees with disabilities, barriers still prevent people with disabilities from gaining full access to technologies that can help them reach their full potential.

DISCUSSION

Technology has the potential to improve the educational, career, and adult living outcomes for people with disabilities. However, this potential will not be realized unless barriers to reaching the following goals are overcome.

- All individuals with disabilities have access to technology that promotes positive academic and career outcomes.
- People with disabilities learn to use technology in ways that contribute to positive postsecondary academic and career outcomes and self-determined lives.
- There is a seamless transition of availability of technology for all people with disabilities as they move from K-12 to postsecondary to career environments.

The specific goals addressed in each discussion section are indicated in parentheses immediately after each question.

ACCOMMODATIONS VS. UNIVERSAL DESIGN

How can the creation of universal design of electronic and information technology be promoted? Designing inclusive environments that are accessible to everyone, with and without disabilities, minimizes the need for individual accommodations. Employing the universal design approach to the development of technology devices, facilities, information resources, and services is a critical step towards ensuring that students with disabilities are provided with full access to programs and activities in the school, workplace, and community.

Promoting the use of electronic and information technology standards established by the federal government can help educational and employment entities move closer to this goal. Librarians, educators, and others who purchase technology products for schools need to demand that accessibility considerations be included in the procurement process.

Similarly, distance learning programme providers must employ universal design principles to make courses accessible to potential students with a wide variety of abilities and disabilities, including those who are blind and use speech or Braille output systems.

A universal design approach to electronic and information technology selection and use in schools can help to reduce technology costs as well as facilitate the transfer of technology from secondary to postsecondary educational settings. It can promote compatibility in education and workplace settings; reduce stigma, cultural, and attitudinal barriers for students with disabilities; and make it easier for service providers to respond to the changing technology needs of students.

FUNDING

Who will assure funding so that children with disabilities can gain access to empowering technology? Funding is often cited as a barrier to technology access for people with disabilities. Although the cost of technology is often lower than anticipated and funding is sometimes suggested as a constraint when issues of selection and management are actually more challenging, technology does cost money and must be paid for in some way.

This issue is likely to grow increasingly important as elementary and secondary educators continue to be faced with implementing the assistive technology requirements of IDEA, as technology in general becomes more widely available as a tool for student learning, and as awareness of assistive technology becomes more widespread. Besides consideration of the overall costs, deciding who (e.g., school, government agency, insurance, family) should pay for technology under specific circumstances and who owns the technology as a person transitions between various levels of education and employment creates additional challenges to be overcome.

Technology choices for people with disabilities should be driven by both short-term and long-term needs. Besides initial purchase, questions about who is responsible for upgrades and technical support during all life stages must be answered.

Funding is needed for training personnel to deliver technology services at various academic and employment levels and during transition periods, as well as for increasing technology awareness among all key stakeholders, including parents, educators, librarians, service providers, employers, and people with disabilities.

SELECTION

Who will select appropriate technology and provide ongoing support for students with disabilities at various levels in the educational and career preparation process? The planning and implementation of effective technology for students with disabilities requires specialized knowledge and skills regarding legislation, policies, and technology applications and products by those in decision-making and support positions.

These individuals include special education teachers, occupational therapists, community service providers, students with disabilities, families, and technology professionals. Increasing the knowledge and skills of these individuals regarding the availability and potential uses of technology is a critical step towards ensuring that students are provided with the tools and supports that will increase readiness and motivation as they transition to postsecondary education and employment.

Service providers need to have the capacity to keep pace with the rapidly changing technology that can benefit students with disabilities. With the growing complexity of computing environments and number of commercially available assistive technology devices, staff at smaller institutions faces special challenges in acquiring and maintaining current information about technology options and the most appropriate applications for students with disabilities.

FULL PARTICIPATION IN ACADEMIC AND EMPLOYMENT OFFERINGS

How can general and special education teachers, career services staff, and employers be better trained to understand the capabilities and accommodation needs of students with disabilities and use technology to help people with disabilities fully participate in academic and employment offerings? Sometimes technology is used in a very limited way to enhance the education of students with disabilities.

For example, a computer might be available to a student in a computer lab, but not used by the student for test-taking because an individual teacher is not aware that the student can use this technology or because they are not sensitive to the need for students with disabilities to complete their work independently as they prepare for postsecondary studies and careers.

Similarly, assistive technology is not always readily available to a student who might, with this technology, be able to participate in work-based learning experiences, such as a summer internship. This problem, in part, can be addressed with increased funding for assistive technology; greater awareness of the availability and potential uses of assistive technology on the part of stakeholders, including educators, career services staff, parents, and employers; and effective coordination between these individuals.

PEER AND MENTOR SUPPORT

How can students with disabilities employ technology to gain access to meaningful peer and mentoring relationships on the Internet? Potential role models who have disabilities and are experiencing success in college and careers are often separated from potential protégés by great distances and both potential mentors and protégés face more complex transportation challenges than individuals without disabilities.

Peer and mentor support can be provided via moderated discussion groups on the Internet. Supportive electronic communities can contribute to the self-sufficiency of people with disabilities. Such activities, however, incur administrative time and costs.

ANYTIME, ANYWHERE ACCESS TO TECHNOLOGY

How can educators and employers assure that appropriate technology is available when and where people with disabilities need it? Sometimes accessible technology is available to a student with a disability in a special education resource centre or other isolated location, when it is most needed in the classroom and at home. Often technology available to students at the secondary school level does not transition with them as they pursue postsecondary education and employment.

Funding and management strategies should be flexible enough to provide maximum benefit of technology access for each individual student. Coordinated education and community service systems are essential in ensuring that transfer of technology is a seamless process. This can be facilitated by the development of interagency and/or cost-sharing agreements that identify specific roles and responsibilities of agencies to address the technology needs of both students with disabilities who have IEPs and those who do not.

PROMOTION OF SELF-ADVOCACY, INDEPENDENCE, AND SELF-DETERMINATION

How can parents, educators, and service providers encourage students with disabilities to use technology to self advocate, perform daily tasks independently, and move toward self-determined lives? Successful transition is integral to a student's realization of postsecondary education, employment, and adult living objectives. Like all other aspects of the transition process, the role of technology should be addressed in a way that maximizes the involvement of the student.

Student transition plans should include self-advocacy objectives in the technology area so that students are able to articulate their technology needs to others (e.g., teachers, professors, employers) and access training and support throughout their lives. Ideally, by high school graduation, students with disabilities are experts on the types of technology that serve them best, the technical support requirements of their systems, and the resources available to them.

WORK-BASED LEARNING

How can students with disabilities gain access to hightech work-based learning experiences to prepare them for the world of work? Internships, job shadows, service learning, and other work-based learning experiences can help students with disabilities gain job skills, explore accommodation options, and learn to use technology in work settings.

Such experiences can improve their chances for a successful school-to-work transition. Individuals who coordinate work experiences for high school and college students as well as participating employers need greater awareness of the potential contributions and accommodation needs, including assistive technology, of students with disabilities.

Stakeholders should work together to assure that students have access to appropriate technology for employment settings and that students are included in the process in such a way that they gain the knowledge and self-advocacy skills they need for success in postsecondary education and careers.

LEGISLATION AND POLICY

How can the maze of confusing and conflicting laws, rulings, and policy be simplified? Policy makers and advocates should explore ways to clarify existing legislation and use consistent terminology and standards. Dissemination of current laws, policies, and resources should be tailored to the needs of various stakeholders and disseminated widely.

Differences that occur as students transition between academic levels and academic and career environments should be clearly addressed. Policy makers and advocates should also identify and correct inconsistencies and gaps in legislation and policies regarding the selection, funding, and support of assistive technology.

AWARENESS

How can we assure that key stakeholders have general knowledge of how technology can benefit individuals with disabilities?

To be assured that good decisions are made by IEP teams and other decision-makers, all stakeholder groups need to be aware of the types of technology options available to enhance the academic and career outcomes for individuals with disabilities.

These groups include general and special education teachers, occupational therapists, rehabilitation counselors, policymakers, paraprofessionals, pre-service and in-service trainers, employers, interagency and community service providers, students, families, technology professionals, postsecondary disabled student services staff, and medical equipment providers. Individuals within these groups represent key stakeholders in the process of ensuring that students are provided with appropriate technology and support services as they pursue education and careers.

If stakeholders are not aware of how technology can support students with disabilities, these students will not have assistive technology adequately considered in the IEP process; they will not have access to the full school curriculum; they will not be provided with developmentally appropriate devices and services; they will fail to use technology effectively; and they will not become prepared to self-advocate regarding their technology needs in future stages of their lives. Because of the large number of students with learning disabilities, stakeholder knowledge of how technology can promote the success of this group in educational and employment settings is especially important.

RESEARCH

How can we promote research that will improve our understanding of issues related to technology access for people with disabilities and its impact on post-school outcomes? Mainstream electronic and information technology and assistive technology are in a constant state of rapid development.

We cannot assume that what was impossible yesterday for people with disabilities is not possible today. The National Science Foundation, the Department of Defence, the U.S. Department of Education and other national and private funding agencies should be encouraged to support basic research and promising practices that employ technology to improve the postsecondary education and career outcomes for individuals with disabilities. The current conditions, legal issues, potential applications, and challenges regarding the use of technology by individuals with disabilities discussed in this chapter thus far lead to the implications for practice listed in the next section.

IMPLICATIONS FOR PRACTICE

Federal legislation, demands by people with disabilities and their advocates that they be included in all life experiences, increased acceptance of diversity, improved medical care, and advancements in electronic and information technologies have contributed to higher expectations and improved preparation of students with disabilities for postsecondary academic programs, careers, and community involvement.

As a result, young people with disabilities are better prepared to pursue higher education and ever-increasing numbers of students with disabilities are attending postsecondary academic institutions. Technology has an important role to play in promoting the success of people with disabilities in employment and careers. However, legal mandates for computer access for students and employees with disabilities are not always reflected in practice, even within organizations that have developed access policies.

Stakeholders are not fully aware of technology options, legal issues, and advocacy strategies. These stakeholders include people with disabilities, parents and mentors, government entities, paraprofessionals, policy makers and administrators, precollege and postsecondary educators, librarians, technical support staff, and employers.

These individuals must diligently work together if the following goals are to be reached:

- All individuals with disabilities have access to technology that promotes positive academic and career outcomes.
- People with disabilities learn to use technology in ways that contribute to positive postsecondary academic and career outcomes and self-determined lives.
- There is a seamless transition of availability of technology for all people with disabilities as they move from K-12 to postsecondary to career environments.

Promising practices to be considered in order to reach these goals include those that follow.

Most recommendations support multiple goals:

- Administrators and policymakers should establish policies, standards, and procedures at all academic and employment levels to assure that accessibility is considered when electronic and information technology is procured.
- Administrators and policymakers should establish policies, standards, and procedures and provide training and support at all educational levels to assure that Web pages, library resources, computing and science labs, and distance learning programs are accessible to everyone, including students with disabilities.
- Policymakers and administrators should assure that funding is available to purchase appropriate assistive technology at all levels of academic programs, in employment settings, and during transition periods between these stages.
- Agencies should collaborate on planning, funding, selecting, and supporting assistive technology to assure continuous technology access and support as students with disabilities transition through academic levels and to employment.
- Educators, librarians, parents, support staff, computer lab managers, and other stakeholders should have access to training so that they will be able to design accessible facilities and activities; select accessible computers and software; purchase appropriate assistive

technology; and assure that students with disabilities use technology for their maximum benefit as they pursue academics, careers, and self-determined lives.

- Legislators and policy makers should take steps to clarify existing legislation; disseminate information about current laws, policies, and resources tailored to the needs of various stakeholders; and use consistent terminology and standards. They should identify and correct inconsistencies and gaps in legislation and policies regarding the selection, funding, and support of assistive technology, especially as individuals transition between all academic and employment levels.
- Students with disabilities should be included at all stages of technology selection, support, and use so that they learn to self-advocate regarding their needs for accessible technology in the classroom and workplace.
- Students with disabilities should be taught to use technology in ways that 1) maximize their independence, productivity, and participation in all academic and employment activities, 2) facilitate successful transitions between all academic and employment levels, and 3) lead to successful, self determined adult lives. Technology should be used to support mentoring relationships, access to electronic information, participation in science labs, communication in class discussions, self-advocacy practice, independent living tasks, work-based learning opportunities, and other academic and career preparation activities.
- Students with disabilities at high school and college levels should participate in internships and other work-based learning experiences where they can practice using technology in work settings.

Besides taking immediate steps to assure that technology is accessible and appropriately used by individuals with disabilities, there is a need for ongoing research to inform future practice.

10

Media Involvement in Explaining Internet Dependency

Mass media in forming and reflecting public opinion, connecting the world to individuals and reproducing the self-image of society. Critiques in the early-to-mid twentieth century suggested that media weaken or delimit the individual's capacity to act autonomously — sometimes being ascribed an influence reminiscent of the telescreens of the dystopian novel *1984*. Mid 20th-century empirical studies, however, suggested more moderate effects of the media.

Current scholarship presents a more complex interaction between the media and society, with the media on generating information from a network of relations and influences and with the individual interpretations and evaluations of the information provided, as well as generating information outside of media contexts.

The consequences and ramifications of the mass media relate not merely to the way newsworthy events are perceived (and which are reported at all), but also to a multitude of cultural influences that operate through the media. The media have a strong social and cultural impact upon society. This is predicated upon their ability to reach a wide audience with a strong and influential message.

Marshall McLuhan uses the phrase "the medium is the message" as a means of explaining how the distribution of a message can often be more important than content of the message itself. It is through the persuasiveness of media such as television, radio and print media that messages reach their target audiences. These have been influential media as they have been largely responsible for structuring people's daily lives and routines. Television broadcasting has a large amount of control over the content society watches and the times in which it is viewed.

This is a distinguishing feature of traditional media which New media have challenged by altering the participation habits of the public. The internet creates a space for more diverse political opinions, social and cultural viewpoints and a heightened level of consumer participation. There have been suggestions that allowing consumers to produce information through the internet will lead to an overload of information. The extent to which an audience engages with a media text can be roughly split into three degrees. The first of these is primary involvement, in which the audience is solely concentrating on consuming the media text. For example, sitting down solely to watch a favourite programme on television.

Secondary involvement is when an audience's concentration is split between the media text and another distraction. For example, working on the computer while watching television. Tertiary involvement is when the media text is merely in the background, with no real concentration upon it at all. For example, glancing at a newspaper on a crowded train. While this theory is somewhat simplistic, it provides a clear and probable explanation as to the changes in audience reception.

Perhaps the most widely accepted theory on audience reception is Denis McQuail's Uses and Gratifications model. This places emphasis on the reasons audiences consumes media. The first reason outlined in the model is the need to reinforce ones own behaviour by identifying with roles, values and gender identities presented in the media.

Secondly, consumers need to feel some kind of interaction with other people which is offered by text such as a soap opera or a lifestyle magazine. The third reason is the need for security. Media offer a window to the world that allows education and the acquisition of information. The final reason is the need for entertainment through both escapism, and the need for emotional release, such as laughter. A strength of the Uses and Gratifications theory is the emphasis on the audience as active in the reception of media.

However, this would suggest no passivity within the audience whatsoever. A person may, for example, be too lazy to turn off their television and as a result consume any media that is available, regardless of need. This theory also pays little attention to the short term and long term effects of media on the audience.

Since its inception, the Internet has been hailed because it is convenient, informative, resourceful, and entertaining. It has been estimated that over 54 million Americans go online each day. That number is still growing. It is of theoretical and practical significance to examine dependency on the Internet. First, this line of study should further researchers' theoretical understanding of media and Internet dependency, and shed light on the relationship between people and new technologies. Second, research on Internet dependency should help integrate the study of interpersonal and mass communication, and provide insight into mediated communication. In this study, the authors examined the influence of key factors, especially motivation and involvement, on Internet dependency.

Investigating relationships among motivation, involvement, and dependency contributes to understanding of the Internet in several ways. First, although each construct has received extensive inquiry in the past, research investigations have been independent of each other so that links among these constructs are not clear.

In particular, the role of involvement in relation to motivation and dependency in the new technology environment remains sketchy. Second, to facilitate researchers' understanding of new media, an inspection of the formative process of communication outcomes is essential. Nonetheless, a lack of empirical evidence supporting such a formative process mitigates researchers' conceptualization of media outcomes such as Internet dependency. Understanding media dependency warrants consideration of the possible influence of motivation and involvement in the process. Third, as Greenwald and Leavitt argued, different media have "different potential for boosting involvement".

The unique attributes of the Internet (e.g., combining personal and mediated channels), for example, may help enhance or mitigate effects on involvement. Fourth, researchers have disagreed about how to conceptualize and operationalize constructs such as involvement and dependency in the Internet context. There is a need to clarify the systematic links among these concepts to advance the theorizing of new media research. Below, relevant literature on motivation, involvement, and dependency are first reviewed. Second, based on the literature, the authors elaborate the rationale for the relationship among these constructs and propose specific research questions and hypotheses. Third, method and results are examined and discussed.

MOTIVATION

Investigators have suggested the effectiveness of combining interpersonal and media motives to examine media use, especially the uses of newer media such as computers and the Internet. Several researchers have suggested that people use the Internet to fulfill interpersonal and media needs.

Flaherty, Pearce, and Rubin, for example, argued that people use the Internet to satisfy interpersonal needs (e.g., affection), needs traditionally gratified by the media (e.g., entertainment), and newer media needs (e.g., meeting others). These different types of needs drive a variety of motives for using the Internet.

INTERNET MOTIVES

Research has shown that traditional media motives explain a significant portion of why people use the Internet. Ferguson and Perse found people watching television for diversion also tend to use the World Wide Web for diversion. Kaye compared Web use motives and television viewing motives and found similarities among them.

Six prominent motives were identified for using the Internet: entertainment, social interaction, pass time, escape, information, and Web site preference. In a later study, Kaye and Johnson found people who obtained political information used the Internet for guidance, information seeking/ surveillance, entertainment, and social utility.

People, though, might have greater incentive for using the Internet than for using traditional media. Ebersole, for instance, found college students used the Internet for research and reading, for easy access to entertainment, for communication and social interaction, to relieve boredom, to access material otherwise unavailable, to obtain product information and technology support, to access games and sexually explicit sites, and to conduct consumer transactions. Sjoberg identified four popular reasons why Swedish teenagers use the Internet: surfing the Net, looking for information, chatting with others, and downloading programs.

MEDIA INVOLVEMENT

In media research, involvement pertains to media users' relationships with messages conveyed by media or with media, media personae, or other media users. A. M. Rubin and Perse conceptualized media involvement as "cognitive, affective, and behavioral participation during and because of exposure". The concept of media involvement places the locus of involvement within the individual rather than within messages.

Moreover, media involvement stresses the interaction between audiences and external factors such as messages or media. This emphasis corresponds with Andrews, Durvasula, and Akhter's argument that consumers, not products, are the foci of involvement with advertising.

To understand involvement, one needs to understand audiences, as involvement is vital for explaining the "role of active interactants in communication".

INVOLVEMENT AND AUDIENCE ACTIVITY

The concept of audience activity has been a focus of many audience studies. The connection between activity and involvement is evident. Lin explained that audience activity is a construct describing audiences' involvement when using the media. Activity is mostly manifested in people's media motives (i.e., utility), selectivity, and involvement with messages. Levy and Windahl identified two dimensions of audience activity: the orientation dimension included selectivity, involvement, and use; the temporal dimension covered activities before, during, and after exposure. They argued audience activity varies across different periods of media exposure.

Levy and Windhal focused on three types of activity: selectivity before exposure, involvement during exposure, and use after exposure. The first type of activity speaks to motives for using the media. The second type speaks to psychological engagement. The third type speaks to media utility and effects. Because these types of activities operate along a temporal dimension, such a relationship between motives, involvement, and uses should hold in a temporal order: media motives [right arrow] involvement [right arrow] media use and effects.

MEDIA INVOLVEMENT AS A MEDIATOR

Several researchers have investigated relationships among media motives, involvement, and effects. Perse found instrumental viewing motivation positively related to elaboration, whereas ritualistic viewing motivation positively related to engaging in distracting behaviors. In other words, cognitive involvement was linked to instrumental motives more than to ritualistic motives. Perse also found utilitarian motives for viewing local news were linked to cognitive involvement and angry feelings, and diversionary motives were related to happy feelings. In addition, A. M. Rubin and Step observed that information-seeking and entertainment motives were positive predictors of involvement with television talk-show content. And, Perse found instrumental motivation predicted cognitive and affective involvement (i.e., positive reactions) with television viewing. Ritualistic motivation predicted affective involvement (i.e., negative reactions), but not cognitive involvement.

Research has shown that cognitive involvement and affective involvement are interrelated and influence media use and outcomes. Perse suggested that people who were cognitively involved and experienced positive affect were less likely to change television channels when viewing. On the other hand, those who were less cognitively involved and experienced negative affect were more likely to change channels. Examining other links between involvement and media use, Henning and Vorderer found that people with a low need for cognition and unhappy feelings usually watched television more often than did their counterparts. They argued television viewing requires less thinking and cognition than other media, such as reading the newspaper; therefore, people who do not enjoy thinking are more likely to watch television. This suggests that cognition and affects influence media use.

In line with this thinking and research, the relationship between media motives, cognitive and affective involvement, and media use and outcomes can be illustrated as follows: media motives [right arrow] cognitive and affective involvement [right arrow] media use/effects. Here, cognitive involvement and affective involvement function as mediators between media motives and media use/effects.

MEDIA DEPENDENCY

Investigators have suggested that media dependency is a relation reflecting how individuals' goals are conditional upon the resources media afford. This conceptualization is crystallized as the individual media dependency (IMD) theory. Moreover, media dependency cannot be simplified as goals because dependency stresses a relation, whereas goals reflect an attribute. IMD theory ties in with uses and gratifications theory (UGT), but also is at variance with such research in some respects. Grant et al. commented that both perspectives address the question "what do people do with media?" They argued uses and gratifications focuses on where individuals go to satisfy their needs, and IMD focuses on why an individual accesses this medium to achieve a goal.

Ball-Rokeach contended that the formation of individual media dependency is determined by structural or macro factors, and social psychological factors of individuals. However, early work on media dependency within the sociological framework may underestimate the role of social psychological factors such as individual needs in the formation of media dependency. Examining media dependency from a uses and gratifications perspective should help illuminate these relationships.

The differing foci of the two approaches have led to distinct operationalization of certain key concepts. For example, media dependency is often treated as a single variable assessing the extent of one's reliance on a medium to achieve goals, whereas uses and gratifications often focuses on dimensions of media experience and outcomes. Further, using a measure to assess one's "global dependency" on a medium has no equivalent in uses and gratifications research. Therefore, it is reasonable to argue media dependency is conceptually and operationally distinct from traditional concepts in uses and gratifications.

Past research has shown consistent support for the conceptualization and operationalization of media dependency. Also, the conceptual domain of prior media dependency research is consistent and comparable across studies and media. For example, Loges demonstrated the conceptualization of media dependency is valid across media types including newspapers, radio, magazines, and television. Thus, it is reasonable to define Internet dependency as a relation reflecting one's reliance on the Internet to achieve goals.

Some become dependent on the Internet as a source of information, entertainment, and interpersonal connection. Researchers have traditionally conceptualized media dependency as a manifestation of one's dependence on media for play, orientation, and understanding. Play speaks to entertainment needs, understanding to information-seeking needs, and orientation to interpersonal connection needs.

LINKS AMONG MOTIVATION, INVOLVEMENT, AND DEPENDENCY

Media System Dependency (MSD) theory and UGT help explicate the relationships among motivation, involvement, and Internet dependency. Ball-Rokeach argued that MSD is a theory of media power instead of media effects. Dependence is the flip side of power, and hence a dependence relationship strengthens when a party to the relationship is motivated to seek another's resources. In other words, whether one is motivated to use a medium will influence the intensity of the user-medium dependency relationship. Seen from MSD, Internet dependency speaks to the power-dependency relations between users and the Internet. That dependency relation is also responsive to individuals' motivational investment, which is equivalent to involvement as identified in UGT.

According to MSD, the individual media dependency relation is asymmetrical. This means that people are less pivotal to the media system's needs than the media system is to an individual's needs. Such an asymmetrical relation is relatively stable at the individual media dependency level. Put differently, people's needs, which drive motivations, play a significant role in the individual media dependency relation. As A. M. Rubin and Windahl argued, individuals' needs and motives cannot be separated; both are precursors of media dependency. Further, in the Uses and Dependency Model, A. M. Rubin and Windahl noted that the media system, societal system, and audience combine to influence people's motives for using media, which correspondingly influence their use of media and functional alternatives.

In addition, media use including consumption, message processing, interpretation, and other activity (e.g., involvement), produce media effects or consequences. Researchers have suggested media dependency often occurs in conjunction with traditional media effects. For instance, the intensity of media dependency relations often makes persuasion or attitude change more salient. In other words, media dependency is a media effect that is contingent on audience involvement with media or media content.

Ball-Rokeach explained that individual media dependency relationships vary along three conceptual dimensions: intensity, goal scope, and referent scope. As for Internet dependency, the first dimension refers to how one perceives the Internet to help fulfill goals or needs; the second dimension refers to goals of understanding (social and self), orientation (interaction and action), and play (social and solitary); and the third dimension refers to the number of Internet functions a user adopts.

Logically, changes in people's motivation for using the Internet should result in variation of individual Internet dependency along the three dimensions. First, the stronger and wider one's motivation to use the Internet, the more likely one would perceive the Internet to be helpful (i.e., intensity). Second, the more diverse one's Internet motives are, the wider the scope of the goals.

Third, the more diverse one's Internet use motives, the wider the referent scope of Internet dependency. Specifically, if an individual is motivated to use the Internet for a range of reasons (e.g., entertainment, information seeking, interpersonal communication), that person is more likely to access a wider spectrum of Internet functions such as e-mail, Web browsing, and online games.

Therefore, motivation for using the Internet might predict Internet dependency along all dimensions, with involvement (i.e., motivation investment) being a precursor of Internet dependency. Furthermore, as noted earlier, involvement is a motivated activity, which serves as a mediator between motivation and media outcomes. Therefore, it is legitimate to propose the following relationship: media motives [right arrow] cognitive and affective involvement [right arrow] Internet dependency.

RESEARCH QUESTIONS AND HYPOTHESIS

The main objective was to examine Internet dependency through a uses and gratifications lens, highlighting the centrality of communication motivation and involvement. In addition, the nature of personal dependency on media is goal-related. Therefore, investigating audience uses and effects requires consideration of the links among communication motivation, involvement, and media dependency.

Although previous Internet motive studies have shown some consistent findings, identifying a comprehensive and generalizable Internet motive typology is a complicated issue. First, the samples used in previous research vary. For example, Katz and Aspden used a national random telephone sample, whereas Papacharissi and Rubin and Charney and Greenberg used college-student samples.

Second, with the rapid development of Internet technology and changes in media environments, researchers may identify additional Internet motives. For instance, Internet access is now easier and less costly, so more people are likely to use the Internet to achieve different goals. Third, researchers have used different measures of Internet motives. Because reliability and validity vary across instruments, it becomes more difficult for researchers to reproduce the same Internet motive typology.

Consequently, the aim is to employ an Internet motives typology that reflects a contemporary portrait of Internet use. Because constructing instruments for measuring Internet motives is still in an early stage, examining the typology of Internet motives should provide insight into measurement issues.

Communication motivation is central to understanding media uses and effects, but has not received sufficient attention in newer media research. Media use, which describes individuals' selecting, consuming, processing, and interpreting media and their content, is a key variable in media effects.

One of the current authors' purposes was to examine how motivation relates to typical uses of the Internet. Focusing on typical use facilitates understanding Internet use because the variety of Internet functions complicates individuals' use patterns. Moreover, establishing a connection between motivation and typical Internet use should reveal why people use the Internet differently.

As A. M. Rubin and Windahl argued, people's motives predict media use, which is constrained and shaped by societal structures and conditions. Examining individuals' typical Internet use enhances understanding of the user-Internet relationship because Internet use leads to media outcomes such as Internet dependency. Therefore, the first research question asked:

[RQ.sub.1]: Which motives best explain individuals' typical uses of the Internet?

Research suggests involvement mediates the relationship between media motives and outcomes. Eveland (2001) found cognitive involvement (e.g., attention and elaboration) mediated the relationship between motivation for using media for surveillance reasons and gaining political knowledge from the media. In terms of MSD, Ball-Rokeach explained that people's motivational investment is a precursor of media dependency. Similarly, from a UGT perspective, A. M. Rubin asserted, involvement is motivated activity. Thus, both MSD and UGT support the proposition that involvement is an antecedent of media dependency.

Moreover, as noted earlier, theoretically, media motives precede media involvement in a temporal order. Examining the role of involvement in Internet dependency adds information about activity in the newer media environment. The current authors sought to examine how involvement mediates the process leading to Internet dependency. This hypothesis was:

[H.sub.1]: Cognitive involvement and affective involvement mediate the relationship between Internet motivation and Internet dependency.

Media dependence follows from heightened needs or motivation to use the media. In line with UGT, a host of intervening variables (e.g., involvement) affect the process from motivation to media outcomes. Because involvement is a motivated activity, it is difficult to separate from media motives. To explain Internet dependency as a result of antecedent factors and mediating variables, and to assess the precise unique contribution of these factors, the second research question asked:

[RQ.sub.2]: What is the relative contribution of motivation and involvement to predicting Internet dependency?

METHOD

Design and Procedure

Research assistants enrolled in a liberal education-required communication class at a large midwestern university were trained to locate male and female participants representing four broad age classifications: 18 to 29, 30 to 39, 40 to 49, and 50 and over. Each assistant was required to contact two male and two female participants. Of these four participants, one participant needed to be within each age group. Following Human Subjects Review Board approval, research assistants attended a training session in which the principal researcher or colleagues discussed research ethics and provided precise instructions for distributing and collecting questionnaires. Research assistants received four blank questionnaires and four envelopes, and were asked to return those finished questionnaires sealed in envelopes with participants' initials across the seal.

SAMPLE

Overall, 471 questionnaires were subjected to data analysis. The sample was 46.9 per cent male (n = 221) and 53.1 per cent female (n = 250); 2.5 per cent of the participants had not completed high school (n = 12); 21.9 per cent were high school graduates (n = 103); 35.2 per cent completed some college (n = 166); 26.8 per cent were college graduates (n = 126); and 13.6 per cent attended or completed graduate school (n = 64). There were 129 participants between 18 and 29 years old (27.4 per cent), 116 between 30 and 39 years (24.6 per cent), 112 between 40 and 49 years (23.8 per cent), and 114 between 50 and 74 years (24.2 per cent); M age = 38.93, SD = 13.38. There were 398 Caucasians (84.5 per cent), 44 African Americans (9.3 per cent), 3 Asian Americans (0.6 per cent), 3 Hispanics/Latinos (0.6 per cent), 2 Native Americans (0.4 per cent), and 21 others (4.5 per cent).

MEASUREMENT

Typical Internet Use

Participants were asked to bear in mind their typical use of the Internet when completing the questionnaire. Descriptive statistics showed 44.2 per cent of the participants typically used e-mail (n = 208), 36.1 per cent typically used general Web browsing (n = 170), 6.8 per cent typically downloaded music or games (n = 32), 6.8 per cent typically used other Internet functions (n = 32), 3.0 per cent typically used newsgroups/bulletin boards/listservs (n = 14), 2.3 per cent typically shopped online (n = 11), and 0.8 per cent typically used chatrooms (n = 4).

So, 80.3 per cent of the participants identified e-mail or Web browsing as their typical use of the Internet. Fewer than 20 per cent of the participants identified the other Internet functions as their typical use. Given the variety and complexity of Internet functions, the focus was on the most salient typical Internet uses rather than all uses. The nature of this study warranted examining the prominent characteristics of participants' typical Internet use. Because the most salient typical use patterns were e-mail and Web browsing, when examining the relationship between factors such as motivation and typical Internet use, the focus was on e-mail and general Web browsing.

Internet Motives

The CMC Motives Scale constructed by Papacharissi and Rubin was used to measure people's Internet use motives. They culled a majority of items from the Interpersonal Communication Motives Scale, and the Television Viewing Motives Scale. The CMC Motives Scale assessed motivation on a 5-point Likert scale ranging from 1 (not at all) to 5 (exactly) "likes my reason for using the Internet." There were several reasons to conduct principal components analysis with the Internet motive typology. First, this study was exploratory in nature. Researchers have not reached consensus about how to measure involvement and Internet motives.

At this stage, it was difficult to say which measure was better, and hence, it was safer to use exploratory instead of confirmatory techniques. Second, prior research on the latent structure of motives is relatively clear. So, the focus of this study was not to uncover the latent motive structure, but rather to reduce the measured variables to a smaller number of composite components.

As Grant et al. argued, the focus of uses and gratifications research is to create a small set of variates from a large set of variables. To that end, principal components analysis was more appropriate than exploratory factor analysis. Moreover, the objective of the study was not to examine the interrelationships among different motives. Motivation was treated as an independent variable for explaining other variables. The principal components analysis technique helps retain as much information as possible in the original variables. Third, due to a lack of the differentiation between motivation, involvement, and affect in past research, it is necessary to achieve a simple structure of the constructs. For that purpose, varimax rotation was a better choice compared to other alternatives.

The analysis yielded five factors accounting for 55.6 per cent of the total variance. Responses to items loading on each factor were averaged to form the motive indexes. Factor 1, Substitution, accounted for 31.9 per cent of the total variance after rotation. The factor included all three pass-time items, all three relaxation items, one habit item, one escape item, and one inclusion/companionship item. The factor reflected a leisure motivation or amotivation, meaning users lacked a very clear intent or purpose. This 9-item factor reflected Internet use as a displacement activity because there was no better alternative. Factor 2, Information, accounted for 9.6 per cent of the total variance. It consisted of all three information items, one convenience item, one economy item, and one surveillance item. This 6-item factor reflected using the Internet for information searching. It was the most salient factor.

Factor 3, Social Interaction, explained 6.4 per cent of the total variance. It included two social interaction items, two surveillance items, one inclusion/companionship item, and two expressive need items. This 7-item factor depicted using the Internet to interact with others and to get others' views. Factor 4, Convenience, accounted for 4.4 per cent of the total variance. It consisted of one social interaction item, one time control item, and one economy item.

This 3-item factor reflected using the Internet because it was a convenient communication medium. Factor 5, Control, explained 3.4 per cent of the total variance. It included two control items and one affection item. This 3-item factor depicted using the Internet to get others to do something. It was the least salient factor.

COGNITIVE INTERNET INVOLVEMENT

The 5-item Elaboration Scale was used to measure cognitive involvement. Response options ranged from 1 (strongly disagree) to 5 (strongly agree). Items in this scale (e.g., "while I am using the Internet, I think about how the online information relates to other things I know") are more applicable to the Internet environment than the other two subscales (i.e., attention, recognition) sometimes used in prior studies. Moreover, elaboration implies attention, and is an appropriate assessment of cognitive involvement.

Eveland and Dunwoody adapted the elaboration scale to assess elaboration of online information. Eveland, Seo, and Marton adapted the elaboration scale to measure people's learning from television news, newspapers, and online news. In the present study, the mean of the five items was used as an index of cognitive involvement.

AFFECTIVE INTERNET INVOLVEMENT

The adapted MACL contains 20 adjectives describing various moods. There are 10 adjectives to measure positive affect (i.e., amused, at ease, calm, cheerful, content, delighted, happy, pleased, relaxed, satisfied) and 10 adjectives to measure negative affect (i.e., angry, ashamed, bored, depressed, embarrassed, fearful, gloomy, miserable, sad, worried). Response options ranged from 1 (strongly disagree) to 5 (strongly agree) with each mood descriptor.

As mentioned before, due to the exploratory nature of the current study, in particular, the disagreement of measuring involvement in an online context, the present researchers used principal components analysis with varimax rotation on the 20 affective involvement items. By using a 60/40 factor loading rule with a minimum eigen value of 1.00 per factor, two interpretable factors were retained. These two factors explained 57.8 per cent of the total variance.

- Factor 1, Positive Affect, explained 30.7 per cent of the total variance after rotation. It included all 10 positive affect items. This 10-item factor reflected Internet users' positive affective involvement
- Factor 2, Negative Affect, explained 27.0 per cent of the total variance after rotation. It included eight of the original negative affect items. The two omitted items were "I feel angry" and "I feel bored." The 8-item factor reflected Internet users' negative affective involvement.

INTERNET DEPENDENCY

To date, researchers have not precisely clarified how to measure Internet dependency. A review of prior research suggests disagreement in constructing such a measure. One reason is that researchers differ in their understanding of Internet dependency. For example, researchers often interchange terms such as Internet dependence, heavy use, and addiction without referring to their conceptual differences.

In addition, research has seldom examined whether it is possible to apply relevant measures of assessing traditional media dependency to the newer media context. Such an attempt, however, is a practical way for constructing an Internet dependency measure, and provides insight into measuring audiences in different media contexts. More importantly, as noted before, the conceptual domain and operationalization of media dependency have been consistent and comparable across different media. Therefore, the most recent version of the Television Dependency Scale developed by Grant was adapted to measure Internet dependency. Grant found the 18 items to be reliable for assessing dependency on different types of media. The revised Internet Dependency Scale includes six dimensions: action orientation, interaction orientation, self-understanding, social understanding, solitary play, and social play.

Sample items include: "In your daily life, how helpful is the Internet to..." (a) "get ideas about how to approach others in important or difficult situations?" (b) "have something to do when nobody is around?" (c) "stay on top of what is happening in the community?" (d) "keep up with world events?" (e) "figure out what to buy?" (f) "decide where to go for services such as health, financial, or household?" and (g) "plan where to go for evening and weekend activities?" Through its wording, the instrument enhanced the "correspondence between the media dependency relational concept and its measurement".

Response options ranged from 1 (not at all helpful) to 5 (extremely helpful). Grant explained that the six dimensions of this scale are highly correlated, and Grant et al. found it was valid and reliable to use all six dimensions to measure media dependency. Thus, combining the six dimensions produced a global measure of media dependency. The mean response to the 18 items was the index of Internet dependency.

DATA ANALYSIS

Data analysis proceeded in several steps. First, the current authors computed descriptive statistics and conducted reliability analyses of all scales. Second, because linear regression was used, data were examined to see whether linear-regression assumptions were violated. Normality, linearity, and homoscedasticity were examined by plotting the residual scores against the predicted scores. Examining these assumptions insured that linear regression, instead of nonlinear techniques, was suitable for the data. The scatter plot indicated these assumptions were not violated with dependency as the dependent variable.

HYPOTHESIS

The current authors posited that cognitive and affective involvement would mediate the relationship between Internet motives and dependency. There were zero-order product-moment correlations of.63 between substitution motivation and Internet dependency,.52 between information motivation and Internet dependency,.62 between social interaction motivation and Internet dependency,.37 between convenience motivation and Internet dependency, and.48 between control motivation and Internet dependency.

After controlling for cognitive involvement and affective involvement, the third-order partial correlations were.41 between substitution motivation and Internet dependency,.42 between information motivation and Internet dependency,.41 between social interaction motivation and Internet dependency,.26 between convenience motivation and Internet dependency, and.28 between control motivation and Internet dependency.

Therefore, controlling for involvement (a) reduced the correlation between substitution motivation and dependency by a magnitude of.22, (b) reduced the correlation between information motivation and dependency by.10, (c) reduced the correlation between social interaction motivation and dependency by.21, (d) reduced the correlation between convenience motivation and dependency by.11, and (e) reduced the correlation between control motivation and dependency by a magnitude of.20.

Taken as a whole, then, cognitive involvement and affective involvement mediated the relationship between Internet motives and Internet dependency. The path analysis provides additional information about this mediation effect. Substitution motivation directly affected cognitive involvement, positive affect, and negative affect.

Cognitive involvement, positive affect, and negative affect directly influenced Internet dependency. Taken as a whole, involvement mediated the relationship between substitution motivation and Internet dependency. But, motivation, except the convenience motive, also had a direct effect on Internet dependency. This suggests that involvement partially mediated the relationship between motivation and Internet dependency, generally supporting the hypothesis.

DISCUSSION

Consistent with prior research, over 80 per cent of the participants typically used the Internet for e-mail or general Web browsing. The results support Eveland and Dunwoody's proposition that the Web as "a system of information delivery can be used to influence information processing". Papacharissi and Rubin observed that information-seeking motivation positively predicted Web browsing but negatively predicted e-mail use.

Their finding is consistent with the results of the current study. It is legitimate to argue that the Web serves as a better information tool than does e-mail. Similar to Teo's finding, women were more likely to use e-mail than were men. Men were more likely than women to use the Internet for Web browsing. As a communication tool, e-mail affords opportunities to express oneself and interact with others.

Teo explained that men are more likely to be interested in using the Internet for learning, whereas women are more interested in communicating with others on the Internet. Teo also suggested that women tended to perceive computer-mediated communication more favorably than did men. The results also provide insight into the "gratification opportunities" a medium can provide, that is, a medium's beneficial attributes.

Researchers have shown that the gratification opportunities e-mail affords (e.g., fast speed, convenience, less expensive) are important reasons for people's preference for using e-mail. In addition, Westmyer, DiCioccio, and Rubin found that being motivated to control others influenced one's evaluation of the effectiveness and appropriateness of communication channel choice.

They observed that people rated oral channels such as the telephone more effective and appropriate to fulfill their control needs than written channels such as e-mail. Although e-mail was not compared with other communication channels in this study, it makes sense that people use e-mail to seek to control others. One can control whether or not to reply and when to reply to others' e-mail. Also, e-mail use might be related to saving face. If one does not want to confront another person directly for the sake of saving face, e-mail may offer more control compared to other channels such as the telephone.

The second research question asked about the relative contribution of antecedent factors to predicting Internet dependency. Demographics accounted for a small proportion of the variance. Younger people were more likely to exhibit Internet dependency than older participants. Again, this might link to the "built-in bias" of the Internet. Some people are more "technologically savvy" than others. Younger people are more likely than older people to be at the frontline of technological developments.

Motivation and involvement were more important predictors of Internet dependency than were demographics. This is consistent with uses and gratifications' emphasis on the role motivation and involvement play in the media effects process. As A. M. Rubin stated, media dependency develops from people's communication motives, attitudes, media use patterns, and available functional alternatives.

Among the various Internet use motives, substitution, information seeking, and social interaction were most salient in explaining and predicting Internet dependency. Substitution motivation reflected a ritualized orientation to fill time, relax, and escape, whereas information seeking and social interaction motivation reflected a more instrumental, goal-directed orientation focusing on informational content of the Internet.

HYPOTHESIS

The results of this study are consistent with the literature. Both cognitive and affective involvement mediates the relationship between one's motives to communicate and media outcomes. Involvement and affect play an important role in media outcomes, including dependence on the Internet. The findings support the proposition that a range of intervening orientations may influence the relationship between audience motivation and media outcomes. The present findings also are consistent with the uses and gratifications argument that audience activity "plays an important intervening role in the effects process". An interesting finding is that motives to interact socially and to control others' behaviour were strong predictors of cognitive involvement, and the motive to fill time, relax, and escape was a strong predictor of positive affect, that is, feeling cheerful, pleased, delighted, calm, relaxed, and at ease. As noted earlier, social interaction and control motivations reflect an instrumental orientation, and substitution motivation reflects a ritualized orientation for using the Internet.

The finding makes sense within the uses and gratifications framework. An instrumental orientation speaks to an active use of media and suggests involvement with media content, whereas a ritualized orientation speaks to a less active use of media and suggests affinity with the medium. The current findings suggest that an instrumental Internet orientation aligns closely with greater cognitive involvement and a ritualized orientation aligns more with affective involvement.

LIMITATIONS

There are several limitations that might influence the generalizability of these findings. First, the cross-sectional data employed in this study do not warrant a claim of any causal relationships among motivation, involvement, and Internet dependency. Indeed, panel data might be a better choice for examining such relationships. A cursory review of extant uses and gratifications literature also attests to a lack of panel data.

Moreover, the quota sample, which excluded people under the age of 18, might restrict the generalizability of findings; more people under age 20 have come online. Research assistants were asked to select an equal number of male and female participants. This was not wholly achieved, nor was the precise quota for age. The Internet population, though, might not be so gender and age balanced.

Second, operationalizing some constructs might limit the scope of the study. For example, although the Internet motives scale and media dependency scale often appear in prior research, some items of these two instruments appear to be similar.

To some extent, such a seeming repetition results from the nature of dependency relationships which implicate motivation. As mentioned before, though, dependency cannot be reduced to motivation or goals because the former is a relation and the latter is an attribute. Accounting for a temporal dimension in a longitudinal design might help future researchers empirically distinguish constructs such as motivation, involvement, and dependency.

Third, the operationalization of typical Internet use provided a viable empirical portrait to examine the research questions and hypothesis, but might not precisely reflect the complexity of an individual's use patterns. It is likely that each individual uses several Internet functions each day. Researchers would benefit from developing a mechanism for capturing the complexity of the Internet and user patterns. Fourth, there are no single, agreed-upon instruments to measure cognitive involvement, affective involvement, and dependency in the context of Internet use.

Although the adapted scales were reliable, their construct validity deserves further examination in Internet settings. Perse, for example, measured cognitive involvement along three dimensions: attention, recognition, and elaboration. In this study, the current authors used the elaboration subscale to measure cognitive involvement, and the MACL to measure affective involvement. It is possible that Internet users have other emotional reactions during Internet use beyond the 20 moods identified in the MACL. Renewed efforts to conceptualize and measure affective involvement are warranted.

FUTURE DIRECTIONS

The Internet affords a variety of functions. To obtain an in-depth understanding of the Internet, researchers may take a close look at dependency on a specific Internet function such as e-mail or instant messaging, or on a combination of Internet functions. Although in this study participants' typical uses of the Internet were e-mail and Web browsing, it could be illuminating to analyse the profile of those who usually use other Internet functions such as chatrooms and bulletin boards.

Comparing those whose typical use of the Internet is different from each other could provide further data about the relationship between individual differences and Internet dependency. As Oliver stated, researchers should pay more attention to individual differences in media effects research; neglecting this might lead to an underestimate or biased assessment of media effects.

This study suggests various forms of involvement are important mediating factors in Internet uses and dependency. Although the relationship between cognitive involvement and affective involvement was not the focus, it is possible that Internet users could shift from cognitive involvement to affective involvement, or vice versa. Moreover, involvement is variable rather than constant.

To understand involvement better, researchers need to investigate changes in involvement during Internet use, and over time. For example, when will users initially become involved with the content and mechanism of the

Internet? When and why will they stop being involved? Investigating such processes will further illuminate the mediating role of involvement, and help clarify how motivation and involvement affect Internet dependency.

We are grateful for Professor C. Edwin Baker's lively response to our article and for the opportunity to clarify the important issues he raises, chiefly about the relationship between theory and evidence in media regulation specifically and law generally. We appreciate in particular his praise of our article's "innovative statistical techniques," given that our primary aim was to provide a new approach to empirically measure substantive viewpoint diversity.

Our empirical measures and methods help to address long-standing questions about whether media consolidation leads to convergence in viewpoints (the "convergence hypothesis"). We are glad that Baker agrees that the article makes progress in the empirical understanding of the media and that it is "far superior methodologically to most empirical studies that [he] ha[s] seen." At the same time, Baker "denies the policy relevance" of our article. At heart, Baker asserts that empirical evidence about viewpoint diversity is "entirely irrelevant" to media regulation. In the place of empirical inquiry, we should conduct "value-based inquir[ies]" (for example, in the form of the theory he espouses) and, he argues, "anecdotal tales of seriously objectionable past abuses by media moguls could be much more informative" than statistical inquiry.

As a result, Baker argues that the FCC should aim to maximize the number of media owners ("source diversity"), as opposed to "viewpoint diversity." We write here to defend the role of empirical research in law, as well as the conclusions of our article. As we explain below, Baker's view suffers from deep ambiguity and internal inconsistency, ignores the empirical turn in communications law, and adopts the extreme position that normative theory should displace what he calls "law schools' recent romance with statistical empiricism [and] welfare economics," which Baker views as "malignant" to the "hermeneutic discipline" of law.

Most disconcerting is Baker's call for anecdotal tales and normative theory to take the place of—and preclude any role for—empirical scholarship (as well as positive and economic theory) in law. Our original article was entirely in that pluralistic spirit, invoking legal analysis and social science, qualitative and quantitative evidence, and drawing positive and normative inferences. Empirical inquiry has the potential to resolve parts of public policy problems that would be irresolvable on normative grounds alone. Its promise is not endless—a point we expressly highlight in our article—but it surely is not "entirely irrelevant."

CLARIFYING THE MUDDLE

OUR CONTRIBUTION

Our Stanford Law Review article makes four contributions to the broad question of federal regulation of media ownership. First, we document a trend that the FCC and numerous commentators have noted, namely the sharp empirical turn that the law on structural media ownership regulations has taken over the past twenty years.

The Telecommunications Act of 1996 requires that the FCC periodically "determine whether any of such [ownership] rules are necessary in the public interest as the result of competition." Under arbitrary and capricious review (review as a matter of administrative—not constitutional—law), the courts have increasingly required the FCC to provide evidence of the convergence hypothesis, and the FCC responded in 2002 by commissioning an unprecedented number of empirical studies on the connection between ownership and viewpoint diversity.

Second, our article surveys existing work and highlights serious limitations to extant measures of viewpoint diversity. For example, editorial endorsements of Democratic presidential candidates result in little variation between media outlets in a two-party system. Alternatively, conventional reading and coding of "bias" of news articles (content analysis) can be fraught with lack of transparency and replicability, as is widely acknowledged (indeed by Baker himself). Third, given limitations of existing empirical approaches, our major contribution is to provide a new, transparent, and replicable measure of editorial viewpoint diversity by capitalizing on rapid advances in statistical measurement methodology.

Much like the concept of "intelligence," the idea of a "viewpoint" is complex and cannot be readily observed in a direct fashion. Nonetheless, intelligence and viewpoints do have observable implications. In educational testing, the measurement of intelligence is commonly dealt with through standardized testing—most importantly, the administration of common questions to place students on a common scale. Our approach capitalizes on that insight to look for instances where newspapers opine on common issues, namely Supreme Court decisions.

For over a year, with the help of a research team of fourteen Harvard and Stanford undergraduate and law students, we engaged in exhaustive data collection to collect every editorial written on Supreme Court decisions across twenty-five newspapers from 1988-2004, personally reading over 1,600 editorial positions in the process. Adapting finely-tuned statistical methods (to account for differences across Justices, outlets, questions, and time) allows us to scale the newspapers on a substantively meaningful dimension of the Supreme Court Justices and to examine the evolution of editorial viewpoints during mergers and acquisitions.

Our results show stability in viewpoints for three conglomerate acquisitions, convergence for the case of the merger of the Atlanta Journal and the Atlanta Constitution to form the Atlanta Journal-Constitution, and divergence for the New York Times's acquisition of the Boston Globe. In short, consolidation does not inexorably lead to convergence or divergence. This purposely adopts a broad view of empirical inquiry as encompassing both quantitative and qualitative research. Indeed, we devote an entire section of the article to an in-depth view of these two cases, drawing on a range of qualitative (e.g., detailed reading of editorials and phone calls with editors from every newspaper in our dataset) and quantitative (e.g., subscriber databases and census data) sources to complement our measures of viewpoint diversity and draw out complexities of these cases.

Fourth, we provide brief, but specific, policy implications based on the difficulty of empirical inquiry. Appellate interpretation of the 1996 Act holds that, unless the FCC finds that an ownership regulation continues to serve the public interest (typically involving evidence of convergence), the FCC shall repeal or modify it.

Our results point to a deep tension in this statutory reading between empirical justification and deregulation—the call for empirical verification subject to a high evidentiary standard may be tantamount to wholesale deregulation. Instead, incremental modification of ownership regulations may better facilitate empirical evaluation while heeding appellate interpretation.

We propose that the FCC collaborate with researchers to incorporate policy evaluation into regulation. Lastly, our case studies also highlight the crucial roles of editorial policies, editorial board organizational structure, and critical distinctions between mergers and acquisitions.

BAKER'S POSITION

Baker's response comes in two sections. In the first, he restates in a substantially similar form to previous writings his normative theory of media consolidation: "The three major reasons to oppose media concentration in general, and mergers in particular, can be labeled: (i) the democratic distribution value; (ii) the democratic safeguard value; and (iii) the media quality value...."

The democratic distribution value posits that everyone should have an "equal voice" in the same fashion of the one person, one vote requirement familiar from election law. Under Baker's view this "lead[s] inexorably to the recommendation of a maximum dispersal of media power... represented ultimately by ownership" so that "everyone [is] able to experience some media as her own." "Increasing ownership dispersal always works in the direction of equalizing the distribution of media power among groups."

The democratic safeguard value posits that ownership dispersal guards against the "danger of demagogic power." Baker relies on a number of illustrations, largely from his other writings, of the problems of media concentration: the support of a media conglomerate for Adolf Hitler; mentioning by news programs of an affiliate quiz show (Who Wants to Be A Millionaire?); pharmaceutical threats against the New York Times for exposes in affiliated magazines; Knight-Ridder's muting of Miami Herald editorial criticism of Edwin Meese due to pending approval of a joint operating agreement; Atlantic Richfield influencing editorial policy at the British Observer; and Richard Nixon's White House conversation about possible retaliation against the Washington Post via its broadcast licenses.

Despite these illustrations, he concludes that "empirical measurement of the effect of interest conflicts is predictably uninformative" as it would be difficult to observe such conflicts: Any informed sense of the degree of danger will likely reflect a structural examination of the possibilities of and incentive for this "corruption" combined with qualitative or ethnographic investigations and, possibly, quantitative surveys of editors' and journalists' self-reports, though with recognition that ingrained, unconscious practices will often be the repositories of the corrupting incentives.

The media quality value stems from Baker's belief that "most conglomerates focus almost exclusively on the bottom line," which, he argues, uniformly undermines quality journalism. Since positive externalities of democratic deliberation and accountability flow from healthy media, Baker favors the following policy to promote quality journalism:

The owners who are most likely to favour journalism over profits include several predictable types:

- Smaller, usually local, owners who take identity from their firms' contributions to their community or from the journalistic product they create;
- Workers who take professional pride in the quality of their product;
- Non-profit entities whose goals include service to their community. Each category justifies policy moves to increase its ranks.

Because these three values (democratic distribution, democratic safeguard, and media quality) are, evidently, sufficient reasons "to oppose media concentration," Baker concludes that our empirical assessment of whether media consolidation reduces viewpoint diversity is entirely irrelevant. The second section of Baker's response more directly addresses our article.

First, Baker points to limitations in our study, namely that:

- News reporting "may be more significant for democratic discourse than editorial positions";
- Our study focuses only on the top twenty-five newspapers;
- Our study only contains "a sample of five mergers"; and
- "The relevant diversity should be qualitative, not simply quantitative."

He hypothesizes that in theory some local newspapers may see convergence in news, but divergence in editorial positions, upon merging.

Second, Baker argues that "[t]he democratic quality of discourse is not measured by the amount of diversity actually occurring" but by three other factors:

- That views are not suppressed,
- That views are not subject to suppression, and
- "That there are meaningful efforts to develop relevant information and perspective."

Lastly, Baker argues that the "problem" with our article "lies in its potentially misdirecting policy discussion by purporting to give an empirical but actually irrelevant basis for deregulation." He ruminates at great length as to whether our "error of not considering the real reasons to oppose concentration... is explicable." He hypothesizes:

- That we were "misled" by "the confusion of other scholars and of the FCC itself,"
- That we are "anti-regulatory advocates strategic[ally],... pick[ing] up on the term 'diversity'" and "then interpret[ing it] in commodified terms" in order to move the discussion to "a battleground on which [we] have the greatest chance to win," and/or
- That our error reflects "economists' occupational inclination to see value in what can be purchased in markets... and a corresponding bias in [our] resulting political recommendations."

Most broadly, he argues that "[l]aw aspires to legitimacy, which in turn ultimately is a matter of values and reasons, not a matter of deductive logic or fact or mere instrumental rationality" and that our major methodological error may stem from, amongst other reasons, "a false image of science, an ingrained fearful desire of originally untenured academics to steer clear of controversy," or "an immature craving to escape uncertainty and indeterminacy." His conclusion is sweeping:

The Court's recent call for empirical evidence while avoiding explanations of how or why it is relevant... and many law schools' recent romance with statistical empiricism, following up on the Court's earlier affair with welfare economics, reflects these impulses [to avoid value judgments].

These hopes of interpretive value avoidance and tendencies toward instrumentalist reductionism are malignant. Economics and empiricism are the easy parts of legal scholarship, appropriate only as handmaidens to its real vocation.

Legal scholarship and inquiry, like all hermeneutic disciplines, though clearly in need of knowledge of the world, have traditionally been at their best when they understood themselves as value-based inquiries. Given these provocative arguments, which indict the entirety of welfare economics and empirical legal studies in a few brushstrokes, we are compelled to respond. Notwithstanding the colorful rhetoric—relegating economics and empiricism as "only handmaidens" to legal scholarly inquiry—we share at least three key agreements with Baker.

First, what Baker terms the "democratic safeguard value" is an important and relevant underlying consideration in media regulation. As we squarely acknowledged in our article, the media plays an important role in the functioning of a healthy democracy. Yet one primary way the FCC has incorporated this concern is precisely via viewpoint diversity: diverse viewpoints foster democratic deliberation and, at least in theory, ultimately, accountability.

We agree that policymakers should carefully evaluate the risk to democracy posed by potential changes of federal communications law. Nonetheless, our more modest aim was to respond to the recent empirical demands of media law and scholarship. Further, as we elaborate below, most such careful risk evaluations will likely contain an important empirical component.

Second, many aspects of media output beyond editorial positions of the top twenty-five newspapers are relevant. None of these are new concerns that Baker raises.

Our article was entirely clear about these limitations and sought to improve on existing empirical work. We explained: "because we only examine major newspapers, our measures may ignore the types of newspapers whose viewpoints are most threatened by media consolidation" and "our focus on editorial positions ignores news reporting."

Of course, convergence in the top newspapers is still of interest—indeed, three of Baker's illustrations of democratic safeguards revolve around top newspapers (each in our dataset): the New York Times, the Washington Post, the Detroit Free Press, and the Miami Herald.

As to news, methods similar to ours may be adapted to study news reporting, and we show below—and in other work—that editorial viewpoints are strongly correlated with news slant.

Our focus on editorial viewpoint diversity is a direct response to the fact that both scholars and the Commission have pointed out editorials as relevant.

Third, we agree with a weak version of Baker's concern, namely that we must recognize the limitations of empirical inference. Our article went on at great length to highlight the difficulties of direct policy evaluation of the ownership rules. Given that there is little variation in ownership regulations, it is extremely difficult to directly assess the causal effect of these regulations.

Yet the fact that empirical inquiry is limited does not mean that it is worthless. To the contrary, across disciplinary fields, empirical inquiry has advanced scholarship and produced tremendous knowledge, which surely explains in part the enthusiasm—not shared by Baker—about empirical legal studies. While we agree on these three major points, Baker's response goes astray in numerous directions.

A VULNERABLE THEORY

The first part of Baker's response, which rehashes in substantially identical form (and with the same examples) the theory already spelled out in his book and another article, is entirely outside the scope of our work. He views his unique normative theory as the sufficient reason to oppose media consolidation. Since the theory, at least according to Baker, has no observable implications, and cannot be proven wrong with data, we do not dwell on it here.

We merely note that it is difficult to have a complete theoretical answer in an empirical vacuum. One could easily question the theoretical grounds: does the theory provide any way to draw the tradeoff between benefits and costs of ownership regulations when his theory provides only reasons to oppose media consolidation?

Does the theory provide any sense of when ownership regulations may be too great when federal law could mandate, for example, that every single individual should own a broadcast station? How does the democratic distribution analogy to one person, one vote operate when social choice theory highlights the difficulties of preference aggregation, which could similarly plague aggregation of voices by media outlets?

Moreover, why doesn't the analogy to election law undercut the notion that empirical evidence is "irrelevant" when election law commonly deals with evidence of vote dilution, fraud, and the effects of electoral rules?

How are the value of democratic distribution and the policy implication of maximum dispersal of media power not a matter of tautology when valuing equal voices "inexorably" leads to more owners of media? It is one matter to state values and another to see how to achieve them—how does Baker's view avoid conflating ends and means?

Although the theory may not be vulnerable to empirical verification, it is vulnerable to each of these deep theoretical ambiguities. We leave it for others to resolve the persuasiveness of these claims. This sought to examine what empirical evidence exists for the convergence hypothesis with a reliable and valid measure of editorial viewpoints, responding directly to the empirical turn in the law and scholarship. We thereby address why systematic empirical inquiry into viewpoint diversity matters and respond to Baker's specific assertions about our article.

THE FCC AND THE COURTS

One of the fundamental misconceptions, Baker argues, is our focus on substantive viewpoint diversity. Instead, he argues, "[m]any FCC policies are most explicable if based on a concern for source diversity without the requirement of any degree of actual content or viewpoint diversity." By source diversity, Baker means the number of owners. In focusing on viewpoint diversity, he argues, we "overread" sources and are "misled" by "the confusion of other scholars and of the FCC itself."

As support for the idea that source diversity is not a means to viewpoint diversity, he cites to a 1970 FCC Multiple Ownership Order (despite the "confusion of... the FCC") and the Supreme Court's 1978 decision in FCC v. National Citizens Committee for Broadcasting (NCCB). This view suffers from two fatal flaws. First, neither the 1970 Multiple Ownership Order nor the NCCB case support the idea that source diversity is to be valued independently—or to the exclusion—of viewpoint diversity. From the 1970 Multiple Ownership Order, Baker selectively quotes the FCC (and omits the last portion of the sentence, relevant since it highlights what was at least perceived as a natural limit in broadcast spectrum): "A proper objective is the maximum diversity of ownership that technology permits in each area." Although that language might suggest source diversity, the same order goes on to say the following:

Although the principal purpose of the proposed rules is to promote diversity of viewpoints in the same area, and it is on this ground that our above discussion is primarily based, we think it clear that promoting diversity of ownership also promotes competition....... Simply stated, the fundamental purpose of this facet of the multiple ownership rules is to promote diversification of ownership in order to maximize diversification of programme and service viewpoints as well as to prevent any undue concentration of economic power contrary to the public interest.

From the NCCB case, Baker admits that the Supreme Court highlighted viewpoint diversity, but argues that the Court also recognized source diversity when it noted the interest in "preventing undue concentration of economic power."

This language itself is vague and does not necessarily implicate source diversity, but more telling is Justice Marshall's discussion for the majority, which at each juncture connects ownership with viewpoint diversity:

[The FCC's] policy judgment was certainly not irrational and indeed was founded on the very same assumption that underpinned the diversification policy itself and the prospective rules upheld by the Court of Appeals and now by this Court—that the greater number of owners in a market, the greater the possibility of achieving diversity of programme and service viewpoints.

Second, even disregarding the 1970 Multiple Ownership Order and NCCB, what is most telling is that Baker fails to discuss any authority within the last twenty years for the primacy of source diversity. Indeed, that would be difficult, as the courts and FCC could not be clearer. In its 2002 Biennial Order, the FCC states:

The Commission has sought, therefore, to diffuse ownership of media outlets among multiple firms in order to diversify the viewpoints available to the public....... We therefore continue to believe that broadcast ownership limits are necessary to preserve and promote viewpoint diversity.

"Source diversity" refers to the availability of media content from a variety of content producers. The Notice explained that source diversity can contribute to our 'retail" goals of viewpoint diversity and programme diversity.... The record before us does not support a conclusion that source diversity should be an objective of our broadcast ownership policies.

The Commission adopted the newspaper/broadcast cross-ownership rule because it believed that diversification of ownership would promote diversification of viewpoint.

In short, the FCC explicitly rejected Baker's position that source diversity is an independent objective. As we stated in our article, the conventional justification for the ownership regulations is as "a means to the ultimate end of furthering substantive viewpoint diversity." Similarly, the D.C. Circuit noted in a series of cases:

The only support the Commission offered for regulation based on this possibility was the idea that every additional chance for a programmer to secure access would enhance diversity.

The stated purpose of the seven-station rule was 'to promote diversification of ownership in order to maximize diversification of programme and service viewpoints' and 'to prevent any undue concentration of economic power.'

The only recent evidence Baker alludes to is from comments filed by the public in the 2002 Biennial Review, which he conjectures may have been animated by concerns about source diversity.

Of course, what was in the mind of each of some 500,000 plus parties filing comments is a matter of pure speculation. Suffice it to say that Commissioner Adelstein, who dissented from the 2002 Biennial Order and highlighted the comments, notes the importance of viewpoint diversity when stating that "[t]he public has a right to be informed by a diversity of viewpoints so they can make up their own minds." Baker's sharp separation of source and viewpoint diversity is an artifact of his own normative theory and has no basis in current law.

THE EMPIRICAL TURN OF THE LAW

Beyond asserting the irrelevance of viewpoint diversity, Baker argues that our statement that "[c]ourts and in turn the Commission have increasingly mandated some form of empirical evidence" is a claim with "unfortunate lack of citation" that may "represent a willingness merely to assume a nonexistent legal mandate that... would require [our] expertise." Indeed, he concludes, "I can find no specific support for their claim that 'measuring viewpoint diversity is... mandated by law.'"

Such a charge is severe. But it plainly misreads the thrust of our article, which had an entire section devoted to the empirical turn in the law of media, documented by dozens of references with copious discussion of the case law. We showed that starting with cases such as Schurz Communications, Inc. v. FCC, Time Warner Entertainment Co. v. FCC, Fox TV Stations, Inc. v. FCC, Sinclair Broadcast Group, Inc. v. FCC, and culminating in the 2002 Biennial

Order, courts and the FCC have increasingly required evidence to sustain the convergence hypothesis, instead of deferring as the NCCB court did several decades earlier.

Little else would account for why the FCC, in an unprecedented fashion, commissioned twelve empirical studies on localism and diversity in its 2002 biennial review, specifically seeking comment on "whether th[e] longstanding presumed link between ownership and viewpoint could be established empirically," and affirmatively stating in that context that "[t]o fulfill our biennial review obligation, we will first define our goals and the ways we will measure them."

Moreover, it would be a strange position for the courts and the FCC not to mandate at least some evidence. After all, the public interest determination under the 1996 Act has to be made every few years. If we are to rely exclusively on normative theory, as Baker desires, what could possibly change every few years about the values (and not evidence) of media quality and democratic distribution and safeguards?

When the Commission makes a policy determination to rescind the newspaper/broadcast cross-ownership rule—adopted initially "because it believed that diversification of ownership would promote diversification of viewpoint"—some record evidence must sustain the policy determination under standard administrative law principles.

Indeed, our description of the empirical turn in the law would be hard to refute. Describing none other than Baker's position, Christopher Terry and Professors David Pritchard and Paul Brewer note that "[s]ome advocates of strict limits on media cross-ownership argue that this kind of empirical evidence is 'simply irrelevant' to media ownership policy, but even they acknowledge that the FCC and the courts require such evidence."

They, in turn, refer to the following passage by Baker: "Recently in the media context, some courts and some policy makers routinely ask for empirical evidence to support governmental policies.... [The] request for more evidence emboldened some lower courts to strike down sensible media laws and regulations for lack of the empirical support that some individual judges wrongly believed relevant to constitutional legitimacy."

This language may also reveal where Baker misconceives the case law: evidence is not required as a matter of constitutional (First Amendment) law, but rather as a matter of administrative law: namely, the Court's application of arbitrary and capricious review.

Lastly, Baker does not appear to distinguish between types of evidence (e.g., qualitative and quantitative empirical evidence). The Supreme Court in Turner remanded for more development of evidence per se, and Baker equates this with "empirical evidence." Whether the empirical turn is normatively desirable is a different matter—a tension explicitly addressed in our discussion of policy implications—but Baker misunderstands our positive description of the empirical turn in the law, one which is resoundingly echoed in assessments by media scholars (and, strangely, by Baker himself elsewhere).

THE DANGERS OF ANECDOTALISM

Given that evidence as to viewpoint diversity plays a central role in media regulation, how do we know what inference the evidence sustains? The key is that the process of gathering evidence has to be articulated. Such formalization of the research process is a chief virtue of well-conducted empirical studies. This for example, articulated each step of the research process, making it transparent how the data was acquired, how observations were chosen, and thereby what inferences could be drawn.

By contrast, Baker's selective use of a handful of "anecdotal tales," which he argues are more informative than statistical inquiry, violates basic rules of inference and fails the fundamental research standard of replicability. Key questions go unanswered about the case he provides to illustrate the democratic safeguard concern: what's the population of units to which he is drawing inferences? How were the cases chosen?

By what process were they observed? How could his theory be falsified? We recognize that Baker, on one level, does not aspire to put forth a falsifiable theory. However, the deep tension is that his normative theory is laden with empirical propositions for which Baker offers only single cases as illustrations. Baker dismisses empirical studies for the following reasons:

Caution... dictates consideration of whether these empirical studies reflect not only particular historical but potentially changeable circumstances. It also dictates a consideration of whether they adequately conceptualize the issue under examination, remove effects of (hold constant) potentially competing, alternative, or additional causes, properly treat any indeterminacy in the findings, consider alternative explanations of the data, and so forth.

Each of these methodological challenges presents a valid concern, but applies a fortiori to the selective use of empirical examples by unarticulated criteria. When drawing a reliable inference from evidence it is no defence to say that the evidence is qualitative: basic rules of inference apply. To illustrate these points, we discuss several of Baker's cases and show the danger of drawing inferences from anecdotal tales alone. A. Who Wants to Be A Millionaire?

To illustrate how conglomerate ownership concentration can undermine journalistic integrity, Baker points to a study by economics Professor James Hamilton that ABC's affiliates mentioned the show Who Wants to Be a Millionaire? In over 80 per cent of local news programs while no NBC affiliate found the ABC programme newsworthy.

While this case appears indicative of network self-promotion, Baker—unlike Hamilton—tells us nothing about how he chose this case. Hamilton actually examined several instances of soft news, such as the reporting by network affiliates of Toy Story 2, an episode involving a lesbian kiss on Ally McBeal, and an interview by Barbara Waiters of Monica Lewinsky promoting her book. The figure demonstrates that Baker singled out the extreme outlier that happened to be consistent with his views.

Worse, Baker has not articulated how Millionaire is even relevant to his theory of democratic safeguards and how it exemplifies that conglomerate ownership undermines journalistic integrity. First, only one of the cases studied by Hamilton—Toy Story 2—is about conglomerate ownership (involving Disney and ABC), and that case does not support the claim that conglomerate ownership influences soft news coverage. The observations are centered around the origin, indicating indistinguishable coverage rates by affiliates and non-affiliates of Toy Story 2 or its stars, Tim Allen and Tom Hanks.

Second, is network self-promotion about Millionaire or Ally McBeal's kiss truly relevant to the grave concerns about democratic deliberation and legitimacy? As we argued, one of the major benefits of empirical measurement is that it forces scholars to conceptualize more concretely what is meant by complex concepts, such as viewpoint diversity and distortion of journalism.

Reasonable people may disagree as to whether the evening news lead-in (e.g., "Coming up next: Millionaire") is innocuous, but measurement itself clarifies what we mean by quality of journalism. Lastly, if they are relevant, that comes into tension with the position that the costs to concentration cannot be measured.

CONGLOMERATE SUPPORT OF FASCISM

To illustrate how the "existence of... concentrated power within the public sphere creates a real danger of abuse," Baker points to a sobering example of the first German media conglomerate's support of Adolf Hitler. "No democracy should accept that risk" of "abuse of the concentrated power implicit in conglomerate media ownership," and ownership regulations, he argues, would guard against such atrocious outcomes of fascism.

As we stated, we agree with the underlying concern of democratic safeguards. Yet Baker also appears to make an empirically falsifiable claim when he states that "at least since the first major German media conglomerate supported the rise of Hitler, various countries... have experienced demographic abuse of the concentrated power implicit in conglomerate media ownership," namely that conglomerate media outlets are more likely to support the abuse of power or fascism.

Unfortunately, we are given little information about the single example he provides (what sources he consulted, what other cases he considered, etc.). What if the only example provided was one of a small, non-conglomerate newspaper supporting Hitler? Would that support the contrary theory? A cursory examination of German media history reveals much more evidence by which one can assess the validity of this conglomerate-fascism connection, as many more newspapers existed. The fact that the only conglomerate supported Hitler may be due to pure chance alone, especially if newspaper support of Hitler was widespread. This might weaken the inference that conglomerate status affected fascist support. Of course, drawing an inference about conglomerates when only one exists is fraught with peril.

The fascism theory may have another observable implication: if concentration matters, perhaps circulation should be associated with support of Hitler. Across three newspapers with small, medium, and large circulation, the lack of correlation remains the same. Of course, we have not said anything about how these cases were chosen. And that is precisely the point.

With more data, representative of a population, we might be able to examine the validity of Baker's hypothesis. The Hugenberg case illustrates the failure to heed basic principles of inference: articulate how observations were gathered, collect as much information as possible, and extract all possible observable implications of the theory.

Baker discusses two more cases to illustrate the "abuse of the concentrated power implicit in conglomerate media ownership." In 1976, the New York Times published several articles on medical malpractice that evidently angered the medical industry.

Medicine-related advertisers threatened to withdraw advertisements from Times-owned medical magazines, which were later sold, arguably in consideration of the threat. Baker argues that the advertising threat demonstrates the danger of conglomerates.

Two problems present themselves in connection with the first case. First, the relationship between medical magazines and the New York Times has nothing to do with extant cross-ownership rules. This is, of course, acceptable if it might inform us more generally about the impact of common ownership.

More importantly, the New York Times did, in fact, run this expose of medical malpractice, which may cut against Baker's strong assumption that conglomerates favour profits over journalism. Indeed, one of the major arguments about the benefits of consolidation is that news resources can be pooled to engage in more investigative journalism.

More generally, recall Baker's supposition: The owners who are most likely to favour journalism over profits include several predictable types: (a) smaller, usually local, owners who take identity from their firms' contributions to their community or from the journalistic product they create; (b) workers who take professional pride in the quality of their product; (c) non-profit entities whose goals include service to their community.

These assertions appear inconsistent with the New York Times and the Washington Post examples. Worse, one strains for how to interpret this statement. Does statement (a) mean that smaller owners are more likely to "take identity" from their journalistic product than larger owners?

Or is the statement simply true by tautology (i.e., owners "most likely to favour journalism over profits" are "owners who take identity... from the journalistic product they create" and "workers who take professional pride in the quality of their product")? Can we define this in a falsifiable way? It is no defence that the theory isn't offered for positive scholarship—for policy purposes the implementation of Baker's rule would require decisionmakers to operationalize these categories.

Decidedly lacking from this statement are citations to vast amounts of empirical work on the topic of conglomerate and chain ownership of newspapers. The Watergate example suggests that a relevant outcome is coverage of political scandals, and we might consult this literature to see whether smaller newspapers are generally more likely to cover political scandals. Examining coverage of thirty-five scandals by 200 newspapers, one recent study finds the exact opposite, namely, "[o]verall coverage of scandals is significantly higher for newspapers with higher circulation" and "[n]ewspapers with higher circulation systematically devote more coverage to political scandals, at least in the news section."

Of course, we have not done a formal examination of all empirical works on this question (metaanalysis), and one may quibble with the exact design and how closely it tracks Baker's conjecture—but that is precisely the virtue of empirical work in helping to clarify theory.

THE RULES OF INFERENCE

Our examination of these cases is not to suggest that case studies are not worthwhile. To the contrary, well-chosen case studies can be tremendously illuminating. Indeed, recall that our article entailed a lengthy exposition of two case studies. The lesson from Baker's cases is that one must be careful about research design, principles of inference, and the dangers of anecdotalism.

In the end, for all the rhetoric about empirical studies being "irrelevant," there is a deep, unanswered tension in Baker's position. He suggests that ethnographic surveys and journalist self-reports (i.e., empirical studies) may be probative evidence of the corruption of concentrated media (and relies on one example from Hamilton's book chock full of empirical results), but dismisses other empirical studies as irrelevant. Further, he says:

I am a great admirer of empirical research. At places where I make empirical predictions—for example, that mergers typically reduce the quality of media performance—I have looked to see if empirical studies support... my claim, in this case finding that, although evidence is meager, apparently mergers did have this negative effect.

Such a statement gets it exactly wrong. Social scientists are not advocates scouring for empirical studies that happen to support the favored position. To the contrary, social scientists look for every reason to falsify their theory, so as to ascertain the truth of the matter. The very study that Baker looked to for support of his claim contains distinct findings that contradict his view on ownership.

That study concludes: "The data offer some evidence to support the argument favoring cross ownership." To draw an inference from scholarly literature, one cannot selectively choose results by unarticulated criteria. One should look for all evidence that may be inconsistent with one's theory.

Only after such vetting can a researcher (or reader) be persuaded that some rival explanation does not account for observed phenomena. Anecdotalism is unlikely to take us far. Systematic measurement is crucial.

SYSTEMATIC MEASUREMENT

THE IMPORTANCE OF EMPIRICAL EVIDENCE WITH CALAMITOUS RISKS

It is precisely because the media plays an important role that empirical inquiry is warranted. Baker argues that evidence is entirely irrelevant due to the strength of his normative theory. Moreover, "empirical measurement... is predictably uninformative" and the "search for empirical evidence" is "misguided."

The danger to democracy is so strong that "[e]ven if, in the past, the risk had never led to bad results (which would make the danger hard to measure by normal statistical techniques), good institutional design—like good structural design of nuclear power plants—should not unnecessarily risk calamitous results."

The example of nuclear power is telling. If anything, it contradicts Baker's privileged and exclusive role for normative theory. While we may not observe many calamitous results of nuclear failure, observable indicators of structural design exist, such as the robustness of the containment structure, shutdown margins, and other operational controls.

How else would we discover what "good structural design" entails, or whether a design imposes "unnecessary risk"? It cannot be the case that empirical evidence is "simply irrelevant" for these determinations. Evidence, science, and expertise should and do inform the design of nuclear power plants.

The analogy is further illuminating because nuclear power presents a kind of "dread risk" feared by the public, but this perception diverges significantly from expert assessments of nuclear risk. Divergence between popular and expert assessments may well be present in the media context as well.

Calamitous disasters are not impervious to empirical scrutiny. One luminary of data visualization, Professor Edward Tufte, cogently argued that the reticence to appropriately examine data may well have contributed to the Challenger space shuttle disaster. While NASA was in possession of compelling evidence that low temperatures were associated with O-ring erosion (the cause of the shuttle explosion), it failed to examine the data in a sufficiently clear form to set off alarm. As Tufte argued, irrelevant icons of side rocket boosters, inscrutable legends of damage, and chronological organization of shuttles distort the relevant relationship in the data between temperature and O-ring failure. The data exhibit a sharp pattern: O-ring erosion on previous shuttle flights occurred overwhelmingly at lower temperatures. Every shuttle below sixty-six degrees experienced erosion.

No failures occurred above seventy degrees. The only instance with three erosions occurred at the lowest observed temperature of fitly-three degrees. And the temperature forecast for the day of the Challenger takeoff was some twenty degrees lower than any previous shuttle flight. Regardless of the exact relationship, extrapolating the pattern should have set off alarm bells. The risk of "calamitous results" warrants more examination—subject to principles of inference—of evidence, not less.

THE ENTERPRISE OF MEASUREMENT

The purpose of systematic measurement is to overcome the speculative nature of anecdotal tales. Yet Baker argues that "the relevant diversity should be qualitative, not simply quantitative." "The democratic quality of discourse is not measured by the amount of diversity," but by (1) the fact that views are not subject to or actually suppressed, and by (2) meaningful efforts to develop relevant information and perspective.

He argues that our measures of viewpoint diversity are "commodified," and thereby we commit a basic error: since consumers value commodities (such as viewpoints) on the market, we miss "non-commodified" democratic values. We agree that there are other relevant media outputs that may be affected by media consolidation. But Baker's charge that viewpoints are irrelevant because they are "commodified" misunderstands the enterprise of measurement.

First, the enterprise of measurement is to capture meaningful outcomes. Prior to our research, indirect and inadequate proxies for substantive viewpoints were used. Statements about whether the Los Angeles Times became more "conservative" upon acquisition by the Tribune Company (or Baker's characterization of the Wall Street Journal as having a "reactionary" editorial stance) were hence difficult to evaluate.

Our approach provides a transparent and neutral way to do this, addressing Baker's charge prior to our work that "the claims of content variation are bedeviled by intrinsic methodological measurement problems that cannot be solved in a value-neutral way." We disagree, and take it that Baker also retreats from the prior conclusion that measurement cannot be solved when he says that our study is "far superior methodologically."

Essentially, our measure recovers what a reasonable person would infer about the viewpoint of a newspaper if she read all editorials about the Supreme

Court and learned about all votes cast by the Justices for a ten-year period. The latent scale represents the "distance" between the Justices based on voting patterns and analogous differences between newspapers based on "phantom" votes on Supreme Court cases, and can be interpreted as running from "liberal" to "conservative."

For example, the New York Times exhibits a phantom jurisprudence just to the left of Justice Stevens, and the Investor's Business Daily is closest in opinion to Justice Scalia. Moreover, the intervals capture the uncertainty in distinguishing newspapers: the San Francisco Chronicle and the Boston Globe are indistinguishable from each other (and closest to Justice Ginsburg). Our measurement approach thereby turned what was likely a subjective assessment into something transparent.

Second, the fact that quality matters does not mean that quality cannot be measured. If observable, it is by definition measurable. In addition, Baker mistakenly assumes that "media quality" cannot be measured in quantitative terms. It may be more challenging, but addressing that challenge was precisely what our measurement approach achieved. While our estimated measure is quantitative, the underlying data is qualitative as to whether a newspaper editorialized in favour of each Supreme Court decision or not. As Edward Lee Thorndike, a founder of educational psychology, stated:

Our ideals may be as lofty and as subtle as you please, but if they are real ideals, they are ideals for achieving something; and if anything real is ever achieved, it can be measured. Not perhaps now, and not perhaps fifty years from now; but if a thing exists, it exists in some amount; and if it exists in some amount, it can be measured.

Third, Baker's assertions—that our measure is market-based and that as "market apologists, [we] then interpret diversity in commodified terms—obfuscate rather than clarify. Our measures are not "market measures" in any classical sense (such as measures from contingent or hedonic valuation studies. The issue is not one of "commodification," but of measurement.

This becomes clear when he argues "[t]ypical market measures provide no direct way to measure purported contributions of separation of powers and legislative bicameralism to improving democratic deliberations and to reducing risks to liberty."

It is unclear what he means by "market measures," but both bicameralism and separation of powers have been studied voluminously by social scientists, including measures precisely relevant to broad concerns of liberty and deliberation, including effects on political accountability, judicial and congressional decision-making, executive appointments, government duration, fiscal deficits, majoritarian tyranny, policy stability, length of legislative bargaining, and the cohesion of a ruling coalition.

To say that this thriving research—studying and measuring the various dimensions of separation of powers and bicameralism—is irrelevant because it uses "market measures" (perhaps because a formal theoretic or quantitative empirical approach is adopted?) is misinformed. The incantation of an arguably ill-defined concept of "commodification" is not talismanic. If media quality has observable outcomes, they are measurable.

Indeed, Baker implicitly measures quality every time he invokes an illustration of the effects of concentration on media. Our methods empower such measurement. Fourth, our measure plausibly incorporates certain elements of Baker's media quality (notwithstanding the fact that it remains loosely articulated).

Viewpoint suppression, such as Tribune-company influence over the Los Angeles Times editorial board, would be captured, at least in part, by changes in substantive editorial viewpoints. And few other items on the pages of a newspaper are as relevant to the notion of "perspective" as editorializing.

Baker's argument effectively reduces to: you've missed something, yet I won't tell you exactly what it is, because it's not measurable. Indeed, it is ironic that he faults the courts for calling for empirical evidence "while avoiding explanations of how or why it is relevant." Yet clarification is precisely a major benefit of formal measurement: it forces the researcher to concretize concepts that are diffuse in the abstract and to refine what exactly it is that we mean by elusive terms such as "viewpoint diversity" and "quality." For example, one might argue that Supreme Court editorials miss "local diversity."

Thinking about how to measure local diversity forces one to conceptualize "diversity," when, for example, each newspaper might endorse candidates in completely different local races. Does the lack of editorial opposition to candidates in given local races still mean diversity (perhaps temporally or across subscription areas)? Measurement serves to clarify concepts and crystallize theory.

THE ROLE OF EDITORIALS AND NEWS

Baker validly points out that our focus on editorials does not capture news reporting. Yet he goes further in arguing that "news may be more significant for democratic discourse than... editorial positions" and that "[c]ritics of the media seldom bemoan a paper's editorial position. Rather, their chorus alleges slanted news presentation and, even more importantly, misguided choices—whether due to ideological bias or structural economic considerations—in not covering certain stories."

While we agree that news should be independently examined (which is possible—albeit with some complications—by adapting measurement methods similar to ours), we take issue with Baker's slapdash dismissal of the relevance of studying editorial viewpoint diversity. First, whether or not news reporting is "more significant" than editorializing is speculation. (Baker admits as much in stating that news "may be more significant for democratic discourse.") Our contribution was to study editorial viewpoints, which serve a crucial role in the development of perspectives on public policy issues. Recall that one of Baker's indicators of "quality" is "meaningful efforts to develop relevant information and perspective." Editorials are at least one crucial output of such efforts to develop relevant perspective.

Second, Baker's own illustrations demonstrate that editorials play a central role. Knight-Ridder's reported influence over Miami Herald's criticism of Edwin Meese manifested itself precisely through editorials.

And although Baker discusses Atlantic Richfield in the context of incentives to "report favorably," at least according to the only source Baker cites, the company intervened in the writing of editorial columns. Moreover, Baker's example of a media conglomerate's "abuse of... concentrated power" is that of Alfred Hugenberg's support of Hitler, but again, one major channel of influence was via editorial policy and newspaper endorsements of Hitler. The very illustrations that Baker invokes are inconsistent with the notion that critics "seldom bemoan a paper's editorial position."

Third, even ignoring Baker's own inconsistency, it is simply untrue that critics seldom focus on editorial positions. None other than Ben Bagdikian, the "dean of American media critics," laments the homogenization of content due to media concentration. He discusses editorials on the fairness doctrine, the uniformity of editorial endorsements of political candidates, and instances of executive pressure influencing editorial endorsement decisions—something we expressly discussed in our article. And of course, as we have already noted, the FCC and existing scholarship consider editorial viewpoints important.

Fourth, Baker's conjecture that consolidation amongst local newspapers might cause convergence in news and divergence in editorials is intriguing, but a red herring. Baker offers not a shred of evidence upon which to assess its validity. One might conjecture the exact opposite: that upon acquisition, local newspapers fire the editorial board and run wire editorials (thereby converging in editorial viewpoints), while devoting resources to local news (thereby diverging in news reporting).

The Palo Alto Daily News, which is owned by the Bay Area News Group, for example, follows pretty much this practice of wire op-eds and local news. Since we have provided exactly one more data point than Baker has, one might even argue that our conjecture is more plausible than his. Yet such conjectures become verifiable only with a measure of editorial viewpoint diversity—such as in the approach we have provided—and more systematic empirical investigation beyond anecdotes.

Lastly, our measures of editorial viewpoint diversity in fact offer considerable insight into news reporting, as they are highly correlated with news output. The measures are highly correlated, with the exception of the Wall Street Journal, which is known to have a conservative editorial desk and a liberal news desk. Of course, one might argue about the precise measurements, but this is strong facial evidence that our measures may tell much about news reporting as well. In the end, Baker is right to point to news as important, but his arguments that editorials are seldom at issue are internally inconsistent and unsupported. Conjecture cannot replace the hard work of developing a method of measuring editorial viewpoint diversity that is transparent, replicable, substantively interpretable, accounts for measurement uncertainty, and is, in principle, adaptable for the study of news diversity.

INFORMATION VERSUS SAMPLE SIZE

A remaining deficiency of our measurement approach, according to Baker, is that it has "a sample size of five." This is plainly wrong. Our data consisted of 10,598 votes by 13 Justices and 1,618 editorial positions by 25 newspapers across 1,186 cases from 1988 to 2004. While there are five mergers and acquisitions, these represent every one that occurred in the sample for this observation period, providing comparisons between some eleven newspapers before and after the transaction.

Moreover, we collected large amounts of information about each newspaper pre- and post-transaction and augmented this data with evidence from county-level circulation statistics, detailed studies of editorial board composition, and qualitative study of the editorials themselves. By Baker's count, studying the effect of the collapse of the Soviet Union on mass political attitudes by conducting pre- and post-surveys of hundreds of respondents would count as a sample size of one.

Fixation on effective sample size is misguided. A sample size of one individual can be greatly informative when mapping the human genome, while a sample size of one million can be irrelevant when the causal factor of interest does not vary.

Similarly, a sample of twenty randomly selected individuals with randomly assigned treatment can be far more informative than a non-random sample of 5,000 individuals who have self-selected into treatment. The purpose of research design is not to maximize the number of observations, but to maximize leverage over quantities of interest so that we can meaningfully learn about the world.

THE NORMATIVE AND THE PERSONAL

While we greatly appreciate the lively response, it is oddly consumed with dissecting our personal motivations and presumed normative pre-commitments. Baker charges that as "anti-regulatory advocates," we "purport to give an empirical... basis for deregulation."

Nowhere do we do so. First, we did not start from a normative pre-commitment. To the contrary, at the outset of this research, we had no preconception as to what to expect about the evolution of viewpoints before and after mergers and acquisitions. And our results do not lend themselves to ready simplification of favoring regulation or deregulation, as we find evidence for convergence, divergence, and stability in light of newspaper consolidation.

Second, nowhere did our policy implications endorse deregulation and, if anything, made exactly the opposite point. We showed that "repealing the rules would exacerbate the already profound difficulties of empirical justification about the effects of a rule." Further, we highlighted an implicit tension between the mandates of the 1996 Act for the FCC to (1) make a public interest determination (wrought by the difficulties of empirical evaluation), and (2) repeal or modify ownership regulations if they no longer serve the public interest.

We expressly argued that the difficulties of empirical inference militate in favour of incremental modification, rather than wholesale deregulation, which would accord with federal law when strong evidence sustaining the convergence hypothesis is lacking. To overcome the difficulties of the public interest determination, we suggested the FCC collaborate with research groups to design programme evaluation and field experiments to facilitate such evaluation.

Nowhere did we "purport to give an empirical... basis for deregulation." Baker oddly imputes implications where they do not exist. Most strangely, Baker's response makes a number of ad hominem claims and conjectures as to why we were personally "misled" and our "inexcusable" errors of failing to articulate his preferred theory.

As answers, he charges us with "making the same mistake" as scholars "driven by free-market ideology," and argues that we suffer of "economists' occupational inclination to see value in what can be purchased in markets" and "a corresponding bias in [our] resulting political recommendations."

In addition, with what he admits to be "intentionally inflammatory" rhetoric, he charges that our empirical measure fails to capture the media reporting about the connection between Saddam Hussein and Osama Bin Laden and argues that we miss the fact that the rise of Hitler had some association with conglomerate media ownership. And (as if that were not enough), our work may suffer from the "ingrained fearful desire of originally untenured academics to steer clear of controversy, [and] an immature craving to escape uncertainty and indeterminacy."

Most disturbing about these charges and this rhetoric is that they miss a fundamental point about scholarly research: ad hominem attacks have no role in scholarship. (Not to mention the fact that these accusations are each factually incorrect—neither of us is an economist, nor does welfare economics share the same intellectual history of statistics, nor do welfare economics and statistics have a corresponding political bias, nor could anyone accurately describe us as "anti-regulatory advocates," nor do we (hopefully) have an immature craving to escape uncertainty.

The merits of an empirical investigation stand apart from the author. Scholarly exchange is not about individuals—who are not "advocates" looking to confirm their favored theories, and are, rather, researchers seeking knowledge of the world—but about the research.

Our article started from the empirical turn that scholarship and the law have taken over the course of the past twenty years. Far from shying away from questioning that turn, our policy implications flowed from what we highlighted as the difficulties of empirical evaluation. Without having engaged in that inquiry, it would be impossible to ascertain the limits of empirical evaluation.

THE VIBRANT ROLE OF EMPIRICAL LEGAL STUDIES

In the end, we agree with Baker on the central contribution of our article: that our study moves forward the empirical literature on the media. Moreover, we appreciate the opportunity Baker has provided to address basic concerns over the role of theory—normative and positive—and empirics in law. Our conclusion is much more limited than Baker's sweeping indictment of welfare economics and empirical legal studies as "malignant" tendencies and as "only handmaidens" within the legal academy.

While we recognize the limits of empirical inquiry, we see a fruitful role for empirical investigation (and positive theory) as complementary to, and synergistic with, value-based inquiry in law. If policy decisions are to be made solely on normative theoretical grounds, as Baker desires, we may give up opportunities to forge consensus on contentious issues based on growing evidence.

Empirical evidence can inform value-laden decisions, particularly in administrative law and regulation where the factual issues become complex. Evidence that airbags save lives surely is useful for safety standards administered by the National Highway Traffic Safety Administration. Evidence that tailpipe emissions contribute to global warming surely is useful for the setting of motor vehicle standards by the Environmental Protection Agency. And, similarly, evidence of whether viewpoints converge with media consolidation surely is relevant for the regulations administered by the FCC, as recognized by the FCC, appellate courts, and a large number of scholars.

In the end, our most basic disagreement is with the notion that empirical evidence is "entirely irrelevant." Value judgments are crucial to legal decisionmaking, but that does not mean we should operate in affirmative isolation of evidence. Baker charges that the empiricist is "a person on hands and knees looking for her keys under the street light despite her belief that she lost them on a dark stretch further down the street."

That may characterize some empirical research. But, to extend the analogy, the aim of our work was to capitalize on statistical methods to build new light poles to conduct new inquiries for where the keys may, in fact, lie.

That is the crucial role of statistical methodology in a discipline where experiments simply cannot be run to obtain policy-relevant knowledge. Legal scholars cannot, and should not, shut their eyes to evidence that can be brought to bear on policy questions of interest. Tools that have been first crafted outside of law, such as the methods we adapt from psychometrics and political science, can powerfully help to address policy questions and resolve disagreement that otherwise would be left to pure theory.

The deep irony in Baker's view—one that espouses pure normative, value-based theory that cannot be falsified—is that, in the end, it amounts to little more than "trust me." For all the rhetoric about democratic values (and diversity), Baker prefers a mode of legal scholarship for philosopher kings to the exclusion of all empirical (and positive) inquiry.

The burgeoning field of empirical legal studies plays in many ways the opposite role: by providing transparent, widely-accepted rules of inference. Science and empirical inquiry democratize the accumulation of knowledge.

One need not be a philosopher king to contribute to knowledge about the legal world, and anyone can be proven wrong by data. The democratization of knowledge about the law, the accumulation of wisdom about how it operates on the ground, and no one's exclusive claim to being right are what we view as progress.

Gauntlett goes on to criticize studies that focus on children by stating that they do not utilize adults as a control group, and that the studies are conducted primarily to further a "barely-concealed conservative ideology." He counters the premise of these studies with the concept that not all depictions of violence are even bad to witness. M.I.T. Professor Henry Jenkins, for instance, suggested in his speech to congress that The Basketball Diaries utilizes violence in a form of social commentary that provides clear social benefit.

David Gauntlett explains further that objects defined as "violent" or "anti-social" may not be judged as such in the minds of the viewer and tend to be viewed in artificial circumstances. These objects are furthermore based on previous studies with flawed methodology, and are not grounded in theory. Additionally, he claims that the effects model makes no attempt to understand the *meanings* of media.

- Historical criticisms situate the 'meta-narrative' of effects theory within a long history of distrust of new forms of media, dating as far back as Socrates's objections to the deleterious effects due to the written alphabet.
- Political criticisms pose an alternative conception of humans as rational, critical subjects who are alert to genre norms and adept at interpreting and critiquing media representations, instead of passively absorbing them.

Supporters of effects theory contend that commercials, advertising and voter campaigns prove that media influence behaviour. In the 20th century, aggressive media attention and negative coverage of trials involving celebrities like Roscoe Fatty Arbuckle or Michael Jackson have influenced the general public's opinion, before the trials effectively started. However, these critics do point out that while the media could have an effect on people's behaviour this isn't necessarily always the case.

Critics of the media effects theory point out that many copycat murders, suicides and other violent acts nearly always happen in abnormal upbringings. Violent, emotionally neglectful or aggressive environments influence behaviour more than watching certain programs, films or listening to certain music. Most people who carry out these acts are also mentally unstable to begin with.

Critics also point out that just because an audience sees acts of violence in media, this does not mean they will actually commit them. Of the millions of people who watch violent films, only a small number have carried out acts of violence as a direct result. People regularly exposed to violent media usually grow up to be completely normal people. If there are any effects from media, they only affect a very small number of people.

11

Role of Advertising Media in Society

MEDIA MANAGEMENT

Media management is a term used for several related tasks throughout post-production. In general, any task that relates to processing your media is considered to be media management, such as capturing, compressing, copying, moving, or deleting media files. However, media management also refers to keeping track of your media files via clip properties such as log notes, comments, scene number, shot/take number, and so on.

The flexibility and power of media management in Final Cut Pro stems from one simple fact: a clip and its media file are treated independently. In Final Cut Pro, a more accurate description of media management would be clip and media management. What makes the separation of clips and media files so powerful?

Here are a few examples:

- Reconnecting clips to new media files: You can create new media files for your project at any time, and reconnect the clips in your project to the new media files.
- Direct access to your media files: You can directly access your QuickTime media files in the Finder at any time. You can also easily create clips by dragging media files directly into your project via the Browser. In fact, you can even edit by dragging media files from the Finder directly into the Timeline or Canvas.
- Logging clip information without media: You can modify clip properties such as log notes, comments, labels, and even In and Out points without the associated media files. This means you can organize your clips and sequences even though your current editing system may not have the media files.
- Trading projects without media files: A Final Cut Pro project file contains clips and sequences, but not media files. Because a project file is so small, you can email or post your project file online. Anyone who has the corresponding media files can open the project file and reconnect the clips to the local media files.

Making a movie is a tremendous logistical undertaking. It's the execution of the details that ultimately determines the quality of the finished product. What does it matter how good the lead actress's performance was in the third take of scene 2 if you can't find it among a thousand other shots? And what use is a week of fine-tune editing, frame by frame, if the final sequence is improperly assembled by the negative cutter because of a faulty edit decision list that you provided? Final Cut Pro has incredibly versatile media management options, allowing you to customize your workflow to fit the needs of your project.

CABLE ADVERTISING

Consider how this data applies to the notion of advertising on cable television. Cable advertising offers the advantage of sight (visual) and sound (tonal) along with the added benefits of motion, color, affordable rates, and the ability to geographically and demographically target specific customer groups. This is a rather compelling argument to seriously consider advertising on cable.

Television reaches a great number of people in a short amount of time. But in many cases, traditional TV advertising may not be affordable for the average small business. Some can afford it only for a limited period of time, especially if they are buying prime-time slots; they are often relegated to nonprime-time slots if they want to have any long-term frequency. That's why more and more small firms are turning to advertising on less expensive, local cable channels.

Here are some advantages to cable advertising:

- It can quickly create awareness of your business, establish your image and educate viewers about your products or services.
- You can micro-target the groups that fit your "best customer" profile.
- You can achieve frequency on a limited budget, which often moves fence-sitters into action.
- You can enhance and stretch the power of other existing advertising you might be doing.
- You may be able to reach a different segment of the population, one that doesn't read newspapers or magazines.

But just because cable advertising offers unique advantages, don't overlook the basic principles that precede any sound advertising decision. Ask yourself:

- What is it I want my advertising to accomplish? Be precise about your goals.
- Who am I trying to reach? Bring into focus exactly who your target market is. Formulate a profile of your more profitable customers - age, buying power, gender, family and so on.
- Address your customers' needs. You might be able to find the right media at the right price, but unless you know what your ads must

say, your efforts will likely fail. You need to persuade viewers that your product or service meets their needs better than anything or anyone else.

Once you determine your advertising goals, know who your ideal customer is, know what market segments you want to attract, and are realistic about your advertising budget, then approach the advertising representatives from your local cable company. Ask questions about the various networks they carry, the number of subscribers they have, the breakdown of package or channel preferences in terms of numbers, gender, age, profession, ethnic background and so on.

Get a complete explanation of the costs, not only in airing the spots but also in producing them. Know in advance what you're looking at in terms of overall expenditures. Talk to other people who have advertised on cable, and find out how well the medium worked for them. Were they satisfied? How did they track the results? You may even want to look into a "cable co-op" of sorts, where several companies collaborate on an ad package that promotes their services or products and highlights a different business with each ad. In other words, be creative.

Finally, remember any advertising effort must be orchestrated so it works in concert with your entire marketing plan. Advertising on cable television can be just one element in that plan but may serve to reach a large number of targeted prospects in a more economical way.

ONLINE ADVERTISING

Online advertising is a form of promotion that uses the Internet and World Wide Web for the expressed purpose of delivering marketing messages to attract customers. Examples of online advertising include contextual ads on search engine results pages, banner ads, Rich Media Ads, Social network advertising, interstitial ads, online classified advertising, advertising networks and e-mail marketing, including e-mail spam.

COMPETITIVE ADVANTAGE OVER TRADITIONAL ADVERTISING

One major benefit of online advertising is the immediate publishing of information and content that is not limited by geography or time. To that end, the emerging area of interactive advertising presents fresh challenges for advertisers who have hitherto adopted an interruptive strategy.

Another benefit is the efficiency of advertiser's investment. Online advertising allows for the customization of advertisements, including content and posted websites. For example, AdWords, Yahoo! Search Marketing and AdSense enable ads shown on relevant webpages or aside of search results of pre-chosen keywords. Another is the payment method. Whatever purchasing variation is selected, the payment is usually relative with audiences' response happly.

ETHICS

Online advertising encompasses a range of types of advertising, some of which are deployed ethically and some are not. Some websites use large numbers of advertisements, including flashing banners that distract the user, and some have misleading images designed to look like error messages from the operating system, rather than advertisements. Websites that unethically use online advertising for revenue frequently do not monitor what advertisements on their website link to, allowing advertisements to lead to sites with malicious software or adult material.

Website operators that ethically use online advertising typically use a small number of advertisements that are not intended to distract or irritate the user, and do not detract from the design and layout of their websites. Many website owners deal directly with companies that want to place ads, meaning that the website linked to by the advertisement is legitimate.

The overuse of technologies like Adobe flash in online advertising has led to some users disabling it in their browsers, or using browser plug-ins like adblock or noscript. Legitimate advertising often is opt-in, or has a clear opt-out option, which differentiates it from spam.

Malware

There is also class of advertising methods which are considered unethical and may even be illegal. These include external applications which alter system settings (such as a browser's home page), spawn pop-ups, and insert advertisements into non-affiliated webpages. Such applications are usually labelled as spyware or adware. They may mask their questionable activities by performing a simple service, such as displaying the weather or providing a search bar. These programs are designed to dupe the user, acting effectively as Trojan horses. These applications are commonly designed so as to be difficult to remove or uninstall. The ever-increasing audience of online users, many of whom are not computer-savvy, frequently lack the knowledge and technical ability to protect themselves from these programs.

Privacy

The use of online advertising has implications on the privacy and anonymity of users. If an advertising company has placed banners in two Web sites. Hosting the banner images on its servers and using third-party cookies, the advertising company is able to track the browsing of users across these two sites. Third-party cookies can be blocked by most browsers to increase privacy and reduce tracking by advertising and tracking companies without negatively affecting the user's Web experience. Many advertising operators have an opt-out option to behavioural advertising, with a generic cookie in the browser stopping behavioural advertising.

REVENUE MODELS

The three most common ways in which online advertising is purchased are CPM, CPC, and CPA:

- CPM (Cost Per Mille), also called "Cost Per Thousand (CPT), is where advertisers pay for exposure of their message to a specific audience. "Per mille" means per thousand impressions, or loads of an advertisement. However, some impressions may not be counted, such as a reload or internal user action. The M in the acronym is the Roman numeral for one thousand.
- CPV (Cost Per Visitor) is where advertisers pay for the delivery of a Targeted Visitor to the advertisers website.
- CPV (Cost Per View) is when an advertiser pays for each unique user view of an advertisement or website (usually used with pop-ups, pop-unders and interstitial ads).
- CPC (Cost Per Click) is also known as Pay per click (PPC). Advertisers pay each time a user clicks on their listing and is redirected to their website. They do not actually pay for the listing, but only when the listing is clicked on. This system allows advertising specialists to refine searches and gain information about their market. Under the Pay per click pricing system, advertisers pay for the right to be listed under a series of target rich words that direct relevant traffic to their website, and pay only when someone clicks on their listing which links directly to their website. CPC differs from CPV in that each click is paid for regardless of whether the user makes it to the target site.
- CPA (Cost Per Action) or (Cost Per Acquisition) advertising is performance based and is common in the affiliate marketing sector of the business. In this payment scheme, the publisher takes all the risk of running the ad, and the advertiser pays only for the amount of users who complete a transaction, such as a purchase or sign-up. This is the best type of rate to pay for banner advertisements and the worst type of rate to charge.
  - Similarly, CPL (Cost Per Lead) advertising is identical to CPA advertising and is based on the user completing a form, registering for a newsletter or some other action that the merchant feels will lead to a sale.
  - Also common, CPO (Cost Per Order) advertising is based on each time an order is transacted.
  - CPE (Cost Per Engagement) is a form of Cost Per Action pricing first introduced in March 2008. Differing from cost-per-impression or cost-per-click models, a CPE model means advertising impressions are free and advertisers pay only when a user engages with their specific ad unit. Engagement is defined as a user interacting with an ad in any number of ways.

- Cost per conversion Describes the cost of acquiring a customer, typically calculated by dividing the total cost of an ad campaign by the number of conversions. The definition of "Conversion" varies depending on the situation: it is sometimes considered to be a lead, a sale, or a purchase.

TYPES

Though, as seen above, the large majority of online advertising has a cost that is brought about by usage or interaction of an ad, there are a few other methods of advertising online that only require a one time payment. The Million Dollar Homepage is a very successful example of this. Visitors were able to pay $1 per pixel of advertising space and their advert would remain on the homepage for as long as the website exists with no extra costs.

- *Floating ad*: An ad which moves across the user's screen or floats above the content.
- *Expanding ad*: An ad which changes size and which may alter the contents of the webpage.
- *Polite ad*: A method by which a large ad will be downloaded in smaller pieces to minimize the disruption of the content being viewed
- *Wallpaper ad*: An ad which changes the background of the page being viewed.
- *Trick banner*: A banner ad that looks like a dialog box with buttons. It simulates an error message or an alert.
- *Pop-up*: A new window which opens in front of the current one, displaying an advertisement, or entire webpage.
- *Pop-under*: Similar to a Pop-Up except that the window is loaded or sent behind the current window so that the user does not see it until they close one or more active windows.
- *Video ad*: similar to a banner ad, except that instead of a static or animated image, actual moving video clips are displayed. This is the kind of advertising most prominent in television, and many advertisers will use the same clips for both television and online advertising.
- *Map ad*: text or graphics linked from, and appearing in or over, a location on an electronic map such as on Google Maps.
- *Mobile ad*: an SMS text or multi-media message sent to a cell phone.
- *Interstitial ad*: a full-page ad that appears before a user reaches their original destination.

In addition, ads containing streaming video or streaming audio are becoming very popular with advertisers.

E-mail Advertising

Legitimate Email advertising or E-mail marketing is often known as "opt-in e-mail advertising" to distinguish it from spam.

Affiliate Marketing

Affiliate marketing is a form of online advertising where advertisers place campaigns with a potentially large number of small (and large) publishers, whom are only paid media fees when traffic to the advertiser is garnered, and usually upon a specific measurable campaign result (a form, a sale, a sign-up, etc). Today, this is usually accomplished through contracting with an affiliate network.

Affiliate marketing was an invention by CDNow.com in 1994 and was excelled by Amazon.com when it launched its Affiliate Program, called Associate Program in 1996. The online retailer used its program to generate low cost brand exposure and provided at the same time small websites a way to earn some supplemental income.

Contextual Advertising

Many advertising networks display graphical or text-only ads that correspond to the keywords of an Internet search or to the content of the page on which the ad is shown. These ads are believed to have a greater chance of attracting a user, because they tend to share a similar context as the user's search query. For example, a search query for "flowers" might return an advertisement for a florist's website. Another newer technique is embedding keyword hyperlinks in an article which are sponsored by an advertiser. When a user follows the link, they are sent to a sponsor's website.

Behavioral Targeting

In addition to contextual targeting, online advertising can be targeted based on a user's past clickstream. For example, if a user is known to have recently visited a number of automotive shopping / comparison sites based on clickstream analysis enabled by cookies stored on the user's computer, that user can then be served auto-related ads when they visit other, non-automotive sites.

Semantic Advertising

Semantic advertising applies semantic analysis techniques to web pages. The process is meant to accurately interpret and classify the meaning and/or main subject of the page and then populate it with targeted advertising spots. By closely linking content to advertising, it is assumed that the viewer will be more likely to show an interest (i.e., through engagement) in the advertised product or service.

AD SERVER MARKET STRUCTURE

Given below is a list of top ad server vendors in 2008 with figures in millions of viewers published in a Attributor survey. Since 2008 Google controls estimated 69 per cent of the online advertising market.

Vendor	Ad Viewers (millions)
Google	1,118
DoubleClick (Google)	1,079
Yahoo!	362
MSN (Microsoft)	309
AOL	156
Adbrite	73
Total	3,087

It should be noted that Google acquired DoubleClick in 2007 for a consideration of $3.1 Billion. The above survey was based on a sample of 68 million domains.

MOBILE MARKETING

Mobile marketing can refer to one of two categories of marketing. First, and relatively new, is meant to describe marketing on or with a mobile device, such as a mobile phone (this is an example of horizontal telecommunication convergence). Second, and a more traditional definition, is meant to describe marketing in a moving fashion - for example - technology road shows or moving billboards.

Although there are various definitions for the concept of mobile marketing, no commonly accepted definition exists. Mobile marketing is broadly defined as "the use of the mobile medium as a means of marketing communication" or "distribution of any kind of promotional or advertising messages to customer through wireless networks". More specific definition is the following: "using interactive wireless media to provide customers with time and location sensitive, personalized information that promotes goods, services and ideas, thereby generating value for all stakeholders".

In November 2009, the Mobile Marketing Association updated its definition of Mobile Marketing: Mobile Marketing is a set of practices that enables organizations to communicate and engage with their audience in an interactive and relevant manner through any mobile device or network. Mobile marketing is commonly known as wireless marketing. However wireless is not necessarily mobile. For instance, a consumer's communications with a Web site from a desktop computer at home, with signals carried over a wireless local area network (WLAN) or over a satellite network, would qualify as wireless but not mobile communications.

MOBILE MARKETING VIA SMS

Marketing on a mobile phone has become increasingly popular ever since the rise of SMS (Short Message Service) in the early 2000s in Europe and some parts of Asia when businesses started to collect mobile phone numbers and send off wanted (or unwanted) content.

Over the past few years SMS has become a legitimate advertising channel in some parts of the world. This is because unlike email over the public internet, the carriers who police their own networks have set guidelines and best practices for the mobile media industry (including mobile advertising). The IAB (Interactive Advertising Bureau) and the Mobile Marketing Association, as well, have established guidelines and are evangelizing the use of the mobile channel for marketers. While this has been fruitful in developed regions such as North America, Western Europe and some other countries, mobile SPAM messages (SMS sent to mobile subscribers without a legitimate and explicit opt-in by the subscriber) remain an issue in many other parts or the world, partly due to the carriers selling their member databases to third parties.

Mobile marketing via SMS has expanded rapidly in Europe and Asia as a new channel to reach the consumer. SMS initially received negative media coverage in many parts of Europe for being a new form of spam as some advertisers purchased lists and sent unsolicited content to consumer's phones; however, as guidelines are put in place by the mobile operators, SMS has become the most popular branch of the Mobile Marketing industry with several 100 million advertising SMS sent out every month in Europe alone. In North America the first cross-carrier SMS shortcode campaign was run by Labatt Brewing Company in 2002. Over the past few years mobile short codes have been increasingly popular as a new channel to communicate to the mobile consumer. Brands have begun to treat the mobile shortcode as a mobile domain name allowing the consumer to text message the brand at an event, in store and off any traditional media.

SMS services typically run off a short code, but sending text messages to an email address is another methodology. Short codes are 5 or 6 digit numbers that have been assigned by all the mobile operators in a given country for the use of brand campaign and other consumer services. The mobile operators vet every application before provisioning and monitor the service to make sure it does not diverge from its original service description. Besides short codes, inbound SMS is very often based on long numbers (international number format, e.g. +44 7624 805000), which can be used in place of short codes or premium-rated short messages for SMS reception in several applications, such as product promotions and campaigns. Long numbers are internationally available, as well as enabling businesses to have their own number, rather than short codes which are usually shared across a number of brands. Additionally, long numbers are non-premium inbound numbers.

One key criterion for provisioning is that the consumer opts in to the service. The mobile operators demand a double opt in from the consumer and the ability for the consumer to opt out of the service at any time by sending the word STOP via SMS. These guidelines are established in the MMA Consumer Best Practices Guidelines which are followed by all mobile marketers in the United States.

MOBILE MARKETING VIA MMS

MMS mobile marketing can contain a timed slideshow of images, text, audio and video. This mobile content is delivered via MMS (Multimedia Message Service). Nearly all new phones produced with a color screen are capable of sending and receiving standard MMS message. Brands are able to both send (mobile terminated) and receive (mobile originated) rich content through MMS A2P (application-to-person) mobile networks to mobile subscribers. In some networks, brands are also able to sponsor messages that are sent P2P (person-to-person).

A good example of MMS mobile originated Motorola's ongoing campaigns at House of Blues venues where the brand allows the consumer to send their mobile photos to the LED board in real-time as well as blog their images online.

IN-GAME MOBILE MARKETING

There are essentially four major trends in mobile gaming right now: interactive real-time 3D games, massive multi-player games and social networking games. This means a trend towards more complex and more sophisticated, richer game play. On the other side, there are the so-called casual games, i.e. games that are very simple and very easy to play. Most mobile games today are such casual games and this will probably stay so for quite a while to come.

Brands are now delivering promotional messages within mobile games or sponsoring entire games to drive consumer engagement. This is known as mobile advergaming or Ad-funded mobile game.

MOBILE WEB MARKETING

Advertising on web pages specifically meant for access by mobile devices is also an option. The Mobile Marketing Association provides a set of guidelines and standards that give the recommended format of ads, presentation, and metrics used in reporting. Google, Yahoo, and other major mobile content providers have been selling advertising placement on their properties for years already as of the time of this writing. Advertising networks focused on mobile properties and advertisers are also available.

MOBILE MARKETING VIA BLUETOOTH

The rise of Bluetooth started around 2003 and a few companies in Europe have started establishing successful businesses. Most of these businesses offer "hotspot" systems which consist of some kind of content-management system with a Bluetooth distribution function. This technology has the advantages that it is permission-based, has higher transfer speeds and is also a radio-based technology and can therefore not be billed (i.e. is free of charge). The likely earliest device built for mobile marketing via Bluetooth was the context tag of the AmbieSense project (2001-2004). More recently Tata Motors conducted one of the biggest Bluetooth marketing campaigns in India for its brand the Sumo Grande and more of such activities have happened for brands like Walt Disney promoting their movie 'High School Musical'

MOBILE MARKETING VIA INFRARED

Infrared is the oldest and most limited form of mobile Marketing. Some European companies have experimented with "shopping window marketing" via free Infrared waves in the late 90s. However, Infrared has a very limited range (~approx. 10 cm – 1meter) and could never really establish itself as a leading Mobile Marketing technology.

LOCATION-BASED SERVICES

Location-based services (LBS) are offered by some cell phone networks as a way to send custom advertising and other information to cell-phone subscribers based on their current location. The cell-phone service provider gets the location from a GPS chip built into the phone, or using radiolocation and trilateration based on the signal-strength of the closest cell-phone towers (for phones without GPS features). In the UK, networks do not use trilateration; LBS services use a single base station, with a 'radius' of inaccuracy, to determine a phone's location.

Meantime, LBS can be enabled without GPS tracking technique. Mobile WiMAX technology is utilized to give a new dimension to mobile marketing. The new type of mobile marketing is envisioned between a BS(Base Station) and a multitude of CPE (Consumer Premise Equipment) mounted on vehicle dashtops. Whenever vehicles come within the effective range of the BS, the dashtop CPE with LCD touchscreen loads up a set of icons or banners of individually different shapes that can only be activated by finger touches or voice tags. On the screen, a user has a frame of 5 to 7 icons or banners to choose from, and the frame rotates one after another. This mobile WiMAX-compliant LBS is privacy-friendly and user-centric, when compared with GPS-enabled LBS. In July 2003 the first location-based services to go Live with all UK mobile network operators were launched.

USER-CONTROLLED MEDIA

Mobile marketing differs from most other forms of marketing communication in that it is often user (consumer) initiated (mobile originated, or MO) message, and requires the express consent of the consumer to receive future communications. A call delivered from a server (business) to a user (consumer) is called a mobile terminated (MT) message. This infrastructure points to a trend set by mobile marketing of consumer controlled marketing communications. Due to the demands for more user controlled media, mobile messaging infrastructure providers have responded by developing architectures that offer applications to operators with more freedom for the users, as opposed to the network-controlled media. Along with these advances to user-controlled Mobile Messaging 2.0, blog events throughout the world have been implemented in order to launch popularity in the latest advances in mobile technology. In June 2007, Airwide Solutions became the official sponsor for the Mobile Messaging 2.0 blog that provides the opinions of many through the discussion of mobility with freedom.

PRIVACY CONCERNS IN MOBILE MARKETING

Mobile advertising has become more and more popular. However, a great part of the overall mobile advertising is sent without a required permission from the consumer causing privacy violations. It should be understood that irrespective of how well advertising messages are designed and how many additional possibilities they provide, if consumers do not have confidence that their privacy will be protected, this will hinder their widespread deployment.

The privacy issue became even more salient as it was before with the arrival of mobile data networks. A number of important new concerns emerged mainly stemming from the fact that mobile devices are intimately personal and are always with the user, and four major concerns can be identified: mobile spam, personal identification, location information and wireless security.

PROPOSED CHANGES TO THE EXISTING LEGISLATION

Because the current telecom regulations are outdated in the EU and in the United States particularly concerning unsolicited commercial communications and the spam issue new legislation should be imposed. New laws should be more clear (simple), flexible and comprehensive but still address only those issues, which are strictly necessary. This is important because laws should promote competition, encourage investment, cut unnecessary costs, and remove obstacles to doing business.

They should be drafted in a technologically neutral way to avoid the need to adapt the legal framework constantly to new developments and independent from the parties involved. Consumers' privacy must be protected and marketers have to be able easily to understand and comply with the rules. Kaspersen Henrik W.K. has proposed that directives with regard to unsolicited commercial communications should regulate not only electronic communications but also paper distribution. Moreover legislator should cooperate with technological and business experts to create a reasonable legal framework.

Application of these rules must be done in a sensible manner thus courts should avoid applying new rules with too much severity because there is a risk of retarding or limiting the development of a very promising industry.But with too loose interpretation of the rules, consumers' may not feel protected which may also limit the development. In other words if consumers concerns about privacy are not addressed, the growth of mobile advertising may be endangered by the same lack of consumer trust that has discouraged the growth of email marketing. The protection of privacy shall be achieved in combination with a number of efforts including legislation, social norms, business practices and technical means.

COLLABORATIVE FILTERING: ADVERTISING EFFICIENCY

Collaborative filtering (CF) is the process of filtering for information or patterns using techniques involving collaboration among multiple agents, viewpoints, data sources, etc. Applications of collaborative filtering typically involve very large data sets. Collaborative filtering methods have been applied to many different kinds of data including sensing and monitoring data - such as in mineral exploration, environmental sensing over large areas or multiple sensors; financial data - such as financial service institutions that integrate many financial sources; or in electronic commerce and web 2.0 applications where the focus is on user data, etc. The remainder of this discussion focuses on collaborative filtering for user data, although some of the methods and approaches may apply to the other major applications as well.

The method of making automatic predictions (filtering) about the interests of a user by collecting taste information from many users (collaborating). The underlying assumption of CF approach is that those who agreed in the past tend to agree again in the future. For example, a collaborative filtering or recommendation system for television tastes could make predictions about which television show a user should like given a partial list of that user's tastes (likes or dislikes). Note that these predictions are specific to the user, but use information gleaned from many users. This differs from the simpler approach of giving an average (non-specific) score for each item of interest, for example based on its number of votes.

METHODOLOGY

Collaborative filtering systems usually take two steps:

1. Look for users who share the same rating patterns with the active user (the user whom the prediction is for).
2. Use the ratings from those like-minded users found in step 1 to calculate a prediction for the active user.

Alternatively, item-based collaborative filtering popularized by Amazon.com (users who bought x also bought y) and first proposed in the context of rating-based collaborative filtering by Vucetic and Obradovic in 2000, proceeds in an item-centric manner:

- Build an item-item matrix determining relationships between pairs of items

- Using the matrix, and the data on the current user, infer his taste

See, for example, the Slope One item-based collaborative filtering family. Another form of collaborative filtering can be based on implicit observations of normal user behavior (as opposed to the artificial behavior imposed by a rating task). In these systems you observe what a user has done together with what all users have done (what music they have listened to, what items they have bought) and use that data to predict the user's behavior in the future or to predict how a user might like to behave if only they were given a chance. These predictions then have to be filtered through business logic to determine how these predictions might affect what a business system ought to do. It is, for instance, not useful to offer to sell somebody some music if they already have demonstrated that they own that music or, considering another example, it is not useful to suggest more travel guides for Paris to someone who already bought a travel guide for this city.

In the age of information explosion such techniques can prove very useful as the number of items in only one category (such as music, movies, books, news, web pages) have become so large that a single person cannot possibly view them all in order to select relevant ones. Relying on a scoring or rating system which is averaged across all users ignores specific demands of a user, and is particularly poor in tasks where there is large variation in interest, for example in the recommendation of music. However, there are other methods to combat information explosion, for example web search, data clustering, and more.

HISTORY

Collaborative filtering stems from the earlier system of information filtering, where relevant information is brought to the attention of the user by observing patterns in previous behaviour and building a user profile. This system was essentially unable to help with exploration of the web and suffered from the cold-start problem that new users had to build up tendencies before the filtering was effective.

The first system to use collaborative filtering was the Information Tapestry project at Xerox PARC . This system allowed users to find documents based on previous comments by other users. There were many problems with this system as it only worked for small groups of people and had to be accessed through word specific queries which largely defeated the purpose of collaborative filtering.

The first system with proven results was the Bellcore Video Recommender USENET Net news furthered collaborative filtering such that it was available for a mass scale of users while having a simpler method for accessing articles. The system allowed users to rate material based on popularity, which then allowed other users to search for articles based on these ratings. One of the largest early collaborative filtering services for music recommendations widely available on the World Wide Web was Firefly, which evolved from early MIT Media Lab research projects. Firefly was bought by Microsoft in 1998. The service itself was closed down in 1999 with much of its technology and staff helping to create Microsoft Passport.

TYPES

Memory-Based

This mechanism uses user rating data to compute similarity between users or items. This is used for making recommendations. This was the earlier mechanism and is used in many commercial systems. It is easy to implement and is effective. Typical examples of this mechanism are neighborhood based CF and item-based/user-based top-N recommendations.

The neighborhood-based algorithm calculates the similarity between two users or items, produces a prediction for the user taking the weighted average of all the ratings. Similarity computation between items or users is an important part of this approach. Multiple mechanisms such as Pearson correlation and vector cosine based similarity are used for this.

The user based top-N recommendation algorithm identifies the k most similar users to an active user using similarity based vector model. After the k most similar users are found, their corresponding user-item matrices are aggregated to identify the set of items to be recommended. A popular method to find the similar users is the Locality sensitive hashing, which implements the nearest neighbor mechanism in linear time.

The advantages with this approach is the explainability of the results, which is an important aspect of recommendation systems. It is easy to create and use. New data can be added easily and incrementally. It need not consider the content of the items being recommended. The mechanism scales well with co-rated items.

There are several disadvantages with this approach. First, it depends on human ratings. Second, its performance decreases when data gets sparse, which is frequent with web related items. This prevents the scalability of this approach and has problems with large datasets. Third, it cannot handle new users or new items.

Model-Based

Models are developed using data mining, machine learning algorithms to find patterns based on training data. These are used to make predictions for real data. There are many model based CF algorithms. These include Bayesian Networks, clustering models, latent semantic models such as singular value decomposition, probabilistic latent semantic analysis, Multiple Multiplicative Factor, Latent Dirichlet allocation, markov decision process based models.

This approach has a more holistic goal to uncover latent factors that explain observed ratings. Most of the models are based on creating a classification or clustering technique to identify the user based on the test set. The number of the parameters can be reduced based on types of principal component analysis.

There are several advantages with this paradigm. It handles the sparsity better than memory based ones. This helps with scalability with large data sets. It improves the prediction performance. It gives an intuitive rationale for the recommendations.

The disadvantages with this approach are in the expensive model building. One needs to have a tradeoff between prediction performance and scalability. One can lose useful information due to reduction models. A number of models have difficulty explaining the predictions.

HYBRID

A number of applications combines the memory-based and the model-based CF algorithms. These overcome the limitations of native CF approaches. It improves the prediction performance. Importantly, it overcomes the CF problems such as sparsity and loss of information. However, they have increased complexity and are expensive to implement.

APPLICATIONS

In Commercial Systems

Commercial sites that implement collaborative filtering systems include:

- Amazon
- Amie Street
- Barilliance
- Barnes and Noble
- Baynote
- ChoiceStream
- Collarity
- Digg.com
- eBay
- Google News
- Gravity R&D
- half.ebay.com
- Heeii
- Hollywood Video
- Hulu
- iLike - music
- Internet Movie Database - movies
- iTunes - music

- Last.fm - music
- LibraryThing - books
- Loomia - software-as-a-service provider of recommendation technologies
- Musicmatch
- MyStrands - developer of social recommendation technologies
- Netflix - In order to improve its algorithm Netflix has launched a competition, the Netflix Prize.
- Simania - Book recommendation site
- Strands - Strands utilizes and commercializes its own recommendation engine for social networks and eCommerce.
- StumbleUpon - websites
- Threadless - T-shirt
- TiVo
- Yelp
- Ramkol - Sophisticated recommendation for local search in Israel

In Non-commercial Systems

Table. Non-commercial Sites that Implement Collaborative Filtering Systems Include

Service	Type
AmphetaRate	RSS articles
Everyone's a Critic	movies
GiveALink.org	websites
Gnomoradio	music (free)
MovieLens	movies
Rate Your Music	music

SHOCK ADVERTISING

Shock advertising or Shockvertising is a type of advertising generally regarded as one that "deliberately, rather than inadvertently, startles and offends its audience by violating norms for social values and personal ideals." It is the employment in advertising or public relations of "graphic imagery and blunt slogans to highlight" a public policy issue, goods, or services. Shock advertising is designed principally to break through the advertising "clutter" to capture attention and create buzz, and also to attract an audience to a certain brand or bring awareness to a certain public service issue, health issue, or cause (e.g., urging drivers to use their seatbelts, promoting STD prevention, bringing awareness of racism and other injustices, or discouraging smoking among teens).

This form of advertising is often controversial, disturbing, explicit and crass, and may entail bold and provocative political messages that challenge the public's conventional understanding of the social order. This form of advertising may not only offend but can also frighten as well, using scare tactics and elements of fear to sell a product or deliver a public service message, making a "high impact." In the advertising business, this combination of frightening, gory and/or offensive advertising material is known as "shockvertising" and is often considered to have been pioneered by Benetton, the Italian clothing retailers which created the line United Colors of Benetton, and its advertisements in the late 1980s. Shockvertising is a portmanteau of shocking and advertising.

THE SHOCK FACTOR

Shock advertisements can be shocking and offensive for a variety of reasons, and violation of social, religious, and political norms can occur in many different ways. They can include a disregard for tradition, law or practice (e.g., lewd or tasteless sexual references or obscenity), defiance of the social or moral code (e.g., vulgarity, brutality, nudity, or profanity) or the display of images or words that are horrifying, terrifying, or repulsive (e.g., gruesome or revolting scenes, or violence). . Some advertisements may be considered shocking, controversial or offensive not because of the way that the advertisements communicate their messages but because the products themselves are "unmentionables" not to be openly presented or discussed in the public sphere.

Examples of these "unmentionables" may include cigarettes, feminine hygiene products, or contraceptives. However, there are several products, services or messages that could be deemed shocking or offensive to the public. For example, advertisements for weight loss programs, sex/gender related products, clinics that provide AIDS and STD testing, funeral services, groups that advocate for less gun control, casinos which naturally support and promote gambling could all be considered controversial and offensive advertising because of the products or messages that the advertisements are selling. Shocking advertising content may also entail improper or indecent language, like French Connection's "fcuk" campaign.

EFFECTS ON CONSUMERS

Advertisers, psychiatrists, and social scientists have long debated the effectiveness of shock advertising. One finding suggests "shocking content in an advertisement significantly increases attention, benefits memory, and positively influences behavior." The same study also shows that consumers are more likely to remember shocking advertising content over advertising content that is not shocking. However, there is still little information on whether shock advertising directly leads to an increase in sales revenue or to changes in behavior. There are social scientists, psychiatrists, media scholars, and child and family advocates who fear that overexposure to shock advertising will result in a public that is "desensitized" to advertisements that employ shock tactics, particularly those with overtly sexual and violent images.

12

The Role of Media Communications in Developing Tourism

Media communications technologies are imperative for frontline investments for sustainable globalised tourism development indicators. The powerful effects of media communications technologies can dawn on the African continent with sweeping changes of attitudes and behaviour among the key actors in local, national and global tourism for peace, security and sustainable development. The social, cultural, economic, political and environmental benefits of tourism would usher in monumental and historic changes in the African Union. As the verdict goes, the media has a social responsibility to enhance the blending of local, national and international cultural values for enriched politics, society and economy in Africa.

Public communications strategy based on access to quality information and knowledge will drive the new global tourism partnership for Africa to heal the current North-South widening gaps through partnership initiatives such as: peace and security, conflict resolutions for eco-tourism, quality tourism, joint ventures, technology transfer, exchange bids, subject-to-subject attitude, being explicit about values, transparency in interests, clear standards, sticking to mutual agreements, capacity building and development, institutional building and observance of tourism ethical standards.

Development communication is one of the best ways to go in developing eco-tourism in Africa. This strategy involves the planned communication component of programmes designed to change the attitudes and behaviour of specific groups of people in specific ways through person-to-person communication, mass media, traditional media or community communication. It is aims at the delivery of services and the interface between service deliverers and beneficiaries where people are empowered to by informed choice, education, motivation and facilitation effecting the expected changes.

This can be done by media advocacy targeting all key stakeholders involved in the tourism industry. Effective use of communication techniques can barriers and promote better uses participatory message design which combines both traditional and modern media. Participatory communication strategy design methodology is used to build on the results of the participatory rural communication appraisal. It involves a systematic process for participatory communication strategy design, and the principles for communication planning, message development, multimedia material production and the implementation of communication activities in the field.

BRITISH WAR-TIME PREMIER SIR CHURCHILL SAW THE "PEARL OF AFRICA"

Some of the basic concepts and principles of ecotourism rotate on catchwords like: environmentally and culturally-oriented tourism; conservation of natural resource enhancement tourism; local community based socio-economic welfare tourism; participatory community development of tourism. Uganda is emerging from years of political instability and entrenched poverty. Soon after 1971 military coup which ousted President Milton Obote from office, Uganda's flourishing tourism industry was dealt a death blow by a series of political upheavals and social turbulence which ravaged tourism industry in the country. Tourism is now waking up once more in Uganda, a country which was once described as the "Pearl of Africa", by the British war-time Premier, Sir Winston Churchill. Uganda's unique rich biodiversity makes it a natural candidate for ecotourism industry because tourism is currently the best product and service which Uganda can market globally with increasing competitiveness.

Some of the key principles of sustainable tourism development include the following:

- Tourism should be initiated with the help of broad-based community-inputs and the community should maintain control of tourism development;
- Tourism should provide quality employment to its community residents and a linkage between the local businesses and tourism should be established;
- A code of practice should be established for tourism at all levels - national, regional, and local - based on internationally accepted standards.

Eco-tourism seeks to provide yardsticks for tourism activities, environment impact assessment and auditing. Sustainable tourism guarantees the optimal use of environmental and natural resources for sustainable development among government, the private sector and communities. Ecotourism is sustainable tourism that caters for the ecological conservation of both human and natural ecology.

THE CHALLENGES AND ISSUES IN DEVELOPING ECO-TOURISM POLICY

There are some basic challenges and issues affecting the development of sustainable tourism policy in Uganda and the rest of Africa. A glance at the current Uganda's Tourism, Trade and Industry policy and working documents, depicts the country more or less as a plausible "work-in-progress". The ministry has a policy desk. The role of ministry is to formulate and support strategies, plans and programs that promote and ensure expansion and diversification of tourism, trade, cooperatives, environmentally sustainable industrialization, appropriate technology, conservation and preservation of other tradable national products, to generate wealth for poverty eradication and benefit the country socially and economically.

Since 1990, the World Bank and Global Environmental Facility have stepped up investment development for conservation potentials of ecotourism. In 1995, GEF initiated a US$4 million ecotourism project in Uganda, and a similar initiative was planned for Zimbabwe. Ugandan law protects national parks and reserves for the highest conservation standards. The main snag here is inadequate resources to monitor legal and policy compliance, although a project component was launched to provide effective patrols and economic incentives to the local communities. The media would be instrumental in communications campaigns and better coverage. Media campaigns could be an effective check on the unscrupulous activities of eco-tourist agents or agencies including the public sector actors.

Although the Ugandan National Environmental Action Plan covers the whole country, its implementation has been ignored in some parts of the country due to poverty. There is a huge uncertainty about the sustainability of the current ecotourism initiatives in the county on the grounds that the current formula for revenue sharing among the stakeholders cheats the operators. The national tourism policy was formulated to promote economy and livelihood of people, especially poverty reduction development of sustainable and quality tourism.

Though the number of tourists has significantly increased by about 68.18 per cent between 2003 and 2004, the visitors' numbers to protected areas is relatively lower due to inadequate security situation in some protected areas, and lack of implementation of a sound marketing strategy and the new tourism safety plan. Tourism plays a major role in Uganda's economic development. But over the years, the industry has suffered bad publicity which has contributed to its slow progress.

For example, the protracted civil strife in Northern and Western parts of Uganda has affected tourism development in the country for peace and security reasons. Uganda has registered low figures from its major tourists' sources like UK and USA. Urgent challenges facing tourism sector in Uganda are: institutional weakness; lack of appropriate legislations and legal framework; pressure on the protected areas; local conversion of land for alternative uses; and lack of funding to run the industry. Greening tourism industry is a multidisciplinary approach aimed at: better dispersion of tourism in time and space; promotion of environmental friendly forms of tourism;

reduction of private car use in favour of public transportation; better management of mass tourism; and eco-awareness of tourists. A lot of local initiatives to prevent gross pollution by waste- soft drink-cans, plastic bags, mineral water bottles.

EU tourism development issues are: public and industry awareness of the dangers of mass tourism; development of eco-tourism; more responsible management of tourism at member-states level; the exponential development of tourism sector; development of environmentally friendly tourist activities; the undermining of environmental policies in sensitive areas by tourist activities; lack of clear regional strategy for promoting a more environmentally friendly tourism; and the fact that tourism sector's environmental impact can't be fully evaluated because of the fragmentary nature of information available.

PEACE AND SECURITY ISSUES IN UGANDA'S TOURISM ECO-INDUSTRY

Gorilla tourism in Uganda was suspended for several years in order to avoid the risks of very frequent gorillas-human interactions for a while. Uganda's tourism industry is quite small owing to the emerging ecosystems investment development in the country. There is cause to fear that some of the ecosystem elements may be affected by local people who are less informed about the current eco-conservation guidelines. There are several environmental problems in and around the biodiversity rich conservation zones in Uganda. In some cases many people found themselves in these areas as a result of civil wars, abject poverty in their villages, and poor social service delivery by both the local and central governments.

Rapid deforestation in Uganda is nationwide in both urban and rural local communities mainly as a result of eco-suicidal government investment projects and the overwhelming national dependence on biomass fuel for cooking, boiling, lighting, drying and space heating. Increasing numbers of visitors also increase demand for fuel. Rich biodiversity are being abused by eco-illiterate tourists who roam their natural habitats. The lands within the Bwindi and Mgahinga parks are part of the threatened Afro-montane forest. The only remaining population of the highly endangered mountain gorilla lives in Uganda. In August 1989, the Ugandan game department stopped gorilla tourism on the advice of biologists.

Deaths of gorillas as a result of human contact and infection had been reported in neighbouring countries. There was also a notable lack of professional supervision over Ugandan gorilla habitats. After the ban, steps to be taken to implement governmental policies for the integration of conservation into tourism were defined. More generally, tourists, even ecotourists, may not be so utterly conscious as to not litter along their way. Uganda's Bwindi Impenetrable Forest is home to not less than 300 mountain gorillas, which stand for about half of the world's species' population.

PROSPECTS AND PROBLEMS OF ECO-TOURISM DEVELOPMENT ACTIVITIES IN UGANDA

In 1991, the local farmers living near Bwindi Rainforest Park in Uganda were legally prevented from accessing the traditional areas where they used to harvest firewood and herbs as a result of a new conservation project set up by an NGO. The alienation of the poor farmers caused a stir but it was rectified by involving the local farmers in environmental, economic and community development activities. Their interests were met when some of the US$4 million GEF project money was used to build health clinics, schools, fund the park management and eco-research. The European Development fund is also funding Uganda sustainable tourism development programme to strengthen tourism industry to benefit the rural communities in the protected areas and to develop the current community tourism projects there.

Due to the current slow performance of the industry in Uganda, there are still very few new investment development initiatives so far. The ministry is under funded and there is little wonder that the result has been minimal development. Uganda's national tourism industry's has some of the most enthusiastic private sector actors. Unfortunately they are less professionally equipped to perform their perceived role in the industry. The current legislations guiding the development of tourism in Uganda are under review and the proposed human resources development programmes have not yet got off the ground. The tourism sector in Uganda is still underutilized, under capitalized, underdeveloped, and the private sector is paying a high price due to low profit margins from their reinvestment. There is a loud cry for a big improvement in the quality and standards of services, products and operations in the business .There is evidence of poor performance and slow investments in the enterprise.

There is weak capacity in both the public and private sectors as the single most difficult challenge. At the same time the lack of capacity in the private sector cannot be ignored. If the overall Government policy of a private sector driven industry is to be achieved, continuing work will be required to achieve success. The EU has funded the private sector foundation of Uganda to implement the institutional strengthening of private sector groups. Uganda's eco-friendliness is attested to by the creation of six more new national parks and many community-based ecotourism projects with components to curb the spread of HIV/AIDS while promoting women's rights. While the local climate is very fine, Uganda has experienced intermittent armed clashes and civil strife in the eastern Democratic Republic of Congo and the influx of refugees into the country's national parks.

Media reports indicate that the UWA is collaborating with the security agencies to monitor the security situation along Uganda's common international border with DRC. Several security measures are being implemented to ensure the safety of the tourists visiting our national parks and all the other tourist areas and the regular influx of refugees into the country is part of the national peace, security and tourism conflict situations to be handled by the government. The three neighbouring countries of Uganda, Rwanda and the DRC have planned to run a single pricing system for gorilla tourism. Each of the three Great Lakes countries provides gorilla trekking services by various tour companies.

All the three have decided to unify the procedures for booking gorilla permits, making payment refunds, providing business incentives to the private tour operators. Until recently, persistent civil and political conflicts, poaching, illegal trade and ecological degradation resulted in the decline of biodiversity loss in many parts of the country. Biodiversity poaching has plagued Uganda's tourism industry at alarming rate countrywide. It is only recently that tens of poachers have decided to either resign or retire from the poaching business in Uganda. The new found hope cuts across many African countries including the Cameroon in West Africa.

The "dark days" of poaching are predictably coming to a sober end as scores of illegal hunters have started to down their tools in response to an open amnesty by the Uganda Wildlife Authority. Until recently, Uganda was dogged by a "loud absence" of the White Rhino species from among its national biodiversity bank. The apparent climb-down by many Ugandan poachers was attributed to a national education and awareness campaigns for behavioural change in Uganda. Uganda now has six more rhinos at Ziwa Rhino sanctuary and this figure is projected reach 20 in the coming years. The country still has to come to terms with the following bottlenecks: low incomes; low public awareness at national and international levels of the potential of tourism, weak collaboration and coordination in the tourism development process and a lax commitment by private actors in the country.

Some of the key issues which put in doubt, the sustainability of Uganda's wildlife management survival are: persistent land use conflicts; cancerous poaching; illegal settlements within protected areas; eco-hostile tourists' behaviour; conflicting national laws and policies. The main objectives of the national wildlife policy 1995 are to: ensure in perpetuity for Ugandans and the global community, the wildlife resources within and outside protected areas and to enable the people of Uganda to derive ecological, economic, aesthetic, scientific and educational benefits from wildlife. The crux of the matter is to include the rural people who share much of the land with wildlife in the new business. Uganda is known for its rich wildlife species some of which are endemic in the country.

Uganda's biodiversity is ranked among the top 10 countries in the world specifically the mammalian species. The country hosts 11 per cent of the global birds and over 50 per cent of the world's mountain gorillas. The major national constraints facing the country's wildlife resources include: land use conflicts, illegal resource harvesting, policy failures, instability and civil strife, and financial constraints. The forest department in Uganda has started pilot activities in ecotourism as a viable option for non-consumptive use of forests. Infrastructure has been development in Mabira, Budongo, and Mpanga forest reserves and both sites are already registering unprecedented figures of the local and foreign eco-visitors, the current trends show.

ICTS PUBLIC CAMPAIGNS AND POLICY STRATEGIES FOR SUSTAINABLE TOURISM

African countries should promote the use of effective information and communication technology public campaigns and policy strategies for widespread adoption of sustainable tourism, peace and conflict resolution, cultural competence and mutual inter-cultural communications in the continent. The audience access to the intended information is the main determinant of the choice of media strategy to adopt for effective tourism campaign strategy. A combined mass media and interpersonal communication approaches would achieve maximum audience exposure to the intended media messages. ICT innovations should allow users to find and use relevant information and give a feedback in a similar fashion. Institutional capacity building project for protected areas management in Uganda in the ministry of tourism, trade and industry and the national tourist board of Uganda has begun.

The funding covers a national information communication and policy strategy for the country. Appropriate use of information communication technologies can increase the credibility and effectiveness of projects to improve access to quality information, transparency in public sector decision-making, capacity building in both the private and public sectors. The policy objectives of the ICTs project are to: develop a national information and communication strategy; establish a national ICT policy; promote the use of ICTs for development; implement an integrated public sector information management system; improve transparency in fiscal accountability oversights; and set up a national web-site.

Developing public communications campaigns for sustainable tourism in Africa is the bedrock for achieving sustainable development for poverty reduction in the African Union. One of the main reasons is that sustainable tourism is the basis for the attainment of sustainable peace on the continent. Tourism in Africa is synonymous with environment and natural resources. Indiscriminative destruction of our natural resources is a sure recipe for the current mass poverty in Africa. It is a living reality which deserves global approach. Awareness campaigns are critical for effective policy, constitutional and legal implementation of sustainable tourism principles, plan, goals and projects in Africa and globally. Effective information and communications strategies are crucial for policy and decision makers themselves who are often the divers of natural resources destructions on the continent.

THE EFFECTS OF MASS MEDIA ON THE CONTEMPORARY CULTURE AND SOCIETY

The media are agencies of mediation in that in reporting events they propose certain frameworks for the interpretations of those events. They mould or restructure our consciousness in socially and politically consequential manner. It can be said that the media is a part of social reality which shape our perception. A case in point is the "reality TV" programming. The reality-defining role of the TV programming is a propaganda function of the press in that each media tends to recruit public support for the political or social philosophy it favours, seeks to sell a particular political or social definition of the events it reports.

Analysts like Evans argue that the invasion of reality TV has begun and the craze is set to grow in United States and its effect will overlap to Africa due to its popularity with young audiences. Media programs such as Survivor and Big Brother have proved to be big winners for the network. Reality TV programming format meets both local and international needs because of its sensationalism and trivializations based on real situation and involving the real people. The internet transcends the censorship and regulation imposed on radio and television.

The internet granted the freedom enjoyed by print media and common carriers such as letters, mails, and cable to the public media. Through audio streaming it is possible to enhance the reach of radio signals to any part of the world. The internet's vast capacity enables each media house to exhaustively investigate and publish in-depth analyses.

Internet radio is not limited to audio as pictures,images, digital files and graphics are accesible to the users. Advertisers and their audiences can easily interact via the internet radio broadcasts. The internet technology provides interactivity with the trainer or educator and other information for business and advocacy services , internet radio could charge for listening or viewing, offer a music or video clip for free, but charge for the full song, album, or video. Chibita in Nassanga, argues that appropriate media content arises if one considers what it takes for the media in a country like Uganda, under the wave of globalization and commercialization to provide citizens with information, advice and analysis to enable them to know and pursue their rights as well as providing them with a decent range of information, the relevance of content determines the extent to which they can participate meaningfully and access vital information of public opinion, make meaningful choices and be culturally competent.

Uganda and most African countries have adopted trade liberalisation policies which have freed the airwaves in the early 1990s. Radio talk shows facilitate political competition through offering opportunities for government leaders, political groups, and civil society organizations to speak directly with and mobilize public support. The government articulates its agenda on the talk shows. At the same time, opposition politicians and civil society groups have an opportunity to challenge the government over the same issues, articulate alternative political agendas, and demand for accountability.

At another level, talk radio has turned into a civic forum through which citizens acquire information about public affairs, attempt to exert influence upward on political leaders, question, challenge, and demand accountability from official power holders, engage in public discourse and debate on collective public problems and policy, or simply let off steam. Broadcasting ranks top high as the most universal means of public communication, conveying information, entertainment, education, and persuasion.

Today the broadcasting industry has evolved into an influx of radio and television networks. In Uganda for instance the number of radio stations has grown from one in the early 1990s to more than 150 to date. Television stations have also increased from one in the same period to six to date. In the United States there are more than 12,000 radio stations, more than 3,500 TV stations, almost 11,000 cable systems and satellitedelivered programming. Frequency modulation has expanded the number of frequencies through which both radio and television broadcasts can be relayed.

Television's VHF channels have also helped to improved visibility and picture quality. The new developments in the media industry has increased the quality and variety of programmes from commercial, entertainment, educational, and infotainment formats.New developments in the broadcasting technology have made it possible to link media access toTV, radio, music, internet, services for information, shopping, games, banking and development services.There are a variety of media contents can be digitally retained, retransmitted and transported, enabling an interaction by the user, exactly at the moment that is convenient to the user.

The new media technologies have influenced most local cultures through the increased access to allien cultures. The radio has today become one of the admirable piece of work as it sells itself as a medium that reaches listeners while they drive, work, shop and jog. Advertisers like radio's ability to reach targeted audiences. The new innovations in the broadcasting industry have led to an increase in internationally syndicated programming on local radio and television in Africa.

Most of the music aired by F.M radio stations in Uganda and several African countries come from foreign productions led by U.S.A. This also applies to TV broadcasts where the bulk of the programmes are foreign content due to the cultural effects of globalisation in Africa.Media industry convergence is an emerging phenomenon in broadcasting sector on the continent. It influences the technology, media content, market shares of the revenues and public broadcasting in Africa. One of the impacts of technology convergence is the development of innovative broadcasting products and services being launched more rapidly in the market.

MEDIA COMMUNICATIONS ISSUES, CULTURE, ECO-TOURISM AND ENVIRONMENT

The media industry in Africa is instrumental in exerting its influence on the society. Rogers argues that awareness and knowledge of an innovation can be best disseminated by the mass media and that there are five stages of adoption process: awareness, interest, evaluation, trial, and adoption of the decision. During awareness stage, an individual is exposed to a new innovation without prior knowledge of it. In the next stage, one gets interested in the new idea and looks for more information on the issue. The eco-tourism industry can do no worse than adopt as its policy, the development of partnership with the media industry as its secret weapon for surviving global tourism competition. Likewise, the application of priming theory by the media would help the public to follow the political behaviour of the policy and decisionmakers on the continent.

Priming refers to the impact of news coverage on the weight assigned to specific issues in making political judgments. The issues that are highlighted in the priming theory are: responsibility, political knowledge and media trust by the audience. Interpersonal communication can mean the ability to relate to people in written or verbal communication in the context of either both a one-on-one, face-to-face and a group contacts. This requires ability to comfortably deal with all kinds of people we meet in different settings. It is body language which is seen through our behaviour or actions such as: gestures, eye contacts, body movement, dressing, appearances or presentations. Interpersonal communication is crucial during listening, talking, counselling, dressing, and conflict resolution.

The African Union should adopt new innovation communications strategy where the media plays a key role to advance eco-tourism industry-led innovation in public policies at all levels for poverty reduction on the continent. Africa should exploit the new media technology to develop the concept and practice of "lead markets" where public authorities, facilitate industry-led innovation by creating conditions for a successful market uptake of focused innovative products, processes and services for global competitiveness. Prime targets should focus on areas that respond to societal demand-driven areas such as local jobs, accommodation facilities, transport or health, peace/security and new eco-innovations. Media communications campaign must consider at least four key challenges: partnership, resources, leadership and duration.

Communications have to be opportunistic about new events, messengers, and allies. Although the campaign use many tactics to deliver its story, mass media over time play a major role in reaching decision makers and other key audiences. Some of the most serious challenges to be addressed in the development of African ecotourism industry communications environment are: media support, developing media professional skills, ensuring public broadcasting programming that meets the audiences' priorities, cultures and languages, and promoting professional ethics among the media communicators.

Media communication should be based on a multi-media approach particularly in implementing major campaigns, in working out campaigns and programmes; there should be a deliberate effort to understand the communication environment, including target groups, appropriate media platforms, messages and forms of interaction. The main measures of impacts should include: the amount of media exposure or media the campaign has gained for example from: television, radio, print, billboard, and internet. The Uganda national environment management authority has been conducting public awareness campaigns on FM radio stations and a weekly interactive TV programme in the country. Media broadcasts can be effectively used to disseminate key eco-tourism media messages across Africa. Media research is crucial because it examines the specific communication medium, the user and use of medium, the effects of the medium, how the medium can be improved, content, and the communicator.

Communication inputs and audience responses reflect on the following message design factors: production related factors, content related factors, media related factors, and audience-related factors. The latter may examine the application of the "uses and gratifications" theory which is based on the idea that media don't do things to people; but people do things with media. Media communications should be well planned and targeted for maximum audience exposure to the messages. Communicators, who wish to inform, persuade or simply hold the attention of their auditors must adapt more closely than in the past to what ordinary people find interesting, relevant and accessible. Berlo argues that there is a need to know the receiver's attitudes, level of knowledge, listening and comprehension abilities, social and cultural background to communicate more effectively.

Public service agencies which commission media campaigns in support of their goals should know that the use of several media channels and multiple presentations in a variety of eye and ear-catching formats is recommended. Slade and Weitz observed that various media such as newspapers, television and radio should be used to promote environmental values and awareness. The use of appropriate theory or model is crucial for any successful media campaigns aimed at creating, raising and sustaining public awareness for behaviour change. Coffman asserts that more theory development and theory integration for public will campaign are needed because part of the problem with the communication campaign is lack of awareness among the campaign practitioners, evaluators and their sponsors about what outcomes and methods are appropriate and available.

Hubley contends that communication strategy decisions should involve surveys to determine communication systems in a community; audience familiarity with and exposure to different media; characteristics of target groups; effectiveness of different media; opinion leaders that can be engaged in the project. Through priming theory, the media can create, raise, and sustain public awareness for sustainable tourism and "eco-guard" behaviour change. The Priming theory which in media is related to the Agenda Setting theory; is the process by which certain portions of media content are 'brought to the forefront' and other portions are relegated to the background for maximum effect. This process allows the media to exercise control over public opinion. Priming is most important when issues are new and information is scarce.

By applying The Frame Theory the media can "frame" new innovations and ecotourism policies, international conventions and best practices, community projects and regional success stories as well as lessons learned for informed public debates and awareness education in Africa. Framing is a process of selective control over media content or public communication. Framing defines how a certain piece of media content or rhetoric is packaged to allow only the desirable interpretations at the expense of others. Ugandan President Yoweri Museveni recently accused the local press of being irresponsible and irrational agents of saboteurs of Africa's future. The Ugandan media had set the agenda which sparked off a fiery nationwide eco-debate against the current government plan to supplant the biggest Uganda's natural forest by a sugarcane plantation, a move which the president himself defended, as a struggle to industrialise the pre-industrial backward African state. Uganda, with a population of over 25 million inhabitants, now has 140 radio stations and 20 TV stations.

In their efforts to inform, educate and entertain the public, the media industry in Uganda triggered off a nationwide and international public debates against the anticipated wanton destruction of about 8000 hectares of ecologically diverse Mabira natural forest which is also the host of Eco-Tourism Centre run by the National Forestry Agency of Uganda. The media according to the public sphere model are defined as central elements of a healthy public sphere-the "space" within which ideas, opinions, and views freely circulate, Croteau and Hoynes. Mwesige found that open-air talk shows provide more opportunities for citizen participation by allowing at least three minutes of talking time to an average of 15 people per show. Members of the public are also able to participate as equals in these debates, which also attract political elites. McQuail argues that according to this principle, truth triumphs over error in the end and leads to free market place of ideas; which seems to bless private ownership and the free enterprise system.

Uganda like many other African countries adopted the free enterprise system and liberalized the airwaves in the early 1990s. According to Chibita in Nassanga under the wave of globalization and commercialization to provide citizens with information, advice and analysis to enable them to know and pursue their rights as well as providing them with a decent range of information, the relevance of content determines the extent to which they can participate meaningfully and access vital information of public opinion, make meaningful choices and be culturally enriched. The media imposes a range of effects which range from insignificant, medium to great or powerful effects on the audiences in the society. Media communications across cultures include: speaking, writing, editing, information gathering, dissemination and community participation in public campaigns.

There are three main components to any communication: subject matter, medium of delivery, and cultural considerations. They are hard to define even for our own culture because we take them in with our mother's language. Global communication, transportation, and changes in living styles have begun to blur many of the surface distinctions between different cultures. There are common denominators in every cross-cultural communications which require cultural competence by tourists and their hosts. Cultural competence refers to the ability to work effectively with individuals from different cultural and ethnic backgrounds, or in settings where several cultures coexist. It includes the ability to understand the language, culture, and behaviours of other individuals and groups, and to make appropriate recommendations.

Cultural competence exists on a continuum from incompetence to proficiency. Cultural sensitivity is a necessary component of cultural competence. Effective communication between providers and clients may be even more challenging when linguistic barriers exist. Cultural competence is a developmental process that requires a long-term commitment. It is not a specific end product that occurs after a two-hour workshop, but it is an active process of learning and practicing over time. People who work among different ethnic and cultures may become culturally competent by developing awareness, acquiring knowledge, and maintaining cross-cultural skills.

Developing cultural awareness involve: admitting personal biases, stereotypes, and prejudices; becoming aware of cultural norms, attitudes, and beliefs; valuing diversity ;willingness to extend oneself psychologically and physically to the client population; recognizing comfort level in different situations; acquiring knowledge; knowing how your culture is viewed by others ;attending classes, workshops, and seminars about other cultures; reading about other cultures; watching movies and documentaries about other cultures ;attending cultural events and festivals ;sharing knowledge and experiences with others; visiting other countries -making friends with people of different cultures; establishing professional and working relationships with people of different cultures; learning another language; learning verbal and nonverbal cues of other cultures; becoming more comfortable in cross-cultural situations; assessing what works and what does not; assessing how the beliefs and behaviours of the cultural group affect the client or family; learning to negotiate between the person's beliefs and practices and the culture of your profession;

being more flexible ;attending continuing education seminars and workshops; learning to develop culturally relevant and appropriate programs, materials, and interventions; learning to evaluate culturally relevant and appropriate programs, materials, and interventions; ongoing evaluation of personal feelings and reactions ;overcoming fears, personal biases, stereotypes, and prejudices.

In order to achieve better communication skills, competitive tourism industry; the tour operators are encouraged to develop and implement a strategy to: recruit, retain, and promote qualified, diverse, and culturally competent administrative staff, clinical, and support staff; promoting and supporting the necessary attitudes, behaviours, knowledge, and skills for staff to work respectfully and effectively with clients and each other in a culturally diverse work environment; developing a comprehensive strategy to address culturally and linguistically appropriate services, including strategic goals, plans, policies, and procedures; hiring and training interpreters and bilingual staff; providing a bilingual staff or free interpretation services to clients with limited English skills; translating and making available sign and commonly used educational materials in different languages; developing structures and procedures to address cross-cultural ethical and legal conflicts, complaints, or grievances by patients and staff; preparing and distributing an annual progress report documenting the organizations' progress in implementing these standards, including information on programs, staffing, and resources.

While cultural competence has increased significantly, there is still much to be done on the personal, organizational, and societal levels. Education and training to enhance the provision of culturally effective health care must be integrated into lifelong learning. As intercultural contact increases, norms from one culture may appear strange or shocking to people from another culture, but the key to improving cross-cultural dialogue is to develop what is known as cultural competence or the ability to recognize cultural differences, rather than judging another culture by the norms of your own. Cultural competence allows educators and communicators to work effectively in cross-cultural situations. Becoming culturally competent means not only learning about other cultures, but also learning which of our own traits and don't have to travel to find different cultures.

All environmental educators and communicators should be culturally competent to reach diverse audiences both at home and abroad. People who work in foreign lands should learn the cultures of their hosts. There are many major world cultures with common patterns of behaviour including common thought, communication styles, actions, customs, arts, beliefs, and values that are all framed by a worldview. Environmental communicators must be aware of how culture, along with gender and other factors, influences how people interpret our messages. Culturally sensitive and appropriate messages are very effective. Effective communication leads to greater homophily between the communicators.

Nonverbal communication methods vary among cultures as such understanding cultural components of nonverbal communication including body language, gestures, and concepts of space and time, are essential to effective cross-cultural communication. The media is the major source of information followed by schools. Effective environmental communicators should consider culture at the first stage of the audience research, followed by pre-testing messages and materials as the message may be interpreted differently across-cultures. The media has drawn the attention of the public on sensitive ecological issues and trends. Uganda media recently locked-horns with the government when it gave extensive coverage on the impending government plan to replace the country's legally gazetted natural forest with a sugarcane plantation. The streets of Kampala capital city soon overflowed with eco-demonstrators with fatal consequences when the police force opened fire on the protesting crowds.

Media communications raised awareness and political impact on public opinion prompted a fresh political rethinking by the government. It is well known that human-induced climate change and the loss of biodiversity are the key global environmental issues today. The media should intensify campaigns to raise awareness and shift public opinion. Conservation communicators must make the issues relevant for a highly confused public. In UK, government targets concerning the quality of protected areas are now embedded in policy. Recent proposals for major infrastructure projects which were expected to impinge on protected sites like the Hastings Bypasses and the Dibden Bay port development were rejected despite a strong economic argument aggressively made in their support. Sustainable tourism plays a pivotal role in the conservation of natural and cultural heritage.

It caters for the welfare of the local and indigenous communities in its development and operation, contributing to their well-being; interprets the natural and cultural heritage of the destination to visitors; and lends itself better to independent travellers, as well as to organized tours for small size groups. Developing public communications campaigns for sustainable tourism in Africa is the bedrock for achieving sustainable development for poverty reduction in the African Union. One of the main reasons is that sustainable tourism is the basis for the attainment of sustainable peace on the continent. Tourism in Africa is synonymous with environment and natural resources. Indiscriminative destruction of our natural resources is a sure recipe for the current mass poverty in Africa. It is a living reality which deserves global approach. Awareness campaigns are critical for effective policy, constitutional and legal implementation of sustainable tourism principles, plan, goals and projects in Africa and globally.

Effective media communications strategies are crucial for policy and decision makers themselves who are often the drivers of natural resources destructions on the continent. Public awareness communications campaigns provide vital information and knowledge for community empowerment for active participation in eco-tourism project planning and management in Africa. An effective media campaign fosters national, regional and international collaboration among the eco-tourism development partners: the private sector investors, the civil society, the policy makers, and the local communities in the industry. Media practitioners, project monitors and evaluators benefit from the awareness campaigns for better insights for improved campaigns strategies. The campaigns help to speed up the implementation of the legal and policy instruments. They provide the energy for the vital attitudinal and behaviour change as they accord respect and transparency to the whole campaign process.

Media campaigns are human rights issues which should be enshrined in the legal provisions for access to public information. Media campaigns, as a strategy, are crucial for objective verification and analyses of key eco-tourism promotional and investment issues on the continent of Africa. Sustainable tourism awareness campaigns could be rapidly created, raised and sustained throughout Africa, Americas, Australia, Europe, Asia and globally. Many media practitioners and professionals agree that media campaigns would result in effective eco-tourism policy and project implementation in Africa. Public service agencies which commission media campaigns in support of their goals should know that the use of several media channels and multiple presentations in a variety of eye and ear-catching formats is recommended. Media campaigns should be guided by informed ethical, theoretical and sustainable tourism factors. The campaigns should be systematic from inputs to outputs.

The process should be evaluated. Public communications campaigns are varied, multifaceted, highly planned, and strategically assembled media symphonies designed to increase awareness, inform, or change behaviour in the target audiences. The goal of environmental communications campaigns is to instil in learners the knowledge about the environment, positive attitudes toward the environment, and competency in communities in environment and natural resources management skills and gender-equity empowerment. Communications campaign models act as road-maps as they guide the campaign managers how to proceed. The measures of effect that come about in the target populations or communities as a result of the campaign include: knowledge and awareness, saliency, attitudes, norms, self-efficacy, behaviour intentions, behaviour, skills, environmental constraints, media frames, policy change and impacts.

Media research examines the medium, user and use of medium, effects of the medium, how the medium can be improved, content, and the communicator as many media scholars have argued. Communication inputs and audience responses reflect on the following message design factors: production related factors, content related factors, media related factors, and audience-related factors. The media can also apply the "uses and gratifications" theory, the idea that media don't do things to people; but people do things with media. Communicators, who wish to inform, persuade or simply hold the attention of their auditors must adapt more closely than in the past to what ordinary people find interesting, relevant and accessible.

We need to know the receiver's attitudes, level of knowledge, listening and comprehension abilities, social and cultural background to communicate more effectively. Public service agencies which commission media campaigns in support of their goals should know that the use of several media channels and multiple presentations in a variety of eye and ear-catching formats is recommended. Multi-media channels like: newspapers, television and radio are vital for promoting environmental values and awareness in Uganda with a focus on community participation in creating awareness among individuals. There is a need for more theory development and theory integration, particularly for public will campaign because part of the problem with the communication campaign is lack of awareness among the campaign practitioners, evaluators, and sponsors about what outcomes and methods are appropriate and available. Media communication strategy decisions should involve surveys to determine communication systems in community; familiarity with and exposure to different media; characteristics of target groups; effectiveness of different media; opinion leaders that can be used in the programme.

Through priming theory, the media can raise awareness about this new gender based convention. Priming theory in media is related to the agenda setting theory. Priming is the processes by which certain portions of media content are "brought to the forefront" while other portions are relegated to the background. This allows the media to exercise control over public opinion. Priming is most effective when issues are new and information is scarce. The media should focus on practical community and gender needs for ecotourism policy. The media can "frame" some of the most important ecotourism issues in Africa for public debates and awareness education. Framing is a process of selective control over media content or public communication. Framing defines how a certain piece of media content or rhetoric is packaged to expose only the desirable frames at the expense of others. The first and foremost main ingredients of successful public communication campaigns that are designed to change behaviour is increasing knowledge and awareness as the starting point.

Communications campaigns are one of the policy areas for non-formal environmental education in Uganda where the key programme areas identified include: networking and co-ordination, development of EE training materials, development of environmental resource and information centres, public awareness media campaigns, research, development of training manuals, strengthening the role of indigenous knowledge and practice in EE and integrating gender issues into environmental policy planning, and implementation. Most "eco-suicidal" decisions made in Uganda and the rest of Africa are motivated by official corruption involving the state actors under the pretext of foreign investments. Corruption is a formidable poverty driver which shows no signs of abetting in most African Union states. Uganda government defines corruption as the use of public office for private gain.

This covers: embezzlement, nepotism, favoritism, selfdealing, insider trading, influence peddling, or the use of public office or assets for political advantage. Official surveys regularly conducted in the country by the national "Ombudsman" show that most Ugandans believe that state corruption by the government is cancerous. Uganda government says it hopes to: strengthen the law enforcement capacity for investigation, prosecution and judgments, procurement system; public sector reform; public financial accountability; coordination of anticorruption agencies; codes of conduct, corruption laws, and "allow" the civil society to monitor official corruption in the country. It is only an informed public that can contribute to the reduction of state corruption in Africa. Media campaigners can frame some of the key eco-tourism issues in Africa for public awareness education.

TEACHING TOURISM, IMAGE AND MEDIA RELATIONSHIPS

CONCEPTUAL FOUNDATION

The relationship between tourism and image has received a lot of coverage in the tourism literature.

The extensive relationship between image and tourism has been presented in the literature for its role in:

- Creating expectations;
- Marketing strategy and market segmentation;
- Destination selection;
- As a form of consumption;
- Construction and reinforcing images of people and place;
- Effects on prospective markets

Conceptually the investigation of these roles provides great insights into the field of tourism. Additionally there are enormous practical implications of these roles of image. This perspective is very much functional, though it is acknowledged and appreciated that the power of image presentation and interpretation creates or reinforce gazes, and in this there is a critical cultural interpretation and definition of what image is, means and does. To briefly expand and clarify, a functional perspective focuses on the function of image, and especially the importance in marketing and destination selection. This perspective also focuses on the formation of image from the individual's perspective.

This initially started in the role for planning and marketing though, as a greater understanding of the significance of destination image has occurred, there has been an orientation towards processes of image formation and building an understanding of the specific parts of image that influence decision-making. It must be noted that the critical cultural perspective related to representation and the cultural, political or social context within which they take place was also included within the unit.

Additionally, the literature is identifying the source of image as coming increasingly from the media and particularly the mass media. Thus, it was concluded that image is a very important conceptual and managerial area of tourism, though this is increasingly being provided and determined by the media.

Additionally it was noted that in image formation that the organic and autonomous agents were perceived as the most credible. Nonetheless, there had instead been a predominate focus on real agents of destinations, and reference to induced agents within the literature. Due to the importance image and of the organic agent it was proposed that this was a crucial area, over and above that of tourism or destination marketing for tourism managers to appreciate and understand. This was especially the case as pertinent to the destination manager was the management of destination image.

This had been noted as the increased competition not only for maintaining vibrant cities, but also to attract tourists in an increasingly competitive tourism environment. For destination managers an inclusive destination management strategy needs to be developed and implemented. Part of this strategy is the management of image. Also important in this process is the potential tourists' source of image, and the decreasing influence destinations have over these images.

Overall, the breadth of importance of destination image in tourism is immense, though it has been identified that image's role in the decision making process was most important for destination managers. In developing the unit there were a number of underpinnings in the relationship between image and the media as derived from the above brief review. This needed to be contextualised within the much broader tourism conceptual foundation. Based on this foundation the pertinent conceptual aspects were identified as destination image, image formation, decision-making, the media and media tourism. Pertinent management aspects identified were image management, media management, promoting place with media, and media tourism management.

STRUCTURE

The unit was designed and delivered at Waiariki Institute of Technology, Rotorua, New Zealand. It was designed as an elective third year unit within the Tourism Management degree. Within this programme, all students had completed at least three tourism units, and thus had an introductory understanding to the study of tourism. At Waiariki semesters are 15 weeks.

Considering the points above, and the need for the inclusion of pertinent aspects, the following learning objectives were identified:

- Identify and discuss the relationship between tourism and image
- Identify and discuss the formation of destination image
- Discuss the role of the media in tourism
- Discuss the role of fictional media in tourism
- Analyse films' role in tourism

The following will briefly outline the main learning achievements of each lecture time. The specific content, learning objectives and tutorial exercises of each class are included in Appendix A. In the first lecture Morgan and Pritchard was the primary reading and was used to establish the role of image in culture. Within this context, and the foundation of students' previous tourism knowledge, connections were established between the three explicit elements of tourism, image and the media.

The main connection of concern identified was between the tourist and the destination and especially how tourists form images of destinations through the media; tourist's perception of a destination, positive or negative, is based on these images; tourists form motivations to visit place and expectations about that place through these images; image is the interface between the tourist and the destination; and the media provides this image. A film, A Passage to India, was watched for this week.

The use of A Passage to India had two purposes. First the film was used to present examples of tourism and exemplify the role of media and image in tourism. Second, the film was used for students to consider the sources of images of place, how these may be modified through the media, and to exemplify the connections identified in the lecture. Students also noted their images of India prior to and after watching the film. The second lecture was to further conceptualise destination image within the framework of previous investigation. Echtner and Ritchie was used as the primary reading and complemented with Jenkins and Gallarza, Gil Saura and Garcý´a.

Within this class the definition and modelling of destination image were presented as well as creating an appreciation of the role of image in tourism. Additionally considerations of previous methods to measure destination image were also presented, including what specifically was measured and how it was measured. In this class the lists of image attributes noted before and after watching A Passage to India were positioned on Echtner and Ritchie's model of destination image.

The two modelled positions were then compared as discussed as the role of the film in changing the position of attributes and the holistic image. Week three looked more especially at the importance of destination image. Woodside and Sherrell was used as the main reading, supplemented by Um and Crompton and chapters in Nielsen. The role of destination image in decision making was especially the focus, though image management and building were also briefly covered. Within decision making the importance of the evaluative components was discussed in more detail. The Beach was watched in this class for two reasons.

First, The Beach portrayed a range of tourists and tourism. Second, it presented an exotic tourism destination with existing images in students' minds. Students noted their images of Thailand before watching the film and they additionally noted the sources of these images. The students then noted their images of Thailand after watching the film. Destination image formation was the topic for the fourth week. In this class Gartner was used as the primary reading and was supplemented with Baloglu, and McCleary, Croy and Kearsley, Fakeye and Crompton, and Mackay and Fesenmaier. Within this class emphasis was placed on the role of different sources or agents of images in creating a holistic destination image.

This was especially to differentiate the role and credibility of different agents and also to note stages within image formation where different agents played roles. The images and sources of images of Thailand were then analysed to identify differing roles of agents in the creation of the holistic image and their perceived credibility. This was also compared to the post film images to identify the role of a film in changing this image. Image management in week five specifically assessed the development of image management, especially for cities, then the advantages and processes of including image management explicitly within destination management processes. In this Barich and Kotler was used as the primary reading, and French, Gregory and Wiechmann and Teleisman-Kosuta provided the additional readings.

In this Barich and Kotler's implied image management model was presented and compared with tourism image changing practices During this week The Vertical Ray of the Sun, set and filmed in Vietnam was watched. This film was selected because it showed an alternate view of Vietnam to most other media. It also depicted a location that was increasingly identified as a tourist destination. Again students noted their images of Vietnam and the sources of these images before watching the film and their images afterwards. The week six class focused on the media. This presented first definitions and description before reviewing the study of the media, and especially the role of media in culture.

The role of this week was to contextualise media in everyday life and in this the importance of the media as a topic of study; as an industry; the interrelationship between culture and the media; and the role of the media in audience assimilation. Altheide was the primary reading for this week, supported by Grossberg, Wartella and Whitney, Nielsen and O'Shaughnessy. The tutorial time analysed the previous week's images of Vietnam, noting the roles of different types of media, their roles in image creation and possible basic strategies that Vietnam could implement to manage image. Tourism and the Media was the topic of the next class.

A chapter from Nielsen was the primary reading and supplemented by Long and another chapter from Nielsen. This week discussed the role of media in creating and enhancing place image and travel behaviour. It additionally discussed the media and tourism relationship and processes to provide for this increasingly important relationship at the destination and attraction level. In the tutorial national and regional tourism and media programmes were assessed and compared to image creation agent roles. The next three weeks looked especially at elements of fictional media tourism. Fictional media tourism is the re-building and re-imaging of associations with literary, television or film icons to promote destinations and to actively induce tourism.

Film tourism was the first of the three discussed. Croy and Walker was used as the primary reading, and supported by Busby and Klug and Riley, Baker and Van Doren. The role of film as a tourism inducing force and its possible tourism promotion role were discussed. New Zealand was then discussed as a case study of film tourism and the promotion of a country with and through film. The Lord of the Rings: The Fellowship of the Ring was watched in this class. This film was selected because it provided a local case, its recent use for destination promotion in New Zealand, and was also partially set at the location of the class fieldtrip, Hobbition. During viewing, students noted places in the film that they would most like to visit, and places they thought international tourists would most like to visit.

The students also noted locations that they recognised in the film. The second of the fictional media topics was television tourism. Tooke and Baker was used as the primary reading and was supplemented by Hanna and Beeton. Within this week the role of television in tourism and its effects were compared to that of film tourism. Though further television specific issues were also discussed including potentially longer production and post production effects. The tutorial was directed at Beeton's review of Sea Change and the identified effects of television production and tourism. Students then evaluated an invented application to produce a locally based television series for its potential impacts, positive and negative. The third fictional media tourism topic was that of literary tourism.

The primary reading for this week was Fawcett and Cormack and was supported by Herbert, Muresan and Smith and Squire. This week discussed the role of literature, past to present, in enhancing tourism. Also discussed were the similarities to film and television tourism, including that books were the basis of many films and television programmes. Additionally noted were other avenues destinations had taken in promoting themselves as book towns or with book festivals. The tutorial was allocated to Anne of Green Gables and its creation a fictional place in a real setting. Especially focused on were the impacts on the community and tourists. Building upon and similar to the previous week, students evaluated the promotion of a destination based on a book.

Week eleven was the fieldtrip to Hobbiton, Matamata. Hobbiton was used in The Lord of the Rings film trilogy depicting where the hobbits lived. In Matamata, the manager of tourism marketing in the area gave a presentation giving a background to tourism in the area, though especially the development of the campaign based on Hobbiton and The Lord of the Rings.

The class then went on a guided tour with the manager of Hobbiton, in which he provide the usual tourist trip as well as providing a lot of further background information on the site's development and use as a tourist attraction. Students also compared their expected to actual experience as a basis to critically review their process of destination image formation and to identify potential tourism impacts. Promoting place with film was the topic of week twelve.

British Tourism Authority, Tourism New Zealand and Riley and Van Doren were used as primary resources for this topic, and were supplemented by Ashworth and Voogd. The practice of destination promotion with the use of film was discussed and reviewed in previous as well as the contemporary cases of Britain and New Zealand. The Piano was the watched. It was selected as it was the first film used by Tourism New Zealand in international promotion and it provided again a local and realisable case. Students noted their images of Waitakere prior and post watching the film.

Additionally students searched for further information of The Piano and The Lord of the Rings with explicit associations with New Zealand. This was to replicate a potential film tourist's search for the actual film location. Managing the impacts of film was the topic of week thirteen's class. Beeton and Croy and Walker were the primary readings, and supported by the review of film impacts of The Lord of the Rings production by NZ Institute of Economic Research. Within this class both enhancing and mitigating the impacts of film were discussed. Potentially impacted groups were identified and then the potential production and post production impacts were discussed.

Discussion focused on different management techniques for the different effected groups and range of impacts. The tutorial assessed inducing agents of film and how these may be best managed. The fourteenth week was on the future of tourism in film. Cetron was the primary reading, and with Muller and Todd presented perspectives of the future of tourism. Total Recall was selected as it portrayed a future of actual and virtual tourism and tourists. The film was watched and the different futures of tourism depicted in the readings and film were compared and discussed. This was very closely linked with the next week where The Fifth Element was watched.

Again this was selected as it depicted another future of tourism and tourists. Again the different tourism futures were discussed. Also discussed was the role of film in the creation of these potential futures. More importantly in these two classes was an ongoing review of the importance, measurement and management of destination image undertaken by Ivan Polunin, editor of Eclipse, a tourism marketing industry journal. Polunin had sent out a list of 23 questions regarding image in tourism covering definitions, sources, roles, managing and so on. These questions were passed onto the students to answer in discussion and as a review for the unit. The experts' responses were then compared to the students' and further discussed the similarities and differences.

ASSESSMENT

In this unit there were three internal assessment items, and no external assessment item. All assessment items were individual. The three items were awarded marks out of 20, 30 and 50 marks respectively making up 100 marks for the unit. The first item was a review and media diary of New Zealand film and tourism. This had the objective to identify the significance of the film or television and tourism relationship in New Zealand, and to analyse the reported effects of this relationship.

For this assessment item students collected and presented an annotated list of at least 10 articles about film and tourism in New Zealand in the previous twelve months. In addition the students, with reference Echtner and Ritchie, Gartner and Woodside and Sherrell wrote a 1,000 word review of the images that these films created to induce tourism as reported in the media. The second assessment item was an analysis of tourism, image and film.

This item had two objectives. The first was to identify the images a film presents to possible tourists and to analyse these in a critical manner. The second objective was to provide recommendations for destination management organisations as to how best use these images for marketing. Students had to base this assessment item explicitly on a film screened in class. From this they had to compare and contrast their images, the film's images and the destination's images identified in the literature. From this basis they then had to identify and discuss the formation of positive and negative tourism inducing images. They also had to provide recommendations regarding the film's effects on image management for that country's tourism authority.

The third assessment item was to identify a film tourism opportunity and develop it. In this students had to identify, explain and put into theoretical context a fictional media site, including a description of its operations and why it exists. From this they had to compare and contrast the chosen site to Hobbiton, Matamata.

On the findings derived from the comparison students then proposed a new fictional media tourism attraction in New Zealand. The proposed new attraction was to be developed in consideration of destination image, image formation, decision making and fictional media-tourism literature. Additionally students also had to provide a brochure to summarise the entire report to attract local support and investors to the attraction.

REFLECTIONS

During and after the implementation of this unit the author undertook an explicit programme of reflections upon content, focus, assessment and student reaction. Overall the content covered the main conceptual areas, and covered them in sufficient detail and depth. This was also reflected in student feedback. The development and progression through the conceptual issues within the tourism, image and media relationship was well received. The reflection on the importance of image at the beginning of many classes also linked the progressions into the overall context of the unit and tourism. The unit, whilst inclusive of other areas of media, was focused on film, this was particularly in the assessment.

Though the students' feedback and evaluation was positive to this focus, reflecting, the author would suggest, the contemporary popularity of film. In the future it would be recommended to broaden this focus to be more explicitly inclusive of other forms of media tourism, especially in the assessment. The focus in the actual classes, tutorials and readings was broader than the assessment. The fieldtrip was an excellent learning exercise, and a great promoter of the unit. The onsite learning and the inclusion of practitioners in student learning was very well received and applied. Most locations do have film, television or literary sets near by, though the numbers that have been developed for tourism may be limited.

In locations without fictional media tourism sites, the fieldtrip could focus more on potential development of locations and the issues that could arise. The first assessment item provided a good foundation of the conceptual issues and also explored a contextual understanding of the relationship between tourism, image and the media in New Zealand. This was quite contextual as New Zealand had had much media coverage of film production and its promotion for tourism during the previous twelve months. The second assessment item did provide a good conceptual application to a film in class. An extensive possible reading list was provided with the outline and was reflected in the submitted assignments.

The objective and how it was to be achieved created confusion, which the reading list helped with, nonetheless it would be recommended to simplify the item, or more explicitly identify the process that students may use in achieving the objective. The third assessment item, again, was laborious in creating clear expectations. This too could be simplified, though would suggest changing it to reflect other management issues within the relationships between tourism image and the media. The assessment, whilst again positively received by students, could be changed to be more reflective of other tourism management issues in regards to image and the media. One tutorial exercise that worked very well and could easily be developed into an assessment item was the evaluation of impacts and development of criteria for the acceptance of film or television production in an area.

A final consideration would be the shortening of the unit for inclusion in most universities 13 week semesters. The introduction lecture and the destination image lecture could be combined. It must be noted that the introduction lecture was found to provide a great context for the unit within the student's prior learning and their knowledge about the relationship between tourism, image and the media. The final two weeks, the future of tourism in film and review could be omitted, though it would be important to include the review questions within prior weeks. It would also be necessary to allocate time to the discussion of responses of these review questions.

EFFECTS OF NEGATIVE MEDIA EVENTS ON TOURIST'S DECISIONS

'Death toll climbs in Fiji cyclone', 'Visiting Great Britain? Beware of Foot And Mouth Disease!', 'Sars Warning over Taiwan', 'Colombia closes popular parks in yellow fever scare', and the headlines about negative events keep coming. What kind of influence do the mass media have on people, and is the tourist's decision-making process influenced by what the mass media are communicating? According to there are two major ways of [re]-creating a destination image in the minds of visitors after an event has occurred. The first one is through communication in the mass media, while the second one is through a real experience. Even though Lombardi's theory seems logical, it can be criticised because there is no final definition of what he calls a 'true' image. What this paper queries is, if the mass media actually paints a true / factual picture of destinations after a crisis, or if they are more interested in boosting sales and thus creates a fictional image that is claimed to be true.

However, the net result of a perceived and real image has more or less the same outcomes which, according to Baloglu & McLeary are reduction in tourist arrivals and tourist receipts, and a change in visitor's perception of the destination. It has been suggested that the mass media also play an important role in the restoring phase after a crise that have led to negative media publicity and damage a destination's image. However, this paper is limited to focus on the role the mass media plays in influencing tourists in their decision making process and the perception they generate about a destination. In conclusion, based on the models related to tourists' decision-making and the communication process, this paper will aim to identify the role of the mass media and which factor it has in influencing tourists' decision-making.

METHODS

Although several researches have been conducted on tourists' decision-making process and destination images, the more complex relationship between tourism and the mass media is under-researched. The definition of a negative media event will be explained, followed by an example, which shows how negative media publicity can result in significant downturn in numbers of tourists visiting the destination. In addition to the role of the international mass media, the concept of freedom of press will be discussed. Many different theorists have discussed the role of the mass media in the tourist's decision-making process.

This paper will present a model, which shows a simplified sequence on how the tourists reach the 'defer', 'decline' or 'decide' stage in the decision-making process. After having established the relationship between travellers and the mass media, this paper raises the issue on how news can destroy a destination image. Examples are used to highlight how negative media events have resulted in consequences for the tourism industry in different parts of the world. For the purpose of this paper, the term tourist destination region will be used, and can be defined as country, state, region or town that is marketed as a place for tourists to visit.

THE ROLE OF MASS MEDIA IN CRISES

According to Nielsen, a negative media event occurs when the mass media is communicating bad news, threats, irritations or other matters that can be seen as unfavourable by the audience. An important point is that the issues communicated by the mass media might or might not be the truth. However, the end result will not be of great difference whether or not the actual event has occurred. People feel shocked or afraid, and their degree of scepticism increases and reflects their decision-making. Sudden changes in the society can have remarkable consequences for individual TDRs, as well as for the global tourism industry in general. A human act or a nature catastrophe can transform the reputation, image and marketability of the most popular tourism destinations overnight.

Amongst incidents that have disrupted the global tourism industry were the terrorist attacks on New York City and Washington DC on September 11 in 2001, hereafter referred to simply as September 11. According to Beirman, these incidents generated a worldwide panic and fear, which especially had an effect on the tourism industry in form of economic downturns . The combination of SARS and the war in Iraq, which took place between March and June 2003, had severe impacts for the tourism industry and caused a steep reduction of tourism visitation globally, especially in the Asia Pacific region. The on-going unrest in the Middle East, after the initial war, continues to fuel global uncertainty.

Haalebos quotes the Co-Director of Curtin University of Technology's Sustainable Tourism Centre, Professor Jack Carlsen, who stated that '...at the World Tourism Organisation Conference in October 2001, it was estimated it would be two years before international tourism recovered. Since then we've had Bali, Sars and the latest events in Jakarta, Baghdad and Israel. Each event has set recovery back six to twelve months'. This is in line with what the

Commonwealth of Australia announced in their White Tourism Paper where it was identified that there has been a strong market decline in travel and tourism receipts within Australia after the incidents concerned with September 11, SARS and the war in Iraq.

In 2003 overseas arrivals to Australia decreased by 10 percent in April and 21 percent in May compared with the year before. At the same time the effects of SARS in China were even more dramatic. According to Zhou, Beijing Airport experienced a decrease of thirty percent fall in passenger arrivals in April 2003, and an estimated loss of $US4.8 billion loss in the tourism industry. When events such as September 11 and the war in Iraq happens, the international media plays an important role both in publishing the actual catastrophe, as well as in reporting recovery and restoration programs. However, the setback is that 'negative' news sell better than 'good' stories.

According to Beirman, there are five different events or circumstances that media should cover which can create negative impacts on a TDR's image, and again can result in a significant downturn in tourism numbers. Firstly, media should cover situations concerned with international wars or conflicts. Secondly, they should keep the public informed about specific acts of terrorism that is affecting tourists. The third type of events that the mass media should report are major criminal acts or crime waves, especially when tourists are targeted. The fourth area that the media has a duty to cover are natural disasters, such as earthquakes, storms or volcanos that are causing damage to urban areas or the natural environment and consequently impacting on the tourism infrastructure.

The fifth and last major type of event that the mass media are interested in is health concerns related to epidemics and diseases, which have an impact on humans directly, or diseases affecting animals. Based on what the media should cover, Beirman does not discuss the relationship between tourism and the effects of negative news reports. Silverstone on the other hand, argues that media has a role of sharing a meaning and provide a 'taste of the everyday life'. By understanding the mass media's role, a link can be drawn to the issues concerned with tourists' motivation and how expectations are related to the tourists' decisions.

Silverstone states that:

- Our stories, our conversations, are present both in the formal narrative of the media, in factual reporting and fictional representations, and in our everyday tales: the gossip, rumours and causal interactions in which we find ways of fixing ourselves in our relationships to each other, connecting and separating, sharing and denying, individually and collectively... it has been suggested that both the structure and the content of media narratives and the narratives of our everyday discourses are interdependent, that together they allow us to frame and measure the experience.

Especially noteworthy in the quote is the realisation that no narrative alone shapes a picture, rather the intertextual links between surface and content and between different sources of information forms the image. By focusing on media's role it may be easier to understand the nature of a tourist's decision making and the following travel experience. Silverstone argues further that an understanding of how the media works, will make travellers more critical to what the media presents. The relationship between the media and tourism is also commented on by Hall, who states '...in the age of global communication events can be played out live and unedited on television screens, and thereby potentially having a great impact on the viewing public'.

This statement supports the argument that it is important to understand media's response to events like September 11, which affects the tourism industry. According to Beirman the role of effective media communication is critical for tourist authorities in democratic countries where the mass media's role is to inform the general public. The concept of freedom of press in these countries means that the public relation management is an especially important tool for tourism operators because they have to 'ensure that recovery and restoration efforts are reported'. Fall confirms Beirman's view and claims that advertising activities has decreased since September 11 in USA while public relation activities have increased. In contrast, the government in non-democratic countries have far more control over what the mass media is publishing. Consequently, the media coverage tends to be managed in a staged process, and all information is filtered through the government.

Although the nondemocratic counties try to 'hide' destinations in crises, there are leakages. Medical epidemiologist and CSTC Professor Aileen Plant sympathised with the way the Chinese government handled the SARS crisis, and stated that 'I could not criticise the Chinese for their closed-door attitude to the virus. They were simply doing what many other countries would have done to protect their travel and trade. We live in a new world – a globalised world. We cannot hide problems any longer'. This shows that when foreign tourists are the victims of a particular event, they are often subject to media attention, and consequently the media coverage can create a negative image for the TDR.

ANALYSIS

In order to determine the impact the mass media have on a tourists' decision-making process, it is necessary to ask the question whether there is a direct relationship between the information presented and the tourist's motivation. There are various decision-making stages by tourists, and theorists like Mansfeld have created different models for tourism planners and information providers. However, these models are complex and very theory based. Nielsen has simplified these models and created a model, which includes the effects of push-and-pull motivations, in addition to information on the tourists' decision-making process.

Even though the model shows the major phases in the tourists' decision makingprocess, it can be criticised that it is generalising tourists' motivations to travel. Morgan and Pritchard have established that there is a change in consumers' holiday needs, and that tourists are searching for greater variety of holiday activities and unique experiences than what Hall defines as 'push' and 'pull' factors. The trend also shows that there is no longer merely a need for relaxation, but also for recharging and rediscovery. This means that it is questionable how reliable Nielsen's model is. However, it gives a basic overview of tourists' decision-making process.

The sequence in the figure starts with the tourists' motivation to travel. Motivations are dependent on a traveller's social status and background, their stage in the personal life cycle, education and family relationships. These factors will also play an important role when evaluating the issues that can influence the tourists' decisionmaking. The figure is based on an assumed motivation to travel, or at least to gather information for possible trips. Hall states that factors like geographical proximity, ease of accessibility and availability, as well as a destination's social, political and economic stability, are the pull factors that support a tourist in the decision making process. Even though the promotion of TDR's have focused on the mentioned pull factors, recent motivational research has showed that the 'push' factors, 'which is the need to have a break from the daily routine', is of greater value for the tourists.

Having established the basic travel motivation; it is possible to identify more specific motives to the selection process. The next step is to search for travel alternatives through information providers. At this stage the tourists are heavily influenced by third parties' opinions. On the right hand side of Nielsen's model the tourists establish alternatives based on the 'pull' factors that draw people's interest to investigate TDRs and then they collect information about the destination. However, the whole information-gathering phase can also be a combination of 'pull' and 'push' factors, but in both cases the person seeks further travel alternatives. According to Manfredo, there is a relationship between the information providers and the tourist's decision-making process, which leads to 'defer' 'decline', or 'decide' upon the travel experience. The stimulation might come from television advertisements, travel programs on television or radio, a brochure, or any other source of information like travel agencies.

This information gathering stage is the most critical stage when it comes to the tourist's decision making on to 'go or not go'. This stage of the process is important for the tourism planners in order to know what the tourist's decision criteria are when they are reaching this point. Theorists have come up with diverse models on how the receiver of a message views the value of different kinds of information. The tourists are influenced by different factors before deciding whether or not to undertake the travel, and it can be concluded that the mass media plays an important role in the decision making process. Furthermore, the relationship between the media and the tourism operators can be discussed.

According to Hall, tourism operators, on the one hand, are primarily engaging with the media when promoting the TDR. However, in these cases they are only focusing on the positive sides in order to motivate tourists to travel to that specific destination. The mass media, on the other hand have, according to Silverstone, a duty to inform the general public about all types of major events affecting the tourism industry. The coupes in Fiji can be used to illustrate how media attention can have negative effects on tourist's decision-making process. Both in 1987 and 2000 Fiji experienced episodes of political instability. These events had serious impacts on the tourism industry because of travel warnings published in the mass media.

Coup leader Colonel Sitiveni Rabuka overthrew the elected multiracial government in the first coup in 1987. Even though, according to King and Berno the coup was a 'bloodless militarydominated takeover', it had an effect on the tourism industry in terms of decreased visitor numbers. The second coup took place in 2000 when a group of political dissidents took hostage over the members of the Cabinet for two months, but failed their attempt in overthrowing the elected multiracial government. According to King and Berno the coups in 1987 and 2000 had severe impacts on the Fijian tourism industry, and especially the coup in 2000 became a global media event where images of unrest and violence where broadcast around the globe. As a result of this the visitor arrivals decreased with almost 70 percent in year 2000.

Findings by Beirman supports this, and both during and after these events the Fijian Ministry of Tourism and its marketing arm, the Fijian Visitors Bureau, carefully planned campaigns together with airlines and tour operators in order to restore Fiji's tourism industry. According to Singh the major reason why tourists did not visit Fiji was because of travel warnings and images of unrest published in the media. During the crises both the Australian and New Zealand governments used the mass media as a communication tool and actively discouraged people to visit Fiji. These findings are strengthened by Brown and Junek who highlights the power government's travel advisories have over individual tourist's decision to travel after disastrous events have happened and the impact these advices have on effected TDRs.

The Fijian case highlights the significance in the role of the media and of government tourism advisories as they are shaping tourism images. According to Beirman a negative media event can result in considerable economic crises, and for individuals it could result in loss of job and income. However, few tourists think about these consequences when they decide to go for holiday. Their major concern is their own well-being and security.

DISCUSSION

The idea that the mass media can influence tourists' in their choice of destination, as well as their perception on a certain TDR, is relatively new. The traditional way of collecting information has been through travel agencies or the tourism operators directly, and the tourists have made their decisions based on this information. However, according to Seaton, the trend shows that more people are likely to search for supplementary information also from other sources, and the mass media are seen as credible. The question to argue is whether tourists are influenced by the mass media. A model created by Lombardi shows that tourists rely on an 'abstract truth'.

According to it there are two major ways of creating a destination image. The first type of image is created through a specific event that the mass media is communicating to the general public. The image that the mass media is creating can be real or not, however, once it is prototyped to the tourists, it is up to the receiver of the message to recall the image when making a choice of holiday destination. The second way that an image can be created is according to Lombardi through a person's experience. In this case the image is based on an event or experience that a person is a witness of. The image is then supported by reality and truth. Lombardi's theory.

Lombardi's model gives a picture that a TDR's image can be created through a real experience, which again leads to a true image. However, it can be argued what the truth is, because it can be perceived in different ways. Understanding how a destination is perceived is fundamental to the image of a TDR. There are several studies that examine this theory of how a destination image is formed, and amongst the most important are those that discuss the relationship between the image and the tourist's motivation. However, Gunn supports Lombardi's theory by stating that there are two dimensions to a destination's image. The first one is based on the tourist's impression of a TDR without visiting, and in this case different communication channels have influenced the tourist. The second dimension is 'included', which is formed by visiting the destination. In this case the image is created by the tourist's own perceptions.

This theory supports Lombardi's model of communication; however the created image is based on the tourist's perception, and not described as the 'truth'. To sum up, travellers' perceptions are formed based on their knowledge about a destination from various sources. Images and the process of creating images can also be explained as a 'mental picturing where pieces of information create individual features and attributes of stimuli'. This can be related back to the example from the coups in Fiji where images where projected around the world showing a shattered and burning TDR in strong contrast to TDR images of a relaxing and peaceful holiday destination. Baloglu and McLeary have developed a model that includes the factors that influence a destination image and the relationship between the various factors.

The model focuses on three main factors, which are personal, social and stimulation factors, which again are related to a perception a person have of a TDR, and these perceptual evaluations do have an affect on travel motivation. The criticised model of communication created by Lombardi can be used to illustrate how the Foot-and-Mouth disease has had an effect the tourism image in the United Kingdom. During the first half of year 2001 the outbreak of the Foot-and- Mouth disease had severe impacts on the British agricultural sector and caused significant harm to the UK's tourism industry. The British farm industry and rural regions had to face negative consequences for a previously wellmarketed tourism infrastructure. According to Reynolds and Balinbin, the intensity and degree of the mass media's coverage resulted in an image of Britain as a country that was damaged by this disease.

Findings by Beirman support this, and explain further that the Foot-and-Mouth disease caused a major downturn in visitor demand, as foreign tourists cancelled trips to the UK. Mass media was contributing to the decrease in tourism, due to the graphic images of burning and slaughtered animals broadcast around the world. As a result of this the overall image of UK as a TDR was severely damaged. However, the way the British Tourist Authority's reacted to the crises of the Foot-and-Mouth disease is interesting. Instead of only using communication channels like television, newspapers and radio that already had contributed in creating the less appealing tourism image of the country, the British Tourist Authority was one of the first in the world to use the Internet to change the image.

With this tool the British Tourist Authority explained the 'real' situation, and actually managed to create a truthful image without using other mass media as communicators. The Internetpages played an important role in the management of Britain's marketing during and after the tourism crisis. The example from the UK, it is evident that the use of mass media can create a 'wrong' perception on a destination. According to Lombardi people believe what they see, hear and read in the media. The general public view the media as an important authority on the same level as government warnings.

When looking at this issue historically it is important to note that it is especially in recent years that the mass media has had a significantly increasing role as a communication tool. The mass media has given a new importance to the society because it is a source people tend to trust. Mansfeld points out that 'one of the main problems facing destinations that were hit by tourism crises resulting from security turmoil is the evolving negative image. Because tourists do not tend to thoroughly check the reality behind conveyed images, these images become highly biased and distorted'. According to Machin, the media gives popular representations of what is going on in the world. Seen in a historical perspective, this has undoubtedly had an impact on people in most developed cultures, as well as it has had an enormous influence on the TDR's images.

Also illustrated in the examples from Fiji and UK, it is clear that some travellers are influenced by the mass media, and that they use it as an educational tool to learn about the wider society. This supports Beirman's argument that reported incidents, like the terrorist attacks on September 11, have had negative effects on the evolution of the global society, as well as tourism images. Depending on whom the news is affecting, one of the major advantages or disadvantages with mass media as a communication tool is that it is seen as credible. This means that news written by a neutral third party is seen as reliable, while an advertisement or commercial presents an image from the advertiser's point of view. 'Bad' news presented in the media is therefore seen by the audience as objective and factual.

This publicity can bee seen as a hazard for tourism operators because it is only the editorial staff of the mass media that control it. In some cases the communicated message is presented in a vague and incomprehensible way, and this may confuse the audience and create problems for the tourism operators. In some cases, according to Hsu and Powers the media also make a situation worse than it actually is. This happens when the editorial staffs chooses to humiliate a tourist operation or publish a story with negative attributes in some other way. The paradox is that both the tourism operators and the mass media are dealing with the same target group, the general public.

However, a clever tourism operator will learn how to deal with the mass media and use it as a part of their marketing strategy. One way to do this is to follow Fall's suggestion and put a greater focus on public relations activities rather than direct advertising. News that can have an effect on a TDR image has captured front-page headings during the last years, and tourists are not only motivated by stories from glossy brochures, but they are searching for a third party's opinion about the TDR. According to Hsu and Powers, the mass media is an effective communication tool because it reaches a wide and enthusiastic audience, and there is no doubt that tourism has achieved a special status in the news.

However, many regions suffer from bad publicity, even if many years have passed since anything was last reported from the region. Few Australians would, for example, consider Belfast in North Ireland as a cheerful city full of character, with people that are warm and friendly. The coverage of unrest by the mass media has discouraged tourists to travel to North Ireland.

The media has drawn a picture of Belfast as an unsafe place to travel to, and according to Hall, it is human nature to prefer to travel to places that are perceived as safe. Sonmez, Apostolopoulos, & Tarlow suggest that TDRs in areas affected by unrest should incorporate crisis management in their overall strategies in order to construct and protect the image of the destination. This should be done in order to have the capabilities needed to manage peoples opinions before during and after unrest has taken place in the TDR for the mass media. Richter furthers this point by stressing that: 'rebuilding tourism requires more than repairs and promotion. A onesize- fits-all mentality will not do. Just as the sources of instability and their manifestations will differ, so too will the appropriate responses'. What she suggests is that managers in the tourist industry start to look more holistically at their practices and appreciate the fact that they are a part of an industry vulnerable to negative publicity. To manage a TDR effectively does not just mean that the product is enjoyable to visitors but also that it is secure.

THE MEDIA AND THE DEVELOPMENT OF THE TOURISM INDUSTRY

Although much has been written about the role of movies and film in the development of tourism attractions and destinations, little research has attempted to synthesise the role of the media in the development of the tourism sector on a broader level. The aim of this study is to gain an understanding of the influence of the media within the context of tourism on this level. In this paper, the term 'media' refers to mass communication, specifically with regard to newspapers, magazines and broadcasting. The study explored the diverse role of the media in this process over an extended period, spanning from the early 20th century into the new millennium. It is important to gain a better understanding of the ways in which the media has interacted with the tourism sector, as this information can provide practitioners and academics with insights as to how the media can best be employed to benefit stakeholders of the tourism sector. Lessons can be learned from the past so that the experience gained from it can contribute to best practice in the future. In this way, strategies can be developed to cushion the tourism industry from damaging or erroneous portrayals of the tourism product.

RESEARCH APPROACH

- The study employed case study methodology which was appropriate given that case studies are '... undertaken because one wants a better understanding of this case ... because in all its particularity and ordinariness, this case itself is of interest'.

In order, to highlight the variety of ways in which the media has had an impact on the development of the tourism industry, however, this paper explores, analyses and reflects upon four individual cases within this context. This approach to analysis serves to reinforce and corroborate the findings and is referred to as a collective case study. Yin noted that this approach is particularly appropriate when the research to be conducted will focus on contemporary situations, does not require control over behavioural events and where the form of the research question is how or why.

Moreover, Strauss and Corbin assert that such inductive processes are particularly appropriate '...to uncover and understand what lies behind any phenomenon about which little yet is known'. In this study, tourism refers to the broad industry that encompasses travel and hospitality. Four specific cases studies were selected because they provide information on a crosssection of the tourism industry.

The cases were also selected because:

- They cover an extensive period of time; and
- They highlight the diverse roles of the media with regard to the activities, and subsequent development, of the tourism industry.

Each of the four case studies, which are presented in chronological order, are notable because they either highlight the consequences of media intervention or a perceived distortion of the event under investigation.

THE 1920'S WAITERS' STRIKE, SAN SEBASTIÁN, SPAIN.

San Sebastián is a Spanish coastal town, located on the Basque border. Since the 12th century, the town has been victim to a number of sieges and, at times, was occupied by the French. During the 18th century, San Sebastián was burned to the ground, when Anglo-Portuguese seized the city from the French, but by the 1840's, Queen Isabel II of Spain resided in San Sebastián, during the summer, which was the catalyst for the city's rejuvenation. Indeed, the port city became a pioneer in the installation of trams, electric street lighting and telephones. By 1925, the city's population was 65,930, which was triple it population almost 40 years earlier.

From the late 1880's, San Sebastián was one of Spain's two most popular seaside resorts. San Sebastián directly competed with San Marco for domestic tourists from Madrid, and for international tourists from a number of countries, including France and South Africa. Considered to be a more elite destination than San Marco, San Sebastián drew upon its association with Spanish Royalty, and the Queen's residence was a major tourist attraction in itself.

In order to become an elite resort destination, San Sebastián experienced substantial socio-economic changes during the 1900-1930's, but this was set within the broader context of the corresponding changes in Spain's socio-economic transformation. There were a number of political factions in Spain during the 1900- 1930's, including socialist and anarchist groups, militant Catholics and Basque nationalists. In San Sebastián, these political factions were represented by a range of newspapers, that reported and commented on tourism development in the resort.

Walton notes that:

- The dominant discourse in the most visible San Sebastián media emphasized the resort as a vehicle for the civilising processes associated with sustaining a secure and comfortable environment for the wealthy visitors and with the introduction and assimilation of new standards of consumption and polite behaviour from the European high society.

Walton, however, also identified that there were contrary reports and opinions on the development of the tourism industry, and its impact on the San Sebastián community, in the local media, despite being less conspicuous than those positive views of the situation in the more popular press of that time. For example, La Constantia, a republican oriented newspaper, reported on the seedier side of tourism development in San Sebastián. These reports focussed on the levels of prostitution; the negative attitudes and behaviours of the local residents towards tourists; the dichotomy that was developing between the rich and the poor; and the impact of the casino, which was dubbed the 'Our Lady of the Roulette'.

The government did not support this type of commentary, as it leant its support to the development of tourism in the port city. One major incident, or event, that took place in San Sebastián was the Waiters' Strike of 1920. This strike, and the manner in which it was reported, provides insights into the potential of the local media in developing tourism in the resort. Before its economy was supported by tourism, San Sebastián was largely an industrial town, and the 'face' of the tourism industry for many of its residents were the camereros, or the waiters. The camereros were well-paid compared to many of the residents, hence the idea of them striking for better wages and conditions was viewed rather negatively by the local community. For the government, however, the issue was that the camereros were striking at the peak of the holiday season.

This was a concern in itself, not only because of the short-terms impacts, but also because of the long-terms negative impacts that the strike may have on the destination's image and, ultimately, the development of tourism. According to Walton and Walton and Smith, what transpired was a plethora of reports in a cross-section of the local media, specifically newspapers.

The reports seem to reflect extreme views in that they either:

- Support the waiters in their efforts; or
- Downplay their power and their impact on tourism in San Sebastián.

Indeed, there seems to be an underlying national political agenda attached to the strike, which may have influenced its exposure in the media. Walton and Smith analysed the strike in detail and their conclusion was that 'in the long run ... the events of August 1920, did not in themselves make much difference to the trajectory of the San Sebastián's development as a resort'. Although it is inconclusive, it appears that the power of the government in controlling the content and frequency of the media reports about the impact of the strike on tourism services in San Sebastián has obscured much of the 'voice' of the San Sebastián local community in relation to tourism development in this town.

SPECIAL EVENTS AND THE QUEST FOR MEDIA COVERAGE

Special events have been one way in which governments have promoted cities as tourist destinations. Using megaevents, in particular, as part of such a strategy is appealing because of the high levels of television coverage and viewer numbers that they command. The telecast of mega-events provides unique opportunities to portray host cities or nations as attractive tourist destinations.

Indeed, Hall asserts that special events, particularly mega-events, can change how host destinations are perceived and that they can provide the new 'middle class tourist' with the impetus to visit the destination in the future. Currently, mega-events are afforded a considerable amount of sustained media coverage, whilst the number of people viewing mega-events, particularly on the television, has grown substantially during the last decade.

In 2003, for example, the telecast of the World Rugby Cup attracted an audience of more than four billion people worldwide. McDaniel, McDaniel and Chalip and Chalip, Green and Hill have conducted research on the relationships between mega-events, media consumption, tourism and consumers. McDaniel, for example, explored the role of consumer characteristics on viewing the network coverage of the 1996 Summer Olympics.

Chalip employed an experimental design approach; to capture the overall telecast of the Honda Indy 300 as well as to test its impact on a sample of students' by presenting them with images of the host destination. These studies have not only highlighted the comprehensive nature of television coverage, or the telecast, of mega-events, but have also reported on the levels and frequency of coverage of the host destination - its landscape, attractions, culture and people.

It was found, for example, that as well as images of Sydney Harbour being catapulted into homes around the globe via the telecast of the 2000 Summer Olympic Games, many other aspects of Australia were conveyed to viewers, including other destinations and available tourist activities around the nation. This has led Chalip, Green and Vander Velden to argue that it may be the associated meanings of sports events that are the core of their product, rather than the sports themselves. The use of special events in destination marketing strategies is underpinned by a range of marketing theories and concepts.

Kim, Allen, and Kardes noted that in the case of television advertising, in particular, associating visual imagery with a brand [i.e. a destination] is an important component of eliciting affective responses in consumers with regard to that brand. Further, Priluck and Till suggested that much of the advertising on television, pairs products with pleasant stimuli such as agreeable images and enjoyable music aimed at evoking positive responses to the stimuli. It is further acknowledged that the growing use of the telecast of special events in sponsorship marketing campaigns has also influenced the overall use of this form of marketing communication in relation to destinations with regard to tourism. Predating these important studies, but no doubt with a view to capitalising on some of the benefits outlined above, the German authorities commissioned a documentary based on the 1936 summer Olympic games in Berlin, "Olympia".

Produced by Leni Riefenstahl, Germany's official documenter, "Olympia" is probably one of the most controversial films in relation to special events. Although, "Olympia" was not specifically commissioned to develop or enhance tourism to Berlin or Germany per se, it portrayed positive images of Berlin and Germany to manipulate viewers' perceptions of Germany and, no doubt, the Nazi regime. Indeed some critics of the film have suggested that the documentary was part of the Nazi Party's propaganda campaign. A major criticism, for example, is that Berlin's image was 'sanitised' for the 1936 Games. Certainly, much of the commentary on the making of "Olympia" indicates that anti-Semitic signage around the city was removed shortly before both the staging of the Games and the filming of the documentary.

EPICUREAN MAGAZINES AND HOSPITALITY INDUSTRY MAGAZINES

A number of epicurean magazines have emerged in the past few decades, with the most notable of these being Vogue Entertaining and Gourmet. Although few studies have been conducted into the impact of these publications on the industry and its customers, Fattorini has found deep disparity in the content of the messages that are presented to consumers and industry employees. Asserting that consumers read epicurean publications, while industry employees rely on hospitality trade magazines, Fattorini contends that this has contributed to tensions between those who work in restaurants and those who dine in them. His conclusion is based on an analysis of the content of these two different types of publications as well as the manner in which the content is presented to their audiences.

Differences are immediately evident in the presentation of these publications. Hospitality trade journals, for example, generally conform to a standard layout, which Fattorini suggested is attributed to the fact that much of the copy is product advertising. Many of the products that are advertised, such as expensive cooking equipment, sophisticated point of purchase software or employee training courses, require the decision of management to purchase them. Consequently, the target audience of trade magazines is generally decision-makers holding management positions within the industry and very little of the material in these publications is directed towards front-line employees. In contrast, Fattorini proposes that epicurean magazines are targeted at middle class audiences with relatively high disposable incomes.

The information presented in epicurean magazines is designed to educate this audience to the latest trends in food and wine, often set within the context of better-quality restaurants. One of the major issues associated with Epicurean magazines is that they generally portray the hospitality industry as a glamorous environment in which to work. Concentrating more on photographic value rather than any sense of reality, chefs are regularly pictured, in their pristine uniforms, sitting leisurely with a glass of wine or a cup of coffee at a table in their restaurant. Indeed, some of the most recent images of chefs in epicurean magazines are quite artistic.

Moreover, the magazines seem to be intent on presenting images of professional chefs who oversee well-managed businesses. In contrast, within hospitality trade magazines, there is very little attention afforded to chefs, or waiters the main emphasis being on white-collared management personnel. Although both epicurean magazines and hospitality trade journals dedicate sections to recipes, the recipes published in epicurean magazines generally include expensive, or unusual, ingredients. This is an attempt to imbue a level of sophistication, based on the exotic nature of ingredients, to dishes that are often simplistic in terms of the preparation and cooking procedures so that novice cooks can recreate the dishes at home.

In comparison, the layout and formatting of trade magazines is quite staid. Sections of these magazines are devoted to recipes, however, they are generally convenience or budget-oriented, rather than focussed on the uniqueness of the ingredients. The resulting portrayals of the hospitality industry in these two forms of the one media are, at best, unrealistic. There are a number of negative impacts associated with these polarised portrayals of hospitality. Fattorini suggests, for example, that epicurean magazines have given rise to the 'psuedo-professional', who has a wide range of knowledge on food and wine, but has little, if any, experience of working in the hospitality industry. Another term for the pseudo-professional would be the 'foodie', coined by Barr and Levy.

It is often at restaurant tables that the tension between those who work in restaurants, particularly those of the front-line, and those who dine in them is most evident. Pseudo-professionals, as noted earlier, are likely to be from a different social class from the front-line employees serving them. Further, the knowledge that the pseudo- professional possesses about food, wine and its service, can far surpass that of the front-line employee. As a result, this can lead to different levels of understanding as to what represents quality food and service thus deepening the divide between expectations and perceptions of service quality.

THE DAWN OF THE NEW MILLENNIUM

In Melbourne in 2000, as the industry geared up for the New Year's eve celebrations Hede and O'Mahony report on the impact of, apparently, spurious media communications on the demand for hospitality provision. For most operators, hosting events on New Year's Eve would involve skilful financial management because expected increases in operating overheads would need to be recouped - invariably by way of increased charges to customers. It was also anticipated that customers would expect an extraordinary event and that additional staff may be required to meet customers' expectations. Media reports during 1999, however, contended that hospitality providers would face a number of challenges because there would be an unprecedented demand for catering and accommodation from the public.

The media predicted that this would result in exorbitantly high costs for food and beverages; and that employees would be able to command substantial loadings on their hourly rates. Indeed, Faroque reported that by mid-December, the price of food and beverages, had, and would continue to 'spiral', whilst Allen predicted that the loading on employees' normal rates would increase by as much as 400 per cent. The report concluded that hospitality employees would be earning up to AUS$50- AUS$70 per hour on New Years Eve. Given the need to develop a marketable product early in 2000, coupled with perceived increases in customer expectations many hospitality operators elected not to open on New Year's Eve. None of the hotels in the city in the three star category hosted events, for example, leaving the market open to four and five star properties. Of the hotels that did open, most were in the five star category and they elected to market the evening as a 'gala event' offering packages for food, drink and entertainment.

However, prices had to be set in advance of negotiations with the unions about the rates of pay that employees would receive for their services. Indeed, employee wage rates were not finalised until a short time before the event and early negotiations were hampered by media reports about the value and availability of hospitality employee labour. Consequently, event organisers were forced to predict grossly inflated wage costs which were built into the product price. Prices for celebratory events that were advertised at this time ranged from AUS$300 to AUS$500 per person which, in some instances, was up to three times higher than the usual price for a similar event. At these prices demand was weak and a number of other hotels chose to abandon their planned events.

In the Hede and O'Mahony study, hospitality managers attributed the high prices of their events to the media because they perceived that the media had increased employees expectations of the value of their labour. Although the official wage rates that were finally agreed were not inordinately high, managers explained that they had been forced to factor in substantial increases in labour before the official wage rates had been negotiated with employee representatives so that they could take advance bookings. Securing the appropriate staff for the evening was of paramount importance for them. Indeed, at one hotel, staff had been advised of their work schedules three months prior to New Year's Eve and asked to sign a contract committing to work on the night.

DISCUSSION

The aim of this paper was to explore the role of the media within the context of the tourism sector, and specifically how the media has intervened with regard to its activities. Four case studies were explored for this purpose. The study has identified a number of ways in which the media has been influential or has been engaged to intervene in events within the context of tourism. The case of the 1920's Waiters' Strike in the resort town of San Sebastián, Spain, for example, shows how the media played an active role in the evolution of the strike and how the media was used, to a large extent by the government, to downplay the significance of negative industrial relations in the hospitality sector. Aligning itself with the local government, which was concerned that newspaper reports of the strike would negatively impact the image of the destination, the media downplayed the power of the camereros, in terms of their organisational skills and the impact that they would have on the service that San Sebastián would be able to provide their visiting tourists.

In the second case study, it was noted that, within the context of special events, media coverage is largely exploited as a destination-marketing tool to project positive images of host destinations in order to enhance the destination to potential tourists. It also clearly illustrated how in telecasts of mega-events, and particularly of the Olympic Games, governments use eventrelated media as part of their image-making strategies. This case also highlights how the media can be manipulated to present a particular image of a destination to potential tourists. The degree of authenticity in media communications is also important given that, although Olympia is considered to be a classical piece of film, the reaction to the documentary was, in the main, one of suspicion. In particular, the 'sanitisation' of Berlin in relation to the removal of any anti- Semitic communications around the city, whilst projecting a 'politically-correct' image, was, considered to be misrepresentative.

In the case of lifestyle magazines, specifically epicurean magazines, the study found that tensions are being developed between industry personnel and consumers of hospitality services. The increasing knowledge that the public has of culinary commodities and techniques, mostly gained through epicurean magazines, means that many of the lower-skilled front-of-house staff are often challenged by customers' expectations. The New Year's Eve case highlights the negative influence of media publications on hospitality provision. Tensions developed at this time were two-fold. In the first instance, tensions emerged between the industry and the media and in the second, tension emerged between the public and the industry. In this case, the media, was blamed for creating a number of unrealistic expectations for hoteliers, hotel employees and their customers. This resulted in financial loss for hospitality providers, whilst the public also missed out on the opportunity to celebrate a special event at a reasonable price. Industry employees were also disadvantaged because many employees lost the opportunity for increased earnings. Collectively these case studies clearly show that the effects of negative media coverage can be detrimental to the tourism sector and to service provision within the industry.

It emerged in this study, that within the context of the tourism industry, the media is a powerful tool that can be used to manipulate the public's perception of tourism-related concepts, including destinations and the industry itself. The study also highlights a political dimension, particularly in relation to tourism development. This was especially evident in the San Sebastián waiters' strike, where the media was used to garner public support for the Government's position on the strike and its perceived impact on tourism development. A political dimension is also evident in relation to special events. Although the Berlin Olympics might be considered atypical, according to Roche the power of internal politics is often manifest in the decision to host special events and the bidding process as well as the opportunities for urban development that is often associated with these events.

Given the consequences of negative media comment, it is suggested that destination managers and tourism organisations should be proactive in developing strategies and engaging the necessary expertise to manage the influences of the media on its operations. A coordinated approach by the industry and its relevant industry associations is recommended, including the provision of accurate information and the development of positive media releases in order to avoid media related losses in the future.

RESEARCH LIMITATIONS AND FURTHER RESEARCH

The study set out to gain an understanding of how the media influences tourism and tourism destination management based on the analysis of four case studies. This is clearly a limitation of the study in that it is selective rather than comprehensive or exhaustive. It is, therefore, acknowledged that generalisation of the results gained is tentative. This approach, however, was appropriate given the contemporary nature of the situation. Further, research, encompassing a greater range of case studies, would be beneficial to uncover more ways in which the media is used, or intervenes, within the context of the tourism industry. The authors of this study would also propose that future research be directed toward developing appropriate strategies with regard to the media so that positive relationships can be developed between the consumers of tourism and the suppliers of tourism products and services.

CONTRIBUTION OF THE MEDIA TO EXPECTATIONS OF SPACE TOURISM

Space travel, until a few years ago, was essentially restricted to professionals. The average individual visited space merely in their fantasies, or vicariously, through the influence of the media such as books, comics, television programs and films. Those who watched Neil Armstrong set foot on the Moon for the first time in history in 1969 might have wished to have joined him, but the likelihood of this happening was practically non-existent until 2001, when Dennis Tito, the world's first space tourist, made space a potential new tourist destination for the super-wealthy. Recent developments would seem to indicate that space may be opened up to the general public this century, although the rate of this growth is hard to predict.

Individuals have thrilled to the exploits of space travellers through the pages of books, such as Jules Verne's From the Earth to the Moon, H. G. Wells' The First Men in the Moon and Kim Stanley Robinson's Red Mars and comics like Mystery in Space and Flash Gordon. In the 1950's, the Collier's magazine's series of illustrated articles on space reached a circulation of 4 million and Walt Disney included a space-themed segment in his Disneyland theme park at Anaheim known as 'Tomorrowland', which became a popular tourist destination. Space-related films include Rocketship the first 'Flash Gordon' escapade, Forbidden Planet, Barbarella, Star Wars, Red Planet and Solaris. Television programs based around space have been endlessly repeated to win new audiences, with well-known examples including Doctor Who, Star Trek, Lost in Space, Battlestar Galactica, and Buck Rogers in the 25th Century.

Cartoons on space such as The Jetsons and Space Ghost and animated films like Disney's Ducktales: Space Invaders and Treasure Planet give children an introduction to space as a fantasy world, where the extraordinary is not only possible but probable, and individuals are generally actively involved in their environment, rather than passive bystanders. Destinations are often colourful, vegetated and populated by 'aliens,' friendly or otherwise. It is a far cry from the "magnificent desolation," noted by astronaut Buzz Aldrin as he became the second human being to walk on the moon. This may be attributed in part to the fact that space movies are not filmed 'on location' and the intended audience's perception of what space is actually like is not generally coloured by experience, unlike films set in well-visited places on Earth such as Paris or the Grand Canyon.

Film-makers are therefore free to invent fantasy space environments rather than representing or recreating its often bleak reality. Cinema and television are regarded as possibly the most influential forms of media in the 21st century. While novels on space-related themes may have a powerful effect on the imagination, it is arguably visual media that is most likely to shape popular views of space travel. As Morkham and Staiff state, "The ability for film to transport audiovisually other worlds into the present is unique ... bringing worlds to the spectator that may otherwise remain out of reach." Most people in Western nations in the modern era have seen space depicted in at least some of the movies or television programs that they have watched, and it is arguable that the images that they have seen have seeped into their consciousness and influenced their perceptions of space and space tourism experiences, even if it is purely on a subliminal level.

Consumer behaviour with respect to space tourism is, as yet, under-researched and we know very little about tourist expectations about possible future space tourism experiences. The experiential aspects of space tourism are also yet to be studied, mainly due to the paucity of potential subjects at this present time and the difficulty of carrying out data collection in situ. One interesting area of future research is to consider the role the media might play in the space tourism experience. This paper will consider how the cinema might colour the public's expectations surrounding space travel, including the amount of active participation in the experience, the type of activities likely to be engaged in while in space and the nature of the surroundings, as well as levels of satisfaction with the 'real' as opposed to the imaginary experience. It will also suggest areas for future research.

SPACE TOURISM: CURRENT AND FUTURE DEVELOPMENTS

Space tourism, while not yet a fully developed industry, is not merely a futuristic vision. It encompasses a number of different experiences, from terrestrial visits to space themed museums and exhibitions, and flights on a MiG fighter jet at more than twice the speed of sound, where the passenger can see the curvature of the Earth and the blackness of space, to orbital flights on a Russian Soyuz spacecraft to visit the International Space Station, such as those undertaken by Dennis Tito in 2001 and Mark Shuttleworth in 2002, and potentially by Greg Olsen in 2005. These latter flights are reputed to have cost $20 million each, a lofty price not within the budget of the average traveller. Smith refers to this as "elite space tourism" but notes that costs are likely to decrease with technological innovation and increased volume of passengers carried.

Research conducted to date, albeit limited, indicates that there is public interest in engaging in space tourism if not demonstrable market demand. The prevailing view seems to be that space travel for the masses is inevitable, but opinions on when it might occur and what form it might take are mixed. For example, a joint NASA/Space Transportation Association study "concluded that private, high priced 'adventure' trips to space with greater than today's commercial airline risk could become possible in the next few years. Much larger scale, lower priced, orbital operations, could commence in the decade thereafter." The former has occurred with the flights of Tito et al, and the latter might eventuate in the near future, depending on the outcome of recent developments, such as the Ansari X-Prize.

This US$10 million prize was established in 1996, to be awarded to the first private team to launch a space vehicle capable of carrying at least three adults to an altitude of at least 100 kilometres, and repeating the feat within a period of two weeks. On October 4, 2004, Scaled Composites from the United States, with SpaceShipOne was successful in their quest to win the X-Prize and their technology is now being adopted by Sir Richard Branson for his newlyannounced Virgin Galactic space tourism venture. There has been some consideration of the factors that are likely to shape development of space tourism in the 21st century.

Aside from the outcome of initiatives such as the Ansari XPrize, its progress is likely to be driven by factors such as the rate of technological development, which makes cheaper and safer reusable vehicles possible, and the nature of future legal and regulatory requirements for the industry, which are not inimical to viable businesses and commercial investment, as well as public support and confidence in a fledgling space tourism industry. Due to cost and safety considerations, most early space tourism experiences are likely to be sub-orbital flights, which might only last for a short duration, allowing the participant to view space for a few minutes and maybe experience some brief moments of 'weightlessness' if they are not required to be strapped in for the entire journey.

Even if space hotels are constructed as potential holiday destinations, they will probably be sparsely furnished and utilitarian, as the cost of transporting construction materials into space will be high based on current technology. Smith paints a picture of future 'frontier' accommodation in space which is less than salubrious and designed to maximise efficiency and functionality. "Of necessity space hotels are new 'techno tourist bubbles' and small in size. Crowding and the regimen of space utilization can be taxing. Sleeping rooms are available to guests on an 8-hour shift basis. Food will be provided from vending-type machines, in packaged solid form. Leisure space will include recreation room for reading, movies and the Internet, earth watching, and exercise."

The first space tourists, Tito and Shuttleworth, found themselves wedged in the cramped Russian Soyuz spacecraft, shoulder-to-shoulder with their crew-mates. Privacy was impossible in such a vehicle, and the ride was uncomfortable. 'Space walks' were not available to them, and they spent much of their time gazing on Earth and taking photographs. This is not travel which is likely to satisfy those who like comfort and luxury, nor is it likely to appeal to individuals who like to actively control their travel experiences, at least in the early years of the fledgling industry.

CONSUMER EXPECTATIONS AND SATISFACTION

The anticipation stage of tourist behaviour and tourist expectations have been the subject of much research and discussion, not least because it would appear that "...expectations play a crucial role in framing satisfaction evaluations". There is still scope however for further research in this area. For example sees the potential for new research on expectations to focus on consumer reactions to technological advances and products "and the psychology of responding to those changes."

Space tourism arguably falls within this category, and there is thus scope to examine space tourist expectations as an example of consumer response to new and innovative technological developments. Lovelock, Patterson and Walker define 'consumer expectations' as "prepurchase beliefs about service provision that act as a standard reference point for judging post-purchase performance ..." Consumer expectations can be formed through such means as past experience, word of mouth, external communications by providers and consumers' general attitudes towards a brand.

Data on expectations is generally gathered by a researcher before an event or purchase takes place, although it has been argued that expectations about future purchases or events can be gathered after a product use experience. Potential space tourists are unlikely to have their expectations pre-flight shaped by either direct prior experience or the feedback from others, due to the small numbers of people who are likely to have actually engaged in sub-orbital or orbital space tourism in the early days of the industry. Promotional literature might be important in helping to frame expectations, but might fail to take into account attitudes to this new emerging form of tourism which have been influenced by popular culture such as cinema.

TRAVEL AND THE MEDIA

The media can have an important influence on consumption, and travel behaviour, through stimulating the imagination or shaping or influencing tastes and ideas. "Daydreaming is not a purely individual activity; it is socially organised, particularly through television, advertising, literature, cinema, photography and so on". In fact, it has been said that to read a book, watch a film, gaze at a painting or pour over a map is to travel.

Celsi, Rose and Leigh acknowledge in their ethnographic study of skydivers that the dramatic worldview presented by the modern media was an important factor motivating participation in this high-risk activity. "In the twentieth-century mass media, the musings of individuals, which were once largely abstract and imaginative fantasy, are concretely instantiated. Thus, possibilities that might never have been previously considered, including high-risk sports, become tangible behavioural alternatives".

Cinema can also be characterised as 'pull factors' for tourism. Many of our films are in turn based on literary works, and literature plays an important role in influencing culture and inspiring visits to places associated with literary works, or literary characters. Hennig highlights the fantasy aspects of travel and its links with the arts, with tourism described as "part of the great and bounteous realm of the imagination," and notes this link between films and literary texts and their influence on "tourists' expectations and experiences".

Riley, Baker and Van Doren comment on the cinema's ability to "construct anticipation and allure that induces people to travel" by creating "exotic worlds that do not exist in reality but can be recreated through a visit to the location where they were filmed."

There have been a number of studies considering the influence of movies or television as inducements to tourism, such as Tooke and Baker; Riley, Baker and Van Doren; and Busby and Klug but none to date has explored how movies might help to shape our pre-travel expectations in the context of an emerging tourism niche, where there are few other influences to guide or frame tourist expectations.

SPACE TRAVEL IN FILM

Space travellers in the movies fly their own vehicles, visit extraordinary destinations, and battle aliens, in surroundings that are a mixture of the familiar and the unfamiliar. Life on the frontier of space is seemingly never tranquil nor dull. Even though we have yet to find evidence of life in other parts of the solar system, extra-terrestrials are a common feature of space-related literature and film. As Wright notes, "In countless movies and stories space warriors suited with fish bowl helmets [have] focused their ray guns on creatures from outer space." Films such as ET the Extra-terrestrial, Contact, and Independence Day feature aliens interacting with human beings. A few are benign but most threaten the continuation of the human race and some are depicted as possessing intelligence beyond that found on Earth.

The irony is that science is now looking at the most likely signs of life in our immediate solar system as Close Encounters of a microbial kind, which mirrors some of the cinematic depictions of aliens in typical horror flicks such as The Andromeda Strain, The Alpha Incident and Toxic Spawn. Most of the likely destinations for future long-duration space tourism are effectively barren wastelands. At present, we know Mars to be a frozen place with a largely sterile surface regolith, subject to violent dust storms and possessing an atmosphere largely composed of carbon dioxide, with some nitrogen and only trace amounts of oxygen and water. The Moon, as a result of the Apollo flights of the 1960's and early 1970's, was found to be "a desolate, lifeless world", hostile to life, even in its most primitive forms.

Will a generation brought up with ET and the Daleks find travel to uninhabited places in our universe a little uninspiring and even boring, let alone being confined to a vehicle or hotel in space with their fellow travellers, rather than roaming the stars like the crew of Star Trek's Enterprise? The narrative of the 'fantastic journey' runs through many of the most popular spacethemed films and television programs, such as the Lost in Space TV series and movie, Star Trek, the movies Journey to the Far Side of the Sun and Star Quest and the TV series Space 1999. Star Trek in particular often uses the imagery of exploring "strange new worlds". According to Adler, story lines or 'tropes' can often form the foundation of travel experiences, and transcend travel styles.

One example is the narrative of the "discovery of new territory," or "voyages of discovery" which Adler describes as "a cultural epic that set the [mould] for many later travel postures." Zurick also refers to these voyages of discovery, grounded in literary works and permeating our consciousness like a half-forgotten dream, propelling "people into the world's remote lands." The level of influence this trope has on the future space tourist and their pre and post travel experiences is yet to be studied but it would seem likely that the level of restrictions and lack of active involvement in early space tourism experiences might frustrate those used to the active experiences depicted onscreen.

Other common narratives in space- themed movies are the rescue of Earth and human beings from some calamity or disaster from space, whether from aliens as mentioned above, the impact of a comet or meteor or impending nuclear doom. These are again active rather than passive experiences. Very few films with space-related themes depict space travel as it really is, complete with space sickness, cramped conditions, isolation and reliance to a degree on others back on Earth, perhaps because the fantasy is more appealing. Examples of more 'realistic' movies are generally based on real-life events such as Apollo 13 and the From the Earth to the Moon TV series.

Their applicability to a modern-day space tourism experience is likely to be limited, given they represent experiences which took place over thirty years ago, by professionals rather than tourists, and had the cachet of 'exploration' or pioneer travel about them, involving the first human beings to visit the Moon. Recent documentaries showing astronauts in space, such as Mission to Mir and Space Station 3D are the most accurate representations of current space travel, as opposed to space tourism, we have on film.

THE CINEMATIC EXPERIENCE

While there have been numerous movies with space-related plots since the first credited science-fiction movie, Le Voyage dans la Lune none so far has utilised space tourism as a major theme. According to Space Future, "While there are plenty of movies from far in the past about space travel, we are unaware of any in which space tourism is a major business activity, or in which realistically portrayed orbiting hotels play a major role. Nevertheless the concept of tourism turns up here and there - just enough to show how the coming reality of space tourism has not been foreseen at all clearly in the movie industry." The movies highlighted in this paper incorporate a space tourism experience which is possibly more faithful to the 'real thing' than space travel is generally portrayed on screen, but still falls short of the likely reality.

In 2001: A Space Odyssey, passengers are shown flying in Pan Am shuttle spacecraft to space stations, where they wait to catch connecting flights to the Moon. The sole passenger in one scene watches movies screened on the back of the chair in front, just like passengers do today on a typical international flight, although the movie version shows a pen floating around in the zero-g environment, and the flight attendants are forced to wear velcro-based shoes to grip to the 'floor.' Food is served in trays, but has to be taken in liquid form through straws. The atmosphere is quiet, efficient and businesslike, far removed from the fantasy elements of some of the space-themed movies discussed in this paper.

The flight is a mixture of the familiar and the novel to audiences, even in the 1960's but less so today, but there are enough of the unique touches to make it seem innovative and 'new' in comparison to a more commonplace aeroplane flight. The revolving space station on the other hand creates its own artificial gravity, so the guests don't have to contend with items floating around or the potential risk of space sickness. There is little of the hustle and bustle of a hotel on Earth. All is calm and relaxed, with an almost eerie hush. Space is a pure, almost spiritual experience. A Hilton Hotel sign can be seen on the space station, which is furnished in sterile, minimalist style and mainly in neutrals, other than touches of bold colour. This adds to the feeling of zenlike tranquillity. Moon Two Zero was billed as the first Moon 'western' and features a futuristic tourist industry which handles regular flights to the Moon and Mars in vehicles such as the 'Pan Am Moon Express,' where cabins are strangely just as empty as those depicted in 2001: A Space Odyssey, and a permanent presence on the Moon, complete with saloon bar.

Artificial gravity inside the structures gives life in space an appearance of normality, although there is still the need to wear a pressurised spacesuit when going outside. Tourists can visit the site where Neil Armstrong landed in 1969, to become the first person to set foot on the Moon, in a portent of future visits to historical space sites and places of interest are pointed out as being sights "no tourist should miss." Space travel is mainly commercial in focus, with one character noting that "passengers [are] where the money is." The Moon is shown as an alien environment, and the tourist as a 'foreigner' is a theme running through the movie, even extending to the local population as distinct from visitors. "We are all foreigners here. Perhaps we should never have come," says Captain Kent. "I suppose bleak is as good a way as any to describe it [the Moon]."

Space tourism in The Fifth Element, which is set two hundred and fifty years in the future, is more like today's luxury travel. Some of the action takes place on an orbiting space hotel above the mythical planet Fhloston, which is described as a "hotel of a thousand and one follies." To get there, one travels by spacecraft which is fitted with individual cubicles like a Japanese hotel, complete with 'sleep regulators' to allow the passenger the opportunity to sleep for the duration of the flight. We are told that the hotel has twelve swimming pools, including one on the "rooftop" and floats in a higher orbit after 5:00 pm "for the view." Guests watch an opera singer perform in a replica of one of the grand opera-houses on Earth. This extravagant space-equivalent of a modern cruise-ship is not the sort of accommodation which is likely to be built for the first space tourists to enjoy.

The space hotel portrayed in The Fifth Element is certainly vastly different to the utilitarian surroundings of the International Space Station, visited by space tourists Dennis Tito and Mark Shuttleworth, as is the spacecraft in which they travelled there from Earth. "Whilst aboard the ISS space, [Mark]

Shuttleworth will not have all the luxury-extras he might be accustomed to in a room on the French Riviera, with day to day life in [space] being sparse given the restrictive environment". Movies from the in-house space station library, rather than live opera performances, are available to the highpaying guests on the ISS, and even a humble shower has yet to be installed for the use of 'guests.' The space tourism experience, as envisaged by the creators of the abovementioned movies, clearly has yet to become reality. As the former space policy analyst for the Federation of America Scientists, John Pike, noted in 2001 in relation to the movie 2001: A Space Odyssey, "Pan Am went bust, there are no bases on the Moon, and the Space Station doesn't have a Hilton". Tourists such as Dennis Tito are essentially passive spectators, lacking a large degree of control over their surroundings and their experience and forced to submit to the authority of others. Neither luxury nor privacy appears to be an element of the space tourism experience, at least for the foreseeable future.

FUTURE AREAS OF RESEARCH

Future research may demonstrate that space tourism in the early years of its development disappoints rather than excites participants, based on pre-flight expectations which may have been fostered by cinematic images viewed since childhood. There is scope for examining these early space tourism experiences to see what types of expectations exist during the 'anticipation stage' and what factors have influenced the development of these expectations. Further phases of the research could then look at whether expectations have been met or exceeded, and the reasons for this, with attention paid to the possible role of the media in framing pre-flight expectations and post-travel satisfaction levels. Multiple item scales could be used to measure expectations, and then post-travel satisfaction ratings could be provided for the same items.

Factor analysis could then be used to examine the underlying dimensions of both expectations and satisfaction. A qualitative study of space tourists, concentrating on expectations and satisfaction, might also assist in uncovering some of the more subtle, unconscious influences, such as movies and literature. Other useful avenues of research could involve comparing the results of the abovementioned study to consumer expectations and levels of satisfaction levels with respect to other examples of new technological developments. Understanding the factors which influence expectations and hence satisfaction with these 'new to world' developments may help providers to 'fill in the gaps,' by focusing on providing information, including promotional literature, which corrects potential stereotypes or myths created or fostered by the media.

INTERNATIONAL TOURISM AND MEDIA CONFERENCE

MAPPING GEOGRAPHIES OF DESIRE AND INCIDENTAL TOURISM

Some essential dichotomies of Australia are the known and unknown, the local and other, and the here and there. Australia's short history as an outpost of European culture is primarily understood as that of a young culture in an ancient land(scape). Driving through the Australian landscape is often as much about necessity as it is about dreams. It is so often the latter that stimulate the road trip, the elements of which both locate and characterise, as well as serving the dual function of being a means to an end and an opportunity to experience new locations, as well offering the possibility of dis-location. Three recent Australian films, however, presented a distinctively different perspective on location and dislocation, that being to introduce Japanese characters – played by Japanese actors – into Australian narrative settings and explore the results.

All three films - Clara Law's The Goddess of 1967, Sue Brooks' Japanese Story and Rachel Lucas' Bondi Tsunami —have narratives of dislocation, both personal and physical and of diverse desire set in iconic landscapes at once both alluring and alienating. The three narratives share the road as a metaphor of both departure and arrival, as well as that of a journey offering not only deeper self–knowledge but also an experience of journeying through the Australian landscape. Here, then, is where the personal landscape meets that of tourism, as each of the journeys is a personal search of sorts. Whilst the touristic nature of the imagery may be incidental to the narrative action it is, nevertheless, emphasising how the elemental qualities of the landscape may echo the inner personal landscapes and journeys of the characters. Two studies of tourism that explore destination image - Wang and Urry —will be utilised to provide a framework of sorts for the discussion.

TOURISM, CITIZENSHIP AND THE REGULATION OF HUMAN MOBILITY

Tourism is a high profile subject that appears regularly in the media. Broadly speaking it is possible to identify two types of tourism features in print, radio, television and web media: 'tourism stories' and 'stories pertaining to tourism'. Where the former record tourism directly, the latter detail happenings with connections to, or implications for, tourism. Clearly, the media has a powerful role to play in the social constructions of place and hence the practices of tourism. The findings from this paper raise a series of methodological observations worthy of further reflection. As historical sources, tourism stories are empirically useful in documenting, charting and benchmarking the development of tourism production and consumption. They signal and simultaneously shape how tourism is perceived by individuals and groups within society, as do stories pertaining to tourism. One obvious but often unarticulated view is that the location of the story will affect the nature and form of texts and how the discourse may unfold. While we are often prepared to examine the content delivered in the attention economy, we sometimes lose sight of the role and importance of production processes.

CONTESTED AND MEDIATED RURALITY

Rural areas have gone through dramatic changes in the developed world. The forces of globalisation, industrialisation and the consequential economic restructuring of rural and, more relevantly, urban economies have had dramatic and far reaching effects on rural areas. The changes have increased importance of new business units to diversify the regional economic base. As rural areas have changed tourism has been identified as means to maintain, diversify and enhance its abilities in the new economy. These changes to rural areas and national populations have also induced changes to national psyche, where largely urban countries personify themselves as rural. The imagery of rurality has established demand for the rural tourism product, though there is often a lack of development of tourism or functional relationships needed for the industry in rural areas. This paper assesses images promoted in the media and how these images have enlivened the contests of rurality and tourism.

First it assesses historic demand for and impacts of tourism experiences in New Zealand's South Island High Country to identify recreation contests in this rural environment. The paper then assesses 'new' media images of the South Island High Country and identifies new rural/reel contests that may occur, especially with the increased interaction with a much broader and international audience. This new contest and discussion is based on the trilogy of The Lord of the Rings films. An introduction to the South Island High Country is presented, before summarising research into High Country tourism. This is followed by the new media images that may present further contests for rurality. Conclusions drawn provide insights into the issues for the sustainability of the visitor experience, the local community and rurality in this now increasing popular and contested environment.

FILM-INDUCED TOURISM CUTS BOTH WAYS

This study explores the linkages between the film and tourism industries, and the potential for the tourist industry to provide support for film production. The aim was to produce recommendations of benefit to both industries, concerning methods of strategic development of tourism marketing, linked with independent film production, creating alliances between these industries. Previous studies have investigated the phenomenon of film-induced tourism, however, a gap exists in that investigation is after the event and from the point of view of examining existent events, and their effect on tourists or on tourism. The study explores linkages between the industries by utilising a case study of the NRS group, an independent film production company based in Canberra. The data obtained revealed that tourism bodies can render practical assistance to film production and benefit in return from the exposure gained, particularly from planned publicity.

FILMS AND TOURISM

The present paper is part of a wider research project focused on the synergy and all the possible connections between film productions and territories. In particular, it deals with the influence of films on tourism motivations as well as their impact on destination images and the role in affecting tourist purchasing behaviour. Two different research methods were used: a web survey and an on-site interview in two Italian regions. The results reveal that the cause-effect relationship between film viewing and travel experiences shows varying intensity degrees along the subsequent phases into which the choosing and purchasing process of tourism products can be divided. More precisely, the influence of film viewing on travel choices gradually weakens as such process goes on, showing decreasing percentages from the first phase to the following ones up to the final purchasing act.

THE INFLUENCE OF DISASTER MEDIA REPORTS ON THE YOUTH TRAVEL MARKET

Few studies of the youth market have considered the influence of negative disaster media reports on their propensity to travel to the affected destination. This study considers the effect of news reports, travel advisories and the Internet on young people's intention to travel to Phuket following the 2004 Asian tsunami. It was found that this market is relatively resilient, however many expressed concerns about travelling to Phuket, preferring to substitute it for another destination. It recommends that destination marketers adopt a positive re-marketing exercise to counter media misrepresentations as soon as possible in order to retain this market.

FESTIVAL IMAGE CREATION: THE ROLE OF THE PRINT MEDIA

The aim of the paper is to consider the images created of a performing arts festival by Australian national and state newspapers. To achieve this, a content analysis of newspaper coverage of the Melbourne International Comedy Festival was conducted before the commencement of the festival, during the festival and immediately following the close of the festival. The Melbourne based papers covered the festival extensively, with previews and reviews of shows, profiles of artists and articles on comedy as an art form. However, there was surprisingly scant coverage by the national and non-Victorian newspapers of the festival, despite the Melbourne International Comedy Festival being the largest cultural event in Australia in terms of ticket sales.

The descriptor words used in the non-Victorian newspaper articles were noted and the related newspaper photographs and illustrations were examined. The images created of the festival by the non-Victorian newspapers appear to be light-heartedness and fun, where the comedians are depicted as experienced, professional performers skilled in the art of making their audience laugh. Opportunities for future research are identified.

EXPLORING LOCATION AND AUTHENTICITY IN FILM-INDUCED TOURISM

Films may represent a place, but be made at another. In the early years of film-making, quite elaborate sets were constructed on studio backlots. In recent years, runaway productions have represented the USA while being shot in other countries. The dissonance between film setting and film location raises the question of which is more likely to attract tourists. It also suggests that tourists may have difficulties with authenticity. This paper seeks to examine these issues by taking an historical approach to the changing ways in which location has been used by film-makers over time.

UNDERSTANDING POPULAR MEDIA PRODUCTION AND POTENTIAL TOURIST CONSUMPTION

Research on the tourism implications of television-induced tourism generally remains limited, with no single agreed approach to its study. In particular, there are methodological difficulties in understanding this phenomenon and a subsequent lack of empirical research into the relationships between films and TV programmes and tourism. Furthermore, there has been limited attention to the underlying mechanisms and structures in the relationships between the production and consumption of films or TV programmes, audiences and potential tourists, particularly in non-Western contexts. Considering these limitations in this subject, the paper aims to provide insights into the complicated inter-communication processes between TV programmes from the production side and audiences/tourists as consumers.

Based on a triangulated approach, this paper delineates an empirical study to investigate theoretical positions and research methodologies that may be used to explore the production end of popular TV programming and the ways in which particular production values may appeal to tourists in diverse settings. Based on a case study of the 'Hallyu' phenomenon, five major elements of the production of popular TV dramas are proposed by this paper and verified by the interviews with professional producers.

Quantitative research supports examining causal relationships between the highlighted major elements of TV drama production and patterns of consumption associated with audience involvement, its sequential loyalty, and destination choice in the context of Hallyu drama tourism. This paper will, therefore, draw attention to uniquely transnational and interdisciplinary approach which will enable the researcher to develop new ideas and perspectives on the relationship and mediation between production and consumption of popular texts and associated tourism.

THE ROLE OF THE MEDIA IN SHAPING MOTIVATIONS BEHIND TRAVEL EXPERIENCES

This paper aims to explore the role of the media in shaping tourism experiences, using examples drawn from a qualitative study of frontier travellers, being those individuals who travel to places which currently lie at the fringes or extremes of our world or experiences, both geographically and socially/culturally. In the first phase, long interviews were conducted with participants and the data analysed using grounded theory. A content analysis of additional data collected from autobiographies and diaries written by frontier travellers formed the second phase.

Many participants referred to seminal experiences, often occurring during childhood, which were considered to be the genesis of their future frontier travel experiences and these often involved image formation agents such as literature, both fiction and non-fiction, cinema, television and pictures or photographs. Findings of this study indicate that literature has had a greater impact on future motivations behind frontier travel than more modern forms of media such as film and television, and that there is a strong mythical element of these travel experiences, which can be particularly linked back to childhood literature. Future marketing of frontier travel experiences might use some of these findings in developing travel products or promotions, including media selection.

DEVELOPING A PLAUSIBLE CONTEXT FOR ESTABLISHING MUTUAL E-COMMERCE MEDIA IN THE TOURISM INDUSTRY

This research applies the 'Scenario Analysis Instrument' adopted by the Stanford Research Institute to simulate the analogic context to establish an E-commerce platform for Taiwan's tourism industry. This research subject is one of three decisive issues voted by the panelists in a Four-year Project of the Institute for Information Industry and sponsored by the Ministry of Economic Affairs. The representative experts are invited from divergent industries, public sectors, academic institutions and R&D units to draw up and decide upon essential issues for upgrading Taiwan's tourism industry. By adopting the Delphi method, three crucial decisive issues dominate over others and this research focuses on one of them: item L emphasizes how to develop a mutual E-commerce platform for effective connection of an information network.

Eventually, we propose two critical findings. Firstly, when establishing mutual E-commerce platforms which transcend across various sub-industries, the coordination and integration of an existing resource commitment is the most critical mission for advanced preparation. Simultaneously, the fulfilment and perfection of law-making for online consumption including the scope of B2B and B2C must be accomplished promptly. Secondly, establishing mutual E-commerce platforms for different sub-industries respectively, distinguishing boundaries among various businesses from different scopes of sub-industries causes a controversial and preceding problem. This paper reports on research that was conducted to discover how film viewing might be related to tourism activities and whether motivations drive people to become film specific tourists or whether visitation to film locations is simply an incidental tourism experience.

A survey was designed to collect data relating to film tourism motivation, film viewing behaviour, general travel behaviour and demographic profiles. The questionnaire contained a range of information including 29 motivational statements drawn from the literature and previously conducted in-depth interviews. Based on empirical evidence, it appears that these respondents were most interested in the novelty, prestige and fantasy elements associated with film-induced tourism. Factor analysis was applied in order to reduce the 29 statements into themes of motivations which were labelled Novelty, Prestige ,and Fantasy. A model, using logistic regression, was then developed to predict likely future film tourist behaviour. It can be concluded that membership of the 'likely to take a film tourism holiday in future' group was most probable amongst those respondents who had taken a film based holiday in the past, had high Novelty motivations and had high Fantasy motivations. The findings of the research also suggest that most tourists are more likely to be incidental film tourists.

TO BE AUTHENTICALLY FREE AND FREE AUTHENTICALLY

In contemporary society, youth travel is understood and represented, by travellers and media alike, as a contemporary rite of passage or significant, transitional moment. It is argued that the rapid accumulation of experience, an inherent component of travel, influences processes of identity construction and reconstruction. Central to these conceptualisations are concerns with authenticity and freedom, discourses that ultimately serve to structure the travel space and influence interactions between travellers and the travel media and industries. Based on semi-structured, in-depth interviews with young Australian travellers and discourse, image and content analysis of key travel publications and advertisements, this paper will examine the interplay between discourses of authenticity and freedom in traveller narratives and travel media.

It will examine how travel media imagine backpackers and the backpacking community and how backpackers' own self and travel-narratives correspond with or contest such representations. Central to this examination is the centrality of discourses of authenticity and freedom, and the tensions that emerge between the two, as they arise in traveller narratives and media and industry representations of travel. Ultimately, I will argue, following Wang that travellers reconcile some of these tensions with reference to existential authenticity, and that this intersubjective awareness, along with heightened reflexivity, gives rise to a concern with 'authentic freedom'.

MEDIA IN THE ANTICIPATION PHASE OF A RECREATION EXPERIENCE

Natural areas around the world have been used as sites of recreation, leisure and tourism for centuries. A key facet of this increased usage of natural and protected areas and a key tool for management is the role of image. Though the significance of image has been asserted, little study has been undertaken in Australia as related to images of natural and protected areas. Importantly it is the role of the media in promoting and providing expectations that can also be used as a tool to manage potential impacts. Within this context research was undertaken at Port Campbell National Park, Victoria, Australia. This research was implemented during the park's tourist off-season to assess satisfaction, crowding and park issues to provide management indications. Around half of the respondents obtained information from the past experiences of family and friends.

Tourism-specific media such as information centres, travel agents and the internet were also popular. This paper performs analysis to identify the role of the media in shaping adequate expectations of the facilities and service provisions at PCNP. In this context relationships between media and expectations matched and unmatched are ascertained. This not only creates awareness of the varied information sources visitor decisions are based on, it also provides valuable insights into the role of the media in shaping expectations of the facilities and services in protected areas. This has practical marketing implications for protected area management groups as a means for enhancing and managing visitor satisfaction.

A STAKEHOLDERS PERSPECTIVE

This paper identifies the impact of movie induced tourism locations that have become popular due to their featuring in a well liked television series. The researcher's hypothesis is that television induced tourism has a significant impact on the development of a destination. The aim of this research is to identify the benefits of such tourism; therefore this paper will investigate the current literature on television induced tourism. The study area for this paper is Yorkshire, U.K., which has been the film location for a number of popular English television series' and is already the subject of much research in the tourism discipline; Mordue and Tooke and Baker. The hypothesis was initially tested on a survey of visitors to Yorkshire in 2003. The main aim of the survey was to assess the linkages between movie induced tourism and destination branding.

The review of the existing literature identifies a gap in previous research, which indicates that there has been little research on the impacts of a television series on the general tourist perceptions of a destination. The survey undertaken by the researcher was an initial attempt to fill this gap. The findings of this survey and the issues from the literature review highlighted a number of implications for the future development of destinations. To proceed to the next stage of the research, strategic conversations were held with the key stakeholders involved in the development of Yorkshire as a tourist destination. This is an ongoing piece of research but for the purpose of this paper, the impact of television induced tourism from the stakeholder perspective will form the basis of the discussion.

CASTLES MADE OF SAND

Until 1992 a handful of scientific researchers and allocentric backpackers were the only foreigners to visit the Indonesia's Mentawai islands – a remote and impoverished regency of West Sumatra plagued by epidemics of preventable disease and infant mortality rates as high as sixty percent. Within five years the global surf media transformed this depressed region into a surfer's nirvana, the most filmed, photographed, written about and desired surfing tourism destination on earth. Despite this local communities are yet to benefit from surfing tourism. This paper provides a brief history of surfing tourism and presents empirical research demonstrating that the surf media has been instrumental in socially constructing mythical surfing tourist space based upon four symbolic elements: perfect surf, uncrowded conditions, cushioned adventure and an exotic tropical environment.

The generic nature of these elements has led to a disembedding of nirvana from its local context and the 'writing out' of local communities. The Mentawai nirvana is a castle made of sand under threatened by a rising tide of surfing tourism development and disgruntled destination communities. A re-embedding of nirvana in the local is advocated to secure the future of local communities in the management of their surf resources.

TRAVELLING COMPANIONS

Guidebooks play an influential role as mediator between the independent traveller, the travel experience and the travelled destination, providing a lens through which travellers come to see and know their travelled and untravelled world. Guidebooks advise their readers of where to go, what to do and what to see at particular destinations, and many aspects of the backpacker travel experience are shaped and framed by these texts. Despite the centrality of guidebooks in the independent travel experience, the question of how travellers use, engage with, and negotiate these texts has received little attention in tourism research. This paper explores the influence of guidebook texts on backpacker experiences with, and interpretations of, Aboriginal Australia.

The empirical data are drawn from interviews with a sample of 28 international backpackers travelling in Australia. The research reveals that guidebooks are negotiated through the lived and imagined experiences of their readers at various times throughout the travel experience. Backpacker engagement with guidebook information at any given destination is interpreted in light of prior knowledge and experiences. Significantly, the interplay between the backpacker travel experience and the guidebook text is dynamic and primarily situational. The findings highlight the role that the text plays as mediator between the traveller and the travelled culture, and the tensions that exist between texts and lived experiences.

THE EFFECTS OF ONLINE SOCIAL MEDIA ON TOURISM WEBSITES

At the close of the 20th century – roughly between 1997 and 2000 – a set of hardware and software technologies collectively known as the Internet had an enormous diffusion and radically changed most of our economic and social life. In the last few years a further "revolution" has impacted the way we communicate, work and conduct business. The buzzword for this is Web 2.0. Not really a technological advancement, since it relies on well developed and known tools, Web 2.0 rather identifies the changes occurred in the ways software developers and people make and use the Web. The applications that facilitate interactive information sharing, collaboration and formation of virtual communities form today a large part of cybernauts' daily activities and may be seen as a natural development of the original Berners-Lee's idea of "a collaborative medium, a place where we all [could] meet and read and write".

Obviously, as it happened for the first Internet revolution, Web 2.0 could not remain unnoticed in activities genetically bound to the human species such as travel. The impact of Web 2.0 on tourism has been (and is) quite important as numerous publications, scholarly and not, continue to state. Most of the analyses conducted so far assess the behaviour, the usage and the effects Travel 2.0 has as an important set of tools in the hands of a tourist and how it affects the image and the business of destinations, companies and organisations. Moreover, the adoption of such tools is considered to be quite important for improving the status of tourism websites. This generates the hypothesis that the role of OSNs in rising the number of visitors to referenced websites is significant. Aim of this paper is to verify this impact.

Two OSNs have been considered: Facebook and Twitter. The pattern of visits to a sample of Italian tourism websites has been analysed and the relationship between the total visits and those having the two OSNs as referrals have been measured. The rest of this paper is organised as follows. Section 2 briefly surveys the role of Travel 2.0 and OSNs. Section 3 describes the methods used. Results and discussion are reported in sections 4 and 5. Some concluding remarks close the paper.

BACKGROUND

The environment called Web 2.0 (or Travel 2.0) is today too well known to be further described here (would it be needed, the paper by Constantinides &

Fountain, 2008, is a good summary of the main issues on Web 2.0). A few considerations, however, are in order for better understanding the general framework in which this work has been conducted. Tourism has long been the one of most important components of the online commerce world, whose impact has profoundly changed the structure of the industry. Online travel has anticipated ever since (and partly continues to do so) the development of new market dynamics and consumer behaviours. With the introduction and the diffusion of the interactive Web 2.0 features and applications, tourism markets have become real conversations on one of the most thrilling subject for a human being.

This happens in particular with OSNs which seem to have rapidly attracted a considerable attention by Internet users of all ages. They are, almost unanimously, recognised as the busiest environments, and this is valid especially for Facebook which has become in few years by way the largest (in number of users) and the most widespread (in geographical terms) online social network in the World. As stated ten years ago by the Cluetrain Manifesto: "people in networked markets have figured out that they get far better information and support from one another than from vendors." In the Web 2.0 era, the boundaries between information producers and users is blurred, and the usual concepts of authority and control are radically changed. Among the other consequences, marketing approaches aiming at improving online reputation are being greatly affected. Brand awareness, one of the objectives of classical marketing practices transforms into brand engagement, purpose of Marketing 2.0.

This engagement is created by the perceptions, attitudes, and behaviours of those with whom the different companies and organisations are communicating. More importantly, especially for tourism, it passes necessarily through the experience (direct or indirect) a customer gains. Contents generated by users (UGCs) have an acknowledged importance in all fields, and in tourism in particular. Their positive effects have recognised repercussions on quantifiable phenomena such as e-commerce, but also on intangible matters such as those related to the image or the informational side of specific products or services (termed sometimes info-commerce). Already in 2007, the annual Country Brand Index (CBI) measuring attractiveness of countries in several areas, stated that the Web had the highest importance (67 per cent) as channel to collect information about a tourism destination.

On the other hand, the continuing growth of UGCs' influence, due to their wideness and deepness, makes them perceived as even more reliable than official sources for a tourist. According to PhoCusWright (2009) nine out of ten cybertravellers read (and trust) online reviews on tourism products and services (hotels, restaurants and destinations).

Three phases are influential in this travel experience formation process:

- Pre-experience, built on other people's travel stories, before travelling;

- Experience during travel or stay, today increasingly shared real-time through mobile applications;
- Post-experience, which disseminates comments, evaluations, emotions.

These issues form the foundations on which specialised Travel 2.0 tourism websites have built their success. Today, however, we see a new phenomenon that can be interpreted as starting a new trend, especially in some countries: generic OSNs are being progressively more used in travel and tourism. Italy is surely one of these countries, being at the first places in the World with regard to diffusion and usage of OSNs, Facebook in particular. According to Facebakers there are almost 17 million Italian Facebook users, 56 per cent of the online population, which put Italy at the sixth place in country rankings. Italians seem to like much conversing and debating their travel experiences, tastes, perceptions and attitudes.

Recent research reports travels as the second most discussed topic on Italian OSNs and a Google Insights for Search query shows an incredible growth of Facebook searches in Italy with respect to other technologically developed countries such as USA, UK, France or Germany. The phenomenon is a social convergence trend: specialised travel websites increase their sociality by adopting applications which enable real-time sharing of contents among the visitors, while giants such as Facebook try to occupy vertical markets through dedicated services or acquisitions of specialised companies as the social travel recommendation site Nextstop. There are little doubts that the importance of Travel 2.0 features and tools, and specifically of social media environments, is growing fast.

Many tourism businesses are, in one way or another, changing their approach to the manners of presenting themselves online. However, most of the studies have assesses so far mainly the social and psychological effects, and have well confirmed the role played as sources of information and areas in which discussing various issues related to travels or stays. Some works have also discussed the effects of these tools on the image and the popularity of destinations or other tourism operators, mainly in the hospitality sector, in which the direct contact, real or virtual, with the customer and their crucial role for the good health of the companies.

The general conclusion to-date in this field is that, beside the repeated statements on importance and role, tourism operators have not yet fully understood the new technological world by and still many concerns are brought forward. Credibility of the information online, possibility to forge for particular interests by unscrupulous competitors, privacy, overload of useless information, in addition to the usual (in the technology arena) lack of resources or skill shortage are the most reported issues. These positions, however create a tension between demand (tourists, travellers, visitors) and supply (tourism businesses and organisations).

As well reported by Xiang and Gretzel:

- "Social media Websites are "ubiquitous" in online travel information search in that they occur everywhere [...] no matter what search keywords a traveler uses. Certain social media Websites [...], which can be considered more comprehensive and travel-specific sites, are becoming increasingly popular and are likely to evolve into primary online travel information sources. [...]. The results confirm that tourism marketers can no longer ignore the role of social media in distributing travel-related information without risking to become irrelevant."

The rest of this paper gives further quantitative support to this stated importance of the role played by OSNs by directly assessing their effects and influence on tourism website visits. This is a topic which has not been discussed in the literature so far, but has an important value in trying to establish the real role of OSNs in supporting the efforts of tourism operators to attract visitors to their websites and influence their attitudes and memories.

MATERIALS AND METHODS

The data analysed in this work were provided by Shiny through their Shinystat service, an online platform specialised in Internet audience analysis and website statistics. The company is well known mainly in Italy, its country of origin and well diffused. More than 275,000 Italian websites use it. Cumulative data were collected concerning the visits to 19,902 websites in the categories: Travel and tourism and hospitality and restaurants. The timeframe spans a little more than two years (26 observations from August 2008 to August 2010 included). To all extent the sample can be considered quite significant, even if a single source of data was used. The data collected consisted of the series of total visits to Italian websites (TOT) and the contributions to these visits having Facebook (FB) and Twitter (TW) as referrals. Shinystat uses a 30 minutes time window to define a visit; that is: all connections to a website coming from the same IP address in a 30 min period are considered as a single visit.

This follows the proposals of the Web Analytics Association. Although not particularly meaningful per se, for the arbitrarity in the definition, when measured consistently over a period of time, visits are a good indicator of the behaviour of website with respect to its popularity. The global series (TOT) is an example of pooled (or cross-sectional) series: a series consisting of the linear composition of a number of different contributions. In order to assess the significance of these contributions to the global series a multiple linear regression can be used.

This technique is well known and has been widely used in many other studies. In addition to the usual requirements of a regression analysis, the critical point in our case is to make sure that the independent variables do not suffer from multicollinearity (i.e. predictor variables are not highly correlated with each other) which may hinder the estimation of the effects of individual predictors. The significance of the contributions due to FB and TW as referrals were assessed with a multiple regression where the time period is the dependent variable and the FB and TW contributions are the predictors. Tests for multicollinearity and normality of residuals were performed. The time series was also examined by using a standard simple decomposition method to derive its main characteristics, seasonality in particular. All analyses have been carried out with SPSS version 17.

RESULTS

The time series for total visits to Italian tourism websites (TOT) and the FB component. It must be noticed that, for space limitations, the figure uses two scale axes (the right one is for the visits from FB) in order to better show the series' behaviour (measurement scales differ of almost two orders of magnitude, for the same reason TW is omitted due to its very low values). The maximum values for the contributions of FB and TW visits are recorded in the month of August 2010: FB = 0.329 per cent; TW = 0.002 per cent. When examining the series transformed into an index with the starting observation taken as base, TOT gets to 120 at the end of the period examined, while FB reaches 9438 and TW achieve 2280. The results of the regression analysis are shown in Table 1. The predictor coefficients are reported along with their standard errors and statistical significance (indicated by a t statistic and its associated p-value).

The last column contains the condition index for which gauges the presence and the extent of multicollinearity (as known when it value is higher than 15 multicollinearity is a concern, when higher than 30 multicollinearity is a serious problem). The coefficient of determination is $R^2 = 0.523$ which can be considered providing a good fit. Residuals are normally distributed, a Kolmogorov- Smirnov (K-S) test produces Z = 0.833 which has a (asymptotic) p-value = 0.492 (the K-S test has a null hypothesis of normality). The multicollinearity diagnostic does not show significant problems. The only slight effect found is for the TW component which has a condition index = 15.809, indicating a limited problem which can be ignored.

DISCUSSION

The results of the analysis lead to a number of interesting considerations. First of all the contribution of the two social media websites examined are of a low level. A higher proportion would have been expected, but this result is in agreement with other investigations, conducted on different bases, that show a limited usage of all Web 2.0 functionalities by tourism websites practically in every country. Little research has been conducted on this issue for what concerns Italy and, besides some popular press articles, no reliable data exist on how much OSNs are employed by the Italian tourism industry.

In general, however, operators have seldom shown in the past highly favourable attitudes towards ICTs and, still today, make poor usage of them. Hence the advanced Web 2.0 features, OSNs in particular in this case, have a limited diffusion, at least at the present time. Despite that, the growth of the FB and TW components is quite remarkable (some thousand times), mainly if we compare with the limited increase in total visits (a little more than one). This is an expected outcome and is in agreement with the many publications, scholarly and not, stating the quick growth in the usage of these virtual social environments. Also the seasonality effect is an expected result. The growth in usage in the first part of the year, peaking in July, is a clear indication of the role FB and TW play as important and reputed sources for travellers and tourists planning their summer travels, the most intense vacation period in Italy.

This is in good agreement with other studies on the role of online social networks as information sources. The regression analysis shows the positive importance and the significance of the FB contributions to the total number of visits to a tourism website. It must be noted here that no information has been analysed in this work regarding the ownership of these Facebook resources (a study on this topic is ongoing). Very probably these contributions come from pages not directly connected with the websites, a further confirmation of the weight and the value of online social environments for the popularity and the success of tourist operators. The usual disclaimers apply when it come to the limitations of this work. A single country has been considered, Italy, and a peculiar one for its very large proportion of Facebook-dependent online population. More studies will have the task of falsifying the outcomes presented here or adding further confirmations to the effects described.

The results presented here have an obvious importance for practitioners. From an academic point of view this work clarifies, for the first time, the role and the influence of OSNs on the popularity and traffic of tourism operators websites. In addition, it provides simple and effective methodological indications for gauging the significance of different contributions to a temporal phenomenon such as the one discussed here. One final consideration is in order. The mere fact that there are many visits to a website does not necessarily imply a good image of the website owner. Many bad realisations exist and, for example, they are used sometimes to show how not to present an organisation online. In cases like these the websites may be visited by many. As already widely known, only good projects, well designed and carefully implemented, have a positive effect on the health of the actors presenting them online. This good consideration of the brand, then, produces a more favourable acceptance of the website which, in turn, reinforces the brand image, creating a virtuous cycle of appreciation. Also, many studies argue that a solid, rich and appreciated website is a necessary foundation for the design of an effective and worthy online social media strategy. In this preliminary analysis these aspects have been neglected, the only aim has been to show the effects an OSN may have. Further investigations, already ongoing, will take care of these issues.

CONCLUSION

The media can spur the current prospects for the African countries to actively collaborate in a wide range of eco-tourism enhancement activities which include: joint product or service development, research, human resource development and management, exchange of tourism experts and tourism information within the existing economic and trading regional blocks like: the Common Market for Eastern and Southern Africa, Preferential Trade Area, Southern African Development Area Coordination Conference, East Africa Community, Economic Community for the Organisation of West African Countries and the African Union. There is a huge virgin market for Africa's ecotourism investment which should be developed and strengthened. Sustainable tourism cannot survive without a working environment management system and regular environment impact assessment.

Legislations and codes should be developed to ensure balanced development of tourism in African tourist destinations to facilitate access to information about African tourism and ecological conservation. A case in point is Kenya where tourism is a major employer accounting for almost 11 per cent of the total national labour force there. The Kenyan ecotourism society aims to market eco-tourism as a tool for the conservation of the natural environment for sustainable community livelihoods in the protected areas. It plans to develop eco-management standards for better tourism and hopes to publish eco-tourism regulations and codes of conduct as well as to develop public awareness campaign strategy to mitigate potential negative ecological, cultural, social and economic impact of tourism in the country. Sustainable tourism will materialise in Africa if we integrate tourism into the overall policy for sustainable development, development of sustainable tourism, and management of tourism.

Index

A

Accommodations 150, 152, 153, 154
Accountable 80, 88, 89
Anecdotalism 188, 191, 192
Authoritarian 46, 48, 49, 50, 52, 53, 57, 59, 60, 62, 63

B

Biodiplomacy 99, 100, 102, 109, 113, 114, 115, 116, 117
Botswana 65, 66, 67, 68, 69, 70, 71, 72, 73, 74

C

Churchill 27, 221
Citizenry 44, 60, 76, 110
Cognitive 126, 128, 150, 164, 165, 168, 169, 172, 174, 176, 177
Collaborative 113, 214, 215, 217, 218, 279
Conglomerate 86, 179, 180, 188, 189, 190, 191, 198
Contextual 204, 208, 244
Critical 32, 38, 39, 60, 61, 66, 67, 82, 84, 85, 91, 99, 100, 102, 105, 109, 110, 116, 117, 118, 123, 124, 125, 147, 154, 155, 180, 200, 226, 234, 237, 238, 243, 248, 249, 275, 282

D

Democratic 23, 24, 25, 29, 32, 33, 39, 40, 46, 47, 48, 49, 57, 59, 60, 64, 71, 91, 92, 99, 109, 110, 114, 122, 124, 185, 186, 187, 188, 189, 190, 193, 194, 195, 199, 200, 202, 207, 230, 253, 254
Dilemmas 12, 44
Disengagement 31, 39, 101, 103, 104

E

Editorials 180, 183, 193, 195, 196, 197
Empirical 1, 7, 10, 100, 139, 140, 161, 163, 177, 178, 179, 180, 181, 182, 183, 184, 186, 187, 188, 189, 191, 192, 195, 196, 197, 198, 199, 200, 274, 276, 278
Empowerment 127, 235
Enhancement 221, 285
Enriched 121, 125, 220, 232
Ethical 87, 88, 99, 101, 102, 108, 115, 116, 220, 233, 235
Evaluated 223, 235, 241

F

Fascism 189, 190
Framework 47, 66, 94, 109, 111, 115, 117, 129, 130, 131, 134, 143, 166, 176, 213, 222, 239, 271, 285

H

Hazards 41, 42, 43, 44, 113
Hypotheses 34, 35, 38, 132, 137, 138, 139, 140, 163

I

Induce 125, 241, 243
Intellectual 1, 6, 12, 15, 16, 17, 18, 24, 25, 26, 31, 54, 63, 103, 107, 109, 110, 112, 134, 229
Intimate 65, 66, 69, 70, 73

L

Legislation 13, 14, 59, 61, 76, 77, 152, 153, 155, 157, 158, 160, 213, 214

M

Malware 205
Modalities 101, 102, 117, 120
Monumental 220

N

Normative 49, 109, 117, 129, 178, 180, 184, 186, 187, 188, 192, 197, 199, 200

O

Opportunities 14, 21, 24, 34, 74, 124, 125, 134, 146, 151, 153, 160, 175, 186, 187, 213, 239, 248, 273, 278, 285
Optimizing 78
Originality 16

P

Pluralization 47, 57, 58, 59
Preferential 57, 285
Protocol 109, 117, 128

R

Regimes 48, 49, 50, 56

S

Semantic 114, 208, 216
Socialization 31, 32, 33, 34, 39, 130, 131, 133, 134, 141, 144, 145, 146, 147
Sustainable 220, 221, 222, 224, 226, 231, 234, 235, 246, 285
Symphonies 235

T

Terminology 148, 157, 160

V

Vibrant 238
Vulnerable 5, 113, 133, 135, 184, 254